The Basque Mediev

D0402010

Current Research Series No. 13

The Basque Medieval City:

The Laws of Estella and San Sebastian in the Twelfth Century

Edited by
Xabier Irujo
Amaia Álvarez Berastegi

Translated by
Cameron J. Watson

Center for Basque Studies
University of Nevada, Reno
2019

This book was published with generous financial support from the Basque Government and in collaboration with the University of the Basque Country and the City Council of Donostia-San Sebastian

Current Research Series, No. 13
Series Editor: Xabier Irujo

Center for Basque Studies
University of Nevada, Reno
Reno, Nevada 89557
http://basque.unr.edu

Copyright © 2019 by the Center for Basque Studies
All rights reserved. Printed in the United States of America.
Translation copyright © 2019 Center for Basque Studies
Cover and series design 2019 by Juan San Martín

Library of Congress Cataloging-in-Publication Data

Names: Fueros de Estella y San Sebastián (Conference) (2018: Donostia-San Sebastián, Basque Country). | Irujo, Xabier and Álvarez Berastegi, Amaia, editors. | Watson, Cameron, 1967 – translator. | Fundación para el Estudio del Derecho; Histórico y Autonómico de Vasconia, sponsoring body. | Donostia-San Sebastián Basque Country). City Council, sponsoring body. | University of Nevada, Reno. Center for Basque Studies, sponsoring body.

Title: The Basque Medieval City / edited by Xabier Irujo and Amaia Álvarez Berastegi;translated by Cameron J. Watson.

Description: Reno: Center for Basque Studies University of Nevada 2019. | Series: Center for Basque Studies current research series; no. 13 | Summary:"This collective work includes presentations given at the conference Los Fueros de Estella y San Sebastián (The Fueros of Estella and San Sebastian), held on July 2 and 3, 2018, in the plenary hall of Donostia-San Sebastian City Hall, and organized by the Iura Vasconiae Foundation, the Center for Basque Studies at the University of Nevada, Reno, and the Donostia-San Sebastian City Council."--ECIP Introduction. | Includes bibliographical references.

Identifiers: LCCN 2019023628 | ISBN 9781949805116 (paperback)
Subjects: LCSH: Municipal corporations—Basque Country—Medieval Law--History—To 1500—Congresses. | Town laws, Medieval—Basque Country --Congresses. | Donostia-San Sebastián (Basque Country) Fuero de San Sebastián--Congresses.

Classification: LCC KKT5674.94 .F84 2019 | DDC 342.46/6109--dc23
LC record available at https://lccn.loc.gov/2019023628

Contents

Introduction | *Amaia Álvarez Berastegi* 7

Notes on the Dating and Nature
of the Fuero of Estella | *Xabier Irujo* 15

An Obscure Past: Gipuzkoa and Navarre from the Tenth to the
Twelfth Centuries | *José Ángel Lema Pueyo* . . . 37

Organization of the Estella Territory
and the Creation of Estella | *Javier Ilundain Chamarro* 73

The Organization of the Territory of San Sebastian and its
Surroundings during the Early Middle Ages:
A Panoramic View of its Evolution
| *Iosu Etxezarraga Ortuondo* 95

Another History of the Fuero of Jaca: A New Reading
and Re-interpretative Essay | *Ana Mª Barrero García* . 129

Law in the Fueros of Estella
and San Sebastian | *Roldán Jimeno Aranguren* . . 197

Social Minorities in the Fuero of Estella | *Xabier Irujo* . 241

The Jewish Minority in the Fuero of Estella
| *Amaia Álvarez Berastegi* 287

The Family of the Fueros of Estella
and San Sebastian from 1200 on
| *Nere Jone Intxaustegi Jauregi.* 307

Notes on the Fuero of San Sebastian:
Its Expansion, Validity, and Modernity,
and an Analysis of its Texts | *Mª Rosa Ayerbe Iribar* . 323

The Development of Maritime Law
Following the Fuero of San Sebastian
| *Margarita Serna Vallejo* 371

List of Contributors 399

Introduction

Amaia Álvarez Berastegi

L{ike all historical analysis, research on medieval law contributes to understanding processes and events in later eras. In the case of studying local *fueros* (charters) in Vasconia (the Basque Country), however, the very link of history is even more significant given the existing connection between medieval law and later juridical regulations. It is impossible to understand Basque juridical particularities without focusing the gaze on the evolution of the fueros in the medieval and modern ages and, in particular, one cannot understand this foral evolution without first addressing the processes that shaped the municipal fueros in the Early Middle Ages. This volume contextualizes and deconstructs the formation process of local fueros through a comparative study of the fueros of Estella (Lizarra in Basque) in Navarre and San Sebastian (Donostia) in Gipuzkoa, two documents intertwined in the same family. The comparative analysis of these two fueros allows us to advance in overcoming several challenges specific to medieval law: understanding legal formation processes from the eleventh century onward as well as clarifying the characteristics of the early medieval urban institutions, society, and economy in Navarre and Gipuzkoa.

The law that took shape in the territories of Vasconia advance axioms that were developed during later eras, such as the fuero understood as a pact between that which held power and the people, and the acquisition of rights through the concept of *vecindad* (residence). The authors contributing to this work have examined the juridical, political, and social aspects of the fueros of Estella and of San Sebastian in order to paint a picture of the era that contributes to a fuller understanding of the origins of *foralidad* (forality).

As well as expanding on the history of medieval law, this work also contributes to specific knowledge about the formation of the local fueros in Navarre and Gipuzkoa. And it does so without overlooking the numerous controversies that have emerged within the field of historiography. As a result of the scarcity of reliable documentation from the era, the formation of municipal fueros since the eleventh century has generated several controversies. No author questions the significance of these medieval texts in the formulation of subsequent law, in the economic and social development of the places in which it was granted, or in the importance of these fueros in the conception of later forality. Nevertheless, disagreements abound as regards the dates and the constitutive elements (influences and origins) of these early foral texts. Traditionally, the fuero of Estella has been presented as the first extensive Navarrese medieval text whose origins lie in the fuero of Jaca (Aragon). More recently, however, both the date and origin of the Estella text have been questioned and, given the various versions of the fuero of Jaca and the absence of any original document, the possibility has even been raised that the fuero of Estella could predate that of Jaca. Whatever the case, there is no doubt at all in contending that the fuero of Estella was the source of the fuero of San Sebastian, even if it is true that the study of this process and its influence on the law and history of Gipuzkoa has also developed significantly in recent years.

The twelfth-century municipal fueros gave political and juridical shape to the territories that adopted them. Through the fuero, the inhabitants of these municipalities acquired a series of rights and privileges that, in turn, were classified according to the different social groups that made up the municipality. From a medieval view, the municipal fueros regulated the normative life of the inhabitants of each municipality and contributed to expanding the principle of legal equality. They offered an opportunity for specific economic conditions, although they also favored economic growth specifically in the municipalities. In the case of Estella, the concession of the first fuero, around 1076–1077, was related to the Camino de Santiago (the Way of Saint James), a space transited and inhabited by freemen that opened up the prospect of financial gain for people living along the route and, besides that, the acquisition through the fuero of certain privileges on the part of specific groups in the municipality. In the case of San Sebastian we link its first municipal fuero (1180) to the development of maritime commerce and political changes in the Early Middle Ages. In San Sebastian, moreover, the concession of the municipal fuero was followed by major political changes, given that Castile conquered Gipuzkoa in the years 1199–1200 and the later concessions of the San Sebastian fuero were undertaken already under Castilian control.

The fueros have been and continue to be a privileged topic of study for legal historians, but also for medievalist historians like José María Lacarra, Ángel Martín Duque, and José Luis Banús y Aguirre, pioneering authors in their day on the study of municipal foral texts who made first-rate contributions. The contributions included in this volume open up new debates and offer new perspectives on the local fueros and bring up to date the state of historiographical, juridical, and even archeological knowledge on the process of forming *villas*. A dialog is, then, created among the advances produced in recent years by legal history, social history, and archaeology.

The work is divided into three major parts. The first of these analyzes the key moments in the Early and Early Middle Ages in Gipuzkoa and Navarre, while the second is located in the field of sources and controversies surrounding the municipal fueros and focuses on the content of the fueros of Estella and San Sebastian. Finally, the third part situates the fueros of Estella and San Sebastian within the corresponding legal, political, and social events that took place through the Late Middle and Modern Ages, such as maritime law and the social and political rights of minorities.

The Historical Context: The Early Middle Ages

The work opens with a general overview on the history of Navarre and Gipuzkoa during this era and two others relative to the configuration of Estella and San Sebastian, respectively.

In his chapter titled "An Obscure Past: Gipuzkoa and Navarre, from the Tenth to the Twelfth Centuries," José Ángel Lema Pueyo, a professor at the University of the Basque Country (UPV/EHU), deconstructs the process by which Estella and San Sebastian were created within the context of the concession of local fueros. The author connects the historical context of municipal forality to the numerous political fluctuations of the period. The formation of these *villas* (chartered towns) coincided with the shaping of increasingly complex, unequal, and hierarchical societies that, in turn, were less isolated and therefore more interconnected.

The following chapter, by Javier Ilundain Chamarro (International University of La Rioja), addresses the history of Estella from the earliest existing documents. Under the title "Organization of the Estella Territory and the Creation of Estella," Ilundain Chamarro explains how the site of Lizarrara was already a castle of some importance in the organization and defense of the Kingdom of Pamplona in the tenth and eleventh centuries. Thus, according to the author, the Estella territory enjoyed a certain political and economic importance prior to the eleventh century, the moment at which the first documentation of the presence of new settlements associated with the Camino de Santiago appears. Therefore, going against most historical explanations, Ilundain Chamarro highlights the political importance of the Estella area before the Camino de Santiago expanded.

Iosu Etxezarraga Ortuondo, who holds a PhD from the University of the Basque Country, is the author of "The Organization of the Territory of San Sebastian and its Surroundings during the Early Middle Ages: A Panoramic View of its Evolution." He presents a historical reconstruction of the evolution of the territory of San Sebastian in the centuries prior to the drafting of its fuero, based on a discourse in which documentary data are blended with new archaeological information. Etxezarraga suggests a new interpretative framework through the combination of different types of sources, in a clarifying interdisciplinary analysis.

The Problem of Sources and their Dating

After introducing the context in which the fueros of Estella and San Sebastian were conceded, the second part of this work enters fully into some of the controversies that have surfaced around the formation of forality during the era. In 2003, the referential author in this topic, Ana M* Barrero, published an exhaustive analysis of foral texts in her groundbreaking work, "La difusión del fuero de Jaca en el Camino de Santiago."[1] Here we include a version of this work, updated by the author, under the title "Another History of the Fuero of Jaca: A New Reading and Re-interpretative Essay." The contribution and originality of this text is significant, bearing in mind that the fueros of Estella and San Sebastian have been located traditionally within the family of the fueros of Jaca. Since the fourteenth century, in fact, the fuero of Jaca has been interpreted as the referential legal source of the later fueros of Estella and San Sebastian. However, this detailed document study of the different versions of the fuero of Jaca demonstrates that, in contrast to the perspective maintained to date, there existed a complex process of formation in which there were different phases by which the foral text was formulated and expanded. Barrero proposes a variety of characteristics in each version of the text and contributes to the formulation of new questions about the chronology of influences and dating the original text.

The Content of the Foral Texts

In "Law in the Fueros of Estella and San Sebastian," Roldán Jimeno Aranguren of the Public University of Navarre (UPNA/NUP) explores the content of the fueros and explains the motivations that preceded their concession to these two municipalities. Thus, in

---

1   Ana M* Barrero, "La difusión del fuero de Jaca en el Camino de Santiago," in *El Fuero de Jaca II: Estudios* (Zaragoza: El Justicia de Aragón, 2003), 113–60.

his opinion, with the first fuero of Estella (1076–1077), there was an attempt to install a new urban nucleus, complementary to the precursory Lizarrara, which gave the new settlers a different legal status, creating an urban network equipped with services on the increasingly frequented Camino de Santiago. For its part, the fuero of San Sebastian demonstrated a pronounced legal dependency on the wording of the fuero of Estella. Jimeno Aranguren develops an exhaustive analysis of the content of both fueros and concludes that the regulation of certain matters, especially those that sought to boost trade, were more advantageous for people in San Sebastian than in Estella.

In "Social Minorities in the Fuero of Estella," Xabier Irujo, from the University of Nevada, Reno, points out how the people who drafted the extensive fuero of Estella (1164) made great efforts to identify, regulate, and formulate the freedoms and liberties of the population of Estella and dedicated a significant number of sections to protecting their prerogatives as residents of the burg of San Martin. Specifically, those sections dedicated to codifying and protecting the rights of some of the most disadvantaged collectives in society, such as women, minors, and the poor, stand out. The fuero contains, likewise, a large number of legal norms that aim to systematize the protection of freedoms and interests of the Jewish minority. Thus, Irujo's chapters explain that the fuero of Estella stands out for its rigorous and innovative content relating to the legal protection of these social sectors, as well as for its originality, given that there are not many legal precedents in such specific environments in Medieval Europe prior to 1164. "The Jewish Minority in the Fuero of Estella" by Amaia Álvarez Berastegi examines more closely this same line of inquiry and deconstructs that part of the fuero relating to the Jewish population. In the Early Middle Ages, Estella had one of the most important Jewish quarters in the kingdom and the fuero demonstrates royal protection of the Jewish population during the era.

The Later Development of Estella and San Sebastian Forality

The development of the local fueros of Estella and San Sebastian stood out in the centuries that followed, with the former being extended to numerous towns in Navarre and the latter, via different enclaves on the Cantabrian coast, to San Vicente de la Barquera. Nere Jone Intxaustegi Jauregi, from the University of Deusto, unpicks this process in "The Family of the Fueros of Estella and San Sebastian from 1200 on."

For her part, Mª Rosa Ayerbe Iribar from the UPV/EHU explores the influence of the fuero of San Sebastian on other towns in Gipuzkoa. In her chapter, "Notes on the Fuero of San Sebastian: Its Expansion, Validity, and Modernity, and an Analysis of its Texts," she examines how the concession of the fuero to San Sebastian by King Sancho VI of Navarre, or Sancho el Sabio (Sancho the Wise), marked a fundamental milestone in municipal organization in Gipuzkoa. The ancient valleys in which the territory was organized thus gave way to a more limited and specific municipal framework from the territorial point of view, but a more developed and compact set-up from the politico-institutional perspective. Following its very confirmation on San Sebastian by King Alfonso VIII of Castile, the fuero was later expanded through its concession to other towns.

Finally, Margarita Serna Vallejo, from the University of Cantabria, contributes a vision of the fuero of San Sebastian based on the development of commercial law following its concession by Sancho VI. From the twelfth century on, and coinciding with the concession of the fuero of San Sebastian and its initial expansion, the town was incorporated into an Atlantic maritime tradition, as testified to by numerous testimonies that document the willingness of its inhabitants and authorities to consolidate and prolong relations with people and places throughout the Atlantic coast of Europe. In this way, in her chapter "The Development of Maritime Law Following the Fuero of San Sebastian," Serna Vallejo goes into the steps taken by the town of San Sebastian to incorporate the tradition of Atlantic law, something that took place immediately after the concession of the fuero.

This collective work includes presentations given at the conference *Los Fueros de Estella y San Sebastián* (The Fueros of Estella and San Sebastian), held on July 2 and 3, 2018, in the plenary hall of Donostia-San Sebastian City Hall, and organized by the Iura Vasconiae Foundation, the Center for Basque Studies at the University of Nevada, Reno, and the Donostia-San Sebastian City Council. The conference brought together several specialists in medieval history, legal historians, and archeologists from the University of the Basque Country, the Public University of Navarre, and the University of La Rioja, and was inaugurated by the mayors of Donostia-San Sebastian, Eneko Goia, and Estella-Lizarra, Koldo Leoz.

Prologue

Notes on the Dating and Nature
of the Fuero of Estella[1]

Xabier Irujo

On June 4, 1076, the king of Pamplona, Sancho IV was assassinated. As José Yanguas y Miranda notes, a group of nobles had invited the king to a hunting banquet, between the towns of Funes and Villafranca, in a forest inhabited by deer and wild boar, and when they had gotten him near to a precipice, made up of a rock on the northern bank of the Rivers Arga and Aragon, called Peñalen, they pushed him off and he fell to his death.[2] Both on account of the singularity of the affair—this regicide is a very unique incident in a thousand years of the history of the Navarrese kingdom—and the effect it had on events occurring immediately afterward—the assassination led to an uncertain and difficult period in the history of the Kingdom of Pamplona, in which it saw its territory curtailed and political independence seriously affected—it is without a doubt one of the most interesting episodes in the medieval history of the Navarrese kingdom.[3]

---

1   The following is a translation of a previously published article: Xabier Irujo, "Sobre la datación y naturaleza del fuero de Estella," *Terra stellae* 7 (2016), 38–55.
2   José Yanguas y Miranda, *Historia compendiada de Navarra* (Donostia: Imprenta de Ignacio Ramón Baroja, 1832), 72–73.
3   On this episode, see likewise: José María Lacarra, *Historia del reino de Navarra en la Edad Media* (Iruñea: Caja de Ahorros de Navarra, 1975); José María Lacarra, *Historia política del reino de Navarra: desde sus orígenes hasta su incorporación a Castilla* (Iruñea: Editorial

After the events of 1076 in Peñalen, Sancho Ramírez was crowned king of Pamplona and he pushed for the fortification of Lizarra, which, following the advance of Alfonso VI of León's troops on Araba and La Rioja, constituted a bastion in the defense of the southwestern border of the kingdom.[4] In this regard, he ordered the construction of a second fortress on the promontory of la Peña de los Castillos, situated opposite the ancient settlement of Lizarra, to the south of the course of the Ega, which stood at just over 100 meters (330 feet) above the town, to a height of 570 meters (1,870 feet).

This is the historical context in which the origins of the Fuero of Estella are framed: wars between kingdoms, regicide, occupation, settlements, and, gaining the favor of a town by means of extending benefits to it in the form of laws. Not without reason did the first norm in the Fuero of Estella stipulate what the rights and duties of the population were in times of war.

Traditionally, the Fuero of Estella has been dated to 1090. This is due to the existence of a document in which it is registered that Sancho Ramírez conceded to the monastery of San Juan de la Peña a tenth of all royal rents (in the form of receiving taxes *de lezeta, de censu, de homicidiis, de iudiciis, de caloniis et de omnibus omnino rebus, ut habeant et possideant iure perpetuo*), all the churches (*omnes parrochitanas ecclesias quas in eadem populatione fuerint facte, cum omnibus iuris sibi pertinentibus*), and a plot in the "new settlement that I want to construct in the town they call Lizarrara" (*illa populatione quam noviter volo facere in villa que vocatur Lizarrara*) in which good houses may be built to live in (*in quo possint facere bonas kasas ad habitandum*).

The document states textually that the monks in that monastery of San Juan de la Peña wanted to create a settlement of Franks in the area of Zaraputz, right on the Camino de Santiago, while the king on the other hand preferred to change the route of the Camino, making it go through Lizarrara, and building there a

---

Aranzadi, 1973); and José María Jimeno Jurío, *Merindad de Estella. I. Historia de Estella/ Lizarra*, Colección Obras completas de José María Jimeno Jurío no. 33 (Iruñea: Pamiela-Udalbide-Euskara Kultur Elkargoa, 2006).

4   *Estudios de Edad Media de la Corona de Aragón*, vol. 8 (Zaragoza: Consejo Superior de Investigaciones Científicas, Escuela de Estudios Medievales, 1945), 772.

castle and settlement of Franks (*et facere ibi castrum et populationem de francos*). This way, given that the royal plot of Lizarrara was, in the monarch's opinion, better situated than that which the monks of San Juan wanted to settle, he offered *cum bona voluntate* to create a settlement that they had in mind for their own area in exchange for a specific economic compensation in perpetuity (*perpetualiter*) with the aim that they would not get annoyed on his account (*et non essent murmurantes adversum me pro hac causa*).[5]

Yet this document does not mention the fuero, or the awarding of a fuero, or even the mere intention to grant privileges to the area. The document only indicates that the monks of San Juan proposed creating a settlement around their monastery in Zaraputz in light of the potential economic harm they perceived with the passage of pilgrims through Lizarra.[6] Prior to the urban growth of old Lizarra, the Santiago pilgrims went directly from Villatuerta to the monastery of Irache, without entering Estella. They crossed the River Ega via the Navarro bridge; climbed a gentle slope to pass through Zaraputz, where there was a small monastery and hospital for pilgrims run by San Juan de la Peña, and via the hillside of Montejurra, arrived at Santa María la Real de Irache. In changing the route of the Camino so it went through Estella, the monarch decided to compensate the monks by conceding substantial economic incentives so that they would settle in what was already the burg of San Martín, which would soon grow outward from the market square. In fact this document indicates the preexistence of a burg whose inhabitants payed amounts in the form of exactions and taxes and that was located in a better and more appropriate setting, which attracted the passage of pilgrims. The reference to taxes, censuses, homicides, trials, slanders, and fines points likewise

---

5   José María Lacarra and Ángel J. Martín Duque, *Fueros derivados de Jaca. Estella-San Sebastián* (Iruñea: Institución Príncipe de Viana, 1969), 53–54.

6   Indeed, Zaraputz experienced a period of decline in the eleventh century to the point that, with time, it became the abandoned settlement it is today. See Bernardo Estornés Lasa, *Historia general de Euskalerria: 824–1234, época pamplonesa* (Donostia: Auñamendi, 1989), 348; José M. Lacarra, "De Estella a Nájera," in *Las peregrinaciones a Santiago de Compostela*, ed. Luis Vázquez de Parga, José M. Lacarra, and Juan Uría Ríu, vol. 2 (Madrid: Consejo superior de investigaciones científicas, Escuela de estudios medievales, 1949), 23, 39, and 133–34; and Miguel Avilés and Guillermo Sena, *Nuevas poblaciones en la España moderna* (Madrid: Universidad Nacional de Educación a Distancia, 1991), 400.

to the preexistence of a normative body or group and the local organization of inhabitants.

The first references to the site of Lizarra date from well before 1090 and are even prior to 1076. The medieval documents register many variations of this original place name, such as Liçarra y Lizarra (1012), Liçarrara (1024), Liçarara (1040–1046), Lizarrara (1058) and Leiçarrara (1074) before 1076, and Liçarraga (1079), Lizarega (1084), Liçarrare (1093), Liszarraga (1098), Lizarreta (1106), Liçarra (1120) and Leyçarra (1257 and 1276) thereafter.[7] The first written evidence of the existence of *seniores* (seigneurs) and *tenentes* (tenants-in-chief) in Lizarra is very early, such as the *Semeno Ogoaiz mandante Liçarrara* of 1024, that of the *senioris* Sancho Fortunionis and Sacho Garceiz de Liçarrara, and Scemeno Garces.[8] He was in all likelihood the *dominator* of the old castle of *Lizarra* under King Sancho IV Garcés *of Peñalén* first and under Sancho Ramírez later between 1058 and 1084.[9] It is quite possible that Garces supported the cause of Sancho Ramírez to get the throne of Pamplona. This explains the fact that his brothers, Sancho Garces, Lope Garces, and Eneko Garces were tenants of the castles of Etxauri, Agoitz, and Sanguesa, respectively.[10]

References to royally designated authorities in *Stella* date from 1031, when Sancho the Great conceded the honor of Estella to Fortuño Lopez (*senior Fortunio Lopez de Stella*).[11] Thereafter, *senioris*

---

7   On the toponymy of the place, see José María Jimeno Jurío, ed., *Nafarroako toponimia eta mapagintza*, vol. 24 (Iruñea: Nafarroako Gobernuaren Argitalpen Fondoa, 1996) and Fernando González Ollé, "Etimología del topónimo Estella," *Revista Príncipe de Viana* 51 (1990), 329–44.

8   From 1064 on, he is registered as *Eximino Garceiz dominator Lizarara*. In March that same year he became the *armiger regis* and, later, the *alferiz* or head of the royal guard. In January 1076 he appears as the *senior* of Uxue.

9   He is registered as such in 1058, 1063, 1064, 1065, 1066, 1072, 1074, and 1083. In José María Lacarra, *Colección diplomática de Irache. Volumen I (958–1222)* (Zaragoza: Consejo Superior de Investigaciones Científicas, Instituto de Estudios Pirenaicos, 1965), 7, 13, 22, 35, 38-39, 42, 45, 49, 66, and 73; and Ángel J. Martín Duque, *Documentación medieval de Leyre. Siglos IX a XII* (Iruñea: Diputación Foral de Navarra, Institución Príncipe de Viana, 1983). See likewise, José Moret, *Anales del reino de Navarra*, vol. 2 (Tolosa: Eusebio López, 1890), 360; Ramón Menéndez Pidal, *España del Cid*, vol. 2 (Madrid: Espasa Calpe, 1969), 694; José María Lacarra, *Estudios de historia de Navarra* (Iruñea: Diario de Navarra, 1971), 137; and Juan José Larrea, *La Navarre du IVe au XIIe siècle: Peuplement et société* (Paris and Brussels: De Boeck Université, 1998), 349.

10   *Estudios de Edad Media de la Corona de Aragón*, vol. 2 (Zaragoza: Consejo Superior de Investigaciones Científicas. Escuela de Estudios Medievales, 1946), 388.

11   Joseph Moret, *Annales del Reyno de Navarra*, vol. 1, book 12 (Iruñea: Imprenta de

are registered in the years 1054 (*Estelava*), 1065 (*Estelara*), 1084 (*Estella*), 1085 (*Stella*), and 1087 (*senior Lop Arnaldez dominator Stella*).[12] In 1084, eight years after Sancho Ramírez was crowned king, the *tenentes* of the old castle of Lizarra were taken off the payroll, that is, Lizarra disappeared "as a designation of the 'tenancy' and its new title holder, Lope Arnal, already figured as in charge of the new castle of Estella, whose construction was not completed until several decades later."[13] And Arnal remained in this service until 1093.[14] He was succeeded by García López Etxabarri (1099–1103), Sancho Garces (1104), Sancho Semenones (1104–1106), and Lope Garces (1110–1124).[15]

The first documented evidence of the existence of the new urban nucleus of San Martín de Estella is likewise early and, as Ángel J. Martín Duque and Roldán Jimeno point out, is prior to 1090. A document dated 1076 mentions a piece of land belonging to Sancho (abbot of the monastery of San Juan de la Peña) located "in the burg beneath the castle of Lizarra" (*in burgo quod est subtus illo castro de Lizarrara, a radice de illa pinna de illo castro, denante illos nostros molendinos*).[16] This means that in 1076 there already existed a

Martín Gregorio de Zavala, 1684), 603; and José Moret, *Anales del reino de Navarra*, vol. 3 (Tolosa: Eusebio López, 1890), 103. See likewise José Goñi, *Colección diplomática de la catedral de Pamplona (829–1243)*, vol. 1 (Iruñea: Nafarroako Gobernua, 1997), 35; and Roldán Jimeno and Aitor Pescador, eds., *Colección documental de Sancho Garcés III, el Mayor, rey de Pamplona (1004–1035)* (Iruñea: Pamiela, 2003), 227.

12 A figure likewise such as Lope Arnaldez or Lope Arnald. See Carlos Corona, *Toponimia navarra en la Edad Media* (Huesca: Consejo Superior de Investigaciones Científicas, 1947), 53-55; and Lacarra, *Colección diplomática de Irache. Volumen I (958–1222)*, 86, 88, 92.

13 Ángel J. Martín Duque, "La formación del primer 'burgo' navarro. Estella," *Príncipe de Viana* 51 (1990), 321. See also Martín Duque, *Documentación medieval de Leyre. Siglos IX a XII*. See likewise, *Jaca en la Corona de Aragón: (Siglos XII–XVIII) Actas* (Zaragoza: Gobierno de Aragón, Departamento de Educación y Cultura, 1994), 344.

14 Segundo Otazu, *De García el de Nájera hasta Alfonso el batallador* (Iruñea: Mintzoa, 1986), 112. See likewise *Jaca en la Corona de Aragón*, 344.

15 Lacarra, *Colección diplomática de Irache. Volumen I (958–1222)*, 86. See likewise Martín Duque, "La formación del primer 'burgo' navarro. Estella," 320–22; Julia Pavón, *Poblamiento altomedieval navarro: base socioeconómica del espacio monárquico* (Iruñea: Ediciones Universidad de Navarra, 2001), 247; and *Jaca en la Corona de Aragón*, 345. One should note that in 1121 Pedro Tizon appears registered as "tenente Marannon et Stella civitate," in Idelfonso Rodríguez de Lama, *Colección diplomática medieval de La Rioja (923–1225). Documentos (923–1168)* (Logroño: Servicio de Cultura de la Excma. Diputación Provincial, 1976), 122.

16 Martín Duque, "La formación del primer 'burgo' navarro. Estella," 765. Roldán Jimeno likewise cites the source: *subtus illo castro de Liçarrara, a radice de illa pinna de illo castro*. In Roldán Jimeno, "El municipio de Vasconia en la Edad Media," *Iura Vasconiae* 2 (2005), 45–83.

burg beneath the rock on which the castle was raised. On all this, a medieval document dating from 1077—only one year after Sancho Ramírez took over control of the kingdom—proves that Lope Arnal was already a *merino* or *señor de la tierra* of Estella (*Lop Arnal merino in Stela*).[17]

In sum, there is documented evidence of the existence of Lizarra since at least 1012 and the new *Stela* was already a population nucleus in 1031 and in 1076 the burg of San Martín (*rua de San Martin de Esteylla*) already existed.[18] This is not a new idea and was suggested by José Moret, chronicler of the kingdom, in 1695, when he argued that some people had imagined that 1090 was the year the first city of Estella was founded "and it has been published as such," "but be aware of the machination on the part of previous memories, which we have displayed in this kingdom, in which don Lope Arnaldez has been noted several times."[19]

Likewise, bearing in mind that Sancho IV Garcés of Peñalen was assassinated on June 4, 1076, we must conclude that, very probably, the idea of granting privileges to a burg in the lands bordering on the old castle of Lizarra was not that of King Sancho Ramírez, given that this would mean accepting that in seven months, between the beginning of June and December 1076, the new monarch had time to negotiate, put in writing, and sanction the fuero and even

---

17 The reference to Lop Arnal as *merino* of Estella in 1077 is registered in the royal certificate DSR, I, no. 14 (donation of the town of Ucar) in José Salarrullana, *Colección de documentos para el estudio de la historia de Aragón*, vol. 3 (Zaragoza: M. Escar, 1907), 32. Martín Duque states that this document (DSR, I, no. 14) constituted "more reliable" documented evidence in Martín Duque, "La formación del primer 'burgo' navarro. Estella," 321. See likewise Pavón, *Poblamiento altomedieval Navarro*, 247. See also *Jaca en la Corona de Aragón*, 345.

18 The documents refer likewise to a *merino* or *señor de la tierra*, which indicates that there was law. To be sure, one could argue that the fact that the *merino*, who was an agent of the king and *señor de la tierra* of Estella, lived in the urban nucleus was not related to the concession of norms, privileges, or a foral document; and, therefore, argue that the existence of a *merino* in a population center did not necessarily imply that this settlement had been given a fuero. However, to say that there was a *merino*, a burg, and a castle with a *tenente* and presuppose that Estella did not have law is definitely risky.

19 José Moret, *Anales del reino de Navarra, Bernardo de Huarte, impresor de la muy noble y muy leal provincia de Guypuzcoa*, vol. 2 (Pamplona, 1695), 34. Yanguas on the contrary states that the settlement of Lizarra grew when King Sancho Ramírez founded and populated the place with Franks in 1090 against the wishes of the monastery of San Juan de la Peña that sought to do so within its area of Zarapuz on what was at the time the Camino de Santiago. See José Yanguas y Miranda, *Diccionario de antigüedades del Reino de Navarra* (Pamplona: Diputación Foral de Navarra, 1840), 316.

have time to construct some of the houses in the new burg of San Martín.[20] This was very unlikely. On the contrary, from reading the sources it can be deduced that work in the burg of San Martín was advanced prior to the assassination of Sancho IV Garcés, to the point that that new population settlement was already termed a "burg" in 1076. In a word, the sources point out that the fuero had already been drawn up in 1076, that both the burg and the castle already existed in an advanced stage of construction on that date, and that, therefore, Sancho Ramírez continued a plan scheduled beforehand, during the reign of the king assassinated in Peñalen.

Ana María Barrero proposes a different chronological order for the concession of the Fueros of Jaca, Estella, and Sangüesa based on the results of a comparative analysis and textual critique of the three fueros and contends that the concession of these statutes of settlement was not carried out simultaneously, but successively.[21] Observing that, in drawing up certain simultaneous sections, or among those that one can establish a relationship, a certain textual progression is produced, she concludes that the fuero would have been granted in first place to Sangüesa, then to Estella, and finally to Jaca (*mea uilla que dicitur Iaka*).[22] One of the first conclusions of the study is that, "the presence of the same cases—six—in the main part of these fueros, despite dealing with typical matters in documents of

---

20 Although the monarchs appear as grantors of the documents that we recognize as fueros, they did not draw them up, or even elaborate them in their chancelleries. The concession of fueros was a complex process that involved both parties, the crown and the inhabitants of a town.

21 She insists that, beyond the paragraph in the Fuero of Jaca in which the king expresses his desire to extend Jaca to the status of city, the allusions always refer to Jaca as a town (*villa*). More specifically, and taking as her guide the Fuero of Jaca by Sancho Ramírez, she proceeds to undertake a complex comparative analysis, focusing on the existing coincidences in the texts, of the following legal documents: the Fueros of Sangüesa of 1117 and 1122, Puente la Reina, Alquézar, Ainsa, Pamplona, Asín, Jaca by Ramiro II, Olite, Berdún, Pueyo de Pintano, Estella, Iriberri, and Pueyo de Castellón. "Beyond this document of the wishes of the sovereign, so widely proclaimed, nor does it seem to have achieved any resonance either at the time, or in the centuries immediately following, although it did in the fourteenth and fifteenth centuries at the municipal level; and today as well." See Ana María Barrero García, "La difusión del Fuero de Jaca en el Camino de Santiago," in *El Fuero de Jaca. Estudios* (Zaragoza: El Justicia de Aragón, 2004), 111–60.

22 In this regard see ibid. Likewise, see Jimeno, "El municipio de Vasconia en la Edad Media," 65–67; Roldán Jimeno, "Lizarrako forua-El fuero de Estella," in *Anuario 2003 Irujo Etxea Elkartea* 3 (2003), 32–34; and Gregorio Monreal and Roldán Jimeno, *Textos histórico-jurídicos navarros I: Historia antigua y medieval* (Iruñea: Gobierno de Navarra, Instituto Navarro de Administración Pública, 2008).

this nature, reveal the existence of a common basis to all of them. This base is only included in its entirety in the Fuero of the new burg of Sangüesa, and not in that of Jaca in the form known to us today."[23] Interesting and clear textual progressions are, likewise, observed, "thus, in the Fuero of the old burg of Sangüesa, *de letzdas et de totas alias causas*, in that of Puente la Reina, *in totas vestras causas et vestras faciendas*, and in that of San Cernín de Pamplona and Iriberri *in totas vestras faziendas et vestros iudicios*," which indicates that that of Sangüesa was written first and that different additions were made later to the fueros that were written thereafter. Barrero coincides with Martín Duque and Antonio Ubieto in dating chronologically the granting of privileges to Sangüesa, Estella, and Jaca between 1076 and 1077.[24] As Roldán Jimeno points out, this Sangüesa, which received its privileges around 1076, was that which, with the creation of the new burg in 1122, would be known as old Sangüesa, today Rocaforte.[25]

Clearly, the Fuero of Jaca mentioned by Amalio Marichalar and Cayetano Manrique and later included in Mauricio Molho's work makes express mention of a fuero granted in 1062 or 1063;[26] and by *Santius, gratia Dei Aragonensium rex et Pampilonensium*.[27] While it is true that Sancho Ramírez made sure to use the title of *Aragonensium rex* from 1063 on, the year in which his father died, he could not call himself king of the people of Pamplona until 1076, the year in which Sancho IV died and his coronation as the very king of Pamplona (*ego Sancius Ranimirus, gratia Dei Aragonensium et Pampilonensium rex*). This is one of the reasons why some authors have preferred to put back the date of the granting of the Fuero of Jaca to 1076, the first during the reign of Sancho Ramírez in both kingdoms. The

---

23   Barrero García, "La difusión del Fuero de Jaca en el Camino de Santiago," 111–60.

24   Vicente Villabriga had already suggested 1076–77 as the most likely date of the granting of privileges to Sangüesa in 1962. See Vicente Villabriga, *Sangüesa ruta compostelana. Apuntes medievales*, no. 4 (Sangüesa: Ayuntamiento de Sangüesa, 1962), 144.

25   Roldán Jimeno, "Espacios sagrados, instituciones religiosas y culto a los santos en Sangüesa y su periferia durante los siglos medievales," *Zangotzarra* 8 (2004), 95–97.

26   T.C. era or 1100, the year 1062 or 1063.

27   Amalio Marichalar and Cayetano Manrique, *Historia de la legislación y recitaciones del derecho civil de España*, vol. 4 (Madrid: Imprenta Nacional, 1862), 480; Mauricio Molho, *El Fuero de Jaca. Edición crítica* (Zaragoza: Consejo Superior de Investigaciones Científicas, 1964), 3 and 5. See likewise another later version in Lacarra and Martín Duque, *Fueros derivados de Jaca*, 107.

text of the Fuero of Estella in 1164 states textually: "*dono et concedo vobis et succesoribus vestris illos bonos foros quos Sancius Rex concessit et dedit antecessoribus vestris quando populavit Stellam.*"[28] This is the only reference to the granting of the fuero to the inhabitants of Estella. According to this document, in 1164 Sancho *the Wise* ratified the fuero that "King Sancho" had granted to the inhabitants of the town when they settled it, extended with many of the legal norms that the assembly had included therein from its foundation to 1164. This "*Sancius rex*" mentioned in the fuero of 1164 is traditionally thought to have been Sancho Ramírez, basically because of the dating of the fuero to 1090 (by which time Sancho IV had already died), but if we bear in mind the previous date, there is no reason not to think that the "*Sancius rex*" mentioned in the fuero of 1164 was Sancho IV, of Peñalen. As Barrero points out, the text of Sancho the Wise in 1164 omits making any reference to him being related to Sancho Ramírez.[29]

In sum, while the debate over dating the Fuero of Estella remains open, the documentation we have on when exactly the new urban nucleus of the burg of San Martín was granted privileges points to the fact that it could have been any time between 1031 and 1076. Without overlooking the fact that the fuero may originally have been applied orally rather than being written down and on the understanding that the old Lizarra must have had a law, the question surrounding when the writing down of the Fuero of the burg of San Martín was sanctioned is narrowed down to a period between 1054 and 1076 during the reign of Sancho Garcés IV. This is clearly the most reasonable option. There exists, however, the possibility that on his death, Sancho Ramírez may have granted the fuero to the inhabitants of the new burg of San Martín during the first months of his reign in 1076. In this case one would have to explain why, with *tenentes* existing since at least 1031 and knowing that the burg of San Martín already existed in 1076, this population nucleus did not have any law prior to that date. In any event, even if one accepts this latter option, it would be necessary to admit that the new king

---

28   Xabier Irujo, *Giving Birth to Cosmopolis: The Code of Laws of Estella (c. 1076)* (Santa Barbara: University of California, Santa Barbara, 2013), 189.
29   Barrero García, "La difusión del Fuero de Jaca en el Camino de Santiago," 119.

restricted himself to authorizing a law that had been composed and drawn up and even agreed on beforehand.

The Fuero of Estella should not be considered a derivative of the Fuero of Jaca, which was granted around the year 1076 or 1077 to the inhabitants of that town.[30] In addition to the fact that the study of the content of the fueros indicates that the Fuero of Sangüesa and that of Estella predate that of Jaca, the three texts would have been drawn up and granted through the second half of the eleventh century. In this sense, the sources only allow us to affirm that the three settlements were granted privileges through the same or a similar fuero. As Lacarra and Martín Duque contend, the first eleven chapters of the Latin edition of the Fuero of Estella in 1164 correspond to the same amount of chapters in the fuero that both authors suggest was granted to Jaca by Sancho Ramírez, which is in effect indicative that both texts could be identical.[31] Yet unfortunately we do not possess the original text of the Fuero of Estella so that nor can we argue with complete certainty that both codes were identical.

Whatever the case and, beyond dating the burg of San Martín de Estella prior to 1076, this cannot be considered a "derivative" of another fuero by virtue of its nature.[32] Both the Fuero of the burg of San Martín de Estella and those of Jaca and Sangüesa all

---

30   The dating of the Fuero of Jaca is likewise subject to debate. Mauricio Molho suggests 1063 as the most likely date of the primitive fuero. This date is also accepted by Jesús Lalinde, while Antonio Ubieto questions this possibility, establishing a broader dating framework between 1063 and 1077, and pointing out that in his opinion 1076–1077 seems more likely. Jesús Delgado points out that, while the most likely date of the primitive fuero is 1077, the chronological interval between 1063 and this date is still acceptable. See "Fuero de Jaca, 1063," in Eugen Wohlhaupter, *Altspanisch-gotische rechte* (Weimar: Böhlau, 1936), 134–41; José María Ramos Loscertales, *La tenencia de año y día en el Derecho aragonés (1063–1247)* (Salamanca: Universidad de Salamanca, 1951); Molho, *El Fuero de Jaca*; Antonio Ubieto, *Jaca: documentos municipales, 971–1269* (Valencia: Anubar Ediciones, 1975); Jesús Lalinde, *Los fueros de Aragón* (Zaragoza: Librería General, 1976); Jesús Delgado, *Los fueros de Aragón* (Zaragoza: Caja de Ahorros de la Inmaculada de Aragón, 1997); and María Luisa Arnal Purroy et al, *El fuero de Jaca. Estudios* (Zaragoza: El Justicia de Aragón, 2004), 320.
31   Lacarra and Martín Duque, *Fueros derivados de Jaca*, 20.
32   Renowned authors have considered that, in effect, the Fuero of Estella was derived from that of Jaca. See Lacarra and Martín Duque, *Fueros derivados de Jaca*. See likewise Luis Oroz, *Legislación administrativa de Navarra* (Iruñea: Imprenta provincial, 1917–1923); Barrero García, "La difusión del Fuero de Jaca en el Camino de Santiago" 111–60; and Mauricio Molho, "Difusión del Derecho pirenaico (Fuero de Jaca) en el Reino de Aragón," *Boletín de la Real Academia de Buenas Letras de Barcelona* 28 (1959–60), 264–352.

constitute compilations of common law juridical norms, that is, they are collections of oral norms that predate any written binding that were grouped together, adapted, and drafted with the aim of granting the inhabitants of Sangüesa, those of the burg of San Martín, and those of the *villa* of Jaca a set of norms on which to organize the common life of their respective settlements. Independently of which of them was written and granted first, none of them derive from another.

None of these three legal texts can be considered "privileges." The fuero was not a concession or royal privilege but rather a compilation of legal norms. The legal tradition in Navarre differentiated the concepts of *fuero, ley, usos, costumbres, privilegios, franquezas,* and *libertades* so that we cannot contend that the concepts of *fuero* and *ley* were completely synonymous. In general terms, it can be deduced from the *Diccionario de los fueros y leyes de Navarra* by Yanguas y Miranda that the word *fuero* referred to pre-fourteenth-century written laws or included in the general Fuero of Navarre and in the improvement of Queen Joan II of Navarre and the king consort Philip III Evreux in 1330, of common law origin, while *leyes* would be, from a generic and not very precise perspective, the legal norms adopted thereafter: included in the *Novissima Recopilación* (1735);[33] and in the parliamentary papers from 1724 to 1818.[34] The *usos* and *costumbres* would be those norms of equally common law origin but not written down and, in most cases, exclusive to specific population centers or valleys. The *franquezas* and *libertades* were, for their part, both fueros and common law norms that were perceived as legal principles on account of their importance or their influence in legal codes and that were therefore present in various sections or articles in the fuero. Finally, the *privilegios* would be those privileges conceded by the crown to specific population centers by virtue of historic events or natural catastrophes or other causes and that, therefore, in contrast to all the other legal norms, constituted

---

33 *Novissima recopilación de las leyes del Reino de Navarra: hechas en sus Cortes Generales desde el año de 1512 hasta el de 1716 inclusive* (Iruñea: Joseph Joachin Martínez, 1735).
34 José Yanguas y Miranda, *Diccionario de los fueros y leyes de Navarra* (Iruñea: Editorial Aranzadi, 1964), 16–17.

exceptions, in most cases recompenses or compensations, within the general norms.

In regard to the case under consideration, the word "fuero" designated a set of legal norms for a specific settlement. In this way, local fueros constituted legal statutes applied to a specific place whose objective was, in general, to regulate local life via a set of legal norms of different origins such as the very uses of the place and more general customs taken from the corpus of common law, ordinances passed by local assemblies and privileges granted by monarchs to each of these localities in view of diverse historical or negotiated events with these in exchange for certain services.

In any of its acceptations, the word "fuero" did not designate or mean "privilege" but, rather, "legal norm," most of them deriving from common law and emanating from popular will represented by assemblies or municipal councils on being ratified by virtue of an agreement with the crown and taking on the force of law.

As regards the sources of law, the norms of the Fuero of Estella stem from and therefore basically "derive" from two legal sources, the common law of the land and the Bible. As regards the Holy Scriptures, the fuero incorporates in some cases sections or norms taken literally or paraphrased from the Bible, fundamentally from certain books in the Old Testament. The Torah, Pentateuch, or written Mosaic Law contains declarations or legal and ethical principles that illuminate the Fuero of Estella, in particular in that referring to matters of penal and civil law. Most of the norms included in the fuero stem basically from the Book of Exodus, more specifically Exodus 22 and Deuteronomy (18 and 24). Moreover, in writing up these norms phrases, statements were taken from the Book of Proverbs, Ecclesiastes, the Book of Job, and, in some perhaps purely accidental cases, from the New Testament. Among the norms taken from the Holy Scriptures we can put forward, for example, certain norms of administering justice relating to the regulation of testimonies by witnesses and, likewise, the regulation of cases of false testimony. Such are the cases of, to cite a few examples, the principle of restitution of stolen goods taken from the Book of Exodus, norms on punishment for breaking and entering, aggression, rape, and injury, and, finally, certain norms on the regulation of pawning, borrowing, and collateral. It is remarkable that the punishments observed in the Fuero of Estella are normatively less rigorous than those of the Bible.

Yet the principal source of law in the Fuero of Estella is the very legal tradition of Pyrenean law. In this sense, the Fuero of Estella included legal norms or institutions that we can see subsequently in diverse fueros of the country such as the general Fuero of Navarre or the brotherhood notebooks and fueros of Gipuzkoa, Bizkaia, and Zuberoa, as well as many other local fueros. The reason for such concomitance was that while the Fuero of Navarre was not written down until the thirteenth century, it clearly preexisted in oral form and constituted, naturally, the principal source for the future composition of the Fuero of Estella and also that of Jaca. Thus, for example, typical legal concepts of Basque historical law included in the Fuero of Estella such as the right to be judged by the very laws of the place and *ius migrationis*, the complex systemization of procedural rights, the conditions that witnesses should meet, the procedures for buying and selling inheritances, and the inviolability of the home were found in the general Fuero of Navarre. In general it is important to mention that there were no norms in civil or criminal matters included in the Fuero of Estella that were not included in the general Fuero of Navarre and it is likewise significant the fact that many of these norms were included in the Fuero of Estella with an almost identical drafting as that of the general Fuero of Navarre, written for the first time in the thirteenth century, from which it can be deduced that these norms were transmitted, from generation to generation, from memory.

Nor can the Fuero of Estella be understood as "conceded" by a monarch, but instead as the expression on parchment of some legal principles that regulated the life of the inhabitants of the kingdom and that bound both the king and the inhabitants of the country together. The formula for confirming the Fuero of Estella in 1164 states that Sancho VI the Wise, as king of Navarre and "in the name of God . . . gives, concedes, and confirms . . . the writing and authority"[35] of the fuero with which the new legal code was sanctioned in the form that "the good fueros that King Sancho [IV or V?] conceded to you and gave to your ancestors when he settled Estella"[36] had been reformed. Following a process of negotiation and common agreement with the people in the city, the king confirmed and sanctioned—but did not impose—the right of the inhabitants of Estella to possess, maintain, and improve the rights that the original fuero included and, likewise, the broad and complex set of new norms introduced in the new fuero of 1164.

As the fuero itself stated in its last section, it was not just the responsibility of the crown to preserve and improve the fueros, but that of the population of Estella itself, which likewise had the legal obligation to maintain it "safe and decent, free and honest in perpetuity."[37] It was, then, a contract that committed both parties and benefited everyone. And the formula of confirming the fueros highlighted the fact that the king had made that decision "of his own accord and of spontaneous will"[38] and by virtue of the services that the city of Estella had undertaken and was undertaking "every day"[39] for the Kingdom of Pamplona. As could be appreciated in the sealing of the fuero, it was the result of a process agreed on by the crown of Navarre and the inhabitants of Estella represented by their judges. As a consequence, the fuero was signed by the monarch but, likewise, the representatives of diverse sectors in the Kingdom of Navarre and representatives of the city of Estella, Mayor Pedro Guillermo, Provost Julián, and the executioner Pedro Guillén de Larraga, also figured in the document. Only the signature of all these figures sealed the pact that was signed before a notary in Estella in April 1164, which conferred it with the force of law.

As can be deduced from the general Fuero of Navarre, the monarch could not alter or suspend individual guarantees without the agreement of parliament. By extension, all legal texts required the sanction of the monarch and the parliament of the kingdom or,

---

35 Irujo, Giving Birth to Cosmopolis, 189.
36 Ibid.
37 Ibid., 270.
38 Ibid., 189.
39 Ibid.

in the case of municipalities, the *batzar* or *conseyll*, the local council. This fact reflects the prohibition of the royal authorities on taking any responsibility for or inquiring legally into the private lives of inhabitants of the kingdom. Only treason could lead to the rights of the city being abolished. As stated in the last section, "save loyalty to my person or my posterity for the rest of time." Consequently, the process of confirming or reforming the fueros constituted a complex agreement in which the interests of the crown and the city of Estella and its inhabitants were debated.

The code of laws of Estella is one of the oldest local fueros in the Kingdom of Pamplona and an important legal reference. It is for that reason that a large number of cities were granted privileges in medieval times, including the city of Donostia (San Sebastian) that Sancho VI the Wise, king of Navarre, awarded privileges with this law around the year 1180. The family of this fuero encompassed the towns of Sangüesa, Estella, Jaca, Gares, Monreal, Urrotz, Tiebas, Pamplona, Torralba, Uharte Arakil, Artajona, Tafalla, Olite, Mendigorria, and San Vicente de la Barquera, as well as the Gipuzkoan towns of Oiartzun, Errenteria, Donostia, Hondarribia, Getaria, Zarautz, Usurbil, Zumaia, Orio, and Mutriku.

The Fuero of Estella reflects a clearly democratic political organization. A study of the text demonstrates that, already in the twelfth century, all of its inhabitants had a voice and a vote in the city assembly and that it was governed by a council made up of members elected pro tempore. In the judicial sphere, parliament was governed by the principle of legality and judicial impartiality, the presumption of innocence, the right to a formal accusation, the right to prepare the defense, the right to contribute witnesses, the right to be judged by competent judges and according to the laws of the city, and many other basic procedural rights. The legislators of the city shunned applying prison sentences and avoided adopting the death penalty until 1307. Through the fourteenth century the norm would be applied only in cases of murder and, always within the context of wars between factions in the city, "the Ponces and the Learzas, the Learzas and the Ponces." It is also especially interesting from the perspective of the study of women's rights and obligations.

The text is conclusive and very explicit in stating that women who are the head of a family have the same obligations as men, with the exception of military service, which implies that they likewise possessed the rights that were consubstantial to those payments or obligations.[40] The treatment of minors in the legal text is likewise very significant within the context of the study of privileges and freedoms (what today we term human rights) in Medieval Europe. Lastly, it is necessary to underscore the guarantees that the fuero offered Jews and Muslims at a moment in which European Christianity did not favor any dialogue among religions or contact among the faithful of different creeds.

Owing to the exceptionally varied and extensive legal content, the Fuero of Estella is one of the most significant legal documents in Europe in the eleventh and twelfth centuries and, as such, a historical document of exceptional interest for the study of medieval European legislation. Yet, above all else, the Fuero of Estella and the privileges and freedoms it contains transformed the city into an authentic medieval cosmopolis whose merchants traveled as far as the Low Countries with documents issued in Estella but recognized by the monarchs of different European kingdoms. The Estella market was very successful not just because of its ideal geographical setting and compatibility with commerce and the needs generated by daily buying and selling and services on the Camino de Santiago through the burg of San Martín, but through the privileges guaranteed by the laws of the city and protected by the crown of Navarre. To the original rights contained in the twelfth-century fuero were added new dispositions such as that of 1249 by which Theobald I, king of Navarre, granted the merchants of Estella fiscal advantages

---

40   On the role of women in Estella, "our documents reflect a vision of women that forms part of an important segment of the strength of urban work. They were independent property owners who assumed the responsibilities of heads of families, in their capacity as "keepers of the hearth [*tenientes de fuego*] or home or heads of families," both in their status as widows or spinsters, in an increasingly organized and strict state when it came to fulfilling the payment of different taxes. In the second aspect addressed, we identify a set of women who also enjoyed financial independence, who traded in specific products, both in their status as producers and in their capacity as intermediaries in retail commerce . . . We can classify the commercial activity of women in the life of the cities studied (Tudela, Estella, and Los Arcos) as prominent." Nelly Ongay, "Visión de las mujeres en el Reino de Navarra desde la perspectiva de las fuentes impositivas (siglos XIV y XV)," *Cyber Humanitatis* 11 (January 1999), 8.

regarding the payment of tolls due in commerce with the coastal city of Donostia in Gipuzkoa. On February 10, 1205, Alfonso VIII of Castile had granted the merchants of the city a license to trade freely throughout the cities and seigneuries of the Kingdom of Castile and Leon, "without any person imposing any obstacles." Equally, on August 7, 1254,[41] while in Estella, King James I the Conqueror of the neighboring Kingdom of Aragon granted merchants in the city the right to travel, remain, deal, and contract freely without hindrance in his lands. He added that he would take under his protection the merchants of Estella with the aim of favoring their activity within the borders of his kingdom.[42]

The trade network of the merchants of the city, coupled with the flow of pilgrims from all corners of Europe, soon obliged the merchants of Estella to have exchange counters, a primitive form of bank in which pilgrims or traders could exchange their money freely. Estella was a city with a large market square, a public council, a bank, a rich Jewish quarter, and a phenomenal castle whose custody was in the hands of a squad made up of just three professional soldiers, because in a fortified city like that, totally walled for defending the interests of its inhabitants, the right to public happiness resided in the wellbeing of each of its inhabitants, both buyers and sellers, men and women, adults and minors, Christians and Jews, as well as convicted criminals, because they were all ingenuous, free, and honest *per infinita secula seculorum*. This is probably the greatest value in the Fuero of Estella, the recognition that social and economic prosperity of the town resided in the right to political equality for its inhabitants in particular and the search for the public happiness of the community in general.

---

41 Merche Oses, *Documentación medieval de Estella (siglos XII–XVI)* (Iruñea: Institución Príncipe de Viana, 2005), 32.
42 Sebastián Iribarren, *Apuntes sobre la historia Antigua de Estella* (Seville: Imprenta y Librería de Eulogio de las Heras, 1912), 272–74.

BIBLIOGRAPHY

Arnal Purroy, María Luisa et al. *El fuero de Jaca. Estudios*. Zaragoza: El Justicia de Aragón, 2004.

Avilés, Miguel, and Guillermo Sena. *Nuevas poblaciones en la España moderna*. Madrid: Universidad Nacional de Educación a Distancia, 1991

Barrero García, Ana María. "La difusión del Fuero de Jaca en el Camino de Santiago." In *El Fuero de Jaca. Estudios*. Zaragoza: El Justicia de Aragón, 2004.

―――. "'A fuero de los francos de…' Sobre la base documental de un debate historiográfico." In Béatrice Leroy et al., eds. *Les Français en Espagne du VIIIéme au XIIIéme siècle / Los Franceses en España desde el siglo VIII al siglo XIII*. Actes Congrès transpyrénalia, conduits sous la direction de Ph. Sénac, J-P Barraque et al. Oloron Sainte Marie: Mairie d'Oloron-Sainte-Marie, 2007.

Corona, Carlos. *Toponimia navarra en la Edad Media*. Huesca: Consejo Superior de Investigaciones Científicas, 1947.

Delgado, Jesús. *Los fueros de Aragón*. Zaragoza: Caja de Ahorros de la Inmaculada de Aragón, 1997.

Estudios de Edad Media de la Corona de Aragón. Volume 2. Zaragoza: Consejo Superior de Investigaciones Científicas, Escuela de Estudios Medievales, 1946.

Estornés Lasa, Bernardo. *Historia general de Euskalerria: 824–1234, época pamplonesa*. Donostia: Auñamendi, 1989.

"Fuero de Jaca, 1063." In Eugen Wohlhaupter, *Altspanisch-gotische rechte*. Weimar: Böhlau, 1936.

Goñi, José. *Colección diplomática de la catedral de Pamplona (829–1243)*. Volume 1. Iruñea: Nafarroako Gobernua, 1997.

González Ollé, Fernando. "Etimología del topónimo Estella." *Revista Príncipe de Viana* 51 (1990): 329–44.

Holmér, Gustaf. *El fuero de Estella, según el manuscrito 944 de la Biblioteca de Palacio de Madrid.* Karlsham: E. G. Johannssons Boktryckeri, 1963.

Iribarren, Sebastián. *Apuntes sobre la historia Antigua de Estella.* Seville: Imprenta y Librería de Eulogio de las Heras, 1912.

Irujo, Xabier. *Giving Birth to Cosmopolis: The Code of Laws of Estella (c. 1076).* Santa Barbara: University of California, Santa Barbara, 2013.

Jaca en la Corona de Aragón (Siglos XII–XVIII). XV Congreso de historia de la Corona de Aragón. Actas. Zaragoza: Gobierno de Aragón, Departamento de Educación y Cultura, 1994.

Jimeno Jurio, José María, ed. *Nafarroako toponimia eta mapagintza.* Voliume 24. Iruñea: Nafarroako Gobernuaren Argitalpen Fondoa, 1996.

Jimeno Jurio, José María. *Merindad de Estella. I. Historia de Estella/ Lizarra.* Colección Obras completas de José María Jimeno Jurío no. 33. Iruñea: Pamiela-Udalbide-Euskara Kultur Elkargoa, 2006.

Jimeno, Roldán. "Lizarrako forua-El fuero de Estella." In *Anuario 2003 Irujo Etxea Elkartea* 3 (2003): 32–34.

———. "Espacios sagrados, instituciones religiosas y culto a los santos en Sangüesa y su periferia durante los siglos medievales." *Zangotzarra* 8 (2004): 95–97.

———. "El municipio de Vasconia en la Edad Media." *Iura Vasconiae* 2 (2005): 45–83.

Jimeno, Roldán, and Aitor Pescador, eds. *Colección documental de Sancho Garcés III, el Mayor, rey de Pamplona (1004–1035).* Iruñea: Pamiela, 2003.

Lacarra, José María. "De Estella a Nájera." In *Las peregrinaciones a Santiago de Compostela*, edited by Luis Vázquez de Parga, José M. Lacarra, and Juan Uría Ríu. Volume 2. Madrid: Consejo superior de investigaciones científicas, Escuela de estudios medievales, 1949.

————. *Colección diplomática de Irache. Volumen I (958–1222)*. Zaragoza: Consejo Superior de Investigaciones Científicas, Instituto de Estudios Pirenaicos, 1965.

————. *Estudios de historia de Navarra*. Iruñea: Diario de Navarra, 1971.

————. *Historia del reino de Navarra en la Edad Media*. Iruñea: Caja de Ahorros de Navarra, 1975.

————. *Historia política del reino de Navarra: desde sus orígenes hasta su incorporación a Castilla*. Iruñea: Editorial Aranzadi, 1973.

Lacarra, José María, and Ángel J. Martín Duque. *Fueros derivados de Jaca. Estella-San Sebastián*. Iruñea: Institución Príncipe de Viana, 1969.

Lalinde, Jesús. *Los fueros de Aragón*. Zaragoza: Librería General, 1976.

Larrea, Juan José. *La Navarre du IVe au XIIe siècle: Peuplement et société*. Paris and Brussels: De Boeck Université, 1998.

Marichalar, Amalio, and Cayetano Manrique. *Historia de la legislación y recitaciones del derecho civil de España*. Madrid: Imprenta Nacional, 1862.

Martín Duque, Ángel J. *Documentación medieval de Leyre. Siglos IX a XII*. Iruñea: Diputación Foral de Navarra, Institución Príncipe de Viana, 1983.

————. "La formación del primer 'burgo' navarro. Estella." *Príncipe de Viana* 51 (1990): 317–27.

Menéndez Pidal, Ramón. *España del Cid*. Volume 2. Madrid: Espasa Calpe, 1969.

Molho, Mauricio. "Difusión del Derecho pirenaico (Fuero de Jaca) en el Reino de Aragón." *Boletín de la Real Academia de Buenas Letras de Barcelona* 28 (1959–60): 264–352.

————. *El Fuero de Jaca. Edición crítica*. Zaragoza: Consejo Superior de Investigaciones Científicas, 1964.

Monreal, Gregorio, and Roldán Jimeno. *Textos histórico-jurídicos navarros I: Historia antigua y medieval*. Iruñea: Gobierno de Navarra, Instituto Navarro de Administración Pública, 2008.

Moret, José. *Anales del reino de Navarra, Bernardo de Huarte, impresor de la muy noble y muy leal provincia de Guypuzcoa.* Volume 2. Pamplona, 1695.

———. *Anales del reino de Navarra.* Volumes 2 and 3. Tolosa: Eusebio López, 1890.

Moret, Joseph. *Annales del Reyno de Navarra.* Volume 1. Book 12. Iruñea: Imprenta de Martín Gregorio de Zavala, 1684.

Novissima recopilación de las leyes del Reino de Navarra: hechas en sus Cortes Generales desde el año de 1512 hasta el de 1716 inclusive. Iruñea: Joseph Joachin Martínez, 1735.

Ongay, Nelly. "Visión de las mujeres en el Reino de Navarra desde la perspectiva de las fuentes impositivas (siglos XIV y XV)." *Cyber Humanitatis* 11 (January 1999).

Oroz, Luis. *Legislación administrativa de Navarra.* Iruñea: Imprenta provincial, 1917–1923.

Oses, Merche. *Documentación medieval de Estella (siglos XII–XVI).* Iruñea: Institución Príncipe de Viana, 2005.

Otazu, Segundo. *De García el de Nájera hasta Alfonso el batallador.* Iruñea: Mintzoa, 1986.

Pavón, Julia. *Poblamiento altomedieval navarro: base socioeconómica del espacio monárquico.* Iruñea: Ediciones Universidad de Navarra, 2001.

Ramos Loscertales, José María. *Fuero de Jaca.* Última redacción. Barcelona: Universidad de Barcelona, Facultad de Derecho, 1927.

———. *La tenencia de año y día en el Derecho aragonés (1063–1247).* Salamanca: Universidad de Salamanca, 1951.

Rodríguez de Lama, Idelfonso. *Colección diplomática medieval de La Rioja (923–1225). Documentos (923–1168).* Logroño: Servicio de Cultura de la Excma. Diputación Provincial, 1976.

Ros, Antonio. *El nacimiento de Estella y sus castillos.* Tafalla: Altaffaylla Kultur Taldea, 2009.

Sáinz, María Inés, and Ángel Elvira, eds. *El fuero de Estella*. Iruñea/ Pamplona: Gobierno de Navarra, Departamento de Educación y Cultura, 1990.

Salarrullana, José. *Colección de documentos para el estudio de la historia de Aragón*. Volume 3. Zaragoza: M. Escar, 1907.

Ubieto, Antonio. *Jaca: documentos municipales, 971–1269*. Valencia: Anubar Ediciones, 1975.

Villabriga, Vicente. *Sangüesa ruta compostelana. Apuntes medievales*. Sangüesa: Ayuntamiento de Sangüesa, 1962.

Yanguas y Miranda, José. *Diccionario de los fueros y leyes de Navarra*. Iruñea: Editorial Aranzadi, 1964.

———. *Historia compendiada de Navarra*. Donostia: Imprenta de Ignacio Ramón Baroja, 1832.

———. *Diccionario de antigüedades del Reino de Navarra*. Pamplona: Diputación Foral de Navarra, 1840.

Chapter 1

An Obscure Past: Gipuzkoa and Navarre from the Tenth to the Twelfth Centuries

José Ángel Lema Pueyo

This chapter is based on a presentation titled "Navarre and Gipuzkoa, 1076–1180." As one can see from the definitive title, the aim is to offer a fuller historical trajectory. In line with certain archaeological evidence and more remote potential writings, there has been a preference to situate the oldest limit in the tenth century, while the most modern would be toward the end of the reign of Sancho VI the Wise, in 1194. In fact, the date 1180 for the Fuero of San Sebastian is still a reasonable approximation. It does not enter into the delicate problem of the incorporation of Gipuzkoa into Castile five years later. The objective here, following a brief introductory explanation of the state of knowledge and available sources, will be, first, to follow the changes in jurisdiction that the territory experienced during that era, underscoring the links with the Kingdom of Navarre, titled the Kingdom of Pamplona until 1162. This initial part will include references to the origins and early development of Donostia-San Sebastian, in its relations with the monarchs Pedro I, García Ramírez, and Sancho VI. Thereafter, paying attention to the base realities, there will be an attempt to offer a general characterization of the population and society in Gipuzkoa during those centuries.

Historiography and Sources of Information

In a historiographical journey it is difficult to do justice to all those who have contributed to knowledge of the medieval past of Gipuzkoa prior to 1200. Without any doubt, the erudite contributions of José Luis Banús y Aguirre, Ricardo de Izaguirre, Manuel de Lekuona, and Serapio de Múgica were of great use. Nonetheless, the starting point came in 1975 with *Guipúzcoa en los albores de su historia* (Gipuzkoa at the dawn of its history) by Gonzalo Martínez Díez, who, through a document approach, included, published, addressed, and commented critically on the available written documents from the tenth to twelfth centuries. To be sure, the scarcity of these sources discouraged him when it came to taking the next step, which would have been to try and write a history of the territory during this era. Six years later, Eusko Ikaskuntza (the Society of Basque Studies) organized a conference on the Fuero of San Sebastian that included over twenty works dedicating to publishing texts and historical and juridical studies. In this academic context, José Ángel García de Cortázar, taking advantage of the sources at his disposal, offered an intriguing overview of Gipuzkoan society during the era, of its economic activity and the transformations in its space through to the era of the Fuero of San Sebastian. He defended the existence of an archaic society, of a tribal nature, dedicated primordially to livestock and forestry, which, through the eleventh and twelfth centuries, evolved toward feudal forms of organization under the effect of external influences, of a Mediterranean nature. Working on and going more deeply into this line of inquiry, in 1989 Elena Barrena published her doctoral dissertation, exploiting fully, in a combined way, documented evidence and the information provided by toponymy and geography. In 1997, in the introductory chapter to her doctoral dissertation, Soledad Tena García defended a similar interpretation, while stressing the capacity to evolve on the part of Gipuzkoan society itself rather than on the basis of external influences.[1]

---

1   Gonzalo Martínez Díez, *Guipúzcoa en los albores de su historia* (San Sebastián: Diputación Provincial de Guipúzcoa, 1975); *Congreso: El fuero de San Sebastián y su época (San Sebastián 19-23 de enero de 1981) / Donostiako forua eta bere garaia (Donostia, 1981ko urtarrilaren 19tik 23ra)* (San Sebastián: Eusko Ikaskuntza / Sociedad de Estudios Vascos, 1982); José

From a more traditional perspective, two works published at the close of the twentieth century have been of considerable interest. On the one hand, a study by Aitor Pescador Medrano that reconstructs, combining documented data from diverse sources, information relating to the Navarrese *tenente* barons in Gipuzkoa up to 1076, together with those of Araba and Bizkaia. And on the other, that of Luis Javier Fortún, who, continuing the tradition of José María Lacarra in questions of political and dynastic history, explains in detail the ups and downs of the sovereignty experienced by the territories of the current Basque Autonomous Community between 1134 and 1200. Likewise, in recent decades, one should mention the contributions of José Luis Orella Unzué to diverse relevant questions that include, among many others, a juridical analysis of the Fuero of San Sebastian and the history of Gipuzkoa as a district (*tenencia*) of the Kingdom of Pamplona.[2]

Research work on this topic runs into a serious methodological problem: the extreme scarcity of written primary sources. There are less than a hundred texts of legal value, what we term commonly "documents." A substantial part of those are brief mentions of monarchs or their delegates that exercise jurisdiction in the territory. Imperfect copies and manipulations—if not pure falsifications—of certain texts complicate still more the work of the researcher. Making up to some extent for this panorama, we have the carefully prepared published edition of the fuero granted by Sancho VI

Ángel García de Cortázar, "La sociedad guipuzcoana antes del fuero de San Sebastián," in *Investigaciones sobre historia medieval del País Vasco (1965–2005)*, ed. José Ramón Díaz de Durana (Bilbao: Universidad de País Vasco / Euskal Herriko Unibertsitatea, 2005), 281–312; Elena Barrena Osoro, *La formación histórica de Guipúzcoa. Transformaciones en la organización social de un territorio cantábrico durante la época altomedieval* (San Sebastián: Universidad de Deusto, 1989); Soledad Tena García, *La sociedad urbana en la Guipúzcoa costera medieval: San Sebastián, Rentería y Fuenterrabía (1200–1500)* (Donostia / San Sebastián: Instituto Doctor Camino de Historia Donostiarra, 1997), 49–88. For a general overview, see José Ángel Lema Pueyo, "De 'Ipuzkoa' a la Hermandad de villas de Gipuzkoa (ss. VI–XV)," in *Síntesis de la Historia de Gipuzkoa*, ed. Álvaro Aragón Ruano and Iker Echeberria Ayllón (Donostia: Diputación Foral de Gipuzkoa, 2017), 145–52.

2   Aitor Pescador Medrano, "Tenentes y tenencias del reino de Pamplona en Álava, Vizcaya, Guipúzcoa, La Rioja y Castilla (1004–1076)," *Vasconia. Cuadernos de Historia-Geografía* 29 (1999), 118–20; Luis Javier Fortún Pérez de Ciriza, "La quiebra de la soberanía navarra en Álava, Guipúzcoa y el Duranguesado (1199–1200)," *Revista Internacional de los Estudios Vascos* 45, no. 2 (2000), 439–94; José Luis Orella Unzué, "Estudio jurídico comparativo de los fueros de San Sebastián, Estella, Vitoria y Logroño," in *Congreso: El fuero de San Sebastián y su época*, 255–300; and José Luis Orella Unzué, "Nacimiento de Guipúzcoa como tenencia navarra de frontera," *Lurralde: investigación y espacio* 34 (2011), 189–217.

to San Sebastian, under the care of Ángel J. Martín Duque and presented on the occasion of the aforementioned conference. In order to explain the reasons for such scarcity, one must bear in mind that, at that time, for the principal centers that generated and, above all, preserved these kinds of texts—diocesan headquarters and monasteries—Gipuzkoa was a peripheral space, given that the essential areas under their domain and patrimony were in other places. Nor are chroniclers of much help; in effect, prior to the Alfonso VIII's campaign of conquest, there was only one express mention of Gipuzkoa—not without interest—in the *Historia Compostelana*.[3]

During the last two decades the possibilities of expanding knowledge and suggesting new interpretations have stemmed from the contributions of archaeology. The findings of this discipline inform us about the materiality of lifestyles: the distribution of space, buildings and facilities, burial sites, technologies, and diets, among other things. In Gipuzkoa, medieval archaeology was given great momentum in 1990 thanks to the institutional support offered at that time by the Basque Law on Cultural Heritage. In this vein there have been contributions by researchers such as Agustín Azkarate, Iosu Etxezarraga, Alex Ibáñez, Alfredo Moraza, Juan Antonio Quirós, and Nerea Sarasola. With the support of bodies from the University of the Basque Country to the Aranzadi Society of Sciences and the Arkeolan Foundation, excavation projects have focused preferentially on what is termed the "archaeology of power" (castles and churches), without forgetting the rural and forestry world, through the trail of productive facilities. Necropolises have often offered clues about village settlements and religious enclaves. On account of their transcendence when it comes to revising dating regarding populating places, special mention should be made of the interventions carried out in Santa María la Mayor in Zarautz, as part of the Menosca Project. Getaria and Mutriku—in the church of San Andrés de Astigarribia, one of the oldest in the territory—have also been the object of excavations. Inland, the oldest evidence

---

3   There is an assessment of the available written sources in Barrena Osoro, *La formación histórica de Guipúzcoa*, 37–47; Tena García, *La sociedad urbana en la Guipúzcoa costera medieval*, 55–58; and *Historia Compostelana*, ed. and trans. Emma Falque Rey, book 2 (Los Berrocales del Jarama, Madrid: Akal, 1994), xx.

found, of a chronology similar to that of Zarautz, is in Bidania. The results of this work open up doors for debating and updating interpretations.[4]

Obscure Origins

When does a territory get a name? The question is not unimportant, since answering it marks the beginning of the existence of a community identified with a space. It is worth revising opinions about this matter.

Some Observations for the Debate

Araba and Bizkaia enter into history in the *Codex Albeldensis*, published in the second half of the ninth century. Traditionally, the Gipuzkoan case has been put back to 1025, which implied a notable delay compared to the neighboring territories. In 2004, an intriguing revision of the issue was proposed. The search leads us to the district of Montes de Oca in Burgos and the lands of High Rioja, more specifically the monastery of San Millán de Hiniestra, included in the domain of San Millán de La Cogolla. The reference, copied in a summarized way in what was termed the *Becerro Galicano*, could not be more brief: "*Ego Gometiza trado ad ipsa regula una ferragine mea, in Gipuzare, iuxta fonte, in valle de Ripa. Era DCCCC^a. LXXX^a. I^a. Ranimiro rex.*" The donation of lady Gometiza—whose interest for this case is highlighted by the researcher David Peterson—alludes to a "*Gipuzare*," a term that can be interpreted as the "*villa* of the Gipuzkoan," understood as a modest rural settlement. The date is significant: the year 943—981 in the Spanish Era—under the rule of Ramiro II of León (931–951). This has consequences because, if we accept this interpretation of the place name, excluding other possible interpretations, this would be the earliest identification of Gipuzkoan geographical space and identity, which were also perceived from "the outside." This would also suggest migrations toward what

---

4   Nerea Sarasola Etxegoien, "El poblamiento medieval de Gipuzkoa: revisión crítica del registro arqueológico." Munibe (Antropologia-Arkeologia) 61 (2010), 339–93; Nerea Sarasola Etxegoien and Alfredo Moraza Barea, *Arqueología medieval en Gipuzkoa* (Donostia / San Sebastián: Diputación Foral de Gipuzkoa, 2011), 9–18.

is today La Rioja and northern Castile from this territory, whose limits and legal nature we do not know.[5]

Some years later, in 952, another written testimony, whose interest was pointed out by Andrés de Mañaricúa and José Ángel García de Cortázar, could offer the first mention of a specific enclave in Gipuzkoa: a place by the name of Salinas, where one Diego Vélez owned several properties that he donated to the monastery of San Millán. Perhaps, as both authors suggest, this would be identifiable as Salinas de Léniz (Leintz Gatzaga in Basque), always on the understanding that there were reasons to rule out other options in Araba.[6]

Gipuzkoa as a District of the Kingdom of Pamplona, 1025–1076

In one way or another, there was a clear mention of the territory, already with a defined jurisdictional category, in 1025: Gipuzkoa was presented as a *tenencia* or district of the Kingdom of Pamplona. The document is well known and was for a long time considered the oldest testimony to the existence of Gipuzkoa. It concerns a donation by the baron García Aznárez and Lady Gayla, his wife, to the monastery of San Juan de la Peña, received by the church of San Salvador de Olazabal, in Altzo. King Sancho III the Great intervened in the act, clearly indicating the subordination of García Aznárez, in his role as seigneur of Gipuzkoa, to the monarch: "*Prefatus ego quidem Sancio regnans in Pampilona et sub eius imperio senior Garsia Açenariz de Ipuscua hoc testamentum decrevimus confirmare.*" The deed, several copies of which exist, raises innumerable queries and doubts. There has been speculation that the *tenente* was originally from Aragón, and that possibly he died in 1048.[7] It appears that

---

5   David Peterson, "Primeras menciones a Guipúzcoa," *Fontes Linguae Vasconum: Studia et Documenta* 97 (2004), 597–608; *Becerro Galicano Digital* , doc. 382, at www.ehu.eus/galicano/id382 (last accessed August 10, 2018).
6   García de Cortázar, "La sociedad guipuzcoana antes del fuero de San Sebastián," 281; Andrés E. de Mañaricúa y Nuere, *Obispados de Álava, Guipúzcoa y Vizcaya hasta fines del siglo XI. En Obispados de Álava, Guipúzcoa y Vizcaya hasta la erección de la diócesis de Vitoria* (Vitoria: Seminario Diocesano, 1964), 169; *Becerro Galicano Digital*, doc. 358, at [doc. 358] (www.ehu.eus/galicano/id358 (last accessed August 10, 2018).
7   Pescador Medrano, "Tenentes y tenencias del reino de Pamplona," 118.

his wife Gayla was Gipuzkoan and possessed extensive patrimonial roots in the territory, as well as in Upper Aragón.[8]

Since when had this "Ipuscua" been linked to the Kingdom of Pamplona? In Araba, there are already indications of Pamplona influence during the reign of Sancho II Garcés (970–994). It was perhaps Sancho III the Great (1004–1034) who, in his hegemonic expansionist efforts, ended up including this primitive Gipuzkoa among his dominions. We do not know the precise borders of the territory, or the range of powers García Aznarez had as the king's representative.[9]

In this journey through the jurisdictional history of the territory we lack documents for more than four decades. In the mid-ninth century there is (not very convincing) mention of a certain Sancho Fortuñones and his wife Blasquita, the daughter of Lady Gayla, without any express link to any responsibility. Whatever the case, the continuing rule of the Kingdom of Pamplona cannot be denied, given that, in 1060, Sancho IV of Peñalén appeared as the king of "Ypuzcoa." The second known authority as a *tenente* with certainty, in 1066, was Órbita Aznárez, who at the same time held similar responsibilities in Araba (1068). We know of his presence in the retinue of the aforementioned king of Pamplona and his intervention as a witness in private patrimonial acts in La Rioja. Most likely, political circumstances, as we will see, would relieve him of his responsibilities in 1076, although he did maintain a connection to the Basque lands.[10]

---

8   Martínez Díez, *Guipúzcoa en los albores de su historia*, 33–45, 175–76; Barrena Osoro, *La formación histórica de Guipúzcoa*, 51–64; Pescador Medrano, "Tenentes y tenencias del reino de Pamplona," 118–20; and Orella Unzué, "Estudio jurídico comparativo de los fueros," 189–217.

9   Gonzalo Martínez Díez, *Álava medieval*, vol. 1 (Vitoria: Diputación Foral de Álava, 1974), 77–79; Juan José Larrea Conde, "La herencia vasca: acción política y arquitectura social en Vizcaya y Álava antes de su incorporación al reino de Alfonso VI." In *Alfonso VI y su época I: los precedentes del reinado (966–1065), Sahagún (León), 4 a 7 de septiembre de 2006*, ed. Etelvina Fernández González (León: Universidad de León, 2007), 77–79.

10   Pescador Medrano, "Tenentes y tenencias del reino de Pamplona," 118–20; Ángel J. Martín Duque, *Documentación medieval de Leire (siglos IX a XII)* (Pamplona: Diputación Foral de Navarra; Institución Príncipe de Viana, 1983), docs. 76 and 83.

A Shared Space, 1076–1109

Gipuzkoa was not removed from the general problems of the Kingdom of Pamplona, which was going through a process of change, and the ambitions of neighboring kingdoms: Aragón and Castile. The consequence of all this would be the division of the Gipuzkoan territory.

The Repercussions of a Dynastic and Political Crisis

On June 4, 1076, Sancho IV of Peñalén, king of Pamplona, was assassinated, the victim of a conspiracy encouraged by his siblings Ramón and Ermesinda. Faced with the power vacuum thus created, the barons reacted in different way. Some transferred their loyalty to Alfonso VI of Castile (1072–1109); others to Sancho Ramírez of Aragón (1063–1094), who assumed the title of "king of the people of Pamplona." That led to a division of territories between the two monarchs that would be confirmed in 1087. Alfonso VI was allocated Pancorbo, La Rioja, Araba, Bizkaia, and the lands of what is today Navarre south of the River Ega. The rest would go to the king of Aragón, who in turn would be a vassal to his counterpart in Castile. Both declared their sovereignty over Gipuzkoa, termed "Ipuzcua" or "Puzcoa." Although there is very little evidence, there is a tendency to think that Sancho Ramírez only included the far northwest, including, at the very least, the lower reaches of the Urumea Valley. The main part, that allocated to Alfonso VI, had a clear western boundary: the lands around what is today Mutriku, in the vicinity of the monastery of San Andrés de Astigarribia, which marked the coastal border with Bizkaia. One supposes that the area inland from this point would extend along the middle and upper reaches of the River Oria and the Urola and Deba Valleys. As well as this division, a new form of understanding the exercise of jurisdiction was gradually imposed, typical of feudalism, given that the nobility—definitely including the barons who were active in Gipuzkoa at the time—gained rights, guarantees, and the collective capacity to act in their vassalage relationship with the monarch.[11]

---

11   José María Lacarra de Miguel, *Historia política del reino de Navarra desde sus orígenes hasta*

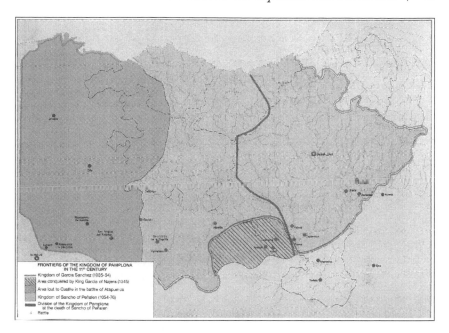

Map 1.
Division of the Kingdom of Pamplona in 1076.

Source: José Luis Orella Unzué, Iñigo Aguirre Querejeta, and
Edorta Kortadi Olano, Atlas de Euskal Herria. Geografía-
Economía-Historia-Arte (Donostia: Erein, 1982), 64.

The Pamplona "Vertex"

King Sancho Ramírez integrated his acquisition into a set of frontier
ditricts in the far northwest of his new domains: Etxauri, the Baztan
and Burunda Valleys, and, lastly, Hernani. The latter area included
the portion of Gipuzkoa that this monarch received as a result
of the division and that his two immediate successors—Pedro I
(1094–1104) and Alfonso I (1104–1134)—inherited. The set of
districts was allocated to the seigneur, Iñigo Vélez, perhaps the son
of Órbita Aznárez.

su incorporación a Castilla, vol. 1 (Pamplona: Caja de Ahorros de Navarra, 1972), 271–75;
Martínez Díez, *Álava medieval*, 92–96; Juan José Larrea Conde, *La Navarre du IVe au*
XIIe siècle: Peuplement et société (Paris and Brussels: De Boeck Université, 1998), 347–60,
480–82; *Becerro Galicano Digital*, doc. 579, at www.ehu.eus/galicano/id579 (last accessed
August 10, 2018).

It is precisely within this context that the first reliable documented mentions of Donostia-San Sebastian appeared.[12] A 1097 papal bull by Pope Urban II in favor of the cathedral of Pamplona speaks about a *"Sanctum Sebastianum in ripa maris."* Another testimony dates from 1101. The document—a deed by Pedro I— reveals the existence of a church dedicated to Saint Sebastian in the current Antiguo neighborhood and of a *villa*, that is, a village, in the surroundings blessed with cultivated land, orchards, grazing land, and fishing rights in what was termed the *pardina* (rural area) of "Izurun." The enclave, which formed part of the previously mentioned district of Hernani, had belonged to the monastery of Leire since the era of one King Sancho of Pamplona, whether Sancho III the Great or Sancho IV of Peñalén we do not know. For his part, Pedro I expanded the local patrimony of Leire, adding a *pardina* and rights over the River Urumea. This was inserted into a process of more general expansion that led certain monasteries in Castile, Navarre, and Aragón to extend their interests along the Cantabrian coast, perhaps taking advantage of the dynamic economy of the area.[13]

The Gipuzkoa of Alfonso VI

The sovereignty of Alfonso VI was imposed on the rest of the territory. That implied the substitution of *tenentes*. Barons linked to the Kingdom of Pamplona disappeared, even though they retained their patrimony and social preeminence in the territory, while new

---

12   King Sancho Ramírez, on being given the church of Santiago de Funes (possibly in 1089), mentions San Sebastian among the areas that the church had rights over. Having said that, the two corresponding deeds offer up problems that call for a thorough and rigorous diplomatic, chronological, and historical analysis. See Ángel Canellas López, *Colección diplomática de Sancho Ramírez* (Zaragoza: Real Sociedad Económica de Amigos del País, 1993), docs. 106 and 108.

13   José Ángel Lema Pueyo, "Los orígenes medievales de San Sebastián: la época anterior al fuero de Sancho el Sabio," in *Geografía e Historia de Donostia-San Sebastián*, ed. F. Javier Gómez Piñeiro and Juan Antonio Sáez García (Donostia / San Sebastián: Diputación Foral de Gipuzkoa, 1999), 56–60; José Ángel García de Cortázar, "Una villa mercantil: 1180–1516," in *Historia de Donostia-San Sebastián*, ed. Miguel Artola Gallego (Donostia / San Sebastián: Editorial Nerea, 2000), 15–19; José Goñi Gaztambide, *Colección diplomática de la catedral de Pamplona. Tomo I (829–1243)* (Pamplona: Gobierno de Navarra, 1997), docs. 68 and 80; and Martín Duque, *Documentación medieval de Leire*, docs. 188 and 212.

representatives of royal power were introduced. The key figure was Lope Iñiguez, who is documented, moreover, as the seigneur of Bizkaia and Araba. His successor in Bizkaia, Diego López (1093–1124), may have held the position of representing the royal authority of Castile and León in Gipuzkoa as well, although that is just a reasoned conjecture. Following a line of action that was also observed in the area under Pamplona influence, the monarch and local barons contributed to expanding the patrimony of foreign monastic centers. That was the case of the monastery of San Andrés de Astigarribia, in Mutriku, which Lope Iñiguez and Alfonso VI transferred to the domain of San Millán.[14]

Jurisdictional Fluctuations under Alfonso I, 1109–1134

This state of affairs would be fleeting. The death of Alfonso VI in 1109 opened up a complex period of crisis in his kingdoms marked by dynastic and noble wars, revolts in burgs on the Camino de Santiago, and peasant uprisings. Alfonso I the Battler, who had married Queen Urraca (the successor to the deceased monarch) that same year, did not manage to consolidate his royal authority in Castile and León. Yet he did get a consolation prize: from 1113 on, he managed to extend the borders of his hereditary kingdoms westward. This is the context in which one must understand how Araba, since at least 1120, ended up under the dominion of the king of Aragón. At the same time, the influence of the seigneur of Bizkaia, Diego López, was declining. This border expansion could be interpreted by some as a plan to restore the limits of the Kingdom of Pamplona to what they were before 1076. That part of Gipuzkoa gained by Alfonso VI, like Araba, was lost for Castile. Since when? Since at least, with any certainty, 1133. In the meantime, Diego López, the seigneur of Bizkaia, disappeared from the scene while, during the final years of the Battler, the rising star was Count Ladrón, the seigneur of Araba and probably of Gipuzkoa as well.[15]

---

14 *Becerro Galicano Digital*, doc. 579, at www.ehu.eus/galicano/id579 and doc. 581, at www. ehu.eus/galicano/id581 (last accessed August 10, 2018); Martínez Díez, *Guipúzcoa en los albores de su historia*, 64–69.
15 José Ángel Lema Pueyo, "Evolución política de los territorios históricos: Álava, Guipúzcoa y Vizcaya en la Edad Media," in *Historia del País Vasco. Edad Media (siglos*

Gipuzkoa in the Restored Kingdom, 1134–1194

It is well known how Alfonso I bequeathed an inapplicable will to posterity: the handing over of his kingdoms in equal parts to three ecclesiastical institutions in the Holy Land—Templars, Hospitallers, and Canons of the Church of the Holy Sepulcher—and a series of disproportionate vows to cathedrals and abbeys, including some well outside his own lands. Nobles in Aragón and Pamplona sought their own solutions. The latter agreed to acknowledge García Ramírez, who was related to the Pamplona dynasty and *tenente* of Tudela (Tutera in Basque), as their sovereign. There would be turbulent years ahead, during which García Ramírez would manage, thanks to a majority consensus on the part of his barons (who were at the same time not above certain disloyalties), to remain at the head of the Kingdom of Pamplona.[16]

García Ramírez, 1134–1150

Gipuzkoa—together with Bizkaia and, in a more discontinuous way, Araba—would remain within the territory of the new monarch. That is attested to by records of the jurisdiction of the king of Pamplona over Gipuzkoa since at least May 1135 and without evidence of any loss of control. Count Ladrón and his son Vela alternated in the district of the territory, within a family game of very subtle and complex feudal loyalties. A mid-twelfth-century Leire forgery highlights Donostia-San Sebastian within the limits of Hernani as the eastern boundary of Gipuzkoa, while its western counterpart was situated in Deba. King García Ramírez intervened in this space in 1141. He donated a set of properties, grazing lands, and royal rights across a wide area, extending from the lower reaches of the River Oria in the Urumea Valley to Altza and, perhaps, as far as Aiako Harria/Peñas de Aia, to the cathedral of Pamplona. The Restorer thus strengthened a Navarrese institution that was a competitor

---

V–XV), ed. Pedro Barruso Barés and José Ángel Lema Pueyo (San Sebastián: Hiria Liburuak, 2004), 126; José Ángel Lema Pueyo, *Colección diplomática de Alfonso I de Aragón y Pamplona (1104–1134)* (San Sebastián: Eusko Ikaskuntza, 1990), doc. 270.

16 Lacarra de Miguel, *Historia política del reino de Navarra*, vol. 1, 330–33 and vol. 2, 11–35; José Ángel Lema Pueyo, *Alfonso I el Batallador: rey de Aragón y Pamplona (1104–1134)* (Gijón: Trea Editorial, 2008), 340–50.

of the Leire monastery. The bishop's interest in the Donostia-San Sebastian hinterland is perhaps explained by the dynamism of an area that was growing demographically and economically and in which he wanted to be involved, as well as by the desire to control the short livestock routes between the Aralar mountain range and the coast.[17]

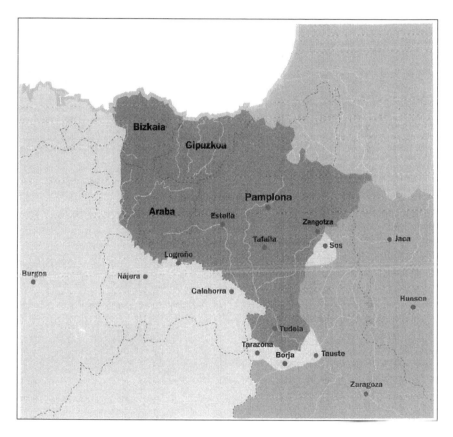

Map 2.
The Kingdom of Pamplona under García Ramírez (1134–1150)

Source: Luis Javier Fortún Pérez de Ciriza and Carmen Jusué
Simonena, eds., Historia de Navarra. I. Antigüedad y Alta Edad
Media (Pamplona: Gobierno de Navarra, 1993), 142.

---

17 Barrena Osoro, *La formación histórica de Guipúzcoa*, 315–28; Fortún Pérez de Ciriza, "La quiebra de la soberanía Navarra," 443–46; Goñi Gaztambide, *Colección diplomática de la catedral de Pamplona*, docs. 221 and 232; and *Becerro Galicano Digital*, doc. 0, at www.chu.eus/galicano/id0 (last accessed August 10, 2018).

Sancho VI, 1150–1194

The Wise king would leave his imprint on Gipuzkoa. Out of all his rulings, the most well-known was the Fuero of San Sebastian, a rich legal text. It responded to the needs of a changing and growing society.

The Definition of a Border, 1150–1179

The beginning of his reign could not have been more hazardous or discouraging, since Sancho VI had to confront serious challenges: a project to divide the kingdom between Alfonso VII and Ramón Berenguer IV (1151) and the dangerous tutelage of the Castilian monarchs. Feudal loyalties, despite the solemn oaths of vassalage, were volatile and complex. In 1153 Count Ladrón and his son Vela—who would succeed him as head of the family two years later—abandoned Sancho VI and went into the service of the Castilian crown. They probably took their fiefs and districts with them, including the lands (partially or fully) of Gipuzkoa.

The situation changed a few years later with the beginning of a period of minorities in the neighboring kingdoms: in Castile in 1158 and in Aragón in 1162. Meanwhile, Vela Ladrón, a cautious realist man, became once more loyal to Sancho VI, and with him came Gipuzkoa. At the same time more significant changes were taking place. A commonly held interpretation argues that the Pyrenean monarchy embarked at that time on a project to assert its sovereignty with the aim of better controlling its lands, resources, and people, and reinforcing its position in relation to the nobility. This was part of a more general trend, since other European monarchies were acting in the same way. This, in the long term, would imply more direct and intense royal control in Bizkaia, Araba, and Gipuzkoa, which was perhaps not so well received.

The years that followed continued to be turbulent and full of territorial disputes: an attempt on the part of Navarre to expand into La Rioja and northern Castile between 1162 and 1167, the belligerent response on the part of Alfonso VIII in 1173, and a not very successful attempt at mediation on the part of Henry II of England between 1176 and 1177. Navarre and Castile would eventually reach an agreement, known as "the pact of friendship and harmony," in April 1179. This established a status quo that would last for two decades. Almost all Gipuzkoa, together with the district around Durango in Bizkaia, would remain in the area allocated to Sancho VI of Navarre. In terms of the object under study here, the western border of Gipuzkoa with the lands of Alfonso VIII ran from Itziar at the mouth of the River Deba to Durango, leaving the Bizkaian castle of Malvecín—whose precise location is disputed—on the Castilian side.[18]

This Gipuzkoan territory linked to Navarre was perceived in different ways from different perspectives. For the monastery of San Millán, according to a mid-twelfth-century forgery, the territory extended from Donostia-San Sebastian to the River Deba, thereby excluding the Bidasoa and Oiartzun Valleys, and from northern limits of Araba to the sea. However, the cathedral of Pamplona, in another forgery that can be dated to the end of the rule of Sancho the Wise, the boundaries were practically those of today: from the Bidasoa to the Deba and from San Adrián—on the understanding we identify it with the port of the same name—to the Cantabrian coast.[19]

---

18   Lacarra de Miguel, *Historia política del reino de Navarra*, vol. 2, 69–76; Martínez Díez, *Álava medieval*, vol. 1, 112–24; Martínez Díez, *Guipúzcoa en los albores de su historia*, 126–29; Fortún Pérez de Ciriza, "La quiebra de la soberanía Navarra," 447–56, with a detailed analysis of the pact of 1179; the idea of the Navarrese monarchy asserting its power comes from Ángel J. Martín Duque, "Sancho VI de Navarra y el fuero de Vitoria," in *Vitoria en la Edad Media*, ed. Pilar Aróstegui (Vitoria-Gasteiz: Ayuntamiento de Vitoria-Gasteiz, 1982), 287–89; Julio González González, *El reino de Castilla en época de Alfonso VIII*, vol. 2 (Madrid: CSIC, 1960), doc. 321; on the general European tendency, see Thomas Bisson, *The Crisis of the Twelfth Century: Power, Lordship, and the Origins of European Government* (Princeton, NJ: Princeton University Press, 2009);

19   *Becerro Galicano Digital*, doc. 0, at www.ehu.eus/galicano/id0 (last accessed August 10, 2018); Goñi Gaztambide, *Colección diplomática de la catedral de Pamplona*, doc. 6. On the date of Sancho III's forgery, see Barrena Osoro, *La formación histórica de Guipúzcoa*, 338–47.

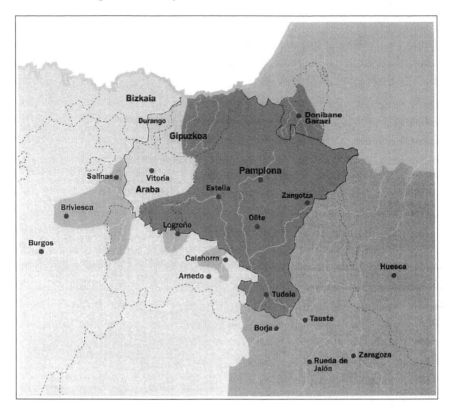

Map 3.
The Kingdom of Navarre under Sancho the Wise, 1150–1194.

Source: Luis Javier Fortún Pérez de Ciriza and Carmen Jusué
Simonena, eds., Historia de Navarra. I. Antigüedad y Alta Edad
Media (Pamplona: Gobierno de Navarra, 1993), 146.

The Reorganization of Space, 1179–1194

From 1179 on, with the relationship with Castile stabilized, Sancho
VI was able to dedicate himself more fully to governing the kingdom,
imposing a more strict control on his administration. In these
circumstances, Gipuzkoa remained integrated into a district that
extended into the eastern part of Araba, with its seat in the castle
of Aizorrotz (Eskoriatza). This was held alternately until the end
of the kingdom by barons that were originally from Araba, Diego

López and Pedro Ladrón, as well as another of Navarrese origin, Iñigo de Oriz, as if there were an attempt to balance the interests of the local nobility with that originating in the ancient Pyrenean kingdom.[20]

It was in this context that Sancho VI encouraged the settling of Donostia-San Sebastian, conceding it a charter of privileges and, with that, the Fuero of Estella in its extensive version of 1164. Other authors in the present work analyze this text in historical and legal terms. Here, I will limit myself to addressing the reasons that drove the monarch to make this decision, which would mark the arrival point of the present study. When was the document granted? The original was lost and the two most reliable copies that were preserved for a critical edition date from much later—1424 and 1474—and are incomplete. In effect, both lack the final part, the so called eschatocol or closing protocol, which contained, among other things, the chronological and topical dates, as well as the list of ecclesiastical and noble authorities, all typical in such deeds. Although other options have been considered, majority opinion—linked to the criterion of José María Lacarra—is inclined, taking into consideration the historical context of the kingdom, to date it around the year 1180; although, in my opinion, there are not sufficient reasons to exclude any other year from 1179 to 1194. The Fuero of San Sebastian was part of a policy to support the urban world. In Araba, between 1181 and 1191, the *villas* of Vitoria, Antoñana, Bernedo, and La Puebla de Arganzón received foundational charters. For the king, this was a means of affirming his control over the territory, reinforcing the seaward passage, and stimulating the loyalty of the communities to which he conceded legal advantages. Likewise, the king was responding to the needs of local development, which were enough to make the area attractive to the (often contradictory) interests of the monastery of Leire and the dioceses of Pamplona and Baiona (Bayonne), among other things. What is more, it was precisely at this moment that both dioceses, via agreements and arrangements that reached the Holy See, had

---

20   Martínez Díez, *Álava medieval*, vol. 1, 125–32; Fortún Pérez de Ciriza, "La quiebra de la soberanía Navarra," 457–58 and 462–70; and Orella Unzué, "Nacimiento de Guipúzcoa como tenencia navarra de frontera," 189–217.

just established their spheres of influence in the area. At the foot of Mount Urgull, not far from the settlement that the monastery of Leire possessed, a community of Gascon settlers had sprung up: fishermen, sailors, haulers, traders, artisans, and innkeepers from Lapurdi (Labourd) and Aquitaine. Their activity was part of a maritime network of communications that, at the very least, extended from Baiona to the Cantabrian coast. They would also make the most of the marketable surpluses produced in the territory itself. In time, these immigrants would form a differentiated group that was aware of its rights and its ethnic and cultural cohesion that, by the end of the twelfth century, received the denomination of "burg." Their arrival and putting down roots must have been the result of a long process that we cannot date with precision. Among the reasons would be, without any doubt, the evident facilities that the setting offered to aid the coastal trade from Bordeaux and Baiona. Other motives have been put forward, including the hypothetical tensions between the Aquitainean population and the English crown, when the area passed from France into the hands of Henry II, Henry Plantagenet, in the mid-twelfth century, which would have induced many Gascons to move to the Gipuzkoan coast. The first written evidence of the parishes of Santa María and San Vicente, the control of which was disputed by the monastery of Leire and the diocese of Pamplona, dates from 1178. There was almost certainly some negotiation between the Navarrese monarch and locals, those that were offered incentives to consolidate their settlement. Perhaps on the eve of offering the charter he called on more Gascons to come. In the final analysis, the Fuero of San Sebastian was indicative of the vitality of the Cantabrian coast, at a time in which, for his part, Alfonso VIII of Castile was conceding privileges to the *villas* of Castro Urdiales, Laredo, and Santander.[21]

---

21   García de Cortázar, "La sociedad guipuzcoana antes del fuero de San Sebastián," 281–312; García de Cortázar, "Una villa mercantile," 17–25; José María Lacarra de Miguel and Ángel Juan Martín Duque, *Fueros de Navarra. Fueros derivados de Jaca 1* (Estella-San Sebastián; Pamplona: Institución Príncipe de Viana, 1969), 28–31; Ángel J. Martín Duque, "El fuero de San Sebastián: tradición manuscrita y edición crítica," in *Congreso: El fuero de San Sebastián y su época (San Sebastián 19–23 de enero de 1981) / Donostiako forua eta bere garaia (Donostia, 1981ko urtarrilaren 19tik 23ra)* (San Sebastián: Eusko Ikaskuntza / Sociedad de Estudios Vascos, 1982), 3–25.

The Basic Realities

In 1120 Bishop Hugo of Porto stopped in Gipuzkoa on his way from Baiona to Santiago de Compostela. The account of his trip, recounted in *Historia Compostelana*, speaks about a fairly uncivilized landscape that conveys the idea of barbarity: "remote isolated places, rough and not very pleasant" that were situated at the edges of the world, where waves crashed against the shore. Such places had to be home to "coarse, fierce, untamed [people] with an unknown language." In fact, the Portuguese prelate required the services of an "indigenous person, who knew the language of the Basques." The account unearths a notable cultural distance in which the language constituted a barrier for understanding, and also the survival of old literary clichés inherited from antiquity about the inhabitants of this part of Europe and, in the final analysis, alluding to the contrast between barbarity and civilization. However, I find it hard to believe that Gipuzkoan society would, in the early twelfth century, be in such a primitive state and that, immersed in such archaism, could have escaped (not without maintaining some singularities) the general tendencies of Western Christianity: a growth in agricultural production and exchange, an increasingly stable rural population, the rise of the urban world, the development of the ecclesiastical framework, and the social hegemony of the nobility.[22]

A Space in Transformation

The root of all medieval development was to be found in the rural world. As in the rest of the Western Christian world, the village, understood as a stable community of farmers and stockbreeders linked to a parish church, must have emerged somewhere between the eighth and ninth centuries. This was testified to in Zarautz and, especially, in the now abandoned village of San Pedro de Iromendi, in which recent digs have revealed a remote early medieval past. By the beginning of the ninth century a network of villages may

---

22 *Historia Compostelana*, book 2, xx; see also García de Cortázar, "La sociedad guipuzcoana antes del fuero de San Sebastián," 337–38.

have already taken shape in the territory, some of which became privileged urban settlements at a later point.[23]

It is complicated to follow any traces of this in written documents. Toward the end of Sancho VI's reign, a document by the bishop of Pamplona, drawn up between 1186 and 1193, during the era in which the Fuero of San Sebastian was conceded, mentions a series of Gipuzkoan place names without any geographical location. Most of them also appear in a forgery of a deed by Sancho III the Great that can be dated around 1032. This may have been forged in the same era as the previous one, in the 1180s, although in the latter case it classifies them as "*vallibus*" or valleys. In my opinion, one should speak in terms of villages or groups of neighboring villages. Two of them match what would later become important Alcaldías Mayores, which in the Late Middle ages constituted rural districts in the king's domain: Areria and Saiatz. Zizurkil, Errezil, and Goiatz now emerged. Perhaps behind this latter reference is the emergence of San Pedro de Iromendi. The reference to Iraurgi could be understood as an allusion to the Urola Valley or to some of the settlements one finds before arriving at Azpeitia or Azkoitia. Likewise, some observers identify pre-urban settlements that in time would be given the category of *villa*: for example, Hernani, clearly differentiated from Donostia-San Sebastian as a population nucleus; and Itziar, which predates historically the *villa* of Deba (of which it is part today). Finally, the mention of Oiartzun would designate a complex space that would be divided later to give rise to a valley of the same name and the *villas* of Errenteria and Hondarribia. This could be compared to the process that divided up the lands of Léniz (Leintz) in the Upper Deba Valley.[24]

---

23   Iosu Etxezarraga Ortuondo, "San Pedro de Iromendi. II Campaña," *Arkeoikuska* 13 (2014), 285–89, "San Pedro de Iromendi. III Campaña," *Arkeoikuska* 14 (2015), 311–17, and "San Pedro de Iromendi. IV Campaña," *Arkeoikuska* 15 (2016), 306–11.

24   Goñi Gaztambide, *Colección diplomática de la catedral de Pamplona*, docs. 6 and 378; Roldán Jimeno Aranguren and Aitor Pescador Medrano, *Colección documental de Sancho Garcés III, el Mayor, rey de Pamplona (1004–1035)* (Pamplona: Nabarralde; Pamiela, 2003). On the era and circumstances in which Sancho III's deed was forged, see Barrena Osoro, *La formación histórica de Guipúzcoa*, 338–47. For this author, the agreement, beyond any juridical appearances, implied a hidden renunciation on the part of the see of Baiona of any permanent claim beyond the Oiartzun Valley. Comparing both texts, we observe that the following place names do not appear in the agreement: Areria and Oiartzun. Likewise, there is no mention of Zizurkil in the forged deed by Sancho III.

With the village, so the church, the basis of parish organization, and the key center of community life took shape. According to the general tendency of the time, such churches would be few in number during the early medieval period, they would be rather extensive in sphere of influence, and with vaguely defined boundaries. In time, their number would increase and their boundaries would be reduced, but better defined and more useful as tools of controlling the space. Some joined an already established settlement; others were able to give coherence to communities resident in diverse areas. Archaeological fieldwork has discovered in Santa María La Real in Zarautz the remains of two small rectangular-floored churches that can be dated, with caution, to the ninth and tenth centuries respectively, with both preceding that which was erected in the thirteenth century in, by that time, an already established *villa*. One should not rule out the possibility that the abovementioned enclave of San Pedro de Iromendi could have had an early medieval church, prior to that constructed around 1100. Through the eleventh century, written sources also mentioned churches in Altzo (San Salvador de Olazabal), Mutriku (San Andrés de Astigarribia), in the area of Bergara (Aritzeta), and in Donostia-San Sebastian (in the El Antiguo neighborhood). During the twelfth century the two aforementioned parishes of the Gascons in Donostia-San Sebastian (Santa María y San Vicente) emerged alongside that of Zaldibia. Archaeological digs have found remains in a chronology that runs from the tenth to the thirteenth centuries in Oiartzun (San Esteban), Irun (Santa Elena), Aia (San Pedro), Tolosa (San Esteban), Irura (San Miguel), and Getaria (San Martín and San Salvador). I will return to some of these examples below. One should understand that this list, although incomplete, indicates the growth of this cell of social organization. Behind these constructions in an initial phase they could act as promoters of local communities of the faithful, even if, in time, noble elites, who were able to pay for more expensive construction materials and attract a specialized workforce, would probably have begun to intervene. They did not do so selflessly, as I will comment on below, but instead with the aim of boosting their social superiority and patrimonial holdings.[25]

Meanwhile, two episcopal powers, the bishops of Pamplona and Baiona, were making an effort to mark out their boundaries in Gipuzkoa, especially from the late eleventh century onward. This process is difficult to follow due to the fact that the relevant documentation—royal, diocesan, and pontifical—does not appear to be free of manipulation. Nor is it straightforward to discern to what point the territorial ambitions of Lapurdi extended. The ultimate phase of this process, which coincided with the era of the Fuero of San Sebastian, culminated with two rulings. The first, dating from sometime between 1186 and 1193, established an agreement between the two sees that allowed Bishop Bernard of Baiona the temporary and conditional benefits of ruling over a series of enclaves, among which included Donostia-San Sebastian and the aforementioned list of place names. The agreement, which would be considered null on the death of either of the two signatory prelates, could have signified a transitory compensation for Baiona. In effect, the second ruling, a papal bull of Pope Celestine III in 1194, assigned the Baiona see the "Otarzu" or Oiartzun Valley, that is, the portion of territory that extends currently from Hondarribia to Errenteria. Donostia-San Sebastian and most of Gipuzkoa would, then, definitively remain within the Pamplona see.

Behind these actions lurked, among other motives, an interest in controlling parish rents. Although almost certainly a lot was charged previously, the abovementioned 1194 bull included new tithes—those received from the harvests of recently plowed terrain—among other incomes for the bishopric of Baiona, which would affect at least that part of Gipuzkoa under its administration. This would be understandable in a context of economic and demographic growth. Likewise, the posture of Baiona could have been associated with the

---

25   Alex Ibáñez Etxeberria, ed., "Santa María la Real de Zarautz (País Vasco), continuidad y discontinuidad en la ocupación de la costa vasca entre los siglos V a.C. y XV d.C," Spec. issue, *Munibe* 27 (2011); Sarasola Etxegoien and Moraza Barea, *Arqueología medieval en Gipuzkoa*, 91–136, 140–41; Iosu Curiel Yarza, *La parroquia en el País Vasco-cantábrico durante la Baja Edad Media (c. 1350–1539)* (Bilbao: Universidad del País Vasco / Euskal Herriko Unibertsitatea, 2009), 73–100.

expansion of Gascon settlers in the northeastern part of Gipuzkoa that underpinned the development of Donostia-San Sebastian.[26]

The silence of this episcopal documentation on the Deba River valley—with the exception of Itziar—is significant and would indicate that, excluding the mouth of the river, the rest of the area was allotted to the bishopric of Araba, which would disappear in 1088 on being absorbed by that of Calahorra.

Different foreign abbeys, which either established dependent centers or integrated already existing ones, had extensive patrimonial networks or, at the least, held the rights to economic exploitation, across much of Gipuzkoa. Most were based in Navarre and Aragón, which would be testimony to the cultural and religious influences that came in from these territories: San Salvador de Leire, San Juan de la Peña (directly, or through its Bizkaian dependency San Juan de Gaztelugatxe), Santa María de Iranzu, San Miguel de Excelsis, and Santiago de Funes (which would end up becoming part of Montearagón). The other great focus of monastic influence came, without any doubt, from the abbey of San Millán de La Cogolla. Of all their lands, as regards the most important monastic centers, Gipuzkoa was a peripheral area, although not lacking in interest.

Meanwhile, between the eleventh and twelfth centuries, castles were constructed. Around ten have been counted, modest constructions in comparison with those of other territories. In part, perhaps raised wooden structures over a moat, like that in Galardi, near Ordizia. In some cases, their position appeared to indicate a clear function of political control, corroborated at times by the documentation. Without any doubt whatsoever, the castle of Aizorrotz (Eskoriatza) monitored the communication between Araba and the High Deba Valley and it was the seat of *tenentes* under Sancho VI. Ausa (Ataun) and Jentilbaratza (Zaldibia) would help to monitor the Aralar mountain range, on the border with Navarre. Other options can be considered: for example, the defense of population centers and the control of mountain herding routes. The scarcity of written testimonies does not help us clarify whether they could,

---

26 Goñi Gaztambide, *Colección diplomática de la catedral de Pamplona*, doc. 378; Martínez Díez, *Guipúzcoa en los albores de su historia*, doc. 29.

in certain cases, have been noble seigneurial power centers, from which exactions were imposed.[27]

Underpinning such changes was the development of productive forces that were capable of generating the surpluses that facilitated the notable commercial activity included in the Fuero of San Sebastian. José Ángel García de Cortázar describes an area dedicated to livestock farming—with a specific mention of cattle in the sources—and forestry, in which there were also signs of a slowly growing grain production. To my mind, this would not have been possible without an effort to open up new lands to cultivation, which would make the previous reference to new tithes understandable. Alongside the omnipresent apple orchards, vegetable gardens and vineyards were developed. The documents on commerce, although scarce until the concession of the fuero, speak about cash transactions in the rural world as well.[28]

This picture, which is familiar, would be incomplete without bearing in mind two other activities. On the one hand, there was fishing, which has been seen as the original driving force of Gipuzkoan ports. And on the other, there was the dynamism of the "*haizeolak*" or "*ferrerías de viento*" (wind forges), located on hillsides and near water sources, as revealed by archaeological digs. Everything points to a surge in activity during the tenth century in Gipuzkoa, which, until recently, had been considered backward in comparison to Araba.[29]

A Hierarchical Society

The documents provide some information about the upper level of secular society. It is the circle of barons that ended up being *tenentes* and that, in some cases, acted (either themselves or through their relatives) in the royal curia of Navarre or Castile-León. Some

---

27 Sarasola Etxegoien and Moraza Barea, *Arqueología medieval en Gipuzkoa*, 76–85; Álvaro Aragón Ruano, "La evolución del hábitat y del poblamiento en el País Vasco durante las Edades Media y Moderna," *Domitia* 12 (2011), 32.
28 García de Cortázar, "La sociedad guipuzcoana antes del fuero de San Sebastián," 297–304.
29 Xabier Alberdi Lonbide and Iosu Etxezarraga Ortuondo, "Proyecto de investigación de las ferrerías de monte o haizeolak en Gipuzkoa y Álava: avance de resultados," *Kobie. Anejos* 13 (2014), 181–92; Francisco Javier Franco Pérez, Iosu Etxezarraga Ortuondo, and Xabier Alberdi Lonbide, "Los orígenes de la tecnología del hierro en el País Vasco: las ferrerías de monte o haizeolak," *Kobie. Serie Paleoantropología* 34 (2015), 267–82.

of them, like García Aznárez, may have been of Upper Aragonese origin; while others, like Órbita Aznárez, Lope Iñiguez, seigneur of Bizkaia, Ladrón and Pedro Ladrón, were from the western part of the Basque Country, or, in the case of Iñigo de Oriz, Navarre. We know almost nothing about their justice or government acts in their role as representatives of their respective kings, or about the vassalage links that bound them to these monarchs. It is not unreasonable to assume that feudal development through the eleventh and twelfth centuries would result in increasing rights when it came to enjoying responsibilities and "honors" in lands, rents, and payments in the service of the respective monarchs. In the same way, they took advantage, in a more than obvious way, of the conflicts among the monarchs of Navarre, Aragón, and Castile in order to obtain honorary titles or increase their own assets. Their strategies were complex and adaptive. Members of the same family could serve different and opposing monarchs. They clearly maintained close relations with the two major monasteries: San Juan de la Peña, which they helped to put down roots in the eastern part of Gipuzkoa; and San Millán de La Cogolla, in its expansion through the western part of the territory.

Likewise, there were nobles of evident Navarrese origin that, withoiut having belonged to the circle of *tenentes*, achieved wealth and influence in Gipuzkoa. In the mid-twelfth century we find the seigneur Lope Iñiguez de Tajonar, originally from the Pamplona basin. He owned the church in Tajonar and extended his holdings, from when we do not know, to Zaldibia. We do not know how: possibly a royal donation for services rendered, an inheritance, or through marriage. Perhaps he belonged to same family as María Iñiguez de Tajonar, who owned properties in neighboring Abaltzisketa.[30]

At the local level, there was another kind of nobility that was more strictly Gipuzkoan. That was the case of Don Sancho, with property and livestock in Bergara, where, among other assets of his, he controlled the church. His connections with the clergy extended

---

30   Goñi Gaztambide, *Colección diplomática de la catedral de Pamplona*, docs. 186 and 242; José María Jimeno Jurío, *El Libro Rubro de Iranzu* (Pamplona: Editorial Aranzadi, 1970), doc. 64.

to the modest Bizkaian monastery of San Juan de Gaztelugatxe, in which his brother, the monk Don Zianna, resided and would end up being its abbot. Once again we must confess ignorance: we know nothing of the vassal or client links that tied these local nobles directly to the king or to the circle of barons, with a stipulation of the obligations of military service, counsel, and protection.[31]

There is less doubt about the control that this secular aristocracy exercised over local ecclesiastical centers, whose expansion was mentioned above, even though it is difficult to determine if this system of its own churches was already dominant by this time. This was the situation, which on most occasions we come to know of when these rights are ceded to a foreign abbey, at least in the eleventh and twelfth centuries, for the churches of San Salvador de Olazabal, San Andrés de Astigarribia, Champayn (the future Santa Fe de Zaldibia), and San Miguel de Aritzeta. In the first two cases, the owners belonged to circles of barons that were *tenentes* (García Aznárez and Count Lope Iñiguez, together with their respective wives), while in the third it was a Navarrese noble (Lope Iñíguez de Tajonar) and in the fourth possibly a Gipuzkoan, the previously mentioned Sancho. They enjoyed—not without conflicts with other powers—the right to choose the head clerics for the churches and one has to suspect that they benefited from the rents generated. One would have to determine what role such control exerted when it came to planning and managing the family assets. It does appear that there was a transmission of such rights via inheritance. The kings intervened to approve the ceding of their churches to foreign monasteries: Sancho III, in the case of San Salvador de Olazabal (1025), and Alfonso VI, in that of San Andrés de Astigarribia (1091). This would indicate that the respective secular patrons obtained their rights through royal donation and that, on behalf of the monarchs, the ceding was not absolute.

In order to prohibit such practices, Celestine III's papal bull in 1194 alluded to the existence of ecclesiastical benefits and

---

31   Soledad Tena García assumes that the Gipuzkoan nobility was organized along some kind of lineage basis, although not understandable in the same way as those that were at the same time coming into shape in northern France in the eleventh and twelfth centuries. See *La sociedad urbana en la Guipúzcoa costera medieval*, 72–74.

cemeteries that were transmitted *"iure hereditario"* in the diocese of Baiona, which may have also affected its portion of Gipuzkoan terrain, the future archpriestship of Hondarribia. This would indicate an attempt on the part of the local nobility to control—we do not know how successfully—the distribution of parish rents and burials linked to certain families.[32]

The rights of these individuals over churches, which oscillated between outright ownership and some kind of patronage prerogative, extended beyond Gipuzkoa, reaching in some cases the Pamplona basin and Upper Aragón, and in others, Araba and La Rioja. One only need cite the example of Órbita Aznárez, who in 1060 figured among the *"barones"* of Araba that handed over the "Huula" monastery to San Juan de la Peña; while in 1080 he ceded a third of another monastery, San Miguel de Albiano, near Haro, to the San Millán monastery.[33]

Within this noble and ecclesiastical context, we have the first (and for a long time only) reliable mention of a professional scribe in Gipuzkoa. I am referring to Cómiz or Gómiz de Urra, who in 1025 wrote or made a scribe in his service write a document detailing the donation of the church in Olazabal. We lack any more information with which to elucidate whether this was a chaplain and grammarian in the regular service of the *tenente* García Aznárez—the last name Urra could indicate Navarrese origins—or one of the clerics that attended to the faithful in this church.[34]

Eleventh-century documents provide the only evidence that show women taking part in legal affairs relating to Gipuzkoa. All the references are to women who part of the elite world: Doña Gayla or Galga, the wife of García Aznárez, Doña Blasquita, their daughter and the wife of Sancho Fortuñones, and Doña Ticlo, the wife of Count Lope Iñiguez. They functioned as one with their spouses or, in the odd case, on their own in acts of buying and selling or in the corresponding confirmations of such activities. At certain

---

32 Martínez Díez, *Guipúzcoa en los albores de su historia*, doc. 29.
33 Pescador Medrano, "Tenentes y tenencias del reino de Pamplona," 119; *Becerro Galicano Digital*, doc. 170, at www.ehu.eus/galicano/id170 (last accessed August 10, 2018).
34 Martínez Díez, *Guipúzcoa en los albores de su historia*, doc. 6.

moments they could participate in prior negotiations, as in the case of Doña Ticlo appearing with her husband before Alfonso VI to speed up the ceding of San Andrés de Astigarribia to San Millán (1091). They exercised the right, like Doña Gayla, to appoint a cleric to be in charge of a church, and in this regard they negotiated with the ecclesiastical authorities. Likewise, at least during the eleventh century, they enjoyed, like the aforementioned Blasquita, rights of substantial inheritances. They controlled foreign ecclesiastical centers. The same Doña Gayla possessed until 1048 a monastery in Pamplona—that of Santiago de "Luquedeng"—at the same time as her daughter Blasquita and son-in-law Sancho Fortuñones were the patrons of the Santa Eufemia de Biniés church in La Jacetania, a region of Aragón, which demanded complex negotiations with San Juan de la Peña.[35]

The formation of the seigneury is well known for the Kingdom of Pamplona. Some indications, which point to the privatization of public functions and exactions deriving from them, could have been mentioned for Araba and Bizkaia. The *tenentes* could have taken advantage of their positions to usurp rights or obtain concessions that safeguarded their estates in the face of royal power. The most telling example in this regard can be observed in the privilege that Diego López, *tenente* of Bizkaia and, perhaps, of Gipuzkoa, obtained from Queen Urraca in June 1110. Thanks to this concession, his disperse *hereditates* would enjoy immunity in all the districts in which they were located, independent of the count or *tenente* who was in control of those lands. We do not know how extensive this process was in Gipuzkoa. Royal predominance seems to have been evident in the urban centers that flourished mainly from the thirteenth century on. Whatever the case, it is always worth asking questions. Could the seigneury have taken root in at least the far southeast, where the Guevaras, in time, would end up imposing their authority?[36]

35   Martínez Díez, *Guipúzcoa en los albores de su historia*, docs. 6, 8, 9, 10, and 12; *Becerro Galicano Digital* , doc. 579, at www.ehu.eus/galicano/id579 and doc. 581, at www.ehu. eus/galicano/id581 (last accessed August 10, 2018).
36   Iñaki García Camino, "Origen y consolidación de la sociedad feudal en el País Vasco (siglos IX–XII)." In *Historia del País Vasco. Edad Media (siglos V–XV)*, ed. Pedro Barruso Barés and José Ángel Lema Pueyo (San Sebastián: Hiria Liburuak, 2004), 274–77; Irene Ruiz Albi, *La reina doña Urraca (1109–1126). Cancillería y colección diplomática* (León: Centro de Estudio e Investigación San Isidoro, 2003), doc. 8.

What was the state of lower social groups? José Ángel García de Cortázar searches for the presence of property owners without any honorary title in witness statements during legal processes. The list includes individuals like Gómez Fortuñones from Ormaiztegi, Iñigo López from Lazcano (Lazkao), and Nunuso Narriátez from Loinaz, which a legal act of 1053 confirms, even if it is true that the identification of some of them as Gipuzkoan solicits grave doubts. We could, following this logic, add Nunuso Narriátez, who appears in a donation of 1025.[37] Conversely, the lack of any information illustrating servile dependence among the population of Gipuzkoa is frustrating. For the moment, there are only two reliable sources, which lead us to the far southwest of the territory, to Salinas de Léniz-Leintz Gatzaga. There, the *senior* Órbita Aznárez disposed of the person of one of its inhabitants, Mamés, whom in 1080 he entrusted with his property, and therefore his family, to the monastery of San Millán. He was not a peasant, given that he seems to have been involved in the production of salt, in which he took part. Seven years later, another baron, Galindo, son of Count Iñigo López, donated to the monastery of San Millán a servant in the same place, which would again have included a family unit. Given the poverty of sources, it is difficult to determine to what extent such a condition of dependence on the secular nobility was extensive in the territory.[38]

One would think that such situations occurred in territories in which monastery power was deep rooted. It is possible that the servants handed over to San Millán in Salinas de Léniz were not the only ones the abbey possessed in the area. One should not rule out the possibility that such things occurred sometimes among the

---

37 García de Cortázar, "La sociedad guipuzcoana antes del fuero de San Sebastián," 306–7; Martínez Díez, *Guipúzcoa en los albores de su historia*, 51–55 and docs. 6 and 11.

38 *Becerro Galicano Digital*, doc. 170, at www.chu.cus/galicano/id170 and doc. 577, at www.ehu.eus/galicano/id577 (last accessed August 10, 2018). Until quite recently, a similar case was mentioned in a certain part of Berastegi in 1141, relating to two servants, Beraxa and Orti Muñoz, but this locality seems more likely to have corresponded to the jurisdiction of the *villa* of Huarte Araquil (Uharte Arakil) in Navarre. See Ernesto García Fernández, "Sociedad, poblamiento y poder en las fronteras de Navarra con Castilla en el Edad Media: las pueblas de Burunda y Araquil," *Anuario de Estudios Medievales* 21 (1991), 41n15.

people in the abbey of Astigarribia or among the inhabitants of the primitive *villa* of Donostia-San Sebastian, donated to Leire.

Conclusion

The time has come to present a series of final considerations and suggestions. There are more questions than certainties. I will not enter in to the thorny problem of the existence of a clannish society as a starting point in the Early Middle Ages, although everything indicates that such outlines were clearly in crisis and in decline. One must assume that progress was being made, in an increasingly populated area, toward an increasingly complex, unequal, and hierarchical society. That is what the written testimonies and, especially, archaeological findings, appear to suggest, and that is how one must interpret the situation on the basis of a comparison with the neighboring territories. Nevertheless, mystery still surrounds crucial questions such as those relating to the basic institutions of the feudal world, including vassalage and client relations, the rootedness of the noble seigneury, and the legal condition of peasants.

Gipuzkoa was not isolated. Its nobility and clerics, linked to diverse ecclesiastical centers, maintained connections, toward the east with Navarre and Upper Aragón; and toward the south and west with Araba, Bizkaia, and Castile. These connections were linked to power and property, but also with cultural and religious influences that we know little about. The very use of writing and, with that, the diffusion of ecclesiastical Latin—in an overwhelmingly Basque-speaking linguistic context—was associated with these phenomena. What of peasant population shifts out of the territory, toward the south, as part of colonization and repopulation processes? The 943 testimony, still to be confirmed, speaks of such tendencies, but it is worth remaining cautious in this regard. Could Gipuzkoans have participated in military campaigns for the kings of Navarre and Castile on the border with al-Andalus? One should not rule out the possibility.

The extraordinary wealth of information on the Fuero of San Sebastian is surprising and contrasts with the extreme lack of prior written information. The foral text reveals all of a sudden an unusual flourishing of the commercial and urban worlds, led by immigrants from Lapurdi and Aquitaine interacting with the local population. It is reasonable to think that such a long period of economic growth, rarely known, made possible the boom that Sancho the Wise's deed reflected. At the very least, there is no doubt that this was a society experiencing growth within that "silent expansion" of Western Christianity during this time.

The reasons behind the settlement of people from Gascony and Lapurdi in Gipuzkoa demand another interpretive effort. Rather than a question of political explanations tied to dynastic changes, one would have to look for these reasons in the attractive nature of Cantabrian commerce and, above all, in the characteristics and evolution of society in the original territories of these people. Their consequences are more evident as regards the decisive push given to the urban world, especially on the coast. Posing the question "what if?" it is likely that, without the participation of these merchants and seafarers, the take-off of Gipuzkoan *villas* would have been delayed until the mid-thirteenth century, the era of Alfonso X the Wise (1252–1284). At the same time, this immigration from Aquitaine, and the economic dynamism it implied, obliged the different powers to better define their boundaries, as happened in the case of the bishoprics of Baiona and Pamplona. This is what urged Sancho VI to promote the port and *villa* of Donostia-San Sebastian and, perhaps, its prosperity must have figured among the incentives that encouraged Alfonso VIII to empower the Gipuzkoan territory.

In the final analysis, any possibility to advance in our understanding of these matters would depend on the intersection of information among the available written sources—which are rather scarce and unlikely to be added to—and, especially, advances in archaeological digs. There is an urgent need for comparative analysis with other territories that share, to some extent, similar characteristics, like Bizkaia and Cantabria. One hopes that new questions, methods, and interpretations help to make progress in this regard.

BIBLIOGRAPHY

Alberdi Lonbide, Xabier, and Iosu Etxezarraga Ortuondo. "Proyecto de investigación de las ferrerías de monte o haizeolak en Gipuzkoa y Álava: avance de resultados." *Kobie. Anejos* 13 (2014): 181–92.

Aragón Ruano, Álvaro. "La evolución del hábitat y del poblamiento en el País Vasco durante las Edades Media y Moderna." *Domitia* 12 (2011): 21–52.

Barrena Osoro, Elena. *La formación histórica de Guipúzcoa. Transformaciones en la organización social de un territorio cantábrico durante la época altomedieval.* San Sebastián: Universidad de Deusto, 1989.

Becerro Galicano Digital. At www.ehu.eus/galicano/. Last accessed August 10, 2018.

Bisson, Thomas. *The Crisis of the Twelfth Century: Power, Lordship, and the Origins of European Government.* Princeton, NJ: Princeton University Press, 2009.

Canellas López, Ángel. *Colección diplomática de Sancho Ramírez.* Zaragoza: Real Sociedad Económica de Amigos del País, 1993.

Congreso: El fuero de San Sebastián y su época (San Sebastián 19–23 de enero de 1981) / Donostiako forua eta bere garaia (Donostia, 1981ko urtarrilaren 19tik 23ra). San Sebastián: Eusko Ikaskuntza / Sociedad de Estudios Vascos, 1982.

Curiel Yarza, Iosu. *La parroquia en el País Vasco-cantábrico durante la Baja Edad Media (c. 1350–1539).* Bilbao: Universidad del País Vasco / Euskal Herriko Unibertsitatea, 2009.

Etxezarraga Ortuondo, Iosu. "San Pedro de Iromendi. II Campaña." *Arkeoikuska* 13 (2014): 285–89.

———. "San Pedro de Iromendi. III Campaña." *Arkeoikuska* 14 (2015): 311–17.

———. "San Pedro de Iromendi. IV Campaña." *Arkeoikuska* 15 (2016): 306–11.

Fortún Pérez de Ciriza, Luis Javier. "La quiebra de la soberanía navarra en Álava, Guipúzcoa y el Duranguesado (1199–1200)." *Revista Internacional de los Estudios Vascos* 45, no. 2 (2000): 439–94.

Fortún Pérez de Ciriza, Luis Javier, and Carmen Jusué Simonena, eds. *Historia de Navarra. I. Antigüedad y Alta Edad Media.* Pamplona: Gobierno de Navarra, 1993.

Franco Pérez, Francisco Javier, Iosu Etxezarraga Ortuondo, and Xabier Alberdi Lonbide. "Los orígenes de la tecnología del hierro en el País Vasco: las ferrerías de monte o haizeolak." *Kobie. Serie Paleoantropología* 34 (2015): 267–82.

García de Cortázar, José Ángel. "Una villa mercantil: 1180–1516." In *Historia de Donostia-San Sebastián*, edited by Miguel Artola Gallego. Donostia / San Sebastián: Editorial Nerea, 2000.

———. "La sociedad guipuzcoana antes del fuero de San Sebastián." In *Investigaciones sobre historia medieval del País Vasco (1965–2005)*, edited by José Ramón Díaz de Durana. Bilbao: Universidad de País Vasco / Euskal Herriko Unibertsitatea, 2005.

García Camino, Iñaki. "Origen y consolidación de la sociedad feudal en el País Vasco (siglos IX–XII)." In *Historia del País Vasco. Edad Media (siglos V–XV)*, edited by Pedro Barruso Barés and José Ángel Lema Pueyo. San Sebastián: Hiria Liburuak, 2004.

García Fernández, Ernesto. "Sociedad, poblamiento y poder en las fronteras de Navarra con Castilla en el Edad Media: las pueblas de Burunda y Araquil." *Anuario de Estudios Medievales* 21 (1991): 41–69.

Goñi Gaztambide, José. *Colección diplomática de la catedral de Pamplona. Tomo I (829–1243)*. Pamplona: Gobierno de Navarra, 1997.

Historia Compostelana. Edited and translated by Emma Falque Rey. Los Berrocales del Jarama, Madrid: Akal, 1994.

Ibáñez Etxeberria, Alex, ed. "Santa María la Real de Zarautz (País Vasco), continuidad y discontinuidad en la ocupación de la costa vasca entre los siglos V a.C. y XV d.C." Special issue, *Munibe* 27 (2011).

Jimeno Aranguren, Roldán, and Aitor Pescador Medrano. *Colección documental de Sancho Garcés III, el Mayor, rey de Pamplona (1004–1035)*. Pamplona: Nabarralde; Pamiela, 2003.

Jimeno Jurío, José María. *El Libro Rubro de Iranzu*. Pamplona: Editorial Aranzadi, 1970.

Lacarra de Miguel, José María. *Historia política del reino de Navarra desde sus orígenes hasta su incorporación a Castilla*. 3 volumes. Pamplona: Caja de Ahorros de Navarra, 1972.

Lacarra de Miguel, José María, and Ángel Juan Martín Duque. *Fueros de Navarra. Fueros derivados de Jaca 1*. Estella-San Sebastián; Pamplona: Institución Príncipe de Viana, 1969.

Larrea Conde, Juan José. *La Navarre du IVe au XIIe siècle: Peuplement et société*. Paris and Brussels: De Boeck Université, 1998.

———. "La herencia vasca: acción política y arquitectura social en Vizcaya y Álava antes de su incorporación al reino de Alfonso VI." In *Alfonso VI y su época I: los precedentes del reinado (966–1065), Sahagún (León), 4 a 7 de septiembre de 2006*, edited by Etelvina Fernández González. León: Universidad de León, 2007.

Lema Pueyo, José Ángel. *Colección diplomática de Alfonso I de Aragón y Pamplona (1104–1134)*. San Sebastián: Eusko Ikaskuntza, 1990.

———. "Los orígenes medievales de San Sebastián: la época anterior al fuero de Sancho el Sabio." In *Geografía e Historia de Donostia-San Sebastián*, edited by F. Javier Gómez Piñeiro and Juan Antonio Sáez García. Donostia / San Sebastián: Diputación Foral de Gipuzkoa, 1999.

———. "Evolución política de los territorios históricos: Álava, Guipúzcoa y Vizcaya en la Edad Media." In *Historia del País Vasco. Edad Media (siglos V–XV)*, edited by Pedro Barruso Barés and José Ángel Lema Pueyo. San Sebastián: Hiria Liburuak, 2004.

———. *Alfonso I el Batallador: rey de Aragón y Pamplona (1104–1134)*. Gijón: Trea Editorial, 2008.

————. "De 'Ipuzkoa' a la Hermandad de villas de Gipuzkoa (ss. VI–XV)." In *Síntesis de la Historia de Gipuzkoa*, edited by Álvaro Aragón Ruano and Iker Echeberria Ayllón. Donostia: Diputación Foral de Gipuzkoa, 2017.

Mañaricúa y Nuere, Andrés E. de. *Obispados de Álava, Guipúzcoa y Vizcaya hasta fines del siglo XI*. En *Obispados de Álava, Guipúzcoa y Vizcaya hasta la erección de la diócesis de Vitoria*. Vitoria: Seminario Diocesano, 1964.

Martín Duque, Ángel J. "Sancho VI de Navarra y el fuero de Vitoria." In *Vitoria en la Edad Media*, edited by Pilar Aróstegui. Vitoria-Gasteiz: Ayuntamiento de Vitoria-Gasteiz, 1982.

————. "El fuero de San Sebastián: tradición manuscrita y edición crítica." In *Congreso: El fuero de San Sebastián y su época (San Sebastián 19–23 de enero de 1981) / Donostiako forua eta bere garaia (Donostia, 1981ko urtarrilaren 19tik 23ra)*. San Sebastián: Eusko Ikaskuntza / Sociedad de Estudios Vascos, 1982.

————. *Documentación medieval de Leire (siglos IX a XII)*. Pamplona: Diputación Foral de Navarra; Institución Príncipe de Viana, 1983.

Martínez Díez, Gonzalo. Álava medieval. Volume 1. Vitoria: Diputación Foral de Álava, 1974.

————. *Guipúzcoa en los albores de su historia*. San Sebastián: Diputación Provincial de Guipúzcoa, 1975.

Orella Unzué, José Luis. "Estudio jurídico comparativo de los fueros de San Sebastián, Estella, Vitoria y Logroño." In *Congreso: El fuero de San Sebastián y su época (San Sebastián 19–23 de enero de 1981) / Donostiako forua eta bere garaia (Donostia, 1981ko urtarrilaren 19tik 23ra)*. San Sebastián: Eusko Ikaskuntza / Sociedad de Estudios Vascos, 1982.

————. "Nacimiento de Guipúzcoa como tenencia navarra de frontera." *Lurralde: investigación y espacio* 34 (2011), 189–217.

Orella Unzué, José Luis, Iñigo Aguirre Querejeta, and Edorta Kortadi Olano. *Atlas de Euskal Herria. Geografía-Economía-Historia-Arte.* Donostia: Erein, 1982.

Pescador Medrano, Aitor. "Tenentes y tenencias del reino de Pamplona en Álava, Vizcaya, Guipúzcoa, La Rioja y Castilla (1004–1076)." *Vasconia. Cuadernos de Historia-Geografía* 29 (1999): 118–20.

Peterson, David. "Primeras menciones a Guipúzcoa." *Fontes Linguae Vasconum: Studia et Documenta* 97 (2004): 597–608.

Ruiz Albi, Irene. *La reina doña Urraca (1109–1126). Cancillería y colección diplomática.* León: Centro de Estudio e Investigación San Isidoro, 2003.

Sarasola Etxegoien, Nerea. "El poblamiento medieval de Gipuzkoa: revisión crítica del registro arqueológico." *Munibe (Antropologia-Arkeologia)* 61 (2010): 339–93.

Sarasola Etxegoien, Nerea, and Alfredo Moraza Barea. *Arqueología medieval en Gipuzkoa.* Donostia / San Sebastián: Diputación Foral de Gipuzkoa, 2011.

Tena García, Soledad. *La sociedad urbana en la Guipúzcoa costera medieval: San Sebastián, Rentería y Fuenterrabía (1200–1500).* Donostia / San Sebastián: Instituto Doctor Camino de Historia Donostiarra, 1997.

Chapter 2

Organization of the Estella Territory and the Creation of Estella

Javier Ilundain Chamarro

S ince 1990, when Ángel J. Martín Duque moved the birth of the first Navarrese burg to 1076,[1] there have been several attempts to explore more deeply the origins of Estella with the aim of clarifying its legal status, its urban shape, and the sociolinguistic profile of its inhabitants. In this regard, the most interesting arguments have emerged from the disciplines of legal history;[2] church history;[3] linguistics;[4] with particular success in the field of onomastics;[5] and archaeology.[6]

---

1   Ángel J. Martín Duque, "La fundación del primer burgo navarro: Estella." *Príncipe de Viana* 190 (1990), 317–28.

2   Ana María Barrero García, "La difusión del Fuero de Jaca en el Camino de Santiago," in *El Fuero de Jaca. Estudios* (Zaragoza: El Justicia de Aragón, 2004), 111–60; Julia Pavón Benito, "Fuero de Jaca y Fuero de Estella. Observaciones críticas," in *XV Congreso de Historia de la Corona de Aragón. Jaca en la Corona de Aragón (siglos XII–XVIII)*, vol. 3 (Zaragoza: Gobierno de Aragón, 1993), 341–55.

3   José Goñi Gaztambide, *Historia eclesiástica de Estella*, 2 vols. (Pamplona: Gobierno de Navarra, 1990–1994); Roldán Jimeno Aranguren, *Terras a suis reperitur semper esse poessessas: la Iglesia en Tierra Estella en la Edad Media* (Pamplona: Lamiñarra, 2007).

4   Fernando González Ollé, "Etimología del topónimo Estella," *Príncipe de Viana* 190 (1990), 329–44; Ricardo Ciérbide, "La lengua de los francos de Estella," *Sancho el Sabio: Revista de cultura e investigación vasca* 3 (1993), 115–48.

5   Ricardo Ciérbide, "En torno a las denominaciones de la ciudad de Estella," *Fontes linguae vasconum: Studia et documenta* 51 (1988), 53–58; Ricardo Ciérbide, "Onomástica personal de los francos de Estella (1090–1222)." In *Actas de las III Jornadas de Onomástica Estella* (Bilbao: Euskaltzaindia, 2008), 165–86; José María Jimeno Jurío, "Estella/Lizarra. Toponimia," *Fontes Linguae Vasconum: Studia et documenta* 77 (1998), 133–64; and José María Jimeno Jurío, "Toponimia rural y urbana de Estella." In *Actas de las III Jornadas de Onomástica Estella* (Bilbao: Euskaltzaindia, 2008), 25–41.

6   José Miguel Legarda Sembroiz, "Estructuras defensivas en la ciudad de Estella.

The texts we dispose of in order to understand what Estella was like and its original shape before the concession of the fuero are, to be sure, scarce. Barely forty documents prior to 1100 offer information in this regard. To this scarcity one should add several additional problems, such as the suspect accuracy of many of them, for being fake altogether, interfered with, or later copies with errors, or just the fact that most of them do not contribute more information than a toponymical reference.

The objective, then, of this chapter is to offer the most complete panorama possible of the historical milestone that was the founding of Estella and its early organization as a settlement, including the latest research on the topic and rereading certain sources in light of this.

The Land of Deyo

Since the origins of the Kingdom of Pamplona, the land of Deyo was considered an integral part of the kingdom;[7] or, rather, one of the areas of which it was made up.[8] Both the chronicles and the documents make a clear distinction when it comes to Pamplona. This is reflected both in the *Crónica de Alfonso III* and the *Crónica Albeldense*, to cite the dominions of Sancho I.[9] In 928, his son García ruled "*in Pampilona et in Deiu.*"[10] Once more, in 958, within the dominions of García I, Fortún Galíndez governed in Nájera;[11] and Queen Toda in Deyo.[12]

Resultados arqueológicos," *Trabajos de arqueología Navarra* 22 (2010), 163–93; Mikel Ramos Aguirre, "Intervenciones arqueológicas en el castillo de Estella (2001–2010)," *Trabajos de arqueología Navarra* 27 (2015), 185–218.

7   "Albelda" (xx) in Juan Gil Fernández, ed., José L. Moralejo, trans., and Juan I. Ruiz de la Peña, study, *Crónicas Asturianas* (Oviedo: Universidad de Oviedo, 1985).

8   This idea is suggested by José María Lacarra, *Historia del Reino de Navarra en la Edad Media* (Pamplona: Caja de Ahorros de Navarra, 1975), 89.

9   See "Alfonso III" (14, 4) and "Albelda" (xv, xx) in Gil Fernández, Moralejo, and Ruiz de la Peña, *Crónicas Asturianas.*

10   Antonio Ubieto Arteta, *Cartulario de San Juan de la Peña* (Valencia: Anubar, 1962), doc. 14.

11   It is significant that, by this time, it seems that Nájera had already overtaken Deyo in importance, with the military and strategic importance of the latter being relegated to a secondary level following the expansion into the Ebro Valley.

12   "Albelda" (24) in Gil Fernández, Moralejo, and Ruiz de la Peña, *Crónicas Asturianas.*

The basis of this differentiation is difficult to perceive. It could be its particular identity that was distinct from other territories or, perhaps, that it had a certain kind of organization as a political entity prior to its incorporation into the kingdom or as a border marker. The persistence of this consideration could also indicate that its incorporation into the Pamplona monarchy was done wholesale, either by military or diplomatic means. It would be a case similar to that of Aragón (incorporated through a matrimonial alliance), Araba (through the vassalage of its seigneurs), or Nájera (through conquest),[13] all territories that maintained their individual identities in the clauses of the ruler. It seems like this separation began to weaken somewhat in the ninth century although, in one way or another, it would be inherited by Estella, under whose denomination a concept of differentiated territorial entity would resurge in the twelfth century, as we will see.

Together with Berrueza, Deyo became the first bastion of the kingdom against Islam on its western border.[14] It was still the object of several attacks by the Muslims in the ninth century.[15] With the arrival of the Jimena dynasty, the area gained special importance as a defensive frontier and point of departure for Pamplona offensives. The supposed sepulture of Sancho I in San Esteban (Monjardín)[16] and, especially, the abundance of small and large fortified points disseminated throughout the area would be reflections of its symbolic and strategic value. In effect, the hilly edges between the Cantabria and Montejurra mountain range were reinforced with a defensive line (Marañón, Punicastro, Desojo, Sorlada, San Esteban, Arróniz, and Allo), on which a dense system of possessions was based.[17] This would survive, in part, until the twelfth century.[18] After this

13 Ángel J. Martín Duque, "Navarra en la Alta Edad Media (711–1234)," in *Nueva Historia de Navarra*, ed. Francisco Javier Navarro (Barañain: EUNSA, 2010), 119–55.
14 "Rot. Seb." (14, 4) in Gil Fernández, Moralejo, and Ruiz de la Peña, *Crónicas Asturianas*
15 "Albelda" (xv) in Gil Fernández, Moralejo, and Ruiz de la Peña, *Crónicas Asturianas*; Juan Antonio Estévez Sola, *Crónica Najerense* (Madrid: Akal, 2003), 23.
16 "Albelda" (xx) in Gil Fernández, Moralejo, and Ruiz de la Peña, *Crónicas Asturianas*.
17 Alberto Cañada Juste, "Honores y tenencias en la monarquía pamplonesa del siglo X. Precedentes de una institución." *Príncipe de Viana*, Annex 2 (1986), 69, 74.
18 José Ángel Lema Pueyo, "Las tenencias navarras de Alfonso I 'el Batallador'," *Príncipe de Viana*, Annex 8 (1988), 63–68.

first containing wall, a second line of defense was put in place as a rearguard on which the castle of Lizarrara was located.

It appears that Deyo, in the same way as Berrueza, was a territorial demarcation more than a specific fortified point. The *Crónica Albeldense* points out that the Muslims sacked Deyo but did not take any of its settlements or castles.[19] This would explain the existence of place names that derived from Deyo in a relatively wide geographical arc: Dicastillo (Deio Castello);[20] San Esteban de Deyo;[21] San Andrés de Deyo;[22] and Yerri (Deyo-*herri* or "village" in Basque).[23] However, through the eleventh century the denomination remained linked closely to one of its most important fortresses: that of San Esteban.

The conquest of Nájera (923) and definitive taking of Calahorra (1045) reduced the military responsibility of these tenancies, and they went from being frontier towns to being interior settlements. Some of them disappeared altogether and in others the principal function of their *tenentes* became, gradually, territorial administration.[24] This new mission would include among its priorities managing royal property in the area as well as repopulating and colonizing the territory. In the case of San Esteban, the once emblematic castle in the kingdom, it first passed into the hands of the monastery of Irache in 1045.[25] Then, in 1081, a community of French monks settled there.[26] Lizarrara, however, would become one of the main tenancies in the area.

---

19 "Albelda" (xv) in Gil Fernández, Moralejo, and Ruiz de la Peña, *Crónicas Asturianas.*
20 José María Lacarra, *Colección diplomática de Irache* (Zaragoza: Instituto de Estudios Pirenáicos, 1965), doc. 9.
21 Ángel J. Martín Duque, *Documentación medieval de Leire (siglos IX a XII)* (Pamplona: Institución Príncipe de Viana, 1983), doc. 62.
22 Antonio Ubieto Arteta, *Cartulario de Albelda* (Valencia: Anubar, 1960), doc. 47.
23 José de Moret, *Anales del Reino de Navarras*, vol. 1 (Tolosa: Casa editorial de Eusebio López, 1890), 130–31.
24 Some, like Marañón, Punicastro and, in another sense, Lizarrara, would recover their importance with the division of the kingdom following the death of Sancho IV in 1076. Ricardo Santamaría, "La muerte de un rey. Repercusiones territoriales del asesinato de Sancho IV Garcés (1076) en el área navarro-riojana," *Príncipe de Viana* 253 (2011): 249–62.
25 Lacarra, *Colección diplomática de Irache*, doc. 8.
26 Ibid., 64.

Lizarrara enjoyed a strategic position[27] that conferred on it a leading role in the tenth and eleventh centuries. That setting, a small prairie with the River Ega flowing through it and surrounded by hills and crags, marked the convergence of various valleys (the Yerri, Amescoa, Guesalaz, San Esteban de la Solana, and Valdega). It was, moreover, one of the main points of contact between the mountains and the Ebro Valley. The old castle[28] sat on a crag by the edge of the river, which allowed it to control both the transit along its riverbank and river crossings in the area. The original population settlement was on the other side of the river (based around the church of San Pedro de Lizarra) and had been furnished with vegetable gardens and mills that can be dated back via documents to the eleventh century. The connection between both spheres, the military and the productive, would be made through one or more bridges. In the same way as happened with Sangüesa (Zangoza) or Puente la Reina (Gares),[29] the existence of a bridge would have been a determining element in the flourishing of Lizarrara. The routes that connected the aforementioned valleys came together at a specific point, protected and controlled by a castle, making the location very favorable for commercial contacts and, later, the settlement of businesses and artisans. The expansion and success of Lizarrara as a settlement would have been determined, as we will see, by a political decision. However, this was based on certain very advantageous geographical and human conditions. The development of the Camino de Santiago would only have reinforced and cemented this.[30]

The tenancy created in Lizarrara would have been, then, the first major step in developing the settlement. And it was stimulated by the presence of the castle and the existence of some seigneurs

27   Alfredo Floristán Samanes, "De Lizarra a Estella una reflexión geográfica," *Príncipe de Viana* 190 (1990), 307–16.
28   See Ramos Aguirre, "Intervenciones arqueológicas en el castillo de Estella."
29   A distinctive feature of both settlements in their respective foral concessions was the presence of a bridge: "*illo borgo novo prope illo ponte.*" See José María Lacarra and Ángel J. Martín Duque, *Fueros de Navarra. I.1. Fueros derivados de Jaca. Estella-San Sebastián* (Pamplona: Institución Príncipe de Viana, 1969), doc. 4; José Ángel Lema Pueyo, *Colección diplomática de Alfonso I de Aragón y Pamplona (1104–1134)* (San Sebastián: Eusko Ikaskuntza, 1990), doc. 113.
30   Luis Vázquez de Parga, José María Lacarra, and Juan Uría Ríu, *Las peregrinaciones a Santiago de Compostela* (Pamplona: Gobierno de Navarra, 1998), 465–97.

there who were sometimes members of the royal family. The strategic location for the town may have also benefited a tenancy from the point of view of controlling and governing the territory. In the lands of Deyo, Lizarrara would have been, alongside San Esteban, the most important *honor*. Clearly, the castle of San Esteban enjoyed an emblematic status on account of its military value. However, when Queen Toda ruled Deyo in the name of her son, she did so from Lizarrara,[31] so that, even if it was not the capital of the territory, it was one of the most important settlements.

The Hamlet and Tenancy of Lizarrara

We know little of the original population nucleus of Lizarrara. The gothic church of San Pedro de Lizarra was constructed, presumably, on the site of previous church, the original parish in the town. In the Late Middle Ages it was the only church in Estella dependent on the Bishop of Pamplona,[32] because it predated the donations that, through the eleventh and twelfth centuries, placed the remaining churches under the jurisdiction of San Juan de la Peña, Montearagón, or Irache.

The royal seigneury would be important in the area and would have served as the basis of the tenancy and, later, the council limits that Estella had as a result of the foral concessions. However, it seems there were several noble families that either resided or had property in Lizarrara. In 1024 the brothers Sancho and Andregoto Galíndez gave the palaces, vineyards, vegetable gardens, and their remaining possessions in Lizarrara and Urtadía to the monastery of Irache.[33] Sancho Garcés de Lizarrara, Sancha de Lizarrara, and Jimeno Ortiz de Lizarrara, cited as witnesses, respectively, in 1045, 1098, and 1120, were also inhabitants of the town.[34] Their use of the titles *senior* or *domna* is indicative of their status as members of the

---

31   "*Et regina Tota donna in Deio in Lizarrara.*" See "Albelda" (24) in Gil Fernández, Moralejo, and Ruiz de la Peña, *Crónicas Asturianas.*
32   Jimeno Aranguren, *Terras a suis reperitur semper esse poessessas*, 80.
33   Lacarra, *Colección diplomática de Irache*, doc. 3. Although the information contained therein seems plausible, the document was possibly manipulated on being incorporated into the cartulary of Irache.
34   Ibid., 8, 73, 103.

lower nobility.[35] Through the twelfth century other individuals that made use of the same toponymical last name can be documented: García Velázquez de Lizarrara;[36] Pedro Sánchez de Lizarrara;[37] and García Lizarceco and his son Fortún.[38] Their onomastics leaves no doubt that this was an autochthonous population.[39]

The *tenentes* of Lizarrara were, likewise, members of the Pamplona aristocracy. In this case, there is documentation of Queen Toda;[40] of Jimeno Ogaoiz in 1024;[41] and, between 1047 and 1084, of Jimeno Garcés. As regards the latter, he could be identified with a seigneur documented since the rule of García III.[42] He was the beneficiary in the will of Queen Estefanía;[43] and occupied the position of standard-bearer for Sancho IV between 1060 and 1064.[44] The frequency with which we find this *tenente* cited contrasts sharply with the presence of other contemporaneous seigneurs and, especially, with that of his predecessors in the post, which could indicate the growing importance of the tenancy in the ancient land of Deyo. If these hypotheses are confirmed, he would be one of the most prominent individuals of the second half of the eleventh century. Following Sancho IV's death in 1076, it seems that Jimeno Garcés would have positioned himself quickly on the side of Sancho Ramírez. To be sure, maintaining control of the tenancy of Lizarrara would have

35 Later, the terms *don* and *doña* also spread among the population. See Javier Ilundain Chamarro, *Los buenos hombres de Olite (siglos XII–XIV). Sociedad, poder y élites urbanas* (Pamplona: Gobierno de Navarra, 2017), 250.
36 Lacarra, *Colección diplomática de Irache*, doc. 125.
37 Ibid., 144.
38 José Goñi Gaztambide, *Colección diplomática de la Catedral de Pamplona* (Pamplona: Gobierno de Navarra, 1997), doc. 255.
39 Predominated by traditional denominators in the Western Pyrenees and their variants: Sancho, García, Fortún, Velasco, and Andregoto. See José Ángel García de Cortázar, "Antroponimia en Navarra y Rioja en los siglos X a XII," in *Estudios de Historia Medieval de La Rioja* (Logroño: Universidad de La Rioja, 2009), 199–200.
40 "Albelda" (24) in Gil Fernández, Moralejo, and Ruiz de la Peña, *Crónicas Asturianas*.
41 Lacarra, *Colección diplomática de Irache*, doc. 3.
42 Margarita Cantera Montenegro, *Colección documental de Santa María la Real de Nájera. Tomo I (siglos X–XIV)* (San Sebastián: Eusko Ikaskuntza, 1991), doc. 8. It would be going too far to identify him as the tutor (*nutrix*) of Ramiro of Aragón for chronological reasons.
43 Ibid., doc. 18.
44 The dominant homonymy among the Pamplona nobility at that moment prevents us from confirming this with certainty. See "Albelda" (42 and 47) in Gil Fernández, Moralejo, and Ruiz de la Peña, *Crónicas Asturianas*; Lacarra, *Colección diplomática de Irache*, docs. 24, 28, 29, 30, 31, 32, 33, 34, and 35; Ildefonso Rodríguez de Lama, *Colección diplomática medieval de la Rioja (923–1225)* (Logroño: Instituto de Estudios Riojanos, 1976–1979), doc. 21; and Goñi Gaztambide, *Colección diplomática de la Catedral de Pamplona*, doc. 19.

been key at that moment in order to safeguard the western part of the kingdom and curb any potential incursion by the new Castilian neighbor, who, following the regicide of 1076, dominated La Rioja and Araba. His loyalty toward the king of Aragón was rewarded by the new monarch entrusting both Jimeno and his family with new tenancies. In 1079 and 1080, Jimeno Garcés was *tenente* of Lizarrara, as well as Salazar, and, even more significantly, his brothers Sancho, Lope, and Íñigo, who were until that time unknown, were given the authority to preside over the tenancies of Echauri, Aoiz, Nagore, Navascués, and Sangüesa.[45]

As regards running the tenancy on the part of Jimeno Garcés, one should point out that, with the expansion into La Rioja in the mid-eleventh century, his function as the administrator of the territory in representation of the king would have been accentuated.[46] His military tasks continued to be active in his role as head of the castle. However, we can verify that the activity he deployed was much broader in scope. No evidence remains of his role as a representative of justice and that as an administrator of royal property is limited to his running of the castle. Nevertheless, it is significant that he was present at all the major events that took place in and around Lizarrara, which was possibly under his charge. Thus, we come across him as a witness and confirmer in numerous donations to the monastery of Irache.[47] In these cases, he was often the only representative of royal authority and an indelible point of reference for the inhabitants and powers of the area. When in 1063 Sancho IV handed over the monastery of San Andrés in Deyo to Gomesano, bishop of Nájera, he did so in the presence of local *tenentes*, among them Jimeno Garcés.[48]

In any event, as regards the focus of this chapter, what is most interesting is his role at the head of repopulating the territory. This was one of the traditional functions of *tenentes*, although not many testimonies about the practice survive. In fact, it was typical,

---

45   Martín Duque, *Documentación medieval de Leire*, docs. 106 and 107.
46   José Ángel Lema Pueyo, *Instituciones políticas del reinado de Alfonso I el Batallador, rey de Aragón y Pamplona.1104–1134* (Bilbao: Universidad del País Vasco, 1997), 172–75.
47   Lacarra, *Colección diplomática de Irache*, docs. 16, 25, 28, 29, 30, 31, 33, 36, 49, 55, and 64.
48   "Albelda" (47) in Gil Fernández, Moralejo, and Ruiz de la Peña, *Crónicas Asturianas*.

in the founding of a settlement or conceding of a fuero, for the monarch to take on the leading role, since it was in his exclusive power to do so. However, certain evidence leads us to speculate that the true promoter of such initiatives was the *tenente* of the area.[49] This would be the case of the settlement known as San Anacleto. In 1065, Gomesano, bishop of Calahorra and Nájera, confirmed to the settlers of San Anacleto the laws that García III had conferred on them and placed them under the authority of San Martín de Albelda.[50] The document itself indicates, moreover, that the place was settled first by King García and then by Jimeno Garcés, *tenente* of Lizarrara. The latter was possibly acting under the authority of Sancho IV, to whom certain concessions were also attributed. While still under the tenancy of Jimeno Garcés, the confirmation and transfer of the property took place. We do not know where San Anacleto was situated, but geographical references, both to the tenancy of Lizarrara (under his tutelage) and the neighboring towns and castles (San Esteban, Arróniz, Arellano, Dicastillo, and *Chegen*[51]) from which the witnesses in the document came, point toward the hillsides of Montejurra as a possible location. There are no later references to this settlement, and its name is not documented either in Navarre or in the bordering provinces, which leads us to believe that it is a copying error on the part of the author of the cartulary of Albelda.

In any event, it is significant that Jimeno Garcés would have participated actively in the creation and legal endowment of a settlement under his tenancy, a clear precedent of what happen later in Estella.

---

49 One paradigmatic case would be that of the conceding of the fuero of Estella to the town of Olite by García Ramírez in 1147, Municipal Archive of Olite, doc. 1. Here, it states clearly that it was Ramiro Garcés, *tenente* of Ujué, who induced the king to concede the fuero.
50 "Albelda" (49) in Gil Fernández, Moralejo, and Ruiz de la Peña, *Crónicas Asturianas*.
51 This latter location remains an unidentified settlement, perhaps also as the result of an error in the reading. It could be Ayegui or even a reminiscent or derivation of Deyo.

The Birth of Estella

In the absence of the discovery of a new document or epigraph, it is impossible to date precisely the funding of Estella. As already noted, the presence of a settlement and especially a bridge and a tenancy would have encouraged people to settle through the eleventh century. To that we should add the already corroborating activity of re-populating the area in which the *tenente* Jimeno Garcés took part and that could have favored the emerging settlement. In the 1076 document by which Irache handed over a plot to San Juan de la Peña,[52] there is mention of a consolidated proto-urban structure, the burg beneath the castle of Lizarrara, in which there already existed mills and it was predicted that it would continue to be built. The denomination of the burg itself could indicate the existence of a wall and even a certain legal-administrative structure. In 1077,[53] Lope Arnaldo, a subordinate of Jimeno Garcés, was appointed the *merino* (akin to a sheriff in the medieval sense of the term) of Estella. This is the first reference to the new name of the settlement that, as we will see, would end up prevailing in 1084 when Lope Arnaldo became the *tenente*.[54] In 1086, Sancho Ramírez awarded the church of Santiago de Funes the crown rents deriving from the Jews and the goods he owned in Estella, as well as the castle church and its accompanying properties.[55] These rents would then be passed on in 1093 to the monastery of Montearagón.[56] The Jewish community of Estella in the late eleventh century would be sufficiently large that the taxes levied on it would be the object of a donation. Both documents are especially interesting for including a reference to another settlement named Lizarrariela, in which Jews also lived. This place name has not been identified with any certainty. However, it could be a derivation of Lizarrara, to which a Romance diminutive suffix was added. This could indicate that it was "little Lizarrara," a neighborhood attached to the old royal

---

52   Martín Duque, "La fundación del primer burgo navarro: Estella," 765–67; Lacarra, *Colección diplomática de Irache*, doc. 58.
53   Archivo Histórico Nacional, CLERO-SECULAR_REGULAR, car. 701, no.21.
54   Martín Duque, *Documentación medieval de Leire*, doc. 113.
55   Mª Dolores Barrios Martínez, *Documentos de Montearagón: 1058–1205* (Huesca: Asociación de Amigos del Castillo de Montearagón, 2004), doc. 3.
56   Ibid., doc. 6.

villa. The fact that, already at the end of the eleventh century, there is a documented Jewish presence, necessarily reveals that it was a settlement of some importance or appeal for this community. It is surprising that a settlement of these characteristics would disappear in the documents without leaving any trace, so the toponymical similarity invites us to speculate that it would have been a foretaste of the future Estella. Lizarrariela, or at least the memory of its population and the rents derived therefrom, survived through the end of the eleventh century, but its identity would disappear as it was eclipsed and its population absorbed by Estella.

The chronicle of San Juan de la Peña (written in the fourteenth century) signaled that Estella was populated in the year 1090 and attributed Sancho Ramírez with the initiative.[57] In effect, that same year the king showed interest in creating a new settlement in the *villa* known as Lizarrara, diverting the Camino de Santiago so that it would go through the new town. The trigger would be a plan on the part of the monks of San Juan de la Peña to create a Frankish settlement in the limits of Zarapuz, a mere two and a half miles from Lizarrara. Faced with the danger that the two settlements could become rivals and, believing the square in Lizarrara to be better protected, Sancho Ramírez beat the monks to it. In order to avoid them talking ill of the king, he granted them a tenth of all the rents deriving from the new settlement, as well as the churches that would be constructed therein. This latter donation would be ratified by the bishop of Pamplona in 1092, with, once more, an explicit reference to the place name Lizarrara and omitting any allusion to Estella.[58]

Several elements in the document by Sancho Ramírez are surprising. On the one hand, he points out his intention to build a "*castrum et populationem de francos,*" when Lizarrara in reality had several centers[59] as well as a castle. Indeed, the existence of a castle and a *tenente* charged with its maintenance would have been a guarantee that, theoretically, made the siting of Lizarrara over that of Zarapuz

---

57 Lacarra and Martín Duque, *Fueros de Navarra*, 1.
58 Goñi Gaztambide, *Colección diplomática de la Catedral de Pamplona*, doc. 52.
59 At that moment Lizarrara and the burg, which would receive the name of Estella, already existed. It is possible that Lizarrariela disappeared in the moment that Estella was created.

preferable. On the other hand, there is always an allusion to the place name of Lizarrara, ignoring completely the already known Estella. One must bear in mind that, since 1084, the tenancy had changed its name to Estella, so that the use of Lizarrara can only be understood as an archaism or, if taken literally, as a project to encourage settlement on or next to the old *villa* of Lizarrara and not underneath the crag. Finally, the fact that he attempted to divert the Camino de Santiago is amazing given that there would be no single route or some fixed stages. The presence of the burg, documented since 1076, would be the first result of the spontaneous redirection of the route toward Lizarrara, whose previously mentioned characteristics would have attracted pilgrims. However, the intention to create a settlement on the part of the monks could have put this diversion at risk, so that royal intervention became necessary in order to secure the Lizarrara-Estella urban project. The main difference between what already existed and what Sancho Ramírez was proposing was the Frankish condition, in its ethnic but mostly legal sense. The settlement he proposed creating would be added to those that already existed,[60] but with legal characteristics that assured its superiority over any other settlement, securing the particularities that would make it preferable for pilgrims on the Camino de Santiago as regards provisions and services. The Frankish legal ratification would be the culmination of the urbanizing process of Estella.

Two events allow us to verify that, by the last decade of the eleventh century, Estella was a consolidated reality with its own identity. First, in 1090 itself, an inhabitant of Estella would promote the construction of some mills in Puente la Reina.[61] His name, Bernero de Estella,[62] confirms, on the one hand, the presence of settlers from the other side of the Pyrenees prior to the new population that Sancho Ramírez was attempting to introduce; and, on the other, the use of the place name with an anthroponymic function indicates that it was a sufficiently consolidated and recognizable reference in order to be used as a last name. Second, in 1094 a document originating

---

60   As in fact had occurred in Sangüesa, Estella, and Pamplona.
61   Lacarra, *Colección diplomática de Irache*, doc. 69.
62   Documented and studied in José María Lacarra, "Una aparición de ultratumba en Estella," *Príncipe de Viana* 15 (1944), 173–84.

in Leire[63] used the "*mensuram de Stella*" to measure wheat, a fact that lays bare the preeminence of Estella as a referential market for the whole kingdom.

Historians and philologists have addressed the etymological origin both of Lizarrara and of Estella for a long time.[64] José María Jimeno Jurío includes in his work on the toponymy of Estella the main arguments in this respect.[65] It appears that the most plausible hypothesis would be to derive Lizarrara from *lizar*, "ash tree" in Basque. It is not by chance that, in 1135, there is a documented reference to a grove of ash trees ("*fraxineta*") next to the church of San Nicolás in Estella.[66] The term was adapted in different ways[67] to Latin spellings when it was written down in the tenth and eleventh centuries. However, already in the twelfth and thirteenth centuries, when copied down in cartularies and registers, the place name Lizarrara was limited strictly to the region of Estella, so that some scribes, unaware of the place name, copied it with errors or assimilated it into other, more widespread names like Lizarraga.[68]

Through the eleventh century the affluence of non-Basque-speaking settlers would have favored a process of adapting the place name to Romance, expressed in two phenomena: first, in the addition of a diminutive suffix, which gave rise to Lizarrariela;[69] and second, the identification of the abbreviated variant Lizarra as a compound article plus the root *izarra* ("star" in Basque). Thus, Lizarra could be translated literally as La Estrella, "The Star." This term was still in use in the twelfth century, as demonstrated by mention of Pedro Tizón as *tenente* of "la Stela."[70] This interpretation could have been aided by the existence of several towns in Europe whose name

---

63 Martín Duque, *Documentación medieval de Leire*, doc. 142.
64 Already in the seventeenth century, the name of the town was linked to a maritime apparition. See Francisco de Eguía y Veaumont, *Historia de la ciudad de Estella y su merindad* (Estella, 1644).
65 Jimeno Jurío, "Estella/Lizarra. Toponimia," 135–37.
66 David Alegría Suescun, Guadalupe Lopetegui Semperene, and Aitor Pescador Medrano, *Archivo General de Navarra (1134–1194)* (San Sebastián: Eusko Ikaskuntza, 1997), doc. I.1.
67 Jimeno Jurío, "Estella/Lizarra. Toponimia," 134.
68 Martín Duque, *Documentación medieval de Leire*, docs. 106, 107, and 112.
69 Barrios Martínez, *Documentos de Monteragaón*, doc. 6.
70 Lema Pueyo, *Colección diplomática de Alfonso I de Aragón y Pamplona*, doc. 231.

was based on the idea of "star."[71] These are all characterized by the existence of a crossroads,[72] as in the case of Lizarrara. The fact that the town was situated along the route of the Camino de Santiago could, equally, have influenced the "star" idea. In 1644 Francisco de Eguía y Beumont narrated the legend of the shepherds of Abartzuza, who in 1985, guided by the stars, had found an image of the Virgin. The fact is that, very soon, the convergence of etymologies, interests, and legends would have favored the consolidation of the new place name to the detriment of the old one. In the twelfth century, the Council of Estella, proud of this identity, reflected a star on its coat-of-arms as an emblem of the town.[73]

We have seen how the presence of the name Estella can be documented since the 1070s.[74] Given that its first appearance was inscribed in a formal context, as part of an official position (that of "*merino in Stela*"), one would expect that its informal use would be already quite extensive by 1077. As a result, the exogenous settlers that fostered the "translation" of the place name would have arrived well before this date. This would confirm the firm nature of their settlement when it received the denomination of burg in 1076.[75] Nevertheless, the definitive consolidation of the place name to the detriment of Lizarrara seems to have been the consequence of a personal decision by Lope Arnaldo. This individual was the *merino* of Jimeno Garcés and, on the death of the latter in 1084,[76] he replaced him as *tenente*. However, the succession brought with it a name change: from that moment on, the seat of the tenancy would

---

71   The place name is associated with a crossroads and the denomination is especially prevalent in France (with towns by the name of L'Étoile in the communes of Jura, Somme, Hautes-Alpes, and Drône), but also in Portugal (Estrela, in the Alentejo region) and Italy (Stella, in the province of Savona). See Ernest Nègre, *Toponymie générale de la France*, vol. 1 (Geneva: Librairie Droz, 1990), 1450.
72   Ciérbide, "En torno a las denominaciones de la ciudad de Estella," 57.
73   Faustino Menéndez Pidal de Navascués, Mikel Ramos Aguirre, and Esperanza Ochoa de Olza, *Sellos medievales de Navarra: estudio y corpus descriptive* (Pamplona: Gobierno de Navarra, 1995), 823–24. Such iconography is also found in the convent of Santo Domingo in the town. See Clara Fernández-Lareda, ed., *El arte gótico en Navarra* (Pamplona: Gobierno de Navarra, 2015), 98–102. On the municipal organization of Estella at this time, see María Raquel García Arancón, "Una posible reforma de las magistraturas de Estella -Navarra- en el siglo XIII," *Vasconia: Cuadernos de historia-geografía* 36 (2009), 37–44.
74   Archivo Histórico Nacional CLERO-SECULAR_REGULAR, car.701, no. 21.
75   Lacarra, *Colección diplomática de Irache*, doc. 58.
76   Martín Duque, *Documentación medieval de Leire*, docs. 112 and 113.

be Estella. We cannot know what led Lope Arnaldo to make that decision, although some data could help to shed some light on the question. On the one hand, the fact that as the *merino* he was using the new place name could indicate that there was a special link between his position and the *villa*. In the twelfth century, *merinos* were the administrators of royal property in certain territories and towns, either directly under royal authority or under that of a seigneur.[77] This could have been the case of Lope Arnaldo, who was assigned to manage royal holdings in the recently founded burg. It is even possible that, by way of contrast to the *senior*, the *merino* would have resided in the burg itself. Already by the twelfth century, the *merinos* of Estella not only resided in the burg, but were of Frankish origin.[78] It is significant that Lope Arnaldo continued to carry out these functions in the new settlement between 1084 and 1093 as a *"dominator Stella."*[79] On the other hand, it is possible that Lope Arnaldo was of Frankish origin himself and, as such, identified more with the new settlers and the name they used than with that of the older inhabitants. Although his name, Lope, had a long tradition in the medieval onomastics of Pamplona,[80] the patronym Arnaldo was completely foreign. Indeed, we cannot document this denominator with a certain frequency until the beginning of the twelfth century, precisely among the Franks of Estella.[81]

Following the foral concessions, there was a legal separation of the urban centers that had been previously united under the tutelage of *tenentes*, and, consequently, a disassociation of the name. The old population, made up mostly of autochthonous, peasant, and lower class people, would maintain the name of Lizarrara and use it as a toponymical last name quite often until the thirteenth century. The burg and the successive neighborhoods that emerged therein were classified under the place name Estella, which the castle would also end up adopting. Between the twelfth and thirteenth centuries both centers were once again integrated within the Council of Estella.

---

77 Lema Pueyo, Lema Pueyo, *Instituciones políticas del reinado de Alfonso I*, 176–78.
78 Lacarra, *Colección diplomática de Irache*, doc. 219.
79 Ibid., doc. 70.
80 See García de Cortázar, "Antroponimia en Navarra y Rioja en los siglos X a XII."
81 Ciérbide, "Onomástica personal de los francos de Estella," 210–14.

The place name Lizarrara, now abbreviated to Lizarra, was still associated with its church of San Pedro, in part with the function of differentiating it from the homonym of the Rúa.

Throughout these centuries the category of these settlements varied. The *castrum* of Lizarra and Estella was a valid reference point both in the ninth and in the twelfth centuries. Still at the beginning of the thirteenth century, when the Occitan-language poet Guilhem de Tudela, author of the *Canción de Cruzada Albigense*, enumerated the dominions of King Sancho VII, he pointed out Pamplona, Tudela, and the castle of Estella.[82]

In 1076 there was a reference to a burg that we associate with Estella,[83] a title that would survive in local toponymy in order to denominate some of the neighborhoods that emerged in the twelfth century. Already in the 1090s both Lizarra and Estella received the denomination of *villa*.[84] On occasion, in 1121, Estella was termed a "*civitate*" under the dominion of Pedro Tizón.[85] This category was incorrect, since the *villa* did not receive the privilege of the "city" title until 1483.[86] However, it emphasized the urban development that had already taken place by that time, which would help it as a counterpoint to the *villa* of Lizarra.

Finally, with the restoration of the Pamplona monarchy under García Ramírez,[87] Estella recovered its preeminent role as a *villa* over which the monarch exercised his authority. The clauses of that rule thus included, alongside Pamplona and Tudela, recognizing its demographic potential as well as its economic and political value in the kingdom. This custom would be maintained until the extension of the title to that of king of Navarre with Sancho VI.

---

82   Guillaume de Tudela, *La chanson de la croisade Albigeoise: texte original*, intro. Michel Zink (Paris: Librairie Générale Française, 1989), strophe 9.

83   Lacarra, *Colección diplomática de Irache*, doc. 58.

84   Lacarra and Martín Duque, *Fueros de Navarra*, 1; Barrios Martínez, *Documentos de Monteragaón*, doc. 6.

85   Antonio Ubieto Arteta, *Cartulario de San Millán de la Cogolla (759–1076)* (Valencia: Anubar, 1976), doc. 302.

86   Ángel J. Martín Duque, "El fenómeno urbano medieval en Navarra," *Príncipe de Viana* 227 (2002), 738.

87   Goñi Gaztambide, *Colección diplomática de la Catedral de Pamplona*, doc. 200.

Conclusion

From the first documented information, Lizarrara appears as a castle of some importance in the organization and defense of the kingdom. The political and territorial fluctuations that shook the Pamplona monarchy in the tenth and eleventh centuries would have meant this its function gradually changed until, finally, it became an especially important tenancy on account of its location within the western dominions of the kingdom. At the end of the eleventh century there is documented evidence of the presence of new settlements associated traditionally with the Camino de Santiago and founded on the foral initiative of certain monarchs.

One cannot rule out, however, the likelihood that the town, bridge (as a meeting point of routes), and castle-tenancy trinomial could have favored the arrival of new settlers attracted by the commercial possibilities there. This initial influx of immigrants would have taken shape in the emergence of a suburb, Lizarrariela, in which there was also a small Jewish community. Possibly, during the era of Sancho IV and under the government of Jimeno Garcés, seeing the success and possibilities of the place, a new settlement with a more defined urban organization and less spontaneous than that of Lizarrariela was promoted. The burg, located under the castle, would have benefited from some privilege of which we have no record, but that would have served to divert Frankish and Jewish immigrants toward the site and attract, likewise, the major monasteries in the kingdom (Irache and San Juan de la Peña). This burg, which differed from the old Lizarrara in both urban and legal ways, would receive a new name, different but derived from the former one, and shortly thereafter would be granted a Frankish legal status that would replace the already existing one and that would position it as one of the most important urban *villas* in the kingdom.

Through the twelfth and thirteenth centuries, successive privileges, urban expansions, and annexations of other settlements (including Lizarra) would end up transforming Estella into one of the major *villas* in the kingdom, preceded in privilege only by Pamplona as the capital and episcopal seat.

BIBLIOGRAPHY

Alegría Suescun, David, Guadalupe Lopetegui Semperene, and Aitor Pescador Medrano. *Archivo General de Navarra (1134–1194)*. San Sebastián: Eusko Ikaskuntza, 1997.

Barrero García, Ana María. "La difusión del Fuero de Jaca en el Camino de Santiago." In *El Fuero de Jaca. Estudios*. Zaragoza: El Justicia de Aragón, 2004.

Barrios Martínez, Mª Dolores. *Documentos de Monteragaón: 1058–1205*. Huesca: Asociación de Amigos del Castillo de Montearagón, 2004.

Cañada Juste, Alberto. "Honores y tenencias en la monarquía pamplonesa del siglo X. Precedentes de una institución." *Príncipe de Viana*, Annex 2 (1986): 67–73.

Cantera Montenegro, Margarita. *Colección documental de Santa María la Real de Nájera. Tomo I (siglos X–XIV)*. San Sebastián: Eusko Ikaskuntza, 1991.

Ciérbide, Ricardo. "En torno a las denominaciones de la ciudad de Estella." *Fontes linguae vasconum: Studia et documenta* 51 (1988): 53–58.

———. "La lengua de los francos de Estella." *Sancho el Sabio: Revista de cultura e investigación vasca* 3 (1993): 115–48.

———. "Onomástica personal de los francos de Estella (1090–1222)." In *Actas de las III Jornadas de Onomástica Estella*. Bilbao: Euskaltzaindia, 2008.

Eguía y Veaumont, Francisco de. *Historia de la ciudad de Estella y su merindad*. Estella, 1644.

Estévez Sola, Juan Antonio. *Crónica Najerense*. Madrid: Akal, 2003.

Fernández-Lareda, Clara, ed. *El arte gótico en Navarra*. Pamplona: Gobierno de Navarra, 2015.

Floristán Samanes, Alfredo. "De Lizarra a Estella una reflexión geográfica." *Príncipe de Viana* 190 (1990): 307–16.

García Arancón, María Raquel. "Una posible reforma de las magistraturas de Estella -Navarra- en el siglo XIII." *Vasconia: Cuadernos de historia-geografía* 36 (2009): 37–44.

García de Cortázar, José Ángel. "Antroponimia en Navarra y Rioja en los siglos X a XII." In *Estudios de Historia Medieval de La Rioja.* Logroño: Universidad de La Rioja, 2009.

Gil Fernández, Juan, ed., José L. Moralejo, trans., and Juan I. Ruiz de la Peña, study. *Crónicas Asturianas.* Oviedo: Universidad de Oviedo, 1985.

Goñi Gaztambide, José. *Historia eclesiástica de Estella.* 2 volumes. Pamplona: Gobierno de Navarra, 1990–1994.

―――. *Colección diplomática de la Catedral de Pamplona.* Pamplona: Gobierno de Navarra, 1997.

González Ollé, Fernando. "Etimología del topónimo Estella." *Príncipe de Viana* 190 (1990): 329–44.

Ilundain Chamarro, Javier. *Los buenos hombres de Olite (siglos XII–XIV). Sociedad, poder y élites urbanas.* Pamplona: Gobierno de Navarra, 2017.

Jimeno Aranguren, Roldán. *Terras a suis reperitur semper esse poessessas: la Iglesia en Tierra Estella en la Edad Media.* Pamplona: Lamiñarra, 2007.

Jimeno Jurío, José María. "Estella/Lizarra. Toponimia." *Fontes Linguae Vasconum: Studia et documenta* 77 (1998): 133–64.

―――. "Toponimia rural y urbana de Estella." In *Actas de las III Jornadas de Onomástica Estella.* Bilbao: Euskaltzaindia, 2008.

Lacarra, José María. "Una aparición de ultratumba en Estella." *Príncipe de Viana* 15 (1944): 173–84.

―――. *Colección diplomática de Irache.* Zaragoza: Instituto de Estudios Pirenáicos, 1965.

―――. *Historia del Reino de Navarra en la Edad Media.* Pamplona: Caja de Ahorros de Navarra, 1975.

Lacarra, José María, and Ángel J. Martín Duque. *Fueros de Navarra. I.1. Fueros derivados de Jaca. Estella-San Sebastián.* Pamplona: Institución Príncipe de Viana, 1969.

Legarda Sembroiz, José Miguel. "Estructuras defensivas en la ciudad de Estella. Resultados arqueológicos." *Trabajos de arqueología Navarra* 22 (2010): 163–93.

Lema Pueyo, José Ángel. "Las tenencias navarras de Alfonso I 'el Batallador'." *Príncipe de Viana*, Annex 8 (1988): 61–70.

———. *Colección diplomática de Alfonso I de Aragón y Pamplona (1104–1134).* San Sebastián: Eusko Ikaskuntza, 1990.

———. *Instituciones políticas del reinado de Alfonso I el Batallador, rey de Aragón y Pamplona.1104–1134.* Bilbao: Universidad del País Vasco, 1997.

Martín Duque, Ángel J. *Documentación medieval de Leire (siglos IX a XII).* Pamplona: Institución Príncipe de Viana, 1983.

———. "La fundación del primer burgo navarro: Estella." *Príncipe de Viana* 190 (1990): 317–28.

———. "El fenómeno urbano medieval en Navarra." *Príncipe de Viana* 227 (2002): 727–60.

———. "Navarra en la Alta Edad Media (711–1234)." In *Nueva Historia de Navarra*, edited by Francisco Javier Navarro. Barañain: EUNSA, 2010.

Menéndez Pidal de Navascués, Faustino, Mikel Ramos Aguirre, and Esperanza Ochoa de Olza. *Sellos medievales de Navarra: estudio y corpus descriptive.* Pamplona: Gobierno de Navarra, 1995.

Moret, José de. *Anales del Reino de Navarras.* Volume 1. Tolosa: Casa editorial de Eusebio López, 1890.

Nègre, Ernest. *Toponymie générale de la France.* Volume 1. Geneva: Librairie Droz, 1990.

Pavón Benito, Julia. "Fuero de Jaca y Fuero de Estella. Observaciones críticas." In *XV Congreso de Historia de la*

Corona de Aragón. Tomo III. Jaca en la Corona de Aragón (siglos XII–XVIII). Zaragoza: Gobierno de Aragón, 1993.

Ramos Aguirre, Mikel. "Intervenciones arqueológicas en el castillo de Estella (2001–2010)." *Trabajos de arqueología Navarra* 27 (2015): 185–218.

Rodríguez de Lama, Ildefonso. *Colección diplomática medieval de la Rioja (923–1225)*. Logroño: Instituto de Estudios Riojanos, 1976–1979.

Santamaría, Ricardo. "La muerte de un rey. Repercusiones territoriales del asesinato de Sancho IV Garcés (1076) en el área navarro-riojana." *Príncipe de Viana* 253 (2011): 249–62.

Tudela, Guillaume de. *La chanson de la croisade Albigeoise: texte original*. Introduced by Michel Zink. Paris: Librairie Générale Française, 1989.

Ubieto Arteta, Antonio. *Cartulario de Albelda*. Valencia: Anubar, 1960.

———. *Cartulario de San Juan de la Peña*. Valencia: Anubar, 1962.

———. *Cartulario de San Millán de la Cogolla (759–1076)*. Valencia: Anubar, 1976.

Vázquez de Parga, Luis, José María Lacarra, and Juan Uría Ríu. *Las peregrinaciones a Santiago de Compostela*. Pamplona: Gobierno de Navarra, 1998.

Chapter 3

The Organization of the Territory of San Sebastian and its Surroundings during the Early Middle Ages: A Panoramic View of its Evolution

Iosu Etxezarraga Ortuondo

For decades, scholarly research on the beginning of the Early Middle Ages in Gipuzkoa has been hampered by a lack of sufficiently rich abundant documented sources that might allow different interpretations in order to encourage progress through historiographical debate. Efforts carried out in the 1980s to construct a story that may explain the evolution of the territory between Antiquity—a historical stage that we are beginning to understand better[1]—and the Late Middle Ages materialized in the historiographical context of post-Francoist historiographical renovation on the part of José Ángel García de Cortázar and the theory of the social organization of space. The main exponent of this trend in the context of Gipuzkoa is Elena Barrena Osoro, who managed to piece together the meager information at her disposal within Cortázar's

---

1   The principal historiographical landmark that marked an advance in research on the ancient era in the Basque Country was Milagros Esteban Delgado's doctoral dissertation, later published as *El País Vasco Atlántico en época romana* (San Sebastián: Universidad de Deusto, 1990)

scheme on the origin of feudal society in the north of the Iberian Peninsula.[2] For nearly two decades this discourse would remain the only interpretative framework, with no debate on the part of either the academy or professionals in the discipline of history.

The development of medieval archaeology from the late 1990s on began to contribute new data with which to construct an alternative discourse,[3] evincing the discrepancies between the current historiographical discourse and material culture. Moreover, other studies carried out through later documentation have led us to discover that the description of the economic foundations of early medieval Gipuzkoan society as described in Barrena Osoro's work had no place in its later development.[4] I am referring in particular to the livestock management system, theoretically the main productive activity in early medieval society, which even came to determine human settlement patterns: the first would have been transhumant and the second itinerant. The increasingly abundant information provided by archaeological research has finally helped us to begin to add to the meager list of documented sources, reflecting an extremely different panorama to that suggested by the previous historiography.

The present chapter seeks to present a new interpretative argument based on the available data in the current state of research. It focuses especially on the population network and on the organization of the territory, given that geopolitical questions and social and power relations will be analyzed elsewhere in the work. Finally, there will be an analysis of other factors of economic change that could have been influential in the transformation of the political and legal structuring of the territory. In general terms, the aim is to outline questions that would merit monographic studies, a task that is still

---

2   Elena Barrena Osoro, *La formación histórica de Gipuzkoa* (San Sebastián: Universidad de Deusto, 1989).
3   There is a synthesis of the main discoveries that archaeology has contributed in Gipuzkoa in Alfredo Moraza and Nerea Sarasola, *Arkeologia 0.5. Arqueología medieval en Gipuzkoa* (San Sebastián: Diputación Foral de Gipuzkoa, 2011). For a more interpretative reading of these remains, focused on the early Middle Ages, see Nerea Sarasola Etxegoien, "El poblamiento medieval de Gipuzkoa. Revisión crítica del registro arqueológico," *Munibe Antopologia-Arkeologia* 61 (2010), 339–93.
4   Álvaro Aragón Ruano, *La ganadería guipuzcoana en el Antiguo Régimen* (Bilbao: Universidad el País Vasco, 2009).

to be done. This contribution may serve to suggest some main areas of inquiry from which to address future research.

Settlement on the Gipuzkoan Coast between the Roma Era and the Middle Ages

One of the areas in which archaeology has been most fruitful and made a major contribution to reconstructing the history of Gipuzkoa is precisely that concerning Antiquity. Thirty years of research has bequeathed quite a rich map of sites that mark out the eastern end of the Cantabrian coast. And these vestiges allow us to begin to reconstruct the evolution of human settlement in Gipuzkoa with the change of eras.

While some of the settlements documented at the beginning of the first millennium are located on sites of previous human occupation, as in the case of Getaria and Zarautz,[5] in other cases it seems that settlement took place in previously uninhabited areas. This seems to have been the case of San Sebastian and the Roman city of Irun-Oiasso. This argument is based on the absence of evidence associated with the Iron Age in these places, although we cannot rule out the possibility that such proof may be found in the future. In this sense, the location of human settlement during the Roman era in San Sebastian is very interesting, given that it took place at the foot of Mount Urgull, a promontory that could have been an ideal position for a coastal fort.

Whatever the case, in the current state of research, the hypotheses put forward tend to toward a change in settlement patterns in the area of San Sebastian with its integration into the heart of the empire. The recent discovery, within the last decade, of late-Iron Age remains in what appears to be a small fortified village on Mount Jaizkibel—Mukitar, in what is today Lezo—that

---

5   Xabier Alberdi Lonbide, Álvaro Aragón Ruano, and Jesús Manuel Pérez Centeno, "Quince años de investigaciones histórico-arqueológicas en torno a Getaria," *Munibe* 57, no. 2 (2005–2006), 435–51; Alex Ibáñez Etxeberria, ed., *Santa María la Real de Zarautz (País Vasco). Continuidad y discontinuidad en la ocupación de la costa vasca entre los siglos V a.C. y XIV d.C*, Suplemento Munibe 27 (San Sebastián: Sociedad de Ciencias Aranzadi, 2009).

was later abandoned, as well as in the settlement of Santiagomendi in Astigarraga[6] that was also abandoned around the beginning of the Common Era, would be indicative of a process of changing settlement patterns in the area close to or surrounding the Concha Bay. In this case, the absence of Iron Age vestiges in the tombolo suggests that this settlement could have come from peripheral locations. In sum, the enclave of San Sebastian could have emerged with the aim of reinforcing coastal trade routes and as a means of making the most of new economic dynamics within the context of this coastal trade. The importance of this corner of the Cantabrian coast for Roman commercial routes is attested to, moreover, by noteworthy discoveries within the context of the Roman city of Oiasso, in the present-day towns of Hondarribia and, especially, Irun.[7]

Thereafter, now in the Late Roman Imperial era, new settlements were developed that were linked to agricultural and artisanal production based around the main towns that had emerged just prior to that time.[8] In the case of San Sebastian, we still do not know of any settlement of this type, while they have been recognized in an around the population centers that had existed since 1 A.D. in the present-day towns of Getaria and Zarautz. Sites such as Urteaga Zahar in Zumaia (which was occupied in proto-historical but late imperial times) and Urezberoetako Kanposantu Zaharra in Aia are examples of how these new spaces and resources were exploited at this time.[9] The site of Irigain is located near San Sebastian, at a prominent point in a meadow by the River Orio, in what is today Usurbil.[10] Although as of yet we do not know the full nature of the

---

6 María Teresa Izquierdo Marculeta, "El poblamiento de la Edad del Hierro en el entorno de Santiagomendi (Astigarraga, Gipuzkoa)," *Kobie, Serie Anejos* 6, vol. 1 (2004), 297–304.

7 There is an extensive description of these discoveries in Mertxe Urteaga and Javier Arce, *Arkeologia 0.4, Arqueología romana en Gipuzkoa* (San Sebastián: Diputación Foral de Gipuzkoa, 2011).

8 For the moment, as regards Gipuzkoa, these changes only affected the Urola Kosta district, but they were framed within the general dynamics of Rome's Atlantic territory. See Milagros Esteban Delgado, "Arbiun. Taller metalúrgico en el enclave romano de la gran bahía de Getaria," *Kobie, Serie Anejos* 13 (2014), 93–110.

9 Ibid., 104–6.

10 Manu Ceberio Rodríguez, "Primeros testimonios de época antigua en el tramo final del valle del Oria: el yacimiento de Irigain (Usurbil, Gipuzkoa)," *Munibe (Antropologia-Arkeologia)* 61 (2010), 243–59.

site, one can speculate that it was used for agriculture and livestock purposes, like the aforementioned sites. Meanwhile, the remains of a metallurgical workshop, in which iron was worked in a preindustrial way, have been unearthed in the excavation of the site at Arbiun, located in Zarautz. We also find evidence of this chronology, although in a state that does not allow us to recreate the history of the plot, in an area close to the parish of San Juan de Lezo, among the remains of what was the ancestral home of Lezo Haundia.[11]

From the fourth century on, some of these enclaves, like Urteaga Zahar, Ureberoetako Kanposantu Zaharra, Iria, and Arbiun, were abandoned. In contrast, the settlements that put down roots at the beginning of the Common Era or earlier, like Getaria and Zarautz, remained and survive to this day.[12] This continuity, although situated within a context of change, would not be an exception with regard to the territories that made up the Roman Empire and that were beginning to be organized into new political entities that succeeded the previous large structure.[13] Thus, not just the continued human presence in these places but also evidence of material culture would suggest the endurance of at least a century or a century and a half of trade routes and commercial relations in the Bay of Biscay; from the coastal area to the Ebro Valley;[14] and even between the Atlantic and the eastern Mediterranean.[15]

---

11   Javier Buces Cabello, "Plaza Lezoaundi," *Arkeoikuska* 10 (2011), 375–76.
12   For the case of Zarautz, see Ibáñez Etxeberria, ed., *Santa María la Real de Zarautz*.
13   For the European context in Late Antiquity, see Chris Wickham, *Framing the Early Middle Ages: Europe and the Mediterranean 400–800* (New York: Oxford University Press, 2006).
14   Milagros Esteban Delgado, "La vía marítima en época antigua, agente de transformación en las tierras costeras entre Oiasso y el Divae," *Itsas Memoria* 4 (2003), 35, 38; Milagros Esteban Delgado, María Teresa Izquierdo Marculeta, Ana Martínez Salcedo, and Jesús Manuel Pérez Centeno, "La difusión de la terra sigillata hispánica tardía (TSHT) y otras cerámicas finas en el Cantábrico oriental," *Ex Officina Hispana* 1 (2012), 139–60; Milagros Esteban Delgado, María Teresa Izquierdo Marculeta, and Ana Martínez Salcedo, "La cerámica de época romana en el País Vasco atlántico: Redes comerciales y consume," *Ex Officina Hispana* 2, vol. 1 (2014), 193–210; Agustín Azkarate Garái-Olaun and José Luis Solaun Bustinza, "La cerámica altomedieval en el País Vasco (siglos V–X d.C.): producciones, modelos productivos y patrones de consume," in *La cerámica de la Alta Edad Media en el cuadrante noroeste de la Península Ibérica (siglos V–X). Sistemas de producción, mecanismos de distribución y patrones de consumo,* ed. Alfonso Vigil-Escalera Guirado and Juan Antonio Quiróa Castillo (Leioa: Universidad del País Vasco, 2016), 193–228.
15   Ana M. Benito, "Cerámicas del yacimiento submarino del Cabo de Higuer (Hondarribia)," *Munibe* 40 (1988), 123–63.

Therefore, while the discourse based on documented references—or, more accurately, lack thereof—points to a clear break between Antiquity and the Middle Ages, archaeology suggests mitigating this hiatus and beginning to ponder the continuities and discontinuities during the era known as Late Antiquity.

Unfortunately, the few archeological interventions carried out in the area in which the oldest remains in the tombolo of San Sebastian were found have not led to any insight into the intermediate era between Antiquity and the Early Middle Ages. The earliest medieval evidence from what would later be the *villa* of San Sebastian dates from no earlier than the tenth century.[16] However, as noted, this is likely the result of the kind of interventions carried out and it is more than probable that future research will strive for datable contexts between the abandonment of the site located around the convent of Santa Teresa and the tombs identified as belonging to the early medieval peripheral necropolis in the church of Santa María del Coro.

There is, though, irrefutable evidence that settlements on the Gipuzkoan coast that had already been consolidated by the late imperial era were, later, the first to receive a fuero.[17] This could be interpreted as a symptom of their endurance through time and deep rooted social and political organization. Possibly, their success was due to their location on coastal trade routes and as logistics hubs at which maritime and inland routes met. Put another way, we could speculate that their endurance through time was down to the economic possibilities that each of these sites offered, which allowed for their survival in more adverse times as well as prosperity as a result of the revitalization of international commercial dynamics.

Whatever the case, of interest here is any evidence that may indicate the endurance of a settlement in San Sebastian as well. Currently, we cannot be sure, but as noted, the reality discovered in

---

16 Marian Gereñu Urzelai, "Las excavaciones arqueológicas de Santa Teresa y La Brecha," in *San Sebastián, ciudad Marítima,* ed. José María Unsain Azpiroz (San Sebastián: Museo Naval, 2008), 163–73.

17 With the exception of Mutriku, which was granted a fuero prior to 1208, although there is some concurrence in the cases of San Sebastián (c.1180), Getaria (before 1200), Hondarribia (1203), and Zarautz (1237).

the case of the Urola Kosta district may not be too different from that of the *villa* of San Sebastian. It should be pointed out that the tombs found in the vicinity of the church of Santa María in the town were located in an area at some distance from the plot of the old church, which would have occupied a smaller space than it does currently. Therefore, possibly, these human remains were part of an area of the necropolis that was occupied later.

In any event, one should remember that the name of the towns employed here evoke current realities, which differ greatly from their older counterparts as regards political and territorial organization, and which are the products of a long-term historical evolution. In this sense, the configuration of enclaves of economic activity around the more thriving settlements during the Late Roman Empire, which began to be known for the jurisdictions of Getaria, Zarautz, and Zumaia, was still incomprehensible for San Sebastian. The only representative remains of the Roman era were found at the foot of Mount Urgull, that is, in the same place as the medieval *villa*, while there have been no discoveries, for the time being, in the remaining part of the jurisdiction of San Sebastian. This is a significant issue when it comes to reconstructing the rural part of the town in the centuries before it was constituted as a *villa*. One must bear in mind that this ample terrain occupied by the municipality of San Sebastian today has been affected and altered in a major way by the growth of the city and urbanization of its ground.

There is a paradigmatic example in the very bay of San Sebastian, namely the small peninsula and promontory Pico del Loro that separates the Ondarreta and Concha beaches. In this geographically prominent area there was an early medieval church that, already by the thirteenth century, was known as "*monasterium Sancti Sebastiani ueteris.*"[18] Two pieces of fundamental data reveal its antiquity: namely, the very inclusion of the word "old" in its name and the fact that the name the settlement on the tombolo took was dedicated to this church, San Sebastian. Unfortunately, archeological

---

18   Gonzalo Martínez Díez, Emiliano González Díez, and Félix Javier Martínez Llorente, *Colección de documentos medievales de las villas guipuzcoanas (1200–1369)* (San Sebastián: Diputación Foral de Gipuzkoa, 1991), 47.

investigation of the plot is extremely difficult owing to the changes caused by a concatenation of constructions in this spot. Very generally, we could list these constructions in the following manner: first, the mid-sixteenth-century construction of the convent of the Dominican Sisters of San Sebastian as an annex to the original church and its razing to the ground in 1836 during the siege of the city by Carlist troops in the First Carlist War;[19] second, the construction of a military turret that occupied the plot in the second half of the nineteenth century,[20] and which was later demolished; third, the rebuilding of the parish church of the Antiguo neighborhood following the last Carlist War;[21] fourth, the construction of a underpass connecting both sides of the peninsula;[22] and finally, the construction of the Miramar Palace in 1893. Although we cannot completely rule out the possibility that there may still some significant remains there, however moved around, it has been impossible to investigate archeologically one of the most important enclaves in San Sebastian and, as such, we cannot resolve the uncertainties that surround the origins of this settlement.

The most widespread version of this history is that the church could have been a primitive rural church that, during an initial moment[23] that we cannot date precisely but prior to the eleventh century, may have been the only one of its kind in the bay. The absence of data prevents us from affirming that such origins would have come toward the end of the Roman era or Late Antiquity, although it is an option to keep in mind. A similar situation has been attested to in the case of the church of San Martín de Askizu, in Getaria. In archeological digs carried out around the altar and the outer part of the apse of the building, a necropolis was discovered whose earliest tombs could be dated to the sixth century.[24] Although the dig did

---

19 For a complete history of the convent, see José Barrado Barquilla, *Las dominicas de San Sebastián el Antiguo. Cuatrocientos cincuenta años de historia en Donostia (siglos XVI–XX)* (Salamanca: San Esteban editorial, 2001).

20 Juan Antonio Sáez García, *Viejas Piedras. Fortificaciones guipuzcoanas* (San Sebastián: Michelena artes gráficas, 2000), 186–89.

21 Txillardegi, *Antigua 1900* (San Sebastián: Instituto Dr. Camino, 1993), 50–51.

22 In reality, this consisted of a ditch resurfaced with soil above a cavity and not a tunnel properly speaking. Ibid., 54–55.

23 José Ángel García de Cortázar, "Una villa mercantil: 1180–1516," in *Historia de Donostia-San Sebastián*, ed. Miguel Artola (Hondarribia: Ed. Nerea, 2001), 20–21.

24 Jesús Manuel Pérez Centeno, Milagros Esteban Delgado, and Xabier Alberdi Lonbide,

not encompass the whole plot of the church and we know hardly anything about the context in which these burials took place, it is undeniable that such findings possess an enormous transcendence insofar as understanding such unknown issues as the process of Christianization in Gipuzkoa and the form in which it was organized at such an early time. The most noteworthy fact, in this case, is that the settlement was located more than a mile, in a straight line, from the enclave inhabited in Roman times on the Getaria peninsula. The parallels with the case of San Sebastian are quite striking. Although it is, for now, an exceptional site, it is possible that the description of "ancient" given to the rural church of San Sebastian could be significant. Whatever the case, for the moment it is more prudent to limit its historical origins to the early medieval period.

The transition from Late Antiquity to the Early Middle Ages in San Sebastian is no less obscure. For that reason, although we lack specific data for the centuries immediately following the Roman period and most of the Early Middle ages, not just for San Sebastian but for Gipuzkoa in general, as a working hypothesis we can extrapolate what we know about the Uribe Kosta district (basically the municipalities of Getaria and Zarautz) in order to apply it to the context of San Sebastian. Thus, we could speculate that the enclave occupied in Roman times sheltered by Mount Urgull persisted in one form or another until early medieval times, a moment in which, most likely, it was transformed into a village.

The Organization of the Terrain of San Sebastian on the Eve of Being Granted the Fuero

From 700 on, approximately, a change took place regarding the circumstances of rural and peasant settlements in the Western Christian world.[25] The settlements that put down roots at an earlier time, as well as those being created during this period, began to

"San Martín de Tours (Askizu)," *Arkeoikuska* 07 (2008), 352–53.

25 Iñaki García Camino, *Arqueología y poblamiento en Bizkaia (siglos VI–XIII). La configuración de la sociedad feudal* (Bilbao: Diputación Foral de Bizkaia, 2002), 185; Juan Antonio Quirós Castillo, "Las iglesias altomedievales en el País Vasco. Del monumento al paisaje," *Studia Historica, Historia Medieval* 29 (2011).

be organized around rural churches,[26] as an antecedent of what, from the Late Middle Ages, we term parishes. Village communities began to have a building that, from that moment on, was extremely important in their religious, political, and social organization. These churches did not just carry out devotional duties but also played an essential political role in local organization during the medieval era.[27]

In the context of the Basque Country, there have been excellent studies of this phenomenon especially in regard to Araba and certain settlements in Bizkaia.[28] Archaeology is also obtaining new discoveries in Gipuzkoa. Vestiges of early medieval occupation in the territory are demonstrating that the guidelines of this development did not differ from the surrounding territories.[29] Unfortunately, in the case of San Sebastian, no excavations aimed at studying ecclesiastical facilities in the ancient town have been carried out, while the discoveries that have been made, as noted, came from the edges of the premises belonging to the church of Santa María. For the moment, then, the oldest remains linked to an early medieval rural church do not predate the year 1000. Yet I believe that this time constraint is the result of the research circumstances; not because San Sebastian constitutes a late example in the process of creating villages and rural churches. As has been mentioned, there are indications to suggest that the Roman population was not completely interrupted from the fifth century on and until the tenth century. Therefore, it is possible that the San Sebastian ecclesiastical network could have become more complex at some point from the eighth century on. In this sense, if we accept that the "Antiguo" time of San Sebastian was the earliest

---

26 This concept is treated widely in the historiography. See for example Francisco Javier Fernández Conde, *La religiosidad medieval en España. Alta Edad Media (siglos VII–X)*, 2nd ed. (Gijón: Ediciones Trea, 2008), 257–58.

27 Iosu Etxezarraga Ortuondo, "Parroquia, hábitat y comunidad en Guipúzcoa. Una propuesta para el estudio de sus relaciones entre los siglos XIII y XV," *Domitia* 12 (2011), 89–112; Iosu Etxezarraga Ortuondo, "El laicado y sus instituciones en la configuración religiosa de Gipuzkoa en la Edad Media," PhD diss., University of the Basque Country, 2017, chap. 1.

28 For a recent synthesis of all these transformations in the northwest quadrant of the Iberian Peninsula, see Alfonso Vigil-Escalera Guirado and Juan Antonio Quirós Castillo, "Arqueología de los paisajes rurales altomedievales en noroeste peninsular," in *Visigodos y omeyas: el territorio*, ed. Luis Caballero Zoreda, Pedro Mateos Cruz, and Tomás Cordero Ruiz (Mérida: Instituto de Arqueología de Mérida, 2012), 79–95.

29 Except, perhaps, in that the development of village networks started later than in the interior. See Ibid., 86–87.

with which to date churches, we could speculate that the Santa María era may also have had an older past, prior to its first documented mention or the earliest remains found to date.

On the contrary, the initial development of the church of San Vicente is more obscure. Archaeological tracking carried out within the context of re-urbanizing work on the streets surrounding it, such as that which shares its name, identified a possible sandstone tomb, among other possibly late medieval archeological remains.[30] No specific dating was carried out on the human remains that may have been in this tomb, although, hypothetically speaking, its typology reminds us of sometime between the ninth and twelfth centuries.[31] What we do know is that, at the end of the twelfth century, this church was mentioned for the first time and this dating matches the stylistic dating of the aforementioned tomb. In any event, we are still unable to propose a construction date for the first church of San Vicente.

In order to try and figure out the origins and role of the future parish of San Vicente in the territorial and social organization of San Sebastian we must focus on other indicators. What was anomalous with regard to other *villas* in Gipuzkoa was the existence of two churches of the same ecclesiastical status or category within the walled enclosure. The location of a church dedicated to the Virgin Mary in a surroundings close to Roman remains, that is, the oldest settlement located in the tombolo of Urgull, which is currently being researched, indicates that it is older than San Vicente. From a topographical perspective, the appearance of a church in an opposing

---

30   Miren Ayerbe and César Fernández, *Memoria de control arqueológico de las obras de rehabilitación de la Parte Vieja de Donostia-San Sebastián (Gipuzkoa). Capítulo 2, Calles Narrica, San Vicente y San Juan*, 1992. Unpublished report in the Archivo de Arqueología del Departamento de Cultura de la Diputación Foral de Gipuzkoa.

31   In the case of the burials found in Zarautz, it has been confirmed that the sandstone tombs were constructed between the tenth and twelfth centuries. See Alex Ibáñez Etxeberria and Alfredo Moraza Barea, "Evolución cronotipológica de las inhumaciones medievales en el Cantábrico Oriental: el caso de Santa María la Real de Zarautz (Gipuzkoa)," *Munibe Antropologia-Arkeologia* 57 (2005): 419–34. For the case of San Pedro de Iromendi, in Bidania-Goiatz, the oldest sandstone tomb found to this point, it dates from the ninth century. See Iosu Etxezarraga Ortuondo, "San Pedro de Iromendi," *Arkeoikuska 2013* (2014), 285–89. By the twelfth century, simple burial plots had already replaced these. See Iosu Etxezarraga Ortuondo, "San Pedro de Iromendi," *Arkeoikuska 2015* (2016), 308.

position on the closest edge to Mount Urgull but at a lower level, that is, more exposed to the onslaught of the ocean, could confirm that chronological disparity. In other words, it may suggest that the most ideal settlement was already occupied when the new church was built. We must take into account that the interventions undertaken on plots located in places farther away from the axis formed by August 31 Street and that connects the two churches within the city walls has offered up materials from the Roman period, but always of secondary importance, that is, moved about or displaced from their original location once they were recovered.[32] In other words, one may think that the Roman remains encountered away from the high point on which the church of Santa María and the convent of Santa Teresa are located do not imply evidence of a growth of the settlement, so that, for the moment, the ancient area of settlement is limited to the northwestern part of the current Old Quarter. This guide could serve also to illustrate a diachrony in land occupation in the tombolo of San Sebastian through the Middle Ages. Possibly, initially the promontory that dominates the current port would have offered a safer and more protected settlement from the inclemencies of the sea, although slowly new peripheral areas would be established, dried out, and consolidated with the aim of extending the inhabited surface space.

Nevertheless, this is not enough to explain the existence of two churches of the same ecclesiastical status in the same local political entity. We still do not possess any evidence to be precise and unequivocal in suggesting interpretative hypotheses, but I think that hazarding an initial outline about them could be useful. In order to explain this duplicity it is necessary to include into our story a heterogeneous social group but one that was made up basically of people from Aquitaine and that received the generic name of Gascons.[33] Historians that have addressed this historical era in the *villa* of San Sebastian have underscored the role of this group in its

---

32   Miren Ayerbe and César Fernández, "Intervención arqueológica en la casa nº3 de la calle Embeltrán de Donostia-San Sebastián," *Zainak* 19 (2000), 215–26.

33   There is a comprehensive account of Gascons in San Sebastian in José Luis Orella Unzue, "La gasconización medieval occidental del Reino de Navarra," *Lurralde* 33 (2010), 177–208.

early political organization. Some say they were seminal in the very founding of the *villa*,[34] even juxtaposing the village inhabited by natives of the area midway along the bay with the initial settlement of the *villa* in the tombolo as the point at which the new predominantly Aquitanian community would have settled. Currently, we know that the area at the foot of Mount Urgull was occupied prior to the arrival of these new settlers, so that it would be more fitting to suggest that the Gascons established themselves beside the original settlement and adopted their own political organization around their own parish. Essentially, the argument here is that the *villa* of San Sebastian, at the moment it was founded, would have had two burgs or neighborhoods that would be privileged by the fuero.

This hypothesis is endorsed by the different treatment the legal text extends to Navarrese, understood as the native inhabitants of San Sebastian and people of the original village, and Franks, in reference to outsiders, among whom those who had come from the area around Baiona stood out. During the original conference that served as the basis for the present work, José Luis Orella Unzué offered a new evaluation that could support this hypothesis: namely, the choice of the fuero of Estella, rather than that of Logroño, as the basis of the San Sebastian text. It was, precisely, the legal characteristics of the fuero of Estella that were able to protect a new *villa* made up of two settlements whose members were different physically and politically, something that the Logroño text did not address. Whatever the case, one would assume that this situation would not endure through time, given that the documents we find about San Sebastian from the Late Middle Ages do not suggest otherwise.

All of this would imply that the fuero of San Sebastian was not just the product of an initiative on the part of the new settlers, but that its goal, among other things, was to offer a legal framework for the complex political and social conglomerate that was taking shape in the town.

---

34 Barrena Osoro, *La formación histórica de Gipuzkoa*, 372–77.

Continuing with this hypothesis, we could also speculate as to why the town would change its name and take that of San Sebastian. We should recall that there was a *villa* (understood in its early medieval sense, that is, a village) on the bay by the name of Izurun that, at a certain point, ceased to be known by this toponym.[35] The progressive transformation of this village reality and initial urban development during the time of or on the eve of drawing up the fuero may explain that the politico-legal entity that was taking shape in the tombolo of San Sebastian was already very different from its early medieval counterpart. Moreover, the adoption of the name "Antiguo" on the part of the rural church in order to designate a new reality that aspired to organize the whole surrounding territory may perhaps be explained by the fact that the idea that this church and its possible village preceded chronologically the rest of the area was already in the minds of those who designed or participated in the making of the new *villa*. It would be a form of granting prestige on the new entity by means of a mythical, to some extent, origin of settlement around the bay of San Sebastian. In any event, this is just one possible explanation.

Finally, in order to conclude this section, I will attempt to outline the territorial organization of San Sebastian in a wider perimeter. If we extend our gaze to the geographical surroundings that encompass the current municipality of San Sebastian, the population evolution there was relatively complex during the Middle Ages. In the immediate limits of the town one would find the church of San Sebastian el Antiguo and that of Santa Catalina located on the edge of the River Urumea. The first mention of the latter church dates from late medieval times and thanks to that we know that it was run by the Zizur charges (*encomiendas*) from the Hospitaller Order.[36] Its location, in a port area upriver, and sixteenth-century testimonies indicate that it offered religious services to the surrounding population outside the city walls.[37] This leads us to think that Santa Catalina was

---

35   The exact documented citation is: "*illam villam qui antiqui dicebant Yzurun.*" Ibid., 437–39.

36   José María Jimeno Jurío, "Iglesias y euskera en Donostia: siglo XVI," *Vasconia* 25 (1998), 217–42.

37   Ibid., 229.

also an early medieval rural church, although we cannot suggest any foundational date. Indeed, it is one of the most mysterious settlements for researchers, due to the fact that, with the urban expansion of San Sebastian, the site was subsequently built on thereby destroying the sequence of occupation it may have preserved. As a hypothesis, I would suggest that both churches served as focal points around which their respective villages emerged.

Toward the west there was another settlement that was first documented in the twelfth century, Igeldo, which was incorporated definitively into San Sebastian in 1379.[38] Conversely, it does not appear that the territory east of the current municipality, made up of Altza, Bidebieta, Intxaurrondo, and the western part of the municipality of Pasaia (Pasai San Pedro), was structured in villages. From early twelfth-century records we know that it was a rural area dedicated to livestock raising, thanks to a series of pens or enclosures located between Mount Ullía and the present-day municipalities of Errenteria and Astigarraga that were donated to the cathedral of Pamplona. In the case of Altza, its inhabitants called for the construction of a new church, dedicated to San Marcial, in 1390.[39] This was the consequence of a growing population and its strengthening as a community. In contrast, the colonization process on the western side of the bay of Pasaia reached a milestone in 1450 with the foundation and construction of the parish of San Pedro.[40] In any event, it seems that, in the context of receiving its fuero, the eastern part of its territory was dedicated to working the hilly terrain, without any stable habitat or its own political organization. The exception to this was the chapel of Our Lady of Uba or Hua, located on the southern slope of the hill of Ametzagaña and presiding over the lower course of the River Urumea, although we have no documented data on this prior to the sixteenth century.[41]

---

38 Archivo General de Simancas, Consejo de Hacienda, Exp. Hacienda, Leg. 217, 6.
39 David Zapirain Karrika and Juan Carlos Mora Afán, "Altza, de los cubilares al concejo. Formación y características del régimen jurídico-político altzatarra," *Boletín de estudios históricos sobre San Sebastián* 32 (1998), 535–78.
40 Iago Irijoa Cortés, *Pasaia: orígenes (siglos XIV–XVI)* (Pasaia: Pasaiko Udala, 2009).
41 Koldo Lizarralde Elberdin and Antxon Aguirre Sorondo, *Ermitas de Gipuzkoa* (Ataun: Barandiaran Fundazioa, 2000), 157.

San Sebastian in the Hernani Valley

The village networks that began to emerge in the eighth century had, by the twelfth century, been integrated into politico-administrative territorial structures known as valleys. As a historiographical concept, the valley was originally addressed in some depth in the published version of Barrena Osoro's doctoral dissertation as well as in studies by García de Cortázar and Mercedes Achúcarro Larrañaga.[42] Later, it was also the object of attention for Iñaki García Camino, although in this case to refer to Bizkaia.[43] In general terms, these authors frame the rise of the valley within a context of changing local circumstances as a result of the influence of external feudal agents, a process they link to the emergence of the village network. Currently, we find ourselves in a position to suggest new alternatives.

In reality, local organization had begun to take shape in the eighth century and developed in the following centuries, reaching its decisive point in the twelfth century.[44] The set of villages on which it was based extended throughout almost the whole of Gipuzkoa at the lower inhabitable levels. In most cases, the most visible evidence of its existence consisted of a religious building that subsequently endured and developed into a parish church, declined to the level of chapel, or, in the most extreme cases, disappeared altogether as a building and ecclesiastical institution.[45] Thus, presumably, the density of villages and rural churches was greater than in the late medieval period, so that, by the end of the Early Middle Ages, the landscape was marked by small settlements held together by humble rural churches.[46]

---

42   Barrena Osoro, *La formación histórica de Gipuzkoa*; José Ángel García de Cortázar, "La sociedad guipuzcoana antes del fuero de San Sebastián," in *Congreso: El Fuero de san Sebastián y su época* (San Sebastián: Sociedad de Estudios Vascos, 1982); José Ángel García de Cortázar, "Álava, Guipúzcoa y Vizcaya en los siglos XIII a XV: de los valles a las provincias," *R.I.E.V.* 45 (2000), 197–234; Mercedes Achúcharro Larrañaga, "La tierra de Guipúzcoa y sus 'valles': su incorporación al Reino de Castilla," *España Medieval* 4 (1984), 13–45.

43   García Camino, *Arqueología y poblamiento en Bizkaia*.

44   See Etxezarraga Ortuondo, "El laicado y sus instituciones," chap. 1.

45   I carry out an initial study of how to detect this process in Etxezarraga Ortuondo, "Parroquia, hábitat y comunidad en Guipúzcoa." See also Etxezarraga Ortuondo, "El laicado y sus instituciones," chap. 1.

46   "The spectacular profusion of small ecclesiastical establishments in Christian Spain, and more particularly in the regions of Asturian-Leonese mobility, is a point of view that is as frequently emphasized as it is incontestable. The valleys that concern us are

These villages appear to have lacked their own jurisdiction, as understood in the late medieval era. The domestic units that formed this agglomeration, together with other auxiliary buildings (dedicated to agriculture and livestock or artisanal endeavors), would be surrounded by individually worked agricultural land and fields for raising livestock. These centers, in turn, were located within larger communal mountain areas.[47] Inhabitants of the villages worked this communal land in a way we are still unfamiliar with. An example of livestock farming in the mountain areas are the pens being studied on the Gipuzkoan side of the Aralar mountain range.[48] Being an area that has been occupied by humans since proto-history, several huts have been discovered within the chronology of interest for the present study, that is, Late Antiquity and the Early Middle Ages. These livestock settlements, by necessity seasonal on account of the adverse winter weather conditions, constitute an example of land use in the communal mountain spaces on the part of peasants.

Within this context, I propose to study valley organization as part of a local and district logic, to use a modern term, and with the implication of political and economic articulation of the territory. The existence of a network of villages by the end of the first millennium that grouped people together in small and numerous population centers making use of shared forest, livestock, and industrial spaces by necessity demanded common administrative and decision-making structures. In this regard, and added to a form of territorial articulation and social organization on the part of external powers, one would think that such geographical demarcations responded to the need to resolve the issue of the everyday use of mountain resources and, possibly, other aspects of local and cross-community interest.

---

certainly very closely linked to the phenomenon." Juan José Larrea and Roland Viader, "Aprisions et presuras au début du IXe siècle: pour une étude des formes d'appropriation du territoire dans la Tarraconaise du haut Moyen Âge," in *De la Tarraconaise à la Marche supérieure d'Al-Andalus, IVe–XIe siècle. Les habitats ruraux. Méridiennes*, ed. Philippe Sénac (Toulouse: CNRS, Université de Toulouse-Le Mirail, 2006), 173.

47 This organization is described in García Camino, *Arqueología y poblamiento en Bizkaia*, 269–74.

48 Jose Antonio Mujika Alustiza and Alfredo Moraza Barea, "Establecimientos de hábitat al aire libre. Los fondos de cabaña de morfología tumular: características, proceso de formación y cronología," *Veleia* 22 (2005), 77–110.

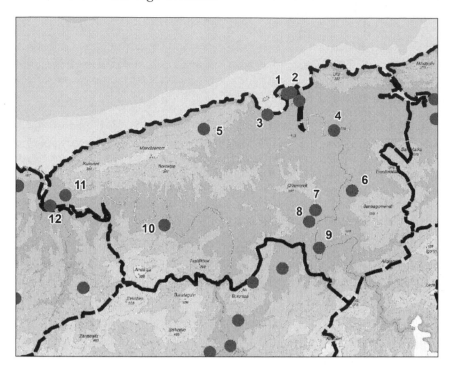

Figure 1.
*Approximate boundaries of the Hernani Valley and possible rural
churches around which population settlement was organized:
1. Santa María; 2. San Vicente; 3. San Sebastián el Antiguo; 4. Nuestra
Señora de Uba; 5. San Pedro de Igeldo; 6. Nuestra Señora de Murgia; 7. San
Martín de Sagastiaga; 8. San Juan de Hernani; 9. Santa María de Zikuñaga;
10. San Esteban de Oa; 11. San Martín de Agirre; 12. San Nicolás de Orio.*

*Source: Author's elaboration based on multiple sources consulted in
Etxezarraga Ortuondo, "El laicado y sus instituciones."*

In the case of San Sebastian, the villages situated around
the Concha Bay were incorporated into the Hernani Valley.[49] This
demarcation, which bordered those of Oiartzun to the east, Lerin
to the southeast, Leitza to the south, Zizurkil to the southwest,

---

49   Proof of that is, for example, the mention in 1101 of the Antiguo church as *"San
Sebastián . . . infinibus Hernani."* Barrena Osoro, *La formación histórica de Gipuzkoa,* 427.

and Saiatz to the west, agglutinated the present-day towns of Orio, Usurbil, Lasarte-Oria, Donostia-San Sebastian, Pasaia San Pedro, and Hernani. The old villages that were included in this valley shared access to different land, forested and for livestock, such as the mountainous Igeldo and Ulia-Altza areas, as well as the broad zone that, from the Late Middle Ages on, would come to be known as the Frankish Mountains of the Urumea.[50] There is evidence to support this suggestion, such as the existence of "enclosures" or primitive pens in the area since at least the twelfth century.[51] The singular nature of such livestock settlements, which were later demarcated in circles emanating from a central boundary marker, resides in the fact that, on the one hand, they were individualized areas on communal land, and, on the other, they granted their owners a series of rights that implied an exception to the system of communal mountain use.[52] The dispersion of pens in the abovementioned area was attested to already at the moment the fuero was granted to San Sebastian, so that, indirectly, the resulting map could have denoted which the communal spaces were in the valley.

As we will see, from the tenth century on, the signs of an economic boom along the western Cantabrian Sea coast were sufficiently clear to consider economic factors as an element to bear in mind in order to understand the political and legal changes that would yield results from the twelfth century on. There is currently archaeological evidence to support the notion of population growth and, consequently, local organizational structures during the High Middle Ages.[53] This transformation was revealed essentially through the changes taking place in the network of rural churches and the abandonment of early medieval necropolises.[54] It is possible that

---

50 On the latter area, there is a detailed study of its historical development in Rosa Ayerbe Iribar, "Los llamados Montes Francos del Urumea. Un ejemplo de desintegración de los comunales supramunicipales guipuzcoanos (s.XIV–XVII)," *BEHSS* 47 (2014): 15–64.

51 Álvaro Aragón Ruano, "Relaciones ganaderas entre Navarra y Guipúzcoa durante la Baja Edad Media y el comienzo de la Edad Moderna," *España Medieval* 38 (2015), 13–35.

52 Iosu Etxezarraga Ortuondo and Álvaro Aragón Ruano, *Entre la explotación pastoril y la forestal. La evolución en el uso y explotación de los seles en el País Vasco* (forthcoming).

53 This process is sustained in Etxezarraga Ortuondo, "El laicado y sus instituciones," chap. 1.

54 Such changes have also been noted in Bizkaia during the same time. See García

the accentuation of the strategic importance of some settlements translated into them becoming a more attractive destination for incomers, with subsequent demographic growth and, as a result, an imbalance in the older structures of territorial organization and legal framing. Currently, this possibility has not been considered or studied in any depth, so we must take it as an interpretative suggestion to bear in mind. Once more, archaeology could offer new data to corroborate, contextualize, or refute this notion.

In any event, the elevation of San Sebastian to a legal status unknown in Gipuzkoa, that of *villazgo* (the privilege of being a *villa*), implied a disruption to the previous territorial organization. While the borders mentioned in the fuero (which, in another way, were not at all specific) may have coincided with those of the valley,[55] in the long run, certain towns in the area such as Orio, Usurbil, and Astigarraga would take it as a defeat of their interests. More proof of the legal and political transformation of the territory of San Sebastian was the creation of a *tenente* that, as a royal representative, defended the interests of Pamplona on the northern borders of the Navarrese kingdom, an issue that is addressed elsewhere in this work.

Camino, *Arqueología y poblamiento en Bizkaia*, 347–48. In reality, it was also a process that went beyond the northeast part of the Iberian Peninsula. See Michel Parisse, "Le recadrement du clergé séculier," in *Histoire du Christianisme des origines à nos jours. Tome V: Apogée de la Papauté et expansion de la Chrétienté (1054–1274)*, ed. Jean-Marie Mayeur, Luce Pietri, André Vauchez, and Marc Venard (Paris: Desclée, 1993), 266–68.

55　While the foundation of *villas* often meant creating new divisions with respect to the early medieval valley, in the case of San Sebastian such an assertion cannot be made. The geographical boundaries mentioned in the text were: from Hondarribia to the River Oria, and from the coast to Errenga and San Martín de Arano (currently a town bordering Navarre). Our current understanding with regard to the origins of settling the *villas* invites us to venture that, in the same way that the village of Arano constituted a demarcation separate from that of the Hernani Valley, in the same way Hondarribia could not be considered a part of the jurisdiction of San Sebastian. The eastern area of the Oiartzun Valley was, probably, experiencing its own process of transformation that would result in its foundation as a *villa* in 1203. On this, see Martínez Díez, González Díez, and Martínez Llorente, *Colección de documentos medievales de las villas guipuzcoanas*, 20. Nor does it seem coincidental that the fuero of this town specified that the settlers of Lezo ("*dono bobis Guillelmum de Lacon et socios suos*") should come under the jurisdiction of Hondarribia, thereby disassociating themselves from the territory to which they belonged, whether Hernani/San Sebastian or Oiartzun. If it was on account of the former then that could explain the late medieval conflicts between the two coastal *villas* and that of Errenteria (Villanueva de Oiartzun) over the ownership and administration of the Bay of Pasaia.

Evidence of Economic Vitality in the Eastern Cantabrian Zone

There is no doubt that the arrival of contingents of foreign peoples, among whom Gascons from the area around Baiona stood out, suggests that the eastern part of Gipuzkoa was experiencing a boom at this time. It is certainly difficult to be specific as regards the particular opportunities the region offered for the new arrivals, but I will try and outline them using the available data.

On the one hand, its strategic position for maritime commerce, with natural anchorages that marked the maritime trade route (the Concha Bay, Pasaia, and Asturiaga-Hondarribia) in the same way as in Roman times,[56] implied an undeniable factor in adding development. These natural ports were located, moreover, at the outlets of river systems that served as communications routes between the coast and inland areas, and this only amplified the strategic potential of the settlements, which functioned as logistics hubs in the flow of commercial traffic.

I believe that, at present, it is clear that the initial boom of the first Gipuzkoan coastal *villas*, and their leading role in Atlantic commerce already during the first half of the thirteenth century, was not just the consequence of being granted a new legal structure and the creation of an urban enclosure. The signing of a commercial treaty between San Sebastian and various ports in the English Channel in 1237[57] had necessarily to have been preceded by a major presence of Basque ships in the Bay of Biscay, sailing both north and west. Thus, the drafting of a fuero with important economic dimensions could be understood as a response to the need to regulate relations between native and foreign settlers in regard to this flourishing activity.

The idea that the eastern Cantabrian coast offered a niche of opportunities for various actors is based on a new interpretation of already known documented sources and a wealth of new archeological

---

56 The influence of this maritime route on population growth in Gipuzkoa is addressed in detail in Milagros Esteban Delgado, "Presencia romana en San Sebastián." In *San Sebastián, ciudad Marítima*, ed. José María Unsain Azpiroz (San Sebastián: Museo Naval, 2008).

57 Wendy Childs, "Commercial Relations between the Basque Provinces and England in the Later Middle Ages, c.1200–c.1500," *Itsas Memoria* 4 (2003), 55–64.

data. It offers a new economic scenario in which intensive rural work was taking place in mountain areas, especially in three activities. First, the numerous pens or enclosures, mentioned in twelfth-century documents, could be considered an indication of intensive land use in mountain areas. Recent studies reveal the existence of a strict system of livestock use in communal lands, in which the herds of foreign stockbreeders were obliged to return to their places of origin at night, as a means of respecting the sunrise to sunset system that existed in Gipuzkoa in the Middle Ages.[58] The owners of larger herds of cattle, such as for example the cathedral of Pamplona, would have made use of the chain of enclosures to be able to move their livestock around from the Navarrese mountains to coastal ranges like Mounts Jaizkibel and Igeldo. Although we lack concrete data, there is no evidence to suggest that the inhabitants of villages in areas in which these animals were moved around did not also make use of the same mountains. On the contrary, as noted, the existence of pens and the need to create spaces or plots so as to respect the sunrise to sunset system constitutes proof of the existence of a management system for livestock use in these same spaces. In other words, I believe that the regulation of an activity is proof of its importance. Sunrise to sunset herding implied limiting potential abuses and favoring those who had access rights to communal land and the enclosures implied a form of response to individual interests.

Second, the work associated with maritime and river resources must have been a strong sector in the economy of the High Middle Ages. Whaling and the commercialization of whale products was a very important activity for the coastal towns of the Basque Country for many generations. Proof of that is, for example, the adoption of iconography related to this work on the coats of arms of numerous towns on the eastern Cantabrian coast. The oldest documented source on this activity in Gipuzkoa dates back to 1200, thanks to which we can verify that the inhabitants of Mutriku were involved at this time in exploiting cetacean resources.[59] New data could attest

---

58 This kind of regulation also exited in the Pyrenean part of Aragón, where it was known as *alera foral*. These issues are covered in detail in Aragón Ruano, *La ganadería guipuzcoana en el Antiguo Régimen*, 32–45.

59 Barrena Osoro, *La formación histórica de Gipuzkoa*, 440–41.

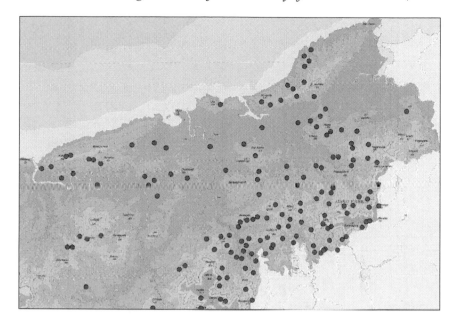

Figure 2.
Map of the pens identified in the northeast quadrant of
Gipuzkoa during the medieval and modern eras.

Source: based on several studies carried out by Iosu Etxezarraga Ortuondo
for the Basque government's Center for Cultural Heritage.[60]

to an even older timeline for this activity, given that early medieval whalebone remains have been discovered at the Zarautz Jauregia site in Getaria, prior to this locality being awarded the fuero.[61] Likewise, twelfth-century documents reveal the existence of river installations used for fishing purposes, known as fishing grounds or traps.[62] One of them figured among the possessions linked to the rural church of San Sebastian el Antiguo and its most recent historical remains have been discovered at the mouth of the Añorga Erreka creek

---

60   The main conclusions are included in Etxezarraga Ortuondo and Aragón Ruano, *Entre la explotación pastoril y la forestal.*
61   I am indebted to Xabier Alberdi for this information. This site is still being studied and one of the tasks being carried out is that of determining a more complete chronology for these whale remains and the archeological context in which they were discovered.
62   Barrena Osoro, *La formación histórica de Gipuzkoa,* 427, 437–39.

at the western end of Ondarreta beach.[63] Unfortunately, we lack information on coastal fishing in Gipuzkoa at this time.

Third and finally, another activity to which special attention has been paid in recent decades is the pre-hydraulic production of iron. Mountain foundries or *haizeolak* were installations used to transform the seam mineral (hematite) into forging iron. Of scarce architectural and structural monumental character, these were complexes made up of calcination ovens, reduction ovens, and other auxiliary dependencies that occupied different positions on mountainsides, generally close to water sources, beside rivers, or at river confluences. While in Bizkaia there is an uninterrupted documented list of such sites since Roman times, the high point of their use in the Cantabrian part of the Basque Country was between the tenth and thirteenth centuries.[64] The discovery of several hundred such preindustrial installations in the coastal stretch of the Basque Country leads me to believe that the first peak of medieval metallurgical activity came before the introduction of hydrological energy in this productive process.

Various examples of such installations have been discovered in Oiartzun and Hernani, especially those documented in the Epele Erreka creek, near the Frankish Mountains of the River Urumea, on the current boundary between Astigarraga and Hernani. Although they still require further study, one could speculate that the production in these installations was not aimed at satisfying just local demand. As an example, the mountain foundries around Aia, alongside the Amaserreka and Manterolaerreka rivers, which could be considered

---

63 Dating from the eighteenth century, it is a system of posts driven into the sand in pairs whose arrangement resembles a parabola open toward the ocean. This was possibly an updated version of an older installation, which had been repositioned in different places within the ria of the Añorga Erreka stream as the topography and morphology of the zone changed. For more n the documentation of this structure, see Xabier Alberdi Lonbide and Jesús Manuel Pérez Centeno, "Estructura lígnea en la playa de Ondarreta," *Arkeoikuska* 3 (2004), 149; Jesús Manuel Pérez Centeno and Xabier Alberdi Lonbide, "Nasa de Ondarreta," *Arkeoikuska* 5 (2006), 469–70.

64 Javier Franco Pérez, Iosu Etxezarraga Ortuondo, and Xabier Alberdi Lonbide, "Los orígenes de la tecnología del hierro en el País Vasco: ferrerías de monte o haizeolak," *Kobie Paleoantropología* 34 (2014), 267–82; Xabier Alberdi Lonbide and Iosu Etxezarraga Ortuondo, "Proyecto de investigación de las ferrerías de monte o haizeolak en Gipuzkoa y Álava. Avance de resultados," *Kobie, Serie Anejos* 13 (2014), 181–92.

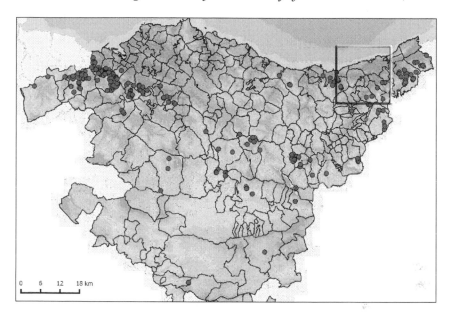

Figure 3.
Map of paleo-metallurgical sites in the Basque Country, in which
the mountain area around San Sebastian is highlighted

Source: Distribution map created by the archeological team at the
Museum of Mining in the Basque Country, based on its own field
surveys and the revision of results from other teams.[65]

precursors of the thirteenth-century iron-producing installations, exported their products via both river and ocean routes.[66]

As regards other production practices, one could conclude that flourishing fishing and commercial activities would have required a concomitant and reasonably important shipbuilding industry. In turn, growth in this industry would have also been reflected in and increasing demand for lumber and hence increased forestry activity.

---

65 Among others, see Franco Pérez, Etxezarraga Ortuondo, and Alberdi Lonbide, "Los orígenes de la tecnología del hierro en el País Vasco."
66 Luis Miguel Díez de Salazar, "El comercio y la fiscalidad de Guipúzcoa a fines del s.XIII," *BRSBAP* 36, nos. 1–4 (1980), 239–77.

However, for the moment and with respect to the timeline under study, we cannot be certain about this and this all remains speculation.

Conclusion

The panorama presented, as noted, is the result of an interpretative effort based on the available evidence to hand right now. Archaeology has demonstrated the need to update the historical record and address new areas of research. I believe we are at the beginning of a new historiographical stage and the argument of this study has been to outline a new starting point that, I hope, will be added to in the near future. In any event, it serves as a working hypothesis to construct new interpretative frameworks.

The fragments we have at our disposal have allowed me to construct a story in which the leading role, once in the hands of external actors that were attempting to transform the territory in order to obtain rents and resources, was now shared by local agents. Far from constituting a territory without history and an isolated society trapped in a never-ending cycle until the reappearance of external influences, we should instead view the local dynamics that unfolded in the region under study between Late Antiquity and the Late Middle Ages as resembling surrounding areas. Furthermore, depending on geographical particularities and baseline political, social, and economic structures, these medieval transformations led to zonal variations. As can be verified, in my opinion, one must consider both internal and external interests and influences in order to reconstruct, in this case, the historical framework in which the fuero of San Sebastian was drawn up.

The process of "founding" new *villas* must be contextualized, generally, within the frame of economic and political strategies on the part of medieval crowns or exogenous power groups, the product of meditated planning. It would appear that, in general terms, royal chancelleries attempted to transform the territory in order to adapt it to their needs. Without underestimating the interests of the respective courts, given the panorama presented here, I believe that local dynamics can help explain the development of the new political and legal organization of the territory. I think that the founding of Gipuzkoan *villas*, each in their own geographical and chronological context, was the consequence of local transformations based on many reasons and that sought to augment, correct, or address these situations through acquiring royally confirmed legislation.

Looking to the future, I believe it would be interesting to continue studying the factors that operated in a local way and that resulted in the evolution of territorial organization. In this sense, urban archaeology may contribute much valuable information and must contribute to the construction of a new portrait of the antecedents and results of the new legal, political, economic, and social model that made up the network of *villas*. In this regard, there is a clear lack of studies addressing the archaeological evidence that may contribute more information on the changes in material culture and the discovery of commercial relations through the artifacts found. In the case of San Sebastian, there is a pressing need to carry out programmed excavations, aimed at researching specific areas and unraveling puzzles like those mentioned above. The mystery of two separate burgs existing side-by-side and the hypothesis of a distribution of settlers within the jurisdictions of each intramural parish in separate fashion depending on their origins could be addressed in this way. In order to do so, multidisciplinary studies on medieval necropolises associated with the churches of Santa María del Coro and San Vicente could be crucial and offer information that either confirms or rejects the hypothesis.

In this sense, a procedural or urgent archaeology that responds to the need to document spaces that are going to be the objects of construction work and, in general, the destruction of the archeological substratum offers interesting data, but its random nature hinders real progress being made to overcome the current state of the issue at hand. Scientific progress requires rethinking the way in which the material remains of the past are dealt with. A strategic plan for archaeological research would constitute the ideal tool so that, in the medium term, progress could be made in our understanding of the remotest past of the city and, especially, of the context in which it was established as a new *villa* around 1180.

BIBLIOGRAPHY

Achúcharro Larrañaga, Mercedes. "La tierra de Guipúzcoa y sus 'valles': su incorporación al Reino de Castilla." *España Medieval* 4 (1984): 13–45.

Alberdi Lonbide, Xabier, and Iosu Etxezarraga Ortuondo. "Proyecto de investigación de las ferrerías de monte o haizeolak en Gipuzkoa y Álava. Avance de resultados." *Kobie, Serie Anejos* 13 (2014): 181–92.

Alberdi Lonbide, Xabier, and Jesús Manuel Pérez Centeno. "Estructura lígnea en la playa de Ondarreta." *Arkeoikuska* 3 (2004): 149.

Alberdi Lonbide, Xabier, Álvaro Aragón Ruano, and Jesús Manuel Pérez Centeno. "Quince años de investigaciones histórico-arqueológicas en torno a Getaria." *Munibe* 57, no. 2 (2005–2006): 435–51.

Aragón Ruano, Álvaro. *La ganadería guipuzcoana en el Antiguo Régimen.* Bilbao: Universidad el País Vasco, 2009.

———. "Relaciones ganaderas entre Navarra y Guipúzcoa durante la Baja Edad Media y el comienzo de la Edad Moderna." *España Medieval* 38 (2015): 13–35.

Ayerbe, Miren, and César Fernández. *Memoria de control arqueológico de las obras de rehabilitación de la Parte Vieja de Donostia-San Sebastián (Gipuzkoa). Capítulo 2, Calles Narrica, San Vicente y San Juan*, 1992. Unpublished report in the Archivo de Arqueología del Departamento de Cultura de la Diputación Foral de Gipuzkoa.

———. "Intervención arqueológica en la casa n°3 de la calle Embeltrán de Donostia-San Sebastián." *Zainak* 19 (2000): 215–26.

Ayerbe Iribar, Rosa. "Los llamados Montes Francos del Urumea. Un ejemplo de desintegración de los comunales supramunicipales guipuzcoanos (s.XIV–XVII)." *BEHSS* 47 (2014): 15–64.

Azkarate Garai-Olaun, Agustín, and José Luis Solaun Bustinza. "La cerámica altomedieval en el País Vasco (siglos V–X d.C.):

producciones, modelos productivos y patrones de consumo." In *La cerámica de la Alta Edad Media en el cuadrante noroeste de la Península Ibérica (siglos V–X). Sistemas de producción, mecanismos de distribución y patrones de consumo*, edited by Alfonso Vigil-Escalera Guirado and Juan Antonio Quiróa Castillo. Leioa: Universidad del País Vasco, 2016.

Barrado Barquilla, José. *Las dominicas de San Sebastián el Antiguo. Cuatrocientos cincuenta años de historia en Donostia (siglos XVI–XX)*. Salamanca: San Esteban editorial, 2001.

Barrena Osoro, Elena. *La formación histórica de Gipuzkoa*. San Sebastián: Universidad de Deusto, 1989.

Benito, Ana M. "Cerámicas del yacimiento submarino del Cabo de Híguer (Hondarribia)." *Munibe* 40 (1988): 123–63.

Buces Cabello, Javier. "Plaza Lezoaundi." *Arkeoikuska* 10 (2011): 375–76.

Caballero Zoreda, Luis, Pedro Mateos Cruz, and Tomás Cordero Ruiz, eds. *Visigodos y omeyas: el territorio*. Mérida: Instituto de Arqueología de Mérida, 2012.

Ceberio Rodríguez, Manu. "Primeros testimonios de época antigua en el tramo final del valle del Oria: el yacimiento de Irigain (Usurbil, Gipuzkoa)." *Munibe (Antropologia-Arkeologia)* 61 (2010): 243–59.

Childs, Wendy. "Commercial Relations between the Basque Provinces and England in the Later Middle Ages, c.1200–c.1500." *Itsas Memoria* 4 (2003): 55–64.

Díez de Salazar, Luis Miguel. "El comercio y la fiscalidad de Guipúzcoa a fines del s.XIII." *BRSBAP* 36, nos. 1–4 (1980): 239–77.

Esteban Delgado, Milagros. *El País Vasco Atlántico en época romana*. San Sebastián: Universidad de Deusto, 1990.

———. "La vía marítima en época antigua, agente de transformación en las tierras costeras entre Oiasso y el Divae." *Itsas Memoria* 4 (2003): 13–40.

———. "Presencia romana en San Sebastián." In *San Sebastián, ciudad Marítima*, edited by José María Unsain Azpiroz. San Sebastián: Museo Naval, 2008.

———. "Arbiun. Taller metalúrgico en el enclave romano de la gran bahía de Getaria." *Kobie, Serie Anejos* 13 (2014): 93–110.

Esteban Delgado, Milagros, María Teresa Izquierdo Marculeta, and Ana Martínez Salcedo. "La cerámica de época romana en el País Vasco atlántico: Redes comerciales y consume." *Ex Officina Hispana* 2, vol. 1 (2014): 193–210.

Esteban Delgado, Milagros, María Teresa Izquierdo Marculeta, Ana Martínez Salcedo, and Jesús Manuel Pérez Centeno. "La difusión de la terra sigillata hispánica tardía (TSHT) y otras cerámicas finas en el Cantábrico oriental." *Ex Officina Hispana* 1 (2012): 139–60.

Etxezarraga Ortuondo, Iosu. "Parroquia, hábitat y comunidad en Guipúzcoa. Una propuesta para el estudio de sus relaciones entre los siglos XIII y XV." *Domitia* 12 (2011): 89–112.

———. "San Pedro de Iromendi." *Arkeoikuska 2013* (2014): 285–89.

———. "San Pedro de Iromendi." *Arkeoikuska 2015* (2016): 306–11.

———. "El laicado y sus instituciones en la configuración religiosa de Gipuzkoa en la Edad Media." PhD diss. University of the Basque Country, 2017.

Etxezarraga Ortuondo, Iosu, and Álvaro Aragón Ruano. *Entre la explotación pastoril y la forestal. La evolución en el uso y explotación de los seles en el País Vasco*. Forthcoming.

Fernández Conde, Francisco Javier. *La religiosidad medieval en España. Alta Edad Media (siglos VII–X)*. 2nd edition. Gijón: Ediciones Trea, 2008.

Franco Pérez, Javier, Iosu Etxezarraga Ortuondo, and Xabier Alberdi Lonbide. "Los orígenes de la tecnología del hierro en el País Vasco: ferrerías de monte o haizeolak." *Kobie Paleoantropología* 34 (2014): 267–82.

García Camino, Iñaki. *Arqueología y poblamiento en Bizkaia (siglos VI–XIII). La configuración de la sociedad feudal.* Bilbao: Diputación Foral de Bizkaia, 2002.

García de Cortázar, José Ángel. "La sociedad guipuzcoana antes del fuero de San Sebastián." In *Congreso: El Fuero de san Sebastián y su época.* San Sebastián: Sociedad de Estudios Vascos, 1982.

———. "Álava, Guipúzcoa y Vizcaya en los siglos XIII a XV: de los valles a las provincias." *R.I.E.V.* 45 (2000): 197–234.

———. "Una villa mercantil: 1180–1516." In *Historia de Donostia-San Sebastián*, edited by Miguel Artola. Hondarribia: Ed. Nerea, 2001.

Gereñu Urzelai, Marian. "Las excavaciones arqueológicas de Santa Teresa y La Brecha." In *San Sebastián, ciudad Marítima*, edited by José María Unsain Azpiroz. San Sebastián: Museo Naval, 2008.

Ibáñez Etxeberria, Alex, ed. *Santa María la Real de Zarautz (País Vasco). Continuidad y discontinuidad en la ocupación de la costa vasca entre los siglos V a.C. y XIV d.C.* Suplemento Munibe 27. San Sebastián: Sociedad de Ciencias Aranzadi, 2009.

Ibáñez Etxeberria, Alex, and Alfredo Moraza Barea. "Evolución cronotipológica de las inhumaciones medievales en el Cantábrico Oriental: el caso de Santa María la Real de Zarautz (Gipuzkoa)." *Munibe Antropologia-Arkeologia* 57 (2005): 419–34.

Irijoa Cortés, Iago. *Pasaia: orígenes (siglos XIV–XVI).* Pasaia: Pasaiko Udala, 2009.

Izquierdo Marculeta, María Teresa. "El poblamiento de la Edad del Hierro en el entorno de Santiagomendi (Astigarraga, Gipuzkoa)." *Kobie, Serie Anejos* 6, vol. 1 (2004): 297–304.

Jimeno Jurío, José María. "Iglesias y euskera en Donostia: siglo XVI." *Vasconia* 25 (1998): 217–42.

Larrea, Juan José, and Roland Viader. "Aprisions et presuras au début du IXe siècle: pour une étude des formes d'appropriation du territoire dans la Tarraconaise du haut Moyen Âge." In

De la Tarraconaise à la Marche supérieure d'Al-Andalus, IVe–XIe siècle. Les habitats ruraux. Méridiennes, edited by Philippe Sénac. Toulouse: CNRS, Université de Toulouse-Le Mirail, 2006.

Lizarralde Elberdin, Koldo, and Antxon Aguirre Sorondo. *Ermitas de Gipuzkoa.* Ataun: Barandiaran Fundazioa, 2000.

Martínez Díez, Gonzalo, Emiliano González Díez, and Félix Javier Martínez Llorente. *Colección de documentos medievales de las villas guipuzcoanas (1200–1369).* San Sebastián: Diputación Foral de Gipuzkoa, 1991.

Moraza, Alfredo, and Nerea Sarasola. *Arkeologia 0.5. Arqueología medieval en Gipuzkoa.* San Sebastián: Diputación Foral de Gipuzkoa, 2011.

Mujika Alustiza, Jose Antonio, and Alfredo Moraza Barea. "Establecimientos de hábitat al aire libre. Los fondos de cabaña de morfología tumular: características, proceso de formación y cronología." *Veleia* 22 (2005): 77–110.

Orella Unzue, José Luis. "La gasconización medieval occidental del Reino de Navarra." *Lurralde* 33 (2010): 177–208.

Parisse, Michel. "Le recadrement du clergé séculier." In *Histoire du Christianisme des origines à nos jours. Tome V: Apogée de la Papauté et expansión de la Chrétienté (1054–1274),* edited by Jean-Marie Mayeur, Luce Pietri, André Vauchez, and Marc Venard. Paris: Desclée, 1993.

Pérez Centeno, Jesús Manuel, and Xabier Alberdi Lonbide. "Nasa de Ondarreta." *Arkeoikuska* 5 (2006): 469–70.

Pérez Centeno, Jesús Manuel, Milagros Esteban Delgado, and Xabier Alberdi Lonbide. "San Martín de Tours (Askizu)." *Arkeoikuska* 07 (2008): 352–53.

Quirós Castillo, Juan Antonio. "Las iglesias altomedievales en el País Vasco. Del monumento al paisaje." *Studia Historica, Historia Medieval* 29 (2011): 175–205.

Sáez García, Juan Antonio. *Viejas Piedras. Fortificaciones guipuzcoanas.* San Sebastián: Michelena artes gráficas, 2000.

Sarasola Etxegoien, Nerea. "El poblamiento medieval de Gipuzkoa. Revisión crítica del registro arqueológico." *Munibe Antopologia-Arkeologia* 61 (2010): 339–93.

Txillardegi. *Antigua 1900*. San Sebastián: Instituto Dr. Camino, 1993

Urteaga, Mertxe, and Javier Arce. *Arkeologia 0.4, Arqueología romana en Gipuzkoa*. San Sebastián: Diputación Foral de Gipuzkoa, 2011.

Vigil-Escalera Guirado, Alfonso, and Juan Antonio Quirós Castillo. "Arqueología de los paisajes rurales altomedievales en noroeste peninsular." In *Visigodos y omeyas: el territorio*, edited by Luis Caballero Zoreda, Pedro Mateos Cruz, and Tomás Cordero Ruiz. Mérida: Instituto de Arqueología de Mérida, 2012.

Wickham, Chris. *Framing the Early Middle Ages: Europe and the Mediterranean 400–800*. New York: Oxford University Press, 2006.

Zapirain Karrika, David, and Juan Carlos Mora Afán. "Altza, de los cubilares al concejo. Formación y características del régimen jurídico-político altzatarra." Boletín de estudios históricos sobre San Sebastián 32 (1998): 535–78.

Chapter 4

Another History of the Fuero of Jaca: A New Reading and Re-Interpretative Essay[1]

Ana Mª Barrero García

Different fourteenth-century testimonies coincide in presenting Jaca as the central generator of its own right that reached a wider diffusion beyond its immediate territorial space, ending up by totally going beyond the borders of the kingdom.

Of these, without doubt, the most expressive and also self-interested was the response given in 1342 by Jaca judges to their colleagues in the city of Pamplona, after the latter had asked for a certified copy and a correction of their fueros with the register of those of Jaca. Therein, it recognizes Pamplona having been settled and privileged with that fuero; there is also the existence of "*muytos libros de fueros que se decian seer de Jaca, los coales en partida non concordaba,*" and, finally, the authorities in the capital of Navarre are reproached with a certain harshness for having interrupted the practice of appealing to the Jaca courts on account of a foral matter and without detriment to their political dependence, as at that time San Sebastian and Hondarribia were doing, "*que son de la seynnoria del*

---

1   This chapter is an adaptation, with minor changes, of Ana Mª Barrero, "La difusión del fuero de Jaca en el Camino de Santiago," in *El Fuero de Jaca II: Estudios* (Zaragoza: El Justicia de Aragón, 2003), 113–60.

Rey de Castiella."[2] This issue of appeals is also included, as a reliable tradition and attributing the interruption of this practice on the part of Navarre to Sancho the Strong, in the *Crónica de los Estados peninsulares.*[3]

Another reference, also relating to Navarre and its diverse forms of forality, is included in a note in the margins of a codex in the General Fuero preserved in the royal archive. Therein, among the seven fueros considered to have been in force in the kingdom are mentioned in second and third place, that is, with their own entity, that of Jaca and that of Estella. In accordance with that, the Fuero of Jaca would have been applied to the city of Pamplona and the *villas* of Sangüesa, Lumbier, Larrasoaña, Villava, Lanz, Echarri, and Villafranca, while that of Estella would have been received by Olite, Puente la Reina, Tiebas, Monreal, and Tafalla.[4]

In both cases, it is about places situated on the Camino de Santiago from the Roncesvalles Pass and on those used habitually by merchants, who were heading either to Pamplona from Jaca, by way of Sangüesa, Lumbier, Urroz, and Villava, to France by way of Villava, Larrasoaña, and Roncesvalles, or to Baiona and San Sebastian by way of Lanz and Santisteban. The coetaneous documentation responds to that, given that the foundational charters of several of the places cited in the abovementioned annotation have been preserved.[5] For its part, the Aragonese documentation preserved reveals how the Fuero of Jaca was also applied to places located along the Aragonese stretch of the Camino, which runs from Somport to

---

2   Mauricio Molho, *El fuero de Jaca. Edición crítica* (Zaragoza: Instituto de estudios pirenáicos, 1964), 7–9. He publishes the document as an Aᵖ wording of the Fuero of Jaca (*El Fuero de Jaca I*, facs. ed.).

3   Even if it does identify the fuero de Jaca with that of Sobrarbe: "*Et dizen mas, que Navarra e Ypuzcoa se goviernan por el fuero de Sobrarbe; que sy los reyes fuessen de Navarra, los privilegios que fueron de Navarra ternian; et oy en dia los de Ypuzcoa apellan al fuero de Sobrarbe, et los de Navarra si fazian, sino que lo vedo el rey don Sancho l'Encerrado.*" Antonio Ubieto, *Crónica de los Estados Peninsulares (Texto del siglo XIV)* (Granada: Universidad de Granada, 1955); cf. José Mª Lacarra and Ángel J. Martín Duque, *Fueros de Navarra I. Fueros derivados de Jaca: 1. Estella-San Sebastián* (Pamplona: Diputación Foral de Navarra, 1969), 20n10. On the Fuero of Sobrarbe as an indicator of Aragonese military forality and its concomitances with the bourgeoisie of Jaca, see Jesús Lalinde Abadía, *Los fueros de Aragón* (Zaragoza: Librería General, 1976), 27–33.

4   The text is reproduced in José Mª Lacarra, "Notas para la formación de las familias de fueros navarros," *Anuario de Historia del Derecho Español* 10 (1933), 206.

5   See under the section "The Diffusion of the Fuero of Jaca" in the present chapter.

Jaca and, following the course of the River Aragón, heads toward the Berdún channel before entering Navarre by way of Sangüesa and Tiebas before joining the main route in Puente la Reina. Berdún and Luesia specifically received the Fuero of Jaca, even though their settlement predated the Camino and they did not have any special relationship with the route of pilgrimage.[6]

All this information basically coincides: the letter from the Jaca judges and the *Crónica* coincide in addressing the same issue, that of appeals, from different perspectives. Yet a doubt remains whether the spreading of the latter with regard to the territories, since it speaks about Navarre and Gipuzkoa, is a mere narrative recourse, or if it responds to a historical reality, given that in this case it would have to include Estella, whose fuero was identified with that of Jaca through San Sebastian and Hondarribia, among the *villas* that would have to attend the Jaca appeals courts. If that were the case, would one have to understand the marked difference between them by the author of the note in the General Fuero as contradictory? Or, perhaps, could that apparent contradiction have had something to do with the variety of versions leading to the confusion of the fourteenth-century Pamplona judges as regards the norms to apply?[7] One should still question the reasons behind such diversity, which seems to date from some time previously, given that the Jaca authorities were obliged to turn to the certificate of their old fueros. And one should even speculate on a possible reason behind this origin, since the silence, if not incongruence, of the manuscripts preserved therein is still surprising, given that none of the Aragonese versions of the Fuero of Jaca mention any royal privilege, or contain any personal reference, while in the Navarrese ones the drafting typified as *D* begins with the charter of the fuero

---

6   See José Ángel Sesma Muñoz, "El camino de Santiago en Aragón," in *Las peregrinaciones a Santiago de Compostela y San Salvador de Oviedo en la Edad Media. Actas del I Congreso Internacional celebrado en Oviedo del 3 al 7 de diciembre de 1990* (Oviedo: Gobierno del Principado de Asturias, 1993), 87–101.

7   This confusion persists, given that, of the different versions that still exist of the Fuero of Jaca, none of them match exactly the register of the old Fuero of Jaca that its judges had in 1342, since one of the corrected norms that the judge's letter includes does not correspond to the content of any of them; yet it does, however, with a norm in the drafting of the fueros of Aragón included in the *códice villarense*. See José Mª Ramos Loscertales, "Textos para el estudio del derecho aragonés en la Edad Media," *Anuario de Historia del Derecho Español* 1 (1924), 403; and, above all, Molho, *El fuero de Jaca*, xxi–xxii.

conceded to San Cernín de Pamplona by the Battler and then, in what follows, attributing the normative text to King Vitiza, in the year 700, in a preamble that not only recalls, but includes literal paragraphs, from the prologue of the Royal Fuero.[8]

This is not, however, the aspect that has most occupied the attention of studies on Jaca law, since the existence of a document by Sancho Ramírez conceding the Fuero of Jaca has been decisive for the historiography to consider this document and this king as the starting point of this law,[9] as well as its coetaneous and later concession to other *villas*, as an extension of this privilege. This being the case and in light of the documents preserved, one's attention is called to the limited manuscript tradition of this privilege, both in its place of origin and among the localities in which it was diffused. To this is added the fact that such diffusion did not take place until a relatively later time, around the second third of the twelfth century, on the initiative of Alfonso I, being only from that moment on when mention of Jaca in the documents became more widespread, and later it became identified with other fueros in the region. And not just this, since an initial reading is also sufficient to verify the substantial difference between the various texts that are considered a concession of the Fuero of Jaca, with or without express recognition of this origin, and the fuero of Sancho Ramírez. These are sufficient arguments to harbor some doubt as to whether this fuero, as it is known today, really corresponds to the content of the activity of this sovereign, and, as a consequence, to proceed to uncover it based on a critical analysis of the texts relating to the Jaca foral family.

---

8   This prologue is also contained in version *E* of the Fuero of Jaca as it appeared in the manuscript originating in the library of the royal palace (nowadays in the University of Salamanca, ms. 2652), recognized by Molho as ms. *E* 1. See Molho, *El fuero de Jaca*, xxvi–xxviii.

9   Thus, for example, Molho understands that, "in principle, the compilations [of the Fuero of Jaca] were written independently in Jaca and in Pamplona on the basis of the Latin fuero of Sancho Ramírez." Ibid., xxxi.

The Foral Documents of Jaca

Medieval documentation relating to Jaca is preserved on having been included in the *Libro de la cadena*. Formed in its totality in 1398 in order to obtain the confirmation of Martin I, the part of this that contains royal privileges seems like it could have been collected as a result of the promise to confer their privileges to cities and *villas* in the kingdom created by King Pedro III on the occasion of the General Privilege, which in regard to Jaca and other towns came into effect on October 20, 1283.[10] Out of the royal privileges included therein, two are of a foral charter nature: one is presented as a concession of Sancho Ramírez and the other of Alfonso II.[11] There are, moreover, several documents confirming the fueros, but only one of them, attributed to Ramiro II, refers to a specific act, that of his father, and to a precise summary it reproduces. That is not the case of his successors on the several occasions they take responsibility for this, always with a generic reach both as regards the content of the fueros and with respect to their grantors. That is how Pedro II did it in a document dispatched in November 1197, by which he confirmed *"illos fueros et consuetudines"* conceded by their serene highnesses, his predecessors, as set out in the instruments they created and authorized, and again in 1208, accompanying the ratification of the fueros with the concession of new privileges.[12] Similarly, Jaime I did this at different moments, in 1225, 1227, and 1269.[13] Other royal acts were aimed at conceding specific privileges, some of which influenced questions contemplated in the fueros. In August 1192, Alfonso II took an interest in securing public order.

10 See Antonio Ubieto, *Jaca: Documentos municipales, 971–1269* (Valencia: Cronista Almela y Vives, 1975), 13–14.
11 For the editions of these and other foral texts mentioned, see Ana Mª Barrero García and Mª Luz Alonso Martín, *Textos de derecho local español en la Edad Media. Catálogo de fueros y costums municipales* (Madrid: CSIC, 1989), corresponding voices. To these one should add, for the Aragonese texts, those in Antonio Ubieto, *Documentos de Ramiro II de Aragón* (Zaragoza: Anúbar, 1988); María Luisa Ledesma Rubio, *Cartas de población del Reino de Aragón en los siglos medievales* (Zaragoza: Institución Fernando el Católico, 1991); and Ángel Canellas López, *La colección diplomática de Sancho Ramírez* (Zaragoza: Real Sociedad Económica Aragonesa de los Amigos del País, 1993). For the Fuero of Jaca by Sancho Ramírez, see also Jesús Morales Arrizabalaga, *Privilegios altomedievales: El fuero de Jaca (c. 1076)* (Zaragoza: Universidad de Zaragoza, 1997). For the Fuero of Tiebas, see Roldán Jimeno Aranguren, ed., *Documentación histórica sobre la villa de Tiebas* (Tiebas: Concejo de Tiebas, 1999).
12 Docs. 23 and 30, Ubieto, *Jaca: Documentos municipales*, 75, 87–89.
13 Docs. 52, 54, and 66, ibid., 128, 130, 149.

In 1197, Pedro II, too, granted the Tuesday weekly market and prohibited the sale of properties to the lower nobility (*infanzones*) and clerics. In 1203, at the request of the inhabitants of the *villa*, he commanded that the sale of meat should only be based on weight. And in 1212 he established the institution of judges.[14]

The Fuero of Sancho Ramírez

Its Manuscript Tradition: The text known as the short Fuero of Jaca has been preserved in two versions, whose most obvious difference lies in the range of their normative content.

The most extensive of the two comes down to us in the form of two examples: one is a pseudo-original on parchment, preserved in the municipal archive of Jaca.[15] It was written in Visigothic script and has been dated to the twelfth century;[16] more specifically still, it has been identified with the first half of that century.[17] Additionally, the fuero was copied in the *Libro de la cadena*, therefore in 1283. Although none of its editors, on the basis of any kind of document, refers expressly to the fact, presumably the thirteenth-century copy was carried out directly from the pseudo-original, which fits not just the accepted chronology but also the extreme literal nature of both documents. Thus, one can confirm, on the basis of Antonio Ubieto' critical approach in his edition of the document, the meager number of these variants (six) and their lack of any entity, except in one specific case, that of the addition in the copy with sixteenth-century script to norm 21 of a final paragraph excluding the freedom to mill to Jews and the flour produced to make bread with commercial ends, which does figure in the pseudo-original. This is interesting in regard to the textual transmission of the document, since it is susceptible to various interpretations, given that it could be a later rectification of what one would think was an involuntary omission, on the part of the copyist, of the *Libro de la cadena*, when he came to transcribe

---

14   Docs. 22, 24, 25, 28 33, and 34, ibid., 74, 76, 77–78, 85, 95–98.
15   Archivo municipal de Jaca, caj. 1, leg. 13, no. 3.
16   Doc. 8, Ubieto, *Jaca: Documentos municipales*, 49; see also doc. 2, Ledesma Rubio, *Cartas de población del Reino de Aragón*, 26.
17   José María Lacarra and Ángel J. Martín Duque, *Fueros de Navarra I. Fueros derivados de Jaca: 2. Pamplona* (Pamplona: Diputación Foral de Navarra, 1975), 105.

the pseudo-original that would serve as his model; or one could also explain the presence of this phrase as the effect of a unilateral addition on the part of the author of the pseudo-original, which would oblige us to think not about a direct relationship between the two documents, but about independent copies of the same model in which the paragraph mentioned did not figure. Lastly, there is a third possibility: that the pseudo-original was based on a copy of the *Libro de la cadena* after the aforementioned addition had been introduced, which would lead us to situate the production of this document in the fourteenth century.

The shortest version is known for having been reproduced in the confirmation of the Fueros of Jaca by Ramiro II, and of Estella by Sancho the Wise, dated in 1164.[18] That of the Jaca document has been considered an incomplete copy of the fuero of Sancho Ramírez inserted into the abovementioned confirmation.[19] Similarly, the version contained in the Fuero of Estella has been related to a concession of this nature to Estella by him at the time the *villa* was founded, which until recently has been dated to 1090.[20] Yet it was never, despite the existence of clear and significant coincidences between both, linked to the collection in the aforementioned confirmation of his son.[21] Nevertheless, the comparative analysis of these two short versions of the Fuero of Jaca in itself, and with that contained in the document by Sancho Ramírez, offers a somewhat different reality, insofar as it shows the immediate relationship of the texts included in both confirmations as opposed to the document considered the original one.

---

18 See note 76.

19 Doc. 1, Lacarra and Martín Duque, *Fueros de Navarra I. Fueros derivados de Jaca: 2. Pamplona*, 105; recognized as model *D* of the fuero of Sancho Ramírez.

20 Thus in Lacarra and Martín Duque, *Fueros de Navarra I. Fueros derivados de Jaca: 1. Estella-San Sebastián*, 17–18. Subsequently, Martín Duque highlighted the apocryphal nature of the document dating the foundation of Estella to that year, as well as including diverse documented testimonies that demonstrate its existence already in 1076 and with complete certainty before 1084. See Ángel J. Martín Duque, "La fundación del primer burgo navarro. Estella," *Príncipe de Viana* 51, no. 190 (1990), 317–27.

21 See the most recent study in this regard by Julia Pavón Benito, "Fuero de Jaca y fuero de Estella. Observaciones críticas," in *XV Congreso de Historia de la Corona de Aragón. Actas. Tomo III. Jaca en la Corona de Aragón (siglos XII–XVIII)* (Zaragoza: Institución Fernando el Católico, 1994), 343–53.

In the first place, worth highlighting is the coincidence of both short versions in including an extensive amount of the same precepts, given that the Fuero of Estella does not contain anything of the fuero of Sancho Ramírez that is not in the confirmation of Ramiro II. In regard to that, both texts dispense with the five initial and the three final paragraphs. For its part, the Fuero of Estella also omits precept 23 in the Fuero of Jaca that, in contrast, does figure in its confirmation.

No less striking is the degree to which the preambles in the confirmations maintain a literal character as opposed to the original Jaca text; a fact that, for similar reasons that could have been the circumstances of the first concession of the fuero to one of the neighboring communities, does not find any justification except in an immediate textual relationship, all the more so based on the fact that its grantors would have to be considered as trained in accordance with their own chancellery customs and the characteristics of each of them.[22] Thus one can observe how variants in the formulation of the clauses in this preamble between one and another document only affect the invocation, which if in that of Jaca is trinitarian, in that of Estella it follows divinity, as is typical in the documents of King Sancho. There are, logically, other differences of a personal and topical nature such as the omission in that of Estella of any reference to the affiliation of the granting sovereign to Sancho Ramírez, and the substitution of the name Jaca with that of Estella. And there is no lack of merely literal differences, such as inverting the word order in the expression "*quotidie faciatis*" and the future projection of royal activity in that of Estella. Other differences of this nature, and this could be significant as regards establishing the genealogy of the Etsella manuscripts, come about just in relation to what is considered the oldest edition, *A*,[23] but not in *B*, hence

---

22   On the Aragonese chancellery of the period, see Ángel Canellas López, "La cancillería real en el reino de Aragón (1035–1134)," in *Folia Budapestina* (Zaragoza: Institución Fernando el Católico; CSIC, 1983), 23–46. On the chancellery of Sancho VI, see Santos García Larragueta and Isabel Ostolaza Elizondo, "Estudios de diplomática sobre fuentes de la época de Sancho el Sabio," in *Vitoria en la Edad Media. Actas del I Congreso de estudios históricos celebrado en esta ciudad del 21 al 26 de septiembre de1981 en conmemoración del 800 aniversario de su fundación* (Vitoria-Gasteiz: Ayuntamiento de Vitoria-Gasteiz, 1982), 115–215.

23   See Lacarra and Martín Duque, *Fueros de Navarra I. Fueros derivados de Jaca: 1. Estella-San

the omission of the conjunction "*et*" and the phrase attributed to Sancho Ramírez, "*qui requies sit*," and the reinforcing of royal activity with the inclusion of the verb "*concedere.*"

This literal nature of both preambles was maintained in the wording of the precepts. Both texts, consistent with the act of including a previous royal act—the fuero of Sancho Ramírez—resort to using the past verb tense when formulating the norms and, likewise, despite the greater formal proximity of the Jaca version in regard to that preceding it, one still observes signs of similarity between the short versions vis-à-vis this, such as the fact that both opt for the option "*ire noluisset*" instead of "*non volet ire*" used by the Fuero of Jaca in the norm that addresses war levies, both use the verb "*habere*" instead of "*dare*" in that relative to statutory rape, and both omit the personal "*vobis*" that appears in the norm establishing the year and one day statute of limitations. Yet, without doubt, the most revealing sign of this dependency appears in the use by these texts of the verb "*pariare.*" This term is open to two meanings: one, which is more common, as a synonym for to pay or settle an account; and another, as an intransitive passive in the sense of matching or being equal.[24] While the Fuero of Jaca by Sancho Ramírez resorts to this term in only the first of the aforementioned acceptances and then only its initial norms that do not have any equivalents in the short versions, in the latter the word is generally used in the sense of paying, but also in addressing the allegation of rape, with a meaning closer to the second of these acceptances. Its presence in this context in the case of Jaca does not seem to have been difficult to understand, yet that was not the case in Estella, where it was necessary to clarify its meaning by means of a corresponding gloss.[25] And this also seems to have been the case in the fuero of Sancho Ramírez, but

Sebastián, 31–32. However, these data highlight the fact the B edition could have been based on a text prior to A and not directly on it. In this regard, Ángel J. Martín Duque's assessment of the textual transmission and genealogy of the Fueros of Estella and San Sebastián is interesting. See "El fuero de San Sebastián. Tradición manuscrita y edición crítica," in *Congreso: El fuero de San Sebastián y su época* (San Sebastián: Sociedad de Estudios Vascos, 1982), 9–10.

24 See Du Cange [Charles du Fresne], *Glossarium Mediae latinitatis et infimae Latinitatis* (Niort: Favre, 1883–1887).

25 FE I, 6.3: "*Hoc est pariare: Si mulier non est digna ut sit uxor illius, debet ille qui forciavit eam dare illi talem maritum unde fusset honorata antequam habuisset eam.*"

on this occasion there was no resort to an explicit gloss but, rather, the direct replacement of the term by the concept.[26] The use of the same meaning by the short versions of the Fuero of Jaca as opposed to the option it followed highlights once more the close link of dependency that existed between them, in which there was no place for the text of Sancho Ramírez. However, the unequivocal understanding of the term *"pariare"* by the latter and the Fuero of Estella points to a possible relationship between the two of them, as well as a fairly distant textual base. In any event, contemplating this fact from a group perspective just underscores the progression observed in the textual transmission of this paragraph—term, gloss, and concept—and even more so as regards how it was produced in an inverse way to that commonly accepted in considering the text of Sancho Ramírez as the original Jaca text.

For their part, the two editions (*A* and *B*) of the Fuero of Estella coincide before those of Jaca (the short and the extended ones) in not accepting certain readings, if not always resolved with the same identical solution;[27] and in the presence of elements that affect the content of the norms either by modifying them or rounding them off.[28]

Its Document Critique: Since its publication by Father Huesca, the Fuero of Jaca by Sancho Ramírez in its longer version has been the object of numerous editions following one or another of the documents preserved that contain it. It is, then, a well-known text whose analysis has not offered scholars any point or doubt

---

26 FJ 12: *"Et si sit causa quod eam forçet, det ei maritum."*

27 FJ 7=FE I, 2.1: *malo cisso]* A: *interdicto vel cisso*, B: *impedimento*; FJ 8= FE I, 2.2: *anno uno et die]* A: *anno et uno die*, B: *uno anno et una die*; FJ 9=FE I, 2.4: *circuitu illius]* A: *illo*, B] *Stelle.*

28 In the regulation of the war levies (J 1=E I, 1.2) Estella contemplates the possibility of failure to pay with a sanction of sixty *sueldos*; in J 4= E I, 2.3 Estella includes water in the statement on communal use; in J 5= E I, 4.1 on legal disputes, Estella omits the approach of assumption among inhabitants, it does not contemplate the preference of the criterion of being local as opposed to that of being an outsider in regard to fulfilling the norm, and finally it adds a positive solution to the assumption with a dual and progressive alternative. For its part, the *B* edition adds clarifications relevant to this part of the norm belonging to the Navarrese formulation; in J 10=E I, 7.2 on the penalty for certain types of aggression Estella increases the amount of the penalty fixed by Jaca at sixty *sueldos*; in J 12= E I, 8, on upsetting public order on account of an indemnity, Estella contemplates the possibility of indemnity under bond; in J 14= E I, 10 on the holding of trials, Estella broadens the assumption in contemplating other circumstances; and finally, in J 15= E I, 11, on the falsification of measures, Estella widens their formulation.

or debate other than that of determining its date of production, owing to the absence of figures numbered in tens and units in mentioning the era in the chronological clause. From among the different solutions that have been pointed out, that of 1077 is accepted as probable nowadays. This was established by Ubieto by virtue of the formula of royal inscription, and on the basis of justifying the numerical deficiency of the data in the difficulty of understanding the corresponding numerals in the original on the part of the scribe who made the copy.[29] Yet at no time has there been any suspicion about the documented authenticity by which, in the absence of other elements of information and contrast, the data contained therein have achieved an axiomatic value when it comes to outlining the history of the first steps in developing this urban nucleus. However, the events previously highlighted when following the trail of documents—the possibility of turning over the preserved pseudo-original later than the copy included in the *Libro de la cadena*[30] and the difficulty of adjusting the publishing sequence of the precept relating to rape in the different versions to the commonly accepted chronology— are offered at least as a means of calling sufficient attention in order to be able to proceed to a new and attentive reading of this document.

From a formal point of view, the text is structured into three clearly differentiated parts, according to documents of the era and especially the privileges issued by the sovereign, who appeared as the grantor: a short section of protocol clauses, a relatively long and unitary body of norms that are distributed by the editors into twenty-four paragraphs, a cautionary clause, and, finally, those of the eschatocol, which are reduced to the chronology and apposition of the marks of King Sancho I and his successor Pedro I.

The document begins with a dual monogrammatic and compound name invocation—to Christ and the Holy Trinity— followed by the two-part notification clause: the first, in line with the document practice of this monarch, opens with a characterization

---

29   On all this see Ubieto, *Jaca: Documentos municipales*, 20–21.
30   This possibility is even more plausible insofar as the precept that was the object of an addition in the fourteenth century offers the same wording, that is, without the said addition, in the short version of the Jaca fuero.

of the document, followed by mention of the grantor with his corresponding titles, and the address. Following those, against what one would expect, there is no step toward the normative body, but instead to a second notification clause referring not to the charter but to the royal will to elevate the *villa* of Jaca to the condition of city; a somewhat surprising clause in its formulation due the scope attempted therein, given that, more than a notification, it is a proclamation to (literally) the four winds of royal wishes, expressed moreover in imperious terms—" *ego volo constituere*" —not at all in keeping with the habitually used formula on similar occasions, "*placuit mihi libenti animo et spontanea voluntate.*"

While it is true that, with the exception of this second notification, the clauses in the protocol present no anomalies, this is not the case with those of a similar nature that close the document. These are, closing the normative nucleus, a comminatory clause, of an exceptional presence in Aragonese royal documents from this era, given that it is not about, as in this case, the fueros, although it is about economic sanctions and not spiritual ones more befitting documents (whether royal or not) elaborated in ecclesiastical studies.[31] As regards the eschatocol, it is made up of just two clauses, the date, and the royal subscription (thereby omitting any prior confirmation of the latter) that, moreover, here, changing the typical order, is put before the chronology. This is reduced to a mere and incomplete mention of the year; there is a lack, then, of any references to the day and month, as well as the subject and the personal characteristics of the Aragonese documents. To these differences is added the fact that the only chronological indication that appears therein is made by the dual calculation of the incarnation and the Hispanic era. Although not exactly related to this document, both the dating of documents from this time by the era of incarnation and the joint presence of both forms has been considered by scholars of this period and region as a clear anomaly and an evident symptom of the false nature of a document.[32] This would, then, on the other

---

31 See Canellas López, "La cancillería real en el reino de Aragón," 36. However, of the fueros conceded by Sancho Ramírez, those of Alquézar and Castellar contained a spiritual sanction clause, even if shorter and simpler.
32 Ubieto, *Jaca: Documentos municipales*, 16. On attaching the false documents contained

hand, appear to confirm the studies by the Catalonian-Aragonese chancellery.[33]

The document ends with the apposition of the marks of Kings Sancho Ramírez and Pedro I, without any record of the confirmation of the executor scribe of the royal mandate.[34] The former's style of signature corresponds fully to that which appears in other documents of his. That is not the case of his son, in which, while the mark does present the Arabic characteristics he adopted after acceding to the throne, it does not correspond to his inscription, here explicitly excessive in relation to his genealogy—*"filius Sancii regis, filii Ranimiri regis"*—given that he appears typically as Pedro Sanç or Sanchiz. Yet nonetheless, it is still very surprising that this document is registered, precisely, in his name (*"Ego, Petrus . . . hec supradicta scribi volui"*), while, literally speaking, his father restricted himself to commanding it (*"hec supradicta iussi"*).

The normative body is made up of precisely worded precepts that the imperative nature of the authority of the grantor transcends. This authority gives the impression frequently of it being a personal act and all that in the present tense, except on one occasion, that can only be perceived as revealing, since measuring just a dozen words the wish that the king had just proclaimed, that of elevating Jaca to the status of a city, is already understood as a thing of the past, so that the immediate nature of this initiative is implied as current, the abolition of the bad fueros by which the inhabitants of Jaca

---

in the *Libro de la cadena* and in reference to those that include the supposed acts of the Council of Jaca (doc. 4) and the donation of thirteen churches to the cathedral of Jaca by Ramiro (doc. 5), both dated in 1063, Ubieto argues that the Aragonese documents were always dated according to the Hispanic era and occasionally by the year of incarnation in those issued by people or institutions outside the kingdom. For his part, in his assessment of the Fuero of Estella, dated 1090 and originating in the monastery of San Juan de la Peña, Martín Duque considers that, "the unusual double dating by era and incarnation reinforces the hypothesis of a manipulation." See "La fundación del primer burgo navarro. Estella," 317n1.

33   In addressing Alfonso II's scribes, José Trenchs Odena observes how, in the chronological clause, "use of the era remains in the documents issued in Aragón, although one observes a certain progress in the style of the incarnation, which—above all in documents written by Catalonian scribes—is juxtaposed with the era." See José Trenchs Odena, "Las escribanías catalano-aragonesas desde Ramón Berenguer IV a la minoría de Jaime I," in *Folia Budapestina* (Zaragoza: Institución Fernando el Católico; CSIC, 1983), 70.

34   On scribes in the chancellery of Sancho Ramírez, see Canellas López, "La cancillería real en el reino de Aragón," 26–27.

were governed "*in hunc diem quod ego constitui . . . esse civitatem*" and, consequently, the concession of other good ones, fueros that, it was said, were requested by the people with the only (and one might say obsessive on the part of the king) aim that the repopulation of the city could be carried out properly. It could not be any other way, since Jaca was transformed on the express wish of the king not just into a *civitas*, but into a *civitas* of the king, as if it were a question of personal rather than patrimonial property. This is insisted on but, it seems, not enough. Outside this paragraph, there is only mention of Jaca and on occasion the reference, even when it is the king who is speaking, is to the *villa*.[35] Nor does the wish of the sovereign, so widely proclaimed, appear to have achieved much resonance outside this document, either at the time or in the following centuries, although it did so in the fourteenth and fifteenth centuries at the municipal level;[36] and it even does so today.[37] For their part, the *populatores* to

---

35 FJ 4: "*Et si aliquis, vel miles vel burguenses aut rusticus, percusserit aliquem et non ante me nec in meo palatio, quamvis ego sum in Iaca, non pariet calonia nisi secundum forum quod habetis quando non sum in villa.*"

36 When the episcopal see was moved to Huesca, twelfth- and thirteenth-century royal documents continued to term Jaca a *villa*, writing *ciutat* above that. See Ubieto, *Jaca: Documentos municipales*, 22. The extent to which mention of Jaca as a city was exceptional in the documents included in the *Libro de la cadena* can be checked in the concords imbued with these in Mª Isabel Yagüe Ferrer, *Jaca: Documentos municipales (971–1324). Introducción y concordancia lematizada* (Zaragoza: Universidad de Zaragoza, 1995). According to these, except in the fuero document and that dated 1063 on the donation of twelve churches to the cathedral of Jaca, considered to be apocryphal (see note 32), mention of the "city of Jaca" is only found in two documents in 1238 and 1324, neither of which originated in the royal chancelleries. Likewise, in the documented corpus of Ramiro II included in Ubieto's work, of the fifteen (with the exception of error or omission) dated in Jaca, the common reference is always to the "*villa* of Jaca," except on two occasions (docs. 66 and 79). They both date from 1135 and refer to the "*urbe*" and never the "*civitas*" of Jaca, while the latter term is applied, though, to Huesca. Nevertheless, there is no shortage of testimonies against this, such as in the *Chronica Adefonsi Imperatoris*, which refers to Jaca as "*civitas regia*" when it discusses the election of Ramiro II in chap. 62. See Luis Sánchez Belda, ed., *Chronica Adefonsi Imperatoris* (Madrid: CSIC, 1950).

37 This fact is fully accepted by historiography, which generally justifies it by relating the requirement of canonical law that episcopal sees be established in cities with the choice of Jaca for its establishment in that of the Aragon, a fact that although 1063 has been established due to the contents of the alleged Acts of the Council held there, Ubieto demonstrates the apocryphal nature of this. See Ubieto, *Jaca: Documentos municipales*, 16 and doc. 4, Molho, *El fuero de Jaca*, 36–41. This leads one to see in the change of Aragon for Jaca in the inscription of its bishops that the documentation registered since 1076. See Lacarra and Martín Duque, *Fueros de Navarra I. Fueros derivados de Jaca: 2. Pamplona*, 107. On the other hand, Martín Duque considers the possible political scope of this in understanding it as an effect of a royal initiative to establish in Aragon a parallel to the *civitas pamplonensis* of the kingdom that he had just received, in order to equate them honorably. See Martín Duque, "La fundación del primer burgo navarro. Estella," 323.

whom the king was speaking here at the beginning seem, equally, to have been forgotten since their presence is only recorded again in the comminatory clause as receivers of the royal charter.

The rest of the normative content, within the very casuistic doctrine of the foral documents, presents a certain unitary appearance, given that the interruption of the sequence in the initial drafting of the early paragraphs (*"Et unisquisque; et si evenerit; Et si aliquis; et si evenerit"*), through the direct and personal form paragraph six begins (*"dono et concedo"*). The use therein of the term *"pariare"* instead of *"pectare"* or *"donare,"* could pass by unnoticed on not being precisely in this way and with this paragraph that the short version included in the confirmations of the Fueros of Jaca by Ramiro II and of Estella by Sancho VI begin, which here is offered in the totality of its content, in the same order of display and with scarce textual differences. Among these the most significant that stand out are the previously analyzed elusion to the term *"pariare,"* especially in the paragraph referring to rape (12); the extension of the mandate to the obligation to pay war levies on the part of the king to his descendants, even more striking insofar as, as noted, the typical formula of perpetual sanction does not appear among the clauses in the eschatocol, and the already mentioned addition in paragraph 21 excluding the Jewish population from the freedom to mill and that undertaken with commercial ends. No less significant are the three final clauses that do not find any equivalent in the short version, in that, through their content, it is clear that this is not a case of omissions in the short version but rather of additions in the text of Sancho Ramírez to the original foral nucleus. Thus, the ban on selling inherited property to people exempt from royal obligations, clerics and the lower nobility, a precept that was on the other hand typical in royally conceded fueros, appears to have been established for Jaca by Pedro II in November 1197.[38] Similarly, the two final norms concerning prison for having debts and servant indemnity have equivalents in the final part of the Fuero of Estella, which is considered to be the formulation of the *villa*'s own legal code.[39]

---

38 See note 14.
39 Norm 23 in the Fuero of Jaca coincides with Estella II, 2. 22 in content as well as in the similar formulation although the two do not literally coincide in everything. As

The document and internal critique of this document leads to results that, while not unexpected, are less obvious. From a formal point of view, the document presents a series of anomalies of this nature, in its preamble and especially in its eschatocol, which are enough to argue that, in the form it has come to us today, it could not have come into shape in the chancellery environment of the sovereign who appears as its grantor. On the other hand, its content reveals a complex composition based on normative elements originating in diverse places: in first place, a wide set of sixteen dispositions (§ § 6–21) that, at least in the time of Ramiro II (1134–1137), was understood as the fuero conceded to Jaca by his father. In any event, the comparative analysis of both versions exposes the fact that what is included in this document was the object of revision before that inclusion, as well as suggesting the possibility that the model transcribed herein does not fully coincide with the other text. To this set, three norms (§ § 22–24) are added from different origins and dating from a previous time.⁴⁰ It is more difficult to establish the origins of norms 2 to 5, or be certain of the common origin of all of them, since the first (§ 2), on account of its content, would appear to come from a town charter to which, possibly, the initial clauses in the protocol of this document would also correspond, while one would perhaps have to link the following ones on the activity of the royal legal authorities to that which, based on his words, Pedro I wanted to write and put his mark on.⁴¹ There

---

regards servant indemnity, it is contemplated in Estella II, 2.26, with a very different formulation, but possibly not as such in its content, if one considers the reading of previous paragraphs on animal indemnity, although in that of Jaca the norm on a humanitarian disposition, which could be located to either a prior time or a clerical environment, is revisited.

40 It was previously stated how norm 22 appeared formulated for Jaca in one of the privileges conceded by Pedro II in November 1197; however, this disposition could be the logical consequence of the validity therein of the ban on the settlement of the clergy and lower nobility that appears formulated expressly in texts as intimately linked to Jaca law as the new burg of Sangüesa, Puente la Reina, and San Cernín in Pamplona (see below). For norms 23 and 24, on the basis of likewise being in the Fuero of Estella, the former with a very similar formulation to that included in its *A* edition, one would be thinking of a common textual origin, even though it is true that such norms are among the Estella dispositions that have been considered an expression of the *villa*'s own development, which is estimated to have been confirmed by Sancho VI in 1164.

41 Nevertheless, although on the basis of its original publication, one would have to link paragraphs 5 and 3, it is a question of a somewhat confusing formulation of a precept, given that the solution given to this for acquittal for a homicide that may take place in Jaca or its limits does not match exactly the proposal of the case, which concerns the

is, however, apparently no document base that seems foreseeable for the norm that heads this complex set, although the reason for elaborating this document is revealed as being on the basis of the normative reviews described, and formally linked to the comminatory and eschatocol clauses, so expressive of its irregular nature.

We find, therefore, a document that does not fully match the fueros conceded by Sancho Ramírez with the aim of fomenting the development of a place of special significance. Instead, it is a set of diverse norms, mostly originating in privileges, which, however, is used at a particular moment as an instrument to give legal recognition to an aspiration that was not just juridical but also symbolic and political.

Having arrived at this point, the when and the why the need to elaborate this document was raised are obligatory questions. One must delay responding, however, until completing this analysis with the remaining Jaca foral texts.

The Confirmation of Ramiro II

There are two preserved documents that include Ramiro II's act of confirming the concession of fueros to Jaca by his father as well as the concession of new fueros, through their respective copies in the *Libro de la cadena*. Although there are clear signs of a close link between the two, not just because of the coincidence as regards the act that both include, but also on account of certain textual parallelisms and similarities, they present very obvious differences both of a formal character and as regards their normative development. This duality of versions of the same fact is not something completely unfamiliar in document practice, whether it is on account of having preserved the testimony of the different periods undertaken in elaborating a document—an initial text in which the royal *actio* is registered, and a second that includes this in a fully formalized document—or, what is typical in foral privileges, whether one of the documents is the

---

death of a thief during the carrying out of the theft, a percept contemplated by the Fuero of Estella, 2.7, in a situation of forced entry of a dwelling and with a similar solution for the owner of the property.

result of granting specific normative content to a generic previous royal concession, on the part of those to whom it was aimed, now outside the realm of royal scribes, so that it is unsurprising that they may present some anomalies or deficiencies of a document nature.[42] In principle, the latter could be an adequate and sufficient explanation on this occasion, given the differences that these documents present, which are both formal and in their substantial development.

The most obvious formal differences are in the eschatocol clauses, given that one of them, as it is known today, is missing from there, despite the fact that it is precisely there, following the confirmation of the grantor, where the signatures of his successors through Pedro II were registered. As regards the content, the fundamental variants stem in the first place from the underlying motives for the monarch's behavior; in second place, from the normative statement of the confirmed fuero, which is missing from one of them; and in third place, from the distinct range of privileges that accompany the act of confirmation, as well as their different formulation in those areas in which the two coincide.

The document put together in a complete way begins with some protocol clauses adapted to the chancellery procedures of the time:[43] a simple nominal invocation to God; the classification of the document as a *carta donationis et libertatis*; mention of the sovereign's name, with the title of *rex*, without any express mention of the territories under his authority and indicating his ancestry. This is followed by the address[44] and notification of the act as well as its motivation: first, the confirmation of the fueros formulated in terms that recall those in the preamble of the document known today that contains them, since similarly it refers to "*illos bonos fueros*" as well as also, but this time in the first person, as if it were his own course of action, in order to abolish the bad ones;[45] second, and on account of

---

42   See on this Ana Mª Barrero García, "El proceso de formación del derecho local medieval a través de sus textos: Los fueros castellano-leoneses," in *I Semana de Estudios medievales. Nájera 1990*, ed. José Ignacio de la Iglesia Duarte (Logroño: Instituto de Estudios Riojanos, 2001), 91–131.

43   On the characteristics of Ramiro II's documents, see Canellas López, "La cancillería real en el reino de Aragón," 32–40.

44   In which there is a clear mistake on the part of the copyist in omitting the term "*presentis.*"

45   There is once more an error in this paragraph, possibly as a result of misreading the

a specific motive—the priority of the men of Jaca to choose him as king—the concession of a privilege that is presented as extraordinary, nothing less than *"illam meliorem libertatem"* that the *"illi burguenses de Montpesstler"* possess, which is thereafter expressed from time to time *"et est talis."* This is developed in just two paragraphs that are clearly related in compositional terms, and yet it is truncated with the insertion of a clause on sanctions, which is reproduced again, although not in the same terms, but with reference to the totality of the document at the appropriate place, as the culmination of the section on dispositions. This is followed by those of the eschatocol without fully adjusting the order established by document practice, given that the dating precedes the subscription of the grantor. The form of dating, as in the document by Sancho Ramírez, is limited to timely chronological indications, dispensing with the ruler's usual formula and any topical or personal references. In contrast, the expression of the date is extremely complete, given that the dual calculation of the incarnation and the Hispanic era is followed by the month, February, and the day, the third ides of that same month that corresponds to the eleventh in the Christian calendar. Such indications are, though, incorrect as regards both the act included in the document and as regards its formulation. The error in the indicated date is obvious since the Battler died on September 7 that year.[46] This is the basis of the criticism that has been levied at it, whether regarding the likely flaw in the unit indicating an era, by which one would have to situate the document in 1135, or whether on account of a misunderstanding on the part of the copyist in interpreting an abbreviation of the month that appeared in the model, reading "February" where it could have said "September."[47] However, scholars have not taken an interest in an issue that is not easy to

---

word *"tolla."*

46   On the testament and death of the Battler, see Ángel J. Martín Duque, "Navarra y Aragón," in Ramón Menéndez Pidal, *Historia de España*, ed. José Mª Jover Zamora, vol. 9, *La Reconquista y el proceso de diferenciación política (1035–1217)*, ed. and intro. Miguel Ángel Ladero Quesada et al (Madrid: Espasa-Calpe, 1998), 309–10.

47   Ubieto, *Jaca: Documentos municipales*, 65. Whatever the case, both dates are adapted to the nominal relationship offered in the document, which allows one to situate it between September 1134, when Viscountess Teresa already appeared as holder of the tenancy of Uncastillo, and August 1135 when Fortún Galíndez ceased to occupy that of Huesca. See Agustín Ubieto, *Los "tenentes" en Navarra y Aragón en los siglos XI y XII* (Valencia: Anúbar, 1973).

justify in a document penned by royal scribes: namely, the method used regarding the fact that besides the dual calculation,[48] the day of the month is mentioned, which is not very typical in Aragonese documents until relatively later dates. And that was in accordance with a formula that does not appear in any other royal document in the *Libro de la cadena*, although there were such documents in among those originating in the episcopal chancellery.[49] The subscription of the king gives way to a long list of characters (no less than twenty-five) that are presented as witnesses to the "*actio*," given that they all function in the past tense ("*fuerunt testes*"). Yet a quick reading of this is sufficient to appreciate that, at the very least, the last nine of those mentioned must have formed part of a personally dated clause that the document lacks.[50] Finally, the document subscribes to the apposition of the corresponding personal sign of the scrivener Pedro, who functioned as such between 1129 and 1138.[51]

There are, then, several diverse anomalies in this document that prevent us from considering it, as has been the case, as a reliable copy of a document created by royal scribes, even though it is true that the correlation of some of its clauses and adaptation of the personal mentions with the chronological indication, with the exception of the numerical error and the previously indicated reading, allow us to pinpoint its elaboration on the basis of an authentic document by Ramiro II.

---

48   Thus, one can see how, in the document corpus of Ramiro II, dual calculation only appeared in documents regarding the cession of the kingdom in favor of Doña Petronila and the count of Barcelona.

49   This formula is characterized by the dual mention of the month, since its precedence over the day forces its repetition as determinant of the latter. A similar formula is used in a document by Bishop García de Gudal when making a donation by the archdeaconry of Soduruel to the church of Jaca. See doc. 31, Ubieto, *Jaca: Documentos municipales*, 90–91.

50   In general, Aragonese documents from this period lack the presence of witnesses and in any event the relationship is not usually wide, reserving for the personal chronological clause the declaration of bishops and *tenentes* with the pertinent topical references of identification relating to the place in which the post was held. In this document one can observe how, from the mention of the bishop of Huesca on, all place names are preceded by the preposition "*in*," and not like in the first part of the relationship, with the preposition "*de*" when the identification of a character with his place of origin is completed. A similarly sufficient sign of the composition of this relationship on the basis of different elements is that which does not begin with the names of bishops and in which they and the *tenentes* occupy a position in the epilogue therein.

51   Canellas López, "La cancillería real en el reino de Aragón," 40.

Could this have been the more extensive document? From a formal point of view, the biggest deficiency in this document is the absence of eschatocol clauses, in contrast to which is its subscription by the successors of the grantor. As regards this absence, as a potential justification one should point to its copy in the *Libro de la cadena* immediately following the last one, which could have led the copyist of the book to omit, for similar reasons, those clauses in this document, but not the subscriptions of those that it lacked.

As regards the preserved part (if at some time it did not lack the eschatocol), it is worth highlighting its greater formal and substantial coherence both in the statement in the preamble and in its normative development. Thus, there one does not come across the copying errors that are maintained in the former,[52] nor the incoherence therein pointed out with regard to the scope of the king's activity, given that here there is no place for the supposed abolishing of bad fueros. Meanwhile, that the text used at a given moment in Estella is the preamble of this document or a reliable version of it is good proof, at least, of its full authority at a relatively near time. Likewise, the coherence in the development of its content and of this with the preamble is evident. The king confirmed the fueros of his father that he related to expressly. We do not know if that is how it was in the original royal document, or if its development was not now under the control of royal scribes, but whatever the case one does not detect any incongruence in the drafting or references that contrast with the content as a whole of the document. After setting forth the fuero, Ramiro II concedes new privileges, as such, by the intent of grace, based on personal reasons, even more fitting in this case on account of their clerical condition and recent events that had taken place. Hence the privilege of general exemption in the kingdom from tributes, elsewhere not exceptional in Navarrese and Aragonese documents (see below), is aimed at the established population of Jaca at the moment King Alfonso died, with a future projection and the express purpose of safeguarding settlement there. The publishing of this clause, despite the referential differences, presents a clear literal similarity in both documents, to such a degree

---

52 Those highlighted in notes 44 and 45.

that the unsuitability of the paragraph relating to the established temporal term—the death of the Battler—therein is overcome not by suppressing it but by substituting it with an improper royal sanction clause, as highlighted previously, by the place in which it appears incorporated and by repetition with respect to the rest of the document. Added to the privilege about tributes, there is still the donation of rents from the royal baths and half a vegetable garden with the express aim of fortifying the *villa*. That is followed by the confirmation and subscription of the sovereign. We do not know if the original document ended with obligatory protocol clauses, but it is entirely possible and even probable, given the formal pulchritude and consistency manifest throughout. Because the content of this document refers to the same act that the previous one dated to 1134, it seems logical that this is the date that should be attributed here as well. However, two references in its final clauses, the interest in a stable population settlement, that is, through the demand for inhabited homes, and the defensive goal of the subsequent donation, lead one to speculate that this was a moment of special difficulty for the *villa*, perhaps unexpectedly on account of the first confrontations with Navarre and the fire in Burnao, located outside the walls of the old center.[53] If that were the case, we would be at a point later than 1134, during the later stages of the kingdom of the monk king. Such chronological precision is interesting from the document point of view insofar as it comes to reveal the apocryphal character of the previously analyzed document, which could have been elaborated on the basis of this one, even predating it,[54] with a concrete goal, which can only be that of presenting Jaca as a place especially deserving of royal favor (since one would expect nothing else from someone who is even owed his own authority) and, as a consequence, in accordance with such non-typical privileges in the kingdom, which are presented as the best among those enjoyed by the people of an important transmountain city, Montpellier. There

---

53 See José Mª Lacarra, "Desarrollo urbano de Jaca en la Edad Media," *Estudios de la Edad Media de la Corona de Aragón* 4 (1951), 139–55.

54 This would imply, moreover, resorting to another document with the aforementioned date of 1134/1135 in order to incorporate at least the final names that appear as witnesses on the list, which although it does appear as somewhat of a forced hypothesis, could explain the strange formation of this list that is presented as made up of witnesses.

is one more connotation besides those in the formal clauses—the reference to the abolition of the bad fueros and the use of dual calculation—that is difficult for any observer to not see evoking the foral document attributed to Sancho Ramírez.

The Concession of Alfonso II

This document includes an act by Alfonso II confirming traditional law in Jaca, which, one would think, is clarified in the subsequent and relatively wide-ranging body of dispositions (thirty clauses according to its editors). The interest raised by this document among scholars is due not so much to the extent of its norms, but rather to the affirmations in its preamble, which refer once again to the special significance of the *villa*; yet on this occasion not in relation to the king, with his devotions or obligations toward the town, but to something that is particular to the place: its law. This law is characterized here by the broad nature of its validity, since it reaches *"tocius ille terre que est ultra serram,"* and also for its singular perfection, to the point of attracting the attention of foreigners. And it is not a question of unfounded rumors or gratuitous affirmations; it is the king himself who acknowledges, *"scio enim,"* how *"in Castella, in Navarra et in aliis terris solent venire Iaccam per bonas consuetudines et fuoros addiscendos et ad loca sua transferendos."* That is how the monarch expressed it, and that is how it has been accepted without any kind of reservation.[55] Yet maybe they did take place? Once more, a document critique is responsible for, at the very least, cautioning us.

---

55 Although it still stands outs as unlikely that the royal statement could correspond to the documented reality. The first editor of this document, Tomás Muñoz y Romero, notes with a certain hint of irony, that "When all the parties went to Jaca to study its habits and customs, one presumes that there were, besides these fueros, many others that were not written down and that may have formed part of its consuetudinary law. If in that era there was no other foral legislation in Jaca other than that written down, the Castilians and Navarrese did not in truth need to go and learn it." See *Colección de fueros municipales y cartas pueblas de los reinos de Castilla, León, Navarra y Aragón* (Madrid: Imp. de José María Alonso, 1847), 243. For his part, in regard to the codices in the Fuero of Jaca, Mauricio Molho considers how, if not for this affirmation, their origins point to their formation in the municipalities of the Aragon plains. See "Difusión del derecho pirenaico (Fuero de Jaca) en el reino de Aragón," *Boletín de la Real Academia de Buenas Letras de Barcelona* 28 (1959–1960), 303.

This testimony has also come down to the present only via its transcription in the *Libro de la cadena*, so as regards its quality as a document, it has no more elements to judge it by than those that may derive from the critique of its formal and normative clauses. Signed by the royal notary, Bernat Desvall, who was active between 1184 and 1194,[56] it seems to stay within the characteristics of documents of this period. There is a short preamble. It contains clauses of invocation, nominal to God, and of notification of the documented act, in which the king, mentioned by name and corresponding titles, gives an account of the scope of the act—the approval, concession, and confirmation of the old customs and fueros—and the circumstances in which it is developed, stating the participation as advisors a series of people ("*multorum bonorum virorum*"), of whom four are mentioned by name, and of those two also by position. Still, in the final lines the king expresses the motives behind his activity, which is just his own realization of the importance and transcendence of this law. The eschatocol clauses play out without any answer to the continuity of the normative body. They lack the habitual royal sanction, although not the subscription, which also on this occasion puts the date back. This, in accordance with the preamble, is in reference to the *actio* and not its *conscriptio*. Expressed in the Aragonese way, it is made up of a topical and chronological indication with mention of the month and the era, and then goes into a nominal list of the witnesses that, clearly, originally constituted a form of personal dating initiated by that of the ruler. Thus, the king himself heads the list in which he presents himself as a witness, without mentioning his name, although there is mention of the territories under his dominion.[57] After the apposition of the royal sign mention is made once more of the figures, who are also attributed (in the singular) with the condition of being a witnesses or "*teste*," presided over by the bishop of Huesca,[58]

---

56   See Trenchs Odena, "Las escribanías catalano-aragonesas," 64.

57   The confusing formulation of this paragraph has given rise to erroneous punctuating on the part of Ubieto, which only contributes to increasing its incoherence.

58   Mentioned as such in the preamble, here he appears at the head of the see of Huesca-Jaca. As regards the way of describing titles of these bishops in the documents, it is very illustrative in my opinion to see how, at least in documents relating to the Ebro Valley collected by Lacarra, from the time of Ramiro II's documents on, bishops only have the title of Huesca. Similarly, among the documents contained in the *Libro de la cadena*, one can observe how, in the royal texts, they only appear as bishops of that see while in ecclesiastical documents they do so with a dual mention.

followed by a series of *tenentes* and an indication of their respective domains, together with a few other high-ranking people from court. Among them, as well as the abovementioned bishop, are the other three figures mentioned in the preamble receiving advice from the sovereign. Here and in the remaining personal references one does not detect any anachronism with regard to the date mentioned above.[59] The form of confirmation on the part of the royal notary does not present the slightest feature of any anomaly. Nonetheless, those identified are sufficiently revealing for it to be considered a document that, as it is known, was the object of clear modifications in these eschatocol clauses.

Yet there were changes elsewhere. A reading of its content also reveals the complex nature of its composition, since therein it is possible to distinguish a series of norms, the initial and final ones (§§ 1–8 and 26–30), in which, on account of the king being present in an immediate way—"*In primis laudo et confirm*" (§ 1), "*mille solidos nobis pectare*" (§ 26), "*et deffensione nostra suscipimus*" (§ 30)—there is no doubt about the nature of its origin. On the contrary, in the remaining seventeen ones references to the king are in the third person ("*merino regis, domno regi, in manu domino regi*"), which leads one to assume a distinct origin for these, which seems like it must be that derived from the statutory capacity of the neighboring authorities. This is reflected in the initial enunciations of some of them—"*De latronibus vero statuimus*" (§ 9), "*De apelitis ita statuimus*" (§ 18)—that, in fact, are just a kind of signature that frame a group of precepts in accordance with a certain thematic unity. Originally, these precepts could have constituted one or several such normative reviews of diverse matters, those previously noted, as well as others on the procedural order (§§ 21, 22, 25) and on the system of transhumance (§§ 16, 17, 23–24), now juxtaposed giving rise even to the odd note in the margin,[60] and

---

59   It is true that some mentions are very limited, thus in regard to Jimeno Cornelio in Ejea, Agustín Ubieto registers this figure in just one document, dated precisely in November that year. See *Los "tenentes" en Navarra y Aragón en los siglos XI y XII*, 137.

60   Such could be the origin of norm 20 on the selection of officials to guard and defend Jaca and other *villas* that are termed "*consules*," which does not seem to have any relation to the previous ones on surnames, except as regards them being the objective of some institution. Although formulated in an imperative way, its beginning with the adversative "*tamen*" leads one to speculate that, in effect, it is a question of an annotation in a previous text. However, the application of the term "*consules*," more befitting of

which, on merging with the normative clauses of the original privilege of Alfonso II, are presented as components of the same normative text of this nature. In the face of such combining of norms with different origins and natures, there remains the doubt over whether those of a statutory character correspond to the traditional law of Jaca that the king was confirming. Even if that were the case, it does not appear that the formulation of such norms took place before, or at the time of, the concession of the document by Alfonso II in order to be incorporated therein, given that, in that case, they would have made up for the inconsistencies highlighted in the mentions of the king. Similarly, a doubt arises over whether such combining was only in the normative sphere, that is, if it took place with the only aim of giving, as a means of updating it, timely and precise content to the act of royal confirmation; or if this combing the original text of the privilege beyond what is implied by the mere incorporation of outside norms to it. From the document analysis undertaken, clear evidence of alteration of the eschatocol clauses is deduced, but it is likely that these changes were greater and more transcendent than the merely formal modification. On examining the protocol clauses, it is still surprising to see the epigonous place in the discourse to that which relegates the statement of determining motives behind the royal actions, even more so to the extent that it situated immediately after a topical reference that likewise appears to be separated from its proper place in the story. It is a question of the phrase "*antiquas Iacce consuetudines et fuoros, et tocius ille terre que est ultra serram, versus montana Iacce, scio enim,*" whose syntax, which is somewhat forced, would not merit any special attention if it were not because something similar appears further along, in paragraph seven: "*Preterea homines de Iacca caveant caucius negociari et de tota illa terra.*" But this is not the case, however, on yet another occasion in which this reference appears—§ 4: "*Si autem fuerit extraneus qui moriatur Iacce vel in illa terra ultra serram*"—that is fully integrated into

---

Catalonian nomenclature, to a local Aragonese judiciary is extremely surprising in this context, insofar as the possible institution to which it refers, judges, was established in Jaca by Pedro II in 1212. See docs. 33 and 34, Ubieto, *Jaca: Documentos municipales*, 95–98. Nevertheless, one should caution that this term appears likewise in one of the clauses of the document by which Pedro II concedes the right to hold a weekly market, dated November 1197.

the normative context and with the appropriate spatial meaning of the (Guara) mountain range, something that does not happen in the first one, which has to be understood in the opposite way, from south to north. The difficulty of such an understanding would not have been lost on the author of the document himself when he realized he would be forced to specify the angle of sight by means of the annotation "*versus montana Iacce.*"[61] In view of these contextual irregularities, one can only suspect that they are the result of altering the original text with the aim of extending the range of validity of Jaca law and, why not, of insisting on its transcendence beyond even the borders of the kingdom. As for the rest, the content and scope of these norms, guarantees for locals and outsiders of the free disposition of their goods and commercial traffic, which foreseeably the original document included, is adjusted fully to the circumstances of the place, given the importance of Jaca as an enclave on communication and commercial routes with Europe at the time it was said to have been conceded (1187), as well as the interest on the part of the sovereigns in fomenting, by means of conceding norms of privilege, the population settlement and economic development of their kingdoms.[62]

Once again we find a document confirming the fueros with clear evidence of widespread self-interested tampering, but which also, like the previous ones, done with the proviso attributed to Ramiro II that contains the reference to Montpellier, appears to be based on reliable document sources.

---

61 This has not been the case for historians, and all the more so insofar as the reference in clauses 16 and 23 to "*Yspania*" has given rise to an understanding that the document differentiates between the "*Montaña*," or primitive Aragon, and the newly conquered land, recognized as Spain; see José Mª Ramos Loscertales, *Fuero de Jaca (última redacción)* (Barcelona: Universidad de Barcelona, 1927), xxii–xxv; Molho, "Difusión del derecho pircnaico," 292–93; Lalinde Abadía, *Los fueros de Aragón*, 26. In my opinion, both references are to the same territory, the mountain range, which came to influence the complex formation of this document on the basis of diverse elements.

62 Hence, similar norms to those granted by Alfonso II would likewise be the object of concession some years later by his homonym in Leon. See App. 77, Luis Vázquez de Parga, José María Lacarra, and Juan Uría, *Las peregrinaciones a Santiago de Compostela. III* (Madrid: CSIC, 1949).

Conclusions Derived from the Document Critique

From the point of view of the technique pursued in these rewritings, in all of them one can observe the same features that evince the alteration of the likely original documents, which are summed up in the tendency to adopt Catalonian chancellery forms as opposed to Aragonese document methods in the dating clauses—resorting to calculating the incarnation, although here linked to the Hispanic era and the transformation of the personal formula into a list of witnesses— and in the presence of a spiritual sanction clause of Visigothic origin, more fitting in the space-time realm of ecclesiastical documents. Moreover, an overall reading of its preambles allows one to see a symptom of its intentions with a sequential cadence: Jaca elevated to the category of *civitas* due to the sovereign, Jaca worthy of royal favor, Jaca recognized for the excellence of its law, expressly by the sovereign, but also by people in Castile and Navarre and other lands that, perhaps, there was a desire to extend the voice of old King Sancho. Everything seems to indicate that it was not a question of diverse specific cases of altering documents, but of a unitary intervention that was revealed in different documents, yet all of them related to law in the *villa* and closely linked to the royal figure.

The document critique undertaken contributes sufficiently expressive data about how this task of rewriting the foral documents unfolded on the basis of combining normative reviews of different origins and natures and their adaptation to the formal structure adopted (and also adapted to some specific conveniences) of some basic documents. Yet there are still questions to be asked of this process, such as those of when, who, and why.

Establishing the cutoff date for the document is no less difficult, given that the copy of all of them in the *Libro de la cadena* offers the year 1283 as the term "*ad quem*," while one must date the term "*a quo*," at the very least, to after 1187, the year the last of the documents analyzed was dated, and in all likelihood after 1197, given that the fuero of Sancho Ramírez includes the norm on the prohibition on selling inherited properties to clerics and the lower

nobility established by Pedro II on that date (see note 14). Within
this wide timeframe of almost a century any other clarification
now enters into the realm of hypothesis, a terrain therefore full of
uncertainty and caution. Nonetheless, the observation of the formulas
used by successive kings that confirmed the Fueros of Jaca is still
illustrative as an approach method. Thus, we come across the first
confirmation, that of Ramiro II, in the precise personal reference
to *"illos bonos fueros quos pater meus Sancius rex . . . missit in Iacca."*
Those that follow, however, are formulated either in ambiguous or
general terms alluding to some *"antiquas consuetudines et fuoros,"*[63] or
are indeed specified, although now not by means of a reference of a
personal but, rather, an involved nature, since royal activity is aimed
specifically at *"illos fueros et illas consuetudines . . . prout in instrumentis
factis et auctorizatis vobis ab illis antecessoribus meis"* (see note 12); or in
an equally specific way, but considerably broader, to *"omnes foros et
consuetudines ac franchitates quos et quas antecessores nostri vobis concesserunt,
et sicut in cartis vestris plenius continentur, et sicut melius hactenus cum cartis
et sine cartis habuistis et rationabilibus posseditis"* (see note 13). Hence,
the continued reading of these documents reveals how, only from
a specific moment on, specifically the year 1197, there was express
recognition of the existence of some normative texts in which
norms of a different nature (*"fueros et consuetudines"*) were included
that, whether originating or not in the royal chancellery, count on
(that is the term used) the due approval of the sovereigns. For that
reason, one cannot overlook the declaration in a document of Pedro
II, dated in Jaca on June 16, 1208.[64] According to this, the monarch,
responding to the demand of the, in this context and without any
precedent, *cives* of Jaca, *"maioribus et minoribus,"*[65] confirms:

> *cartas vestras omnes super quolibet facto vel casu vel negocio vobis a
> predecessoribus nostris factas atque concessas vobis omnibus supradictis
> et cuncte generationi vestre laudamus, concedimus et confirmamus, sine
> aliqua retentione ad plenum, et presentis scripti patrocinio conmunimus*

63 A privilege of Alfonso II in November 1187, discussed above.
64 Doc. 30, Ubieto, *Jaca: Documentos municipales*, 87–89.
65 See note 36. The terms *"maioribus"* and *"minoribus"* appear in the preambles of the confirmation documents of Ramiro II and in the confirmation of the Fuero of Estella by Sancho VI.

> *per nos et successores nostros et eas bonas, veras, legales et omni vitio et*
> *falsitate carentes perpetuo iudicamus, volentes statuentes atque mandantes*
> *eas omnes in omnibus et per omnia obtinere robur et vigorem perpetue*
> *firmitatis, salva tamen fidelitate nostra.*

This was an unheard of concession, however much a grateful king was able to proceed, given that it implied acceptance on his part of the possibility that such a dubious reputation could fall back on the documents elaborated by royal scribes. And it was even more unheard of insofar as it appears inserted in an apparently correct receipt document confirmed by the royal notary since 1203, Ferrer.[66] However, the fact that, in the notarial confirmation, one perceives the simultaneous use of his two characteristic formulas,[67] separated by the reference to the incorporation into the document of a normative clause after the dating, allows one to harbor the suspicion that this reference, together with the norm to which it alludes, were added to the original document after its creation. In doing so, this opens up the possibility of other alterations like the inclusion of the previously highlighted norm, so striking in its formulation and scope, as well as other elements of a formal nature, such as the use of the term "*cives*" in the address or the comminatory clause of spiritual sanction preceding here that of the typical incursion into royal wrath and economic sanction, alongside the use of the dual dating calculation.[68] It does not seem, then, too audacious to assume that these alterations in the document of Pedro II may be related to previous ones and come from the same hand, perhaps making the most of the presence in the original document itself of some clause or paragraph confirming previous royal actions. The fact that, in

---

66   See Trenchs Odena, "Las escribanías catalano-aragonesas," 76–77.

67   The first of these records that, "*Ego Ferrarius, notarius domini regis scribi fecit mandato ipsius et apponi post diem et annum linea ultima.*" See ibid., 81. The second simpler one is characterized by not making any explicit reference to the place in the document in which the royal mandate for underwriting the text is registered. See docs. 154–56 in Ledesma Rubio, *Cartas de población del Reino de Aragón.*

68   Just as the use in this document of spiritual sanction is even stranger insofar as under this king there was a demonstrated greater simplification of document formulas, although not as such in dating since this was also the time when, in Aragonese documents, there was a return to the Hispanic era to the point that, only in very specific cases did it feature as the only element of dating. See Trenchs Odena, "Las escribanías catalano-aragonesas," 89. Nevertheless, one can observe that in the various documents of Pedro II included in the *Libro de la cadena*, none contain the formula of spiritual sanction, nor is there any other chronological reference than that of the Hispanic era.

order to do so, the privilege of this monarch was used and not that of his successor, Jaime I, who likewise ratified Jaca law on several occasions (see note 13), seems to indicate that the rewritings of the document could have been carried out under the mandate of the former, and more specifically between 1208 and 1213.

On contemplating the formation of these documents as a joint act with sufficient indications that it could have taken place during the second decade of the thirteenth century, the interest in allocating Jaca the status of *civitas*, so evident in the first document analyzed, loses impact as the decisive reason in this process at the same time as it excuses any other possibility of explaining it for ecclesiastical reasons. One could say the same for the only political event of any transcendence mentioned in them, the coronation in Jaca of Ramiro II, brought up for its symbolic value in a context of already scarce not political but nor even judicial relevance. It seems more, since legal documents are concerned, that this nature was behind the reason for this procedure and on which Alfonso II's document provides some evidence in showing us Jaca as the home of its own widely recognized law school, in Castile and also (and perhaps one would have to add, above all) in Navarre. On this point and at the height of the thirteenth century, that is, right in the middle of the mandate of this kingdom of Sancho the Strong, would this be a demonstration of discontent by the Jaca authorities caused by the loss of rights to appeal originating in the neighboring kingdom? If in 1342 this question as still capable of hurting the susceptibility of the judges, it is not implausible that those who suffered from it at the time would react in some way, as could have been this of disguising their right to the maximum authority and guarantees by means of elaborating some documents that, as well as including it, giving credible reason to their origins and recognition, would serve to be presented and claimed at a given moment.[69] It being, therefore,

---

69 This way of reacting in the face of the right of appeal of neighboring communities privileged with the fueros of others does not constitute an isolated incident. A similar incident appeared to have taken place in Jaca, but in an opposite sense, occurred sometime later in Carmona with the aim of avoiding the obligatory appeal to Seville. On this, see Ana Mª Barrero García, "El fuero de Carmona," in *Actas del I Congreso de Historia de Carmona. Edad Media. Congreso conmemorativo del 750 aniversario de la conquista de la ciudad de Carmona por Fernando III. 1247. Carmona (Sevilla), 22 al 25 de septiembre de 1997* (Sevilla: Centro de Estudios Ramón Areces, 1998), 387–413.

a question that impacted the neighboring community, one must assume that the initiative had to have come from the municipal realm, even if the analysis of the documents points to one single material author, probably a jurist and, if not from Jaca, then linked to the *villa*, perhaps with some religious connection and, whatever the case, trained in or at least aware of and impressed by the study of Montpellier.[70]

But if the results of the document critique have allowed us to uncover the history of these foral documents, by themselves they are insufficient to test the reconstruction of the process of forming Jaca law during its early life. For that it is necessary to turn to other testimonies, those which provide the documents that give an account of its diffusion.

The Diffusion of the Fuero of Jaca

The Documented Testimonies

There are plenty of testimonies about the diffusion of the Fuero of Jaca in Navarre, either in direct or mediate form, and to somewhat less extent in Aragon. This expansion of Jaca law was due, to judge from the documents preserved, to royal initiative[71] and it appears

---

70 One could deduce the possible ecclesiastical nature of the author from the resort in these documents to certain formulas, such as spiritual sanction, whose use in this era seems limited to documents of this type, as well as the appreciation of a certain humanitarian tendency evident in certain norms (see note 39). Likewise, the patent tendency toward Catalonian ways in rewriting these documents forces us to doubt their Jaca origin, while mention of Montpellier in relation to tributes, in some way in accordance with the legal reality of the region at this and previous times, as well as situating a legal educational environment in Jaca allows one to presuppose at least direct knowledge by this jurist of the neighboring French city. See Carlo Guido Mor, "A l'origine de l'ecole de Montpellier: Rogerius ou Placentinus?" *Recueil de mémoires et travaux. Société d'Histoire du Droit et des Institutions des Anciens Pays de Droit Ecrit* 6 (1967), 145–55; André Gouron, "Autour de Placentin à Montpellier: Maître Gui et Pierre de Cardona," *Studia Gratiana* 19 (1976), 337–54.

71 All the documents on the concession of the fuero to Jaca or those related to them are presented as royal concessions, except in the case of an initiative on the part of Abbot Jimeno de Leire, in 1173, to establish a settlement originating in Yesa, Benasa, San Vicente, and Centulifontes opposite the old gatehouse of the monastery that must have been regulated by the Fuero of Jaca, reserving for the monastery a monopoly on baking bread and the rights that, according to Jaca law, corresponded to the king. The project did not prosper. The document is published as doc. 332, Ángel J. Martín Duque, *Documentación medieval de Leire (siglos XI a XII)* (Pamplona: Institución Príncipe de Viana, 1983), 429–30.

intimately tied, especially in Navarre, to the repopulating process generated along the Camino de Santiago route.

The first concessions of the Fuero of Jaca, according to general acceptance, go back to Sancho Ramírez, even if the relevant documents have not been preserved. The settlements they were destined for were those of the original burgs of Sangüesa and Estella. On the former, the reference comes from his son, the Battler, when he confirmed, possibly in 1117, the fueros given by his father, whom he does not identify specifically,[72] either then or even years later after extending it to the new burg (1122) or even when he granted that of this to Asín (1132). However, in mid-century, in 1158, this similarity was revealed as an indubitable fact, since Sancho VI, on confirming the fueros of the new burg, established that "*secundum vestrum forum de Iaka habeatis vestrum iudicium*," and also in 1186, when, in extending the settlement to Pueyo de Castellón, he did so by means of "*el fuero de Jaca que an los francos del burgo de Sangüesa.*"[73] The concession of the fuero to Estella by King Sancho is only verified to by its confirmation by his homonym the Wise; however, there is evidence that, in 1122, its population had a normative body that was granted to the settlers of Puente la Reina by Alfonso I. Nothing is said in the first concession of the Estella fuero nor in other later ones about the origins of its norms, which as in the case of Sangüesa, were understood as coming from Jaca, at least at the time of its confirmation.[74] Perhaps it was always like this, but in any event one must still be aware of the different attitude of the Battler toward these two *villas*, in both of which he recognized their own law as his, while wherever he sought to establish a new settlement, whether in Aragon (Ainsa and the new burg of Alquézar in 1127) or in Navarre (San Cernín in Pamplona in 1129), he did not hesitate

---

72   On the error in the dating, see Lacarra and Martín Duque, *Fueros de Navarra I. Fueros derivados de Jaca: 2. Pamplona*, 115.

73   On the date of the Fuero of Pueyo de Castellón, see Ángel J. Martín Duque, "Sancho VI de Navarra y el fuero de Vitoria," in *Vitoria en la Edad Media. Actas del I Congreso de estudios históricos celebrado en esta ciudad del 21 al 26 de septiembre de1981 en conmemoración del 800 aniversario de su fundación* (Vitoria-Gasteiz: Ayuntamiento de Vitoria-Gasteiz, 1982), 292n6.

74   Thus one must deduce that the Fuero of Estella begins with clauses from the Fuero of Jaca reproduced in the confirmation of Ramiro II, but no document exists in which it is specifically stated as relating to Sangüesa. On the Fuero of Estella, see note 76.

to turn to the Fuero of Jaca. With the separation of the kingdoms, its diffusion would follow its own rhythm in each one of them: in Aragon, making Zaragoza the capital and its repopulation on the basis of the Fuero of Sobrarbe would relegate its importance to a secondary level, which thereafter would only extend, on the initiative of Ramón Berenguer, to the settlements of Luesia (1154) and Berdún (1158),[75] and of Alfonso II to Pueyo de Pintano (1162)

---

75 I do not know if this fuero has been published. In any event and given that it does not appear in the collection collected by Mª Luisa Ledesma Rubio in *Cartas de población del Reino de Aragón en los siglos medievales*, I believe it opportune to transcribe it here, taken from AHN, Clero, San Juan de la Peña, carp. 714, no. 20:
Jaca, 1158, March.
In nomine sanctisimi et incomparabilis boni quod Deus est. Ego Raimundus, Dei gratia comes Barchinonensis et princeps aragonensis facio hanc cartam ingenuitatis sive franchetatis vobis populatoribus de Berdun. Placuit mihi libenti animo et spontanea voluntate et propter amorem:
[1] Quod populetis in Berdun a fuero de Iacca et fichetis de bono corde.
[2] Facio vobis franchos et liberos sine cisso malo de Starrun in iuso et de cuello de Bailo en entro et de illo cuello de Sangorrin en entro et de illo cuello de Baos en entro et de Mianos en suso et de Osoast en suso et de illa Cote en suso.
[3] Et de ista terminera en entro mando ad totos meos realencos qui ibi veniatis populare com vestro capomaso de ista pascha ad unno anno quod similiter sedeatis franchos et ingenuos et habeatis vestras hereditates liberas.
[4] Et non detis iuditio ad nullum hominem neque accipiatis in Berdun sicuti in Iacha.
[5] Et in vestro bobulares vetatos, si mataverit baca quod matetis eam, et si ovis ibi mataverit, similiter.
[6] Et mando de Larota et de la Rosselga et de Artasso, de istis tribus villis quod veniat illa decima ad Berdun, illo directo de episcopo exiendo.
[7] Et de totos illos scalidos de ista terminera suprascripta quod veniat illa decima tota ad Berdun.
[8] Et si aliquis infanzon venerit populare ibi talem habeat hereditatem quam habeat unde venit.
[9] Et in ista terminera en entro et in toto meo regalenco mando quod talgetis mattera et ligna.
[10] Et mando adhuc quod habeatis ibi mercato in die iovis post illos martes mercato de Iacca.
[11] Et ullus homo qui fecerit disturbo ad illos homines de mea terra qui venerit ad illo merchato in venita aut in ita pectabit mihi mille solidos.
[12] Et nullo francho aut iudeo qui ibi populaverit non donet letzda in tota mea terra.
Et hoc meum donativum vel ingenuamentum sicut superius est scriptum a fuero de Iacca laudo et confirmo ut habeatis et possideatis vos et filii vestri et omnis generatio vel posteritas vestra, salva mea fidelitate et de omni mea posteritate per cuncta seculorum secula, amen.
S[ignum] + RAIMUNDI COMES
Signum Adefonsi + Regis Aragonensium et comes barchinonensium
Facta carta in era Mª Cª LXª VIª, in mense marcio, in villa quod vocatur Iacha. Regnante me, Dei gratia in Barchinona et in Aragone et in Superarbe vel in Ripacurcia et in Lerida atque in Tortosa. Episcopus Petrus in Caesaraugusta, episcopus Martinus in Tarazona, espiscopus Dodo in Oscha, episscopus Guillelmus Petre in Lerida, comes Arnal Mir palgariemsis in Fraga et in Boil, don Fertungo in Estata, Fertun Dat in Barbastro et in Petraselze, Galin Xemenonis in Alkala, Ferriz in Oscha et in Sancta Eulalia, Arnal de Lascun in Boleia, Arpa in Luarre, Sancio de Borgia in Agierbe, Corneige in Morello, Loherrenc in Auguero, don Marcho in Biele, Petro Lopez in Luesia, Deus Aiusa in Sos et in Argedas, Alaman in Luna, Garces Almorabet in Exea, Balles in Toguste, Fortunio

and Santa María de Uncastillo (1169). This was not how it happened in the neighboring kingdom, where it was most widely diffused, although through its own matrixes, Estella and Pamplona, but not so much Sangüesa, whose expansion barely passed the limits of its own surroundings. The projection of the Estella fuero was the first temporally, that of greater spatial transcendence, and the most intimately tied to the phenomenon of pilgrimages. Thus, following its already mentioned concession to Puente la Reina by the Battler, Olite (1147) and Monreal (1149) as well as Villavieja received it from his successor. A second moment marks the activity of Sancho VI, who did not restrict himself to recognizing formally the Estella law by means of its specific confirmation.[76] Instead, he was conscious of its efficacy, and used it to favor the development of the *villa* with new settlements in San Juan and the Arenal, but also that of distant settlements like San Sebastian, thereby opening up a new

---

Acenariz in Tiraza et in Unocastello, don Blascho, maiordomo, in Borga, Palazin in Alagon et Hariza, Petrus de Castellazola in Calataiub, Sancio Enecones in Darocha et in Mercuello, Galin Xemenez in Belgit.

Ego Petrus de Anguero iussu domini mei comitis hanc cartam scripsit et de manu mea hoc signum + feci.

76 The Latin publication of the oldest Fuero of Estella, recognized as edition *A* buy its editors, concludes, in accordance with the attribution of its preamble, with the eschatocol clauses in a document of Sancho VI, issued in Estella in the month of April 1164, a date that fully corresponds to the personal mentions that accompany the ruler's formula, as well as with the functions of the scribe who confirms it, Jimeno. Of the manuscripts know today, it is estimated that the oldest, preserved in the municipal archive, could be an original twelfth-century document. However, the analysis carried out here on this document in comparison with the Fuero of Jaca and its confirmation by Ramiro II allow us to harbor some doubts about the registering of this document, as well as King Sancho's scope of confirmatory activity. As regards its potential original reputation, the verification of literal similarities between the text in edition *B* and the Jaca text that do not appear in *A*, included in the Estella document (see above), incline one to speculate about the possibility of a model prior to both publications closest to that. From the document point of view attention is called, in the supposition that it is a case of a chancellery document, to the servility of the protocol clauses in relation to the document of Ramiro II, while those of the eschatocol correspond with the chancellery practice of the grantor monarch, even if one can appreciate an excessive parallelism in the formulation between the confirmatory clause and the preamble, and the omission of the king's name in the ruler's formula. This being the case and always subject to more expert opinions, one could advance the possibility that the Fuero of Estella that we know today may not be the text confirmed by Sancho VI but, on the contrary, was instead shaped in the heart of the council, on the basis of royal activity of this nature, whether of a generic reach or with specific reference to the Fuero of Jaca (which at that time would be the content in the confirmation of Ramiro II), duly documented, whose final clauses were used to shape formally the foral document. Moreover, one can detect this practice in other local Navarrese settings at this time and even later. See Ana Mª Barrero García, "Las redacciones navarras del fuero de Logroño," *Príncipe de Viana* 53, no. 196 (1992), 409–28.

and broad frame of expansion for this law. A third moment, already late, occurred under Theobald II, who, following the steps of his antecessor, did not just concern himself with updating the fuero by means of opportune expansions and reforms,[77] but who also conceded it to Tiebas and Torralba. Hence, when in the fourteenth century there was a move to collect in a codex the texts of Navarrese law, it would appear among them, as itself, the *Libro de los fueros de Estella, de Olite, de Mont Real, e del Puente et de Tebas.*[78] The second focus of temporal (although not so much of intense) diffusion of Jaca law in Navarre was Pamplona following, as is well-known, the progressive extension of the fuero conceded by Alfonso I to the Frankish population settled in San Saturnino to other neighborhoods in the city, first to the new settlement of San Nicolás, and finally also to the episcopal district of Navarrería. Thus, the reason for the first concession of this fuero to the Frankish enclave in the Navarrese capital was based on its position on the western route of the Camino de Santiago;[79] while its gradual application to the rest of the urban area responded to the political necessity to put an end to the rivalries that had emerged among the different peoples who lived therein.[80] Nevertheless, the privilege of King Alfonso lost its original character, and thus in 1174 Sancho VI conceded it to the Franks that had settled in the plain of Iriberri. However, after this initial settlement did not prosper, when ten years later the monarch tried to revive the site by founding a new *villa*, Villava, he had to turn to the statute of San Nicolás to fit the Navarrese town into that, as was done some years after that with Alesves (later Villafranca), in which there is no record that outsiders settled.[81] Nonetheless, these differences that affected the personal condition of the settlers

---

77   This is a text included in edition B. On the scope of this reform, see Lacarra and Martín Duque, *Fueros de Navarra I. Fueros derivados de Jaca: 1. Estella-San Sebastián,* 33.

78   This codex is preserved in the library at the University of Salamanca, ms. 2652, originally from the royal library, ms. 944; the Fuero of Estella is in folios129r.–138. See ibid., 33.

79   In fact, among the first fuero charters for the settlements in which the Fuero of Jaca was applied, it was only in this one that a norm relating to pilgrims appeared, except, of course for the treatment to which they were subject in that corresponding to the seal of the Fuero of Estella (II, 8).

80   On all this, see Lacarra and Martín Duque, *Fueros de Navarra I. Fueros derivados de Jaca: 2. Pamplona,* 27–37.

81   Ibid., 76.

did not impede them from being governed according to the same normative body, the Fuero of Jaca, as proof of the fact that one of the extensively published codices preserved to this day is a translation of that publication into Navarrese Romance by a notary from Villafranca, García Martínez.[82] However, that did not mean that the Fuero of San Cernín lost its specific character as a statute for the Frankish population, as was evident by its concession by Theobald II to the *villa* of Lanz, nor its symbolic value as a privileged fuero, since there can be no other motive in extending it to the villa of Urroz, somewhat extemporaneously, as it was also in that of the Fuero of Jaca to Santisteban de Lerin.[83]

Thus, following the diffusion of the Fuero of Jaca via the documents preserved provides one with a clear idea of how exhaustive this was and of how wide-ranging it was in space and time. Less expressive, though, it seems, are the texts we have at our disposal when it comes to figuring out what law was hidden beneath this label of guarantee that constituted the mere mention of the Fuero of Jaca. The fact is that, in general, although these documents usually accompany that concession of a normative body of varying extension, but in any event shorter than that held to be the original one of Jaca, there is a tendency to consider it as particular dispositions of each place, only coinciding in minimal ways, except in the case of Estella, with the norms contained therein. That said, we have seen how document critique, in suggesting the possibility that it was a later re-elaboration of the Aragonese *villa* law, obliges the scholar to begin from other starting points. In this respect, one fact is extraordinarily revealing: when Ramón Berenguer conceded the Fuero of Jaca to Luesia in 1154, he did so generically without specifying its content, except to mark out an exception relating to the war levy obligation, of which, it would seem, the Jaca townspeople were free for seven years. The fact that this norm also appeared in the Fuero of Asín (which received that of Sangüesa), clarifying that once the period signaled ended, they would have to come to the aid of the king in battle, leads one to assume that, under the conditions

82   See Molho, *El fuero de Jaca*, xxiv–xxvi.
83   See Lacarra and Martín Duque, *Fueros de Navarra I. Fueros derivados de Jaca: 2. Pamplona*, 76.

established by that stipulated in the edition of Ramiro II and also in that of Sancho Ramírez, this norm could have appeared among those of the first foral privilege of Jaca, conceded probably by King Sancho himself.[84] On the basis of this clue it does not seem to bold to attempt a hypothetical reconstruction through the comparative study and textual collation of the different texts that, on being a concession of the Fuero of Jaca or its similes, make up this foral family.

Comparative Analysis of the Texts Related to the Fuero of Jaca

Logically, from among the documents previously alluded to on the extension of the Jaca fuero, those that offer information about normative development, which is not always the case, are the only ones of use in this regard. As in the case of Luesia, the documents Monreal and Tiebas are limited to a mere mention of the fuero conceded. In others, meanwhile, such as those relating to the settlements of San Juan and the Arenal as regards the Fuero of Estella, or that of Santa María de Uncastillo and Torralba, the scarce dispositions they contain refer to matters such as a demand for payment for a specific census, the rights of the church of Santa María, or the conditions of settlement for the lower nobility (an issue in which one observes the variants imposed by repopulating needs), which affect privately each one of them. Hence, I have opted to leave out some of these on account of their irrelevance for the task.

Thus, taking as my guide the Fuero of Jaca by Sancho Ramírez,[85] I will proceed to undertake a comparative analysis by means of collating the following texts: those of Sangüesa in 1117 and 1122, Puente la Reina, Alquézar, Ainsa, Pamplona, Asín, Jaca by Ramiro II, Olite, Berdún, Pueyo de Pintano, Estella, Iriberri, and Pueyo de Castellón.

---

84 Moreover, this possibility allows one to explain the strange addition in the norm about the war levy obligation in the fuero known today as that of Sancho Ramírez, establishing the perpetual character of this norm with respect to his successors (see above) as a preventative measure before any potential allegation of original privilege.

85 Similarly, this analysis takes into account Ramiro II's confirmation that reproduces the normative content as well as the norms themselves that form part of this privilege. However, the privilege of Alfonso II has been left out of this analysis because it does not present any concurrence with the documents of interest.

As a prior step, it is worth noting that as regards the nature of all the documents, in no case do we have access to the original texts themselves, given that they are only known through later copies, more or less close to the date of their concession. Nonetheless, their document analysis reveals a high degree of accuracy in relation to the originals,[86] since no appreciable anomalies appear therein in their document clauses. The only exceptions to this include some errors in dating that have been detected and which, conveniently, have been corrected by critiques;[87] and the presence of additions to the original normative body in those of the new burg of Sangüesa, Alquézar, and Asín.[88]

Securing the Existing Concurrences Among the Texts

The comparative study of the different texts has been undertaken on the basis of establishing existing similarities among them on the basis of the treatment of the same suppositions, independent of the degree of similarity in their approach, formulation, and solutions adopted in each case. The similarities thus established are included in the following relations of concurrences.[89]

---

86 Only in one case, that of the Fuero of Pueyo de Castellón, does it seem to not be a question of a faithful copy of an original text, but of a Romance version elaborated on the basis of the original, but conveniently updated, as becomes evident in the clause relating to the delimitation of the boundaries of the *villa*, which is excessively detailed and meticulous in comparison to what is typical in documents of a foundational character.

87 For example, 1117 is established as the year of confirming the fuero for the old burg of Sangüesa in Lacarra and Martín Duque, *Fueros de Navarra I. Fueros derivados de Jaca: 2. Pamplona*, 115; for Alquézar in Lacarra, "Alfonso el Batallador y las paces de Támara," *Estudios de Edad Media de la Corona de Aragón* 3 (1947–1948), 461–73; for Ainsa in José Mª Lacarra, *Documentos para el estudio de la reconquista y repoblación del valle del Ebro (números 1 a 319)* (Zaragoza; Anúbar, 1982), 165; and for Pueyo de Castellón in Martín Duque, "Sancho VI de Navarra y el fuero de Vitoria," 292n6.

88 The last norm in the Fuero of Sangüesa appears inserted between royal confirmations and the dating clause and is just an enlargement of a previous norm referring to use of the term; in that of Alquézar between the date and confirmation of the scribe a norm is introduced regarding the day the market is held, and in that of Asín the additions appear incorporate between the comminatory clause and that of royal sanction and between this and the diverse royal confirmations.

89 In order to create this, it was necessary to proceed to the distribution of its normative content in paragraphs and to the numeration of these following the guidelines established by the texts in their editions, except in the case of the confirmation of the Fuero of Jaca by Ramiro II in relation to the numeration offered by Lacarra, adapted to the concurrences therein with the fuero of Sancho Ramírez. The signatures that appear in the first column are merely indicative of the material under study in the supposition, those that follow correspond to each of the texts indicated by its corresponding

	J	S	Sn	PR	Al	A	P	As	JR	O	B	PP	E	I	C
Fuero Concession	1	3	2	8	3	1	1	3	pr	1/3	1	4	pr	2	1
New arable land	2	-	-	3	2	-	-	14	-	6	-	2/5	-	1	-
Crime against King	3	-	-	-	-	-	-	-	-	-	-	-	-	-	-
Idem	4	-	-	-	-	-	-	-	-	-	-	-	-	-	-
Homicide / theft	5	-	-	-	-	-	-	-	-	-	-	-	II.7	-	-
War levy	6							8	1				1.1		
Exemption	7	-	4	-	1	-	-	-	2	-	2/33	2.1	7	7	-
Year and day	8	-	-	9	-	-	-	-	3	-	-	-	2.2	-	-
Plains	9	2	11	5	-	5	2	2	4	-	9	6	3	4	6
Trial by combat	10	-	-	-	-	-	-	5	5	-	-	-	4.1	-	-
Securities	11	-	-	-	-	-	-	-	6	-	-	-	5	-	-
Statutory rape	12	-	-	-	-	-	-	-	7	-	-	-	6	-	-
Arms	13	-	-	-	6	-	-	-	8	-	-	-	7.1	-	-
Homicide	14	-	-	-	7	-	-	-	9	-	-	-	7.2	-	-
Assault	15	-	-	-	-	-	-	-	10	-	-	-	7.2	-	-
Idem	16	-	-	-	-	-	-	-	11	-	-	-	7.2	-	-
Public order	17	-	-	-	-	-	-	-	12	-	-	-	8	-	-

initial(s), arranged in chronological order.

Fine for false accusation	18	-	-	-	-	-	15	13	-	-	-	9	-	-
Trials	19	-	-	2	-	4	14	-	4	-	-	10.1	-	-
False measures	20	-	-	-	-	-	15	-	-	-	-	11	-	-
Mills	21	-	-	2ª	-	13	16	-	-	-	-	-	-	-
Lower nobility	22	6	7	-	4	-	-	2	8	7	13	5	-	-
Prison for debt	23	-	-	-	-	-	-	-	-	-	2.22	-	-	-
Servant indemnity	24	-	-	-	-	-	-	-	-	-	2.26	-	-	-
Town limits	-	1	1	4	-	1	-	5	2	8	-	3	4	-
Tributes	-	3ª	-	3	-	7	17	-	12	-	-	-	5	-
Burg foundation	-	1	-	-	-	-	-	-	-	-	-	-	-	-
Donation	-	7	-	-	-	-	-	-	-	-	-	-	-	-
Royal seigneury	-	8	-	-	-	-	-	-	-	-	-	-	-	-
Royal protection	-	9	-	7	-	-	-	4	-	-	-	-	-	-
Donation	-	10	-	-	-	-	-	-	-	-	-	-	-	-
Use of waters	-	-	2	-	-	-	-	-	-	-	-	-	-	-
Tithes	-	-	4	-	-	11	-	-	6-jul	-	-	-	-	-
Market	-	-	-	4	3	-	-	-	10	-	-	-	-	-
Protec. market	-	-	-	5	-	-	-	-	11	-	-	-	-	-
Tributes to merchants	-	-	-	9	-	-	-	-	-	-	-	-	-	-
Market day	-	-	-	10	-	-	-	-	-	-	-	-	-	-

Equality of fuero	–	–	–	–	–	–	5	–	–	–	–	7	–	6
Sales to pilgrims	–	–	–	–	–	–	6	–	–	–	–	–	–	–
Construction	–	–	–	–	–	–	7	–	–	–	–	–	–	–
Freedom to buy	–	–	–	–	–	–	–	6	–	–	–	–	–	–
Churches	–	–	–	–	–	–	–	10	–	–	–	–	–	–
Clerics	–	–	–	–	–	–	–	12	–	–	–	–	–	–
Excused	–	–	–	–	–	–	–	16	–	–	–	–	–	–
Baths	–	–	–	–	–	–	–	–	18	–	5	–	–	–
Pastures	–	–	–	–	–	–	–	–	–	–	–	8ª	–	–
Responsibility	–	–	–	–	–	–	–	–	–	–	–	–	I.12	–
Quarrels	–	–	–	–	–	–	–	–	–	–	–	–	I.14	–
Authorities	–	–	–	–	–	–	–	–	–	–	–	–	–	2
Settlers	–	–	–	–	–	–	–	–	–	–	–	–	---	3

Table 1: Table of Concurrences

Results of the Table of Concurrences

An examination of the data contained in this list of concurrences both from the perspective of the set as a whole (reading horizontally) and each of the texts individually in their relation to Jaca (vertically) reveals some facts worth highlighting:

In first place, only one supposition, that of the express concession of the fueros, is included in all the texts examined.

Several others are contained by a variable number, but in most, of the texts examined. Of these, most are found in the Fuero of Jaca, but not two: one, relating to the concession of terms that does not appear in the Fuero of Jaca (nor in its confirmations or that of Estella), is included by all the rest except that of Pamplona; another, relating to the foral plains, is addressed by all the texts except those of Alquézar and Olite. Two suppositions, on the exemption from franchises (either personal or on goods) and settlement by the lower nobility, do not appear in six texts, but not always the same ones. Both are lacking in the Fueros of the old burg of Sangüesa, Ainsa, and Asín, while the former is also missing from those of Puente la Reina, Pamplona, and Olite, while the latter, however, is not in that of Alquézar, the confirmation of the Fuero of Jaca (though not of Estella), and that of Pueyo de Castellón.

Besides these suppositions included in most of the texts, two more are also addressed in a good number of them. One, relating to the appropriation of space, is in the Fuero of Jaca by Sancho Ramírez (although not in its confirmation, nor in that of Estella), and in those of Puente la Reina, Alquézar, Asín, Olite, Pueyo de Pintano, and Iriberri. The second, the exemption from tributes, whose concession to Jaca was due to Ramiro II, appears included in the Fueros of the old burg of Sangüesa, Asín, and Pueyo de Castellón, and also in those of Alquézar, Ainsa, and Berdún.

The remaining concurrences appear in four texts, or a number lower than that of the fueros involved. The precept relating to the holding of trials in the *villa* is included in those of Jaca, Ainsa, Asín, and Berdún. And also, apart from the Fuero of Jaca, there is a fourfold concurrence in relation to the supposition on royal protection of urban limits, which is in the texts of the new burg of Sangüesa, Puente la Reina, and Olite, and Ainsa.

Five suppositions appear in three texts: two of them, on homicide and the exemption from the royal monopoly on milling, are common to the Fueros of Jaca, Alquézar, and Asín; while another, on payment of tithes, is in those of Puente la Reina, Asín, and Berdún. The latter in turn is consistent with those of Alquézar and Pamplona in the norm on holding markets. And finally, that of Pamplona is consistent with those of Pueyo de Pintano and Iriberri in establishing the equality of the fuero as a supposition independent of any other formulation.

Finally, there are six concurrences that occur in just two texts: the Fuero of Jaca coincides with that of Asín in the approach to the war levy and trial by combat, with that of Puente la Reina in establishing the prescription as one year and one day, and with that of Alquézar in sanctioning the use of arms in the *villa*. For its part, the Fuero of Berdún is consistent with that of Alquézar in concerning itself with protection of the market, and with that of Pueyo de Pintano in addressing enclosures.

Apart from these concurrences, several fueros present a series of precepts that should be considered exclusive to each of them. The highest number corresponds, logically, given its greatest reach, to the Fuero of Jaca by Sancho Ramírez, with eleven; followed by those of the new burg of Sangüesa and Asín, with four; then Alquézar, Estella, and Pueyo de Castellón, with two; and just one, the donation of rents from baths by Ramiro II to Jaca on confirming its fuero.[90]

Looking at the list according to the so-called Jaca model, the first thing to point out is that the text that presents the greatest number of similarities, in line with its greatest extension (sixteen), is that of Asín, with nine. However, such concurrences are in no

---

90   This same character of privileged concession and not norm of a perceptive scope of other clearly singular ones in each place, such as 1,7, and 10 in Sangüesa, 7 in Pamplona, and 3 in Pueyo de Castellón, which makes them of little significance for our purposes here. This is not the case of those norms likewise of a privileged character that are included in several texts, like the exemption from tributes.

way proportional to the normative content of the corresponding texts, nor either does the chronological factor seem to have less of an effect on that. Thus, following the order in which they are presented, one can observe how, of the three norms contained in old burg of Sangüesa, two correspond to that, and of the eleven in the new burg, the figure is four; of the nine in Puente la Reina, five; of the ten in Alquézar, six; of the seven in Ainsa, three, figures comparable to those of Pamplona; of the six in Olite, likewise three; of the twelve in Berdún, five; the same number out of the nine in Pueyo de Pintano and seven in Iriberri; and finally, only three of the seven contained in the text of Pueyo de Castellón.

Second, it is also significant that these concurrences are in all of them related to one or another of the same suppositions, those previously mentioned in the perspective of the set as a whole, as well as the fact that, in the case of several fueros there are no similarities with that of Jaca except in the said suppositions. What is more, these always correspond, except in the case of Puente la Reina, to Navarrese towns, while their Aragonese counterparts,[91] that is, those developed outside or tangential to pilgrimage phenomenon, demonstrate a greater relationship, even though these are in any event limited, since as a group they resemble eight precepts in the Jaca model.

These observations allow one to highlight some initial results in relation to the genesis of this law and its formulation, to the point of summarizing the fueros that have come down to us today.

First, despite dealing with typical matters in documents of this nature, the presence of the same suppositions, six in total, in most of these fueros reveals the existence of a base common to all of them. This base is only included in its totality in the Fuero of the new burg of Sangüesa,[92] and not in that of Jaca in the form it is known today.

---

91 With the exception of Pueyo de Pintano, whose five concurrences with the Fuero of Jaca occur, precisely, in the five suppositions common to all or most of the texts.

92 It is true that, as it appears in the table of concurrences, the extension of tributes does not appear to be formulated explicitly in that text, perhaps because this is the only specific reference of a normative character included in the confirmation of the fuero of the old burg by Alfonso I, which, just five years later, would be extended to the new

Furthermore, one must caution that the nominal relationship that exists through the texts does not always match the normative content. Thus, while Asín was conceded *"fueros tales quales donavi ad illo burgo novo de Sangüesa,"* several of the norms therein have do not appear in them, but instead in the suppositions addressed in the Fuero of Jaca. No less significant is the case of the Fuero of Iriberri with respect to its Pamplona matrix, given that, of its seven precepts, two of them do not appear formulated in the model followed.

Other concurrences that emerge in only some of the texts, all of them in Aragonese towns, seem to indicate a closer relationship among themselves. The most obvious one, on account of concerning five suppositions, appears in the Fueros of Jaca, Alquézar, and Asín insofar as they all coincide in contemplating two suppositions, to which one should add two more that Alquézar does not include, and a third that Asín lacks.

Finally, there are still concurrences among texts whose only relationship, among themselves, is that derived from the possible community of origin that, however, does not correspond to that recognized specifically in their texts. Such is the case with the supposition on the decimation obligation in the Fueros of Puente la Reina (Estella), Asín (Sangüesa), and Berdún (Jaca). On the contrary, the concurrence in regulating markets between Alquézar and Berdún finds its raison d'être, if not in the fuero, then in Jaca practice.[93] Although theres is still the possibility of a normative relationship based on an independent and casuistic formulation of fairly extended consuetudinary law in the Upper Aragon region, such as that between Berdún and Pueyo de Pintano in regulating livestock grazing land.[94]

---

town.

93   The holding of the market in Jaca was not recognized officially until 1197, and was thus established through a privilege of Pedro II. However, the Fuero of Berdún (§ 10), dated 1158, demonstrates at least a de facto reality of this accepted as such, which conditions its regulations as regards the very day it is held.

94   In this respect, it is worth recalling, in account of their connection with this topic, the previously analyzed norms in the confirmation of the Fuero of Jaca by Alfonso II (see above). Among those of possible statutory origin are several regarding theft and livestock indemnity that, in some ways, recall that established in the Fuero of Berdún.

Textual Analysis of the Concurrences

A comparative analysis of the different texts on the basis of the concurrences established in accordance with the Fuero of Jaca reveals their different behavior with respect to the fuero according to how the diverse suppositions are treated. These suppositions can be differentiated in the following way.

Suppositions in which there is greatest concurrence: As regards the suppositions common to Jaca and other fueros, there are five, all of them relating to population settlement, and characterized by their essential similarity, even though one still detects some variants that are more evident than others, whether in their approach or in the solutions, which frequently respond to the need to adapt the norms to the special space-time circumstances of each place. As to their formulation, in no case is there a fully expressive literal relationship among some of the fueros analyzed; yet they still offer hints at the existence of possible textual models, which, however, cannot be identified with any of them.

With regard to the variants in the approach of these suppositions, the most obvious affect those relating to the state of exemption (§ 7);[95] land appropriation (§ 2); and the settlement of certain groups of people (§ 22). In the first of these, as opposed to the Fuero of Jaca and those of Navarre, in which the privilege applies to properties acquired by settlers, those of Alquézar, Berdún, and Pueyo de Pintano apply it to the settlers themselves. If this difference of approach could give rise to doubts about the similarity of this norm, these are resolved when checking how, precisely, the Aragonese texts follow the literal nature of that of Jaca in clarifying their scope in identical terms by means of the expression "*sine ullo malo cisso*," a characteristic of the Jaca text and, it seems, not easy to comprehend in this context, at least some time later.[96] The use of

---

95   Reference to the paragraph number must be understood in relation to the Fuero of Jaca when it is included therein, or on the contrary to the oldest fuero that includes it.

96   Although this norm presents the same formulation in the fuero of Sancho Ramírez and in its confirmation by Ramiro II, conversely, it seems that it was necessary to clarify the term in the Fuero of Estella, already in its *A* edition, given that it had to resort to the expression "*sine ullo malo interdicto vel cisso*," and even more in the *B* edition, in

this phrase by the texts of Alquézar and Berdún reveals their mutual relationship, whether immediate or derived from the ue of the same model, which is obviously not the known one of Jaca and would not be too different from the model followed by the new burg of Sangüesa, since they coincide with this in adding the terms *"libre"* and *"ingenuo"* used by Jaca, that of *"franco."* For its part, the Fuero of Pueyo de Pintano does not contain the phrase of the bad census, but in its formulation coincides to the letter with that of Alquézar, while that of Pueyo de Castellón offers its own out of the precept of Sangüesa, as does Iriberri with respect to that of Jaca, whatever this may be.

The norm on the disposition of space, with its approach and solution being one and the same, that is, its free appropriation, presents diverse formulations in the various fueros that include it. In contrast to the greater abstraction in the Fuero of Jaca in which the precept seems to be aimed at guaranteeing the property acquired freely as opposed to third parties (*claudat suam partem secumdum suum posse*), the rest specify their scope whether concerning inheritance (Asín and Olite), land (Pueyo de Pintano and Iriberri), or both (Puente la Reina and Alquézar). For their part, those of Puente la Reina, Alquézar, Asín, and Olite coincide in expressing the logical limitation to non-cultivated lands in a specific space, which in the first is detected in the possibility of returning daily to the *villa*, while in those of Alquézar and Asín this faculty affects royalty without any express limit, although, as in the case of Olite, it is understood in relation to the term assigned. Of the other two fueros, that of Pintano refers only to the person allocated the dwelling, while that of Iriberri contemplates with an expressive *"et cetera"* that of all useful buildings. From an editing point of view one should point out a dual similarity: once again, that of Iriberri with Jaca in the use of the same formula, *"secundum suum posse,"* so characteristic of the Jaca text as in that of the precious supposition; on the other hand,

---

which both terms are replaced by *"sine aliquo impedimento"* (see note 27). For kits part, the Fuero of Iriberri, which includes it, avoids the expression and replaces it with its precise content *"nichil redditus inde redentes."* Concerning this, one should likewise point out the expression *"ullo malo fuero,"* which in the text of Alquézar precedes, by means of the linking verb *"atque,"* that commented on.

that of the five remaining places, with the particularity that on this occasion the absolute literal nature of the text of Pueyo de Pintano comes about in relation to not that of Alquézar, but that of Puente la Reina.

There is an essential difference in the approach of the supposition on non-burg population settlement in the Fuero of Jaca and the others that include it. Nevertheless, it is a question of the validity of the same principle, the refusal or admission of specific social groups according to their fiscal condition, which all the texts formulate specifically, while in that of Jaca does so in an indirect way by means of prohibiting the transfer of inheritances via their donation or sale. Given that this norm included in the fuero of Sancho Ramírez seems to have not been formulated for Jaca until 1197 (see note 40), one would think that its presence therein could have been due to an urge to update the original text in which the old principle of exclusion would have appeared, as it appears formulated in some foundational texts that define it like that. Apart from this, there are still differences among the texts that offer the same approach to the question. The most important of these affects the solution, given that the Navarrese ones, except that of Olite, define exclusion, while the Aragonese ones choose the opposite. For their part, among those, one observes a gradually more liberal application of the norm when obligatorily mediating the consent of the people in Iriberri, and in Estella also by the king,[97] the raison d'être of which could have been demonstrated with the passing of time, as well as also in the population needs of each locality. Similarly, variants show up in the scope of the norm, since it is aimed at the lower nobility in the new burg of Sangüesa (and here too to those of the old burg) and in Puente la Reina, it is maintained as it is in those of Berdún and Pueyo de Pintano, while in the Fuero of San Cernín (and following it in that of Iriberri) it would be extended to include Navarrese and clerics. The latter are not mentioned in that

---

97 It is worth recalling that this norm in the Fuero of Estella appears thereafter, in its precepts, to coincide with the Jaca text of Ramiro II. That which refers to the Navarrese and foreign clerics, excluding the lower nobility, seems to indicate that it is about extending the norm regarding the lower nobility to these groups, in all likelihood valid in Estella since it appears included in that of Puente la Reina.

of Olite, and nor are the lower nobility in the Estella precept. From the perspective of editions, the duality between the Navarrese and Aragonese texts remains with the exception of that of Olite, which also in this aspect resembles the Aragonese ones, while among those, which are very similar, one should underscore a formulary total similarity among those of Puente la Reina, Pamplona, and Iriberri.

The two remaining precepts only offer incidental variants in their formulation. In relation to the concession of fueros (§ 1), perhaps what most stands out with respect to the enunciation that the norm presents in that of Jaca is the absence in all of them of any reference (positive or negative) to the quality of the fueros and the circumstances in which they were requested by the settlers. As for the rest, the difference stems from presenting those of Sangüesa, as well as the respective confirmations of those of Jaca and Estella, as fueros conceded as particular to the place, referring the rest to a specific statute—that of Jaca, Estella, or Sangüesa—given that the dual identification is only found in the latest of the texts analyzed, that of Pueyo de Castellón. For its part, the text of Puente la Reina offers the singularity widening its extension to the Fuero of Estella with that of the prevailing "*usaticos vel consuetudines*" therein. The differences in the wording of the precept, which are very similar, occur in the verb(s) used to designate royal activity;[98] in the objective or subjective form (whether in relation to the king or to settlers) of referring to the statute conceded;[99] and in the way of specifying the generic scope of the precept when this is expressed.[100]

---

98   They are the following: "*concedo et confirmo*" in those of Jaca and Ainsa, "*confirmo*" in the old burg of Sangüesa, "*dono*" in those of the new burgs of Sangüesa and Asín, Alquézar, Olite, and Pueyo de Pintano, "*concedo*" in that of Puente la Reina, and, lastly, "*dono et concedo*" in those of Pamplona and Iriberri and in the confirmations of those of Jaca and Estella. The Fuero of Berdún links directly the concession of the fuero to the formula of protocol notification "*placuit mihi*."

99   The Fueros of Alquézar, Ainsa, Berdún, and los Pueyos de Pintano and Castellón present an objective formulation, with the particularity that all of them adhere to the Fuero of Jaca (identified in Castellón with that of Sangüesa); while there is a subjective formulation with reference to a royal act in those of Sangüesa and Asín and the confirmations of Jaca and Estella, and a subjective formulation in relation to settlers, which is unusual in that it refers to their request, in that of Jaca by Sancho Ramírez, and with reference to the statute of the place whose fuero was conceded in those of Puente la Reina and Olite, Pamplona and Iriberri.

100   With the particularity in this case of clear textual progression, such as in the Fuero of the old burg of Sangüesa ("*de letzdas et de totas alias causas*"), in that of Puente la Reina ("*in totas vestras causas et vestras faciendas*"), and in that of San Cernín in Pamplona and

The precept about the free use of grazing land and forests (§ 9) does not present any substantial variant in its formulation other than that of the delimitation of space, which is always the town limits of the place in question.[101] This was fixed by means of pertinent toponyms in this or another norm in the fuero, or it was done by concurrence with the surrounding territory whose extension did not impede the daily return to the *villa*, as in the case of the Fueros of Ainsa and Asín, a spatial measure that likewise applied the Fuero of Jaca and its confirmation, as well as that of Estella, to this norm;[102] and also the Battler's concessions to Navarrese towns for this surpassing the limits granted.[103] The wording of the precept, while there is no exact match in any case, presents a notable similarity that is less marked in Jaca text, although clearer in the second paragraph dedicated to this matter by the new burg of Sangüesa, and those of Ainsa, Asín, and Pintano, and to a lesser extent in that of Berdún, with a variation occurring however in the enunciation of rights that is also produced in those of Puente la Reina and Pamplona.[104] That one, without losing its formal similarity with the rest, appears closer to that of Jaca, which, in turn, resembles that of the old burg of Sangüesa in using the term "*silva*," a not irrelevant detail unless one treats it as a purely chance coincidence. For its part, the Fuero of Iriberri seems to follow the Pamplona model, although with its own formulation, as is the case also of that which offers the norm in that of Pueyo de Castellón.

As regards the suppositions that are not in the Fuero of Jaca, it is the case that, as in the second of the previous ones in the two suppositions linked closely to population settlement, the exemption

---

Iriberri ("*in totas vestras faziendas et vestros iudicios*").

101 With the exception of the Fuero of Pueyo de Castellón, which refers to "*todo meo regno*," which, possibly, has no other basis than an erroneous interpretation on the part of the author of this Romance version of the royal term that may have appeared in the transcript model.

102 With the particularity of extending the time to a full day for each trip (see F E I, 2).

103 That this extension to what the right to work in mountainous and grazing land recognized could have affected the town limits of other *villas* is acknowledged clearly by one of the norms dedicated to it in the Fuero of the new burg of Sangüesa, in referring expressly to the "*terminos alias villas in circuytu de Sangossa*."

104 It is once more a variant caused possibly by the difficulty of understanding a particular word, in this case that used by both the Sangüesa texts, "*lignare*." The Fuero of Puente la Reina overcomes the term by turning to the expression "*incidatis ligna*," which presents it as a disjunctive of "*talliare*," while the rest opt for its omission.

from tributes usually accompanies the particular core privileges in foundational charters. The absence of the norm regarding the concession of town limits (§ 1) in the Jaca texts known today does not rule out the possibility of its existence in a previous document, while in those of San Cernín and Alquézar it seems to be justified by being aimed at established settlements in a predetermined setting.[105] In the remaining texts, given their content, the formulation presents an autonomous nature in each of them, and one can only point out any evident formal and substantial similarity in the Fueros of Ainsa and Asín.[106]

It could be that, because they were necessary places of passage on the Camino de Santiago, there was no mention of exemption from tributes in the first statutes conceded to Jaca, Estella, and Pamplona.[107] However, it does appear to have prevailed in Sangüesa, perhaps on account of it being considered the main privilege conceded by Sancho Ramírez to the old burg, highlighted specifically by the Battler in confirming his fueros. And while it is true that it does not refer specifically to an exemption, it seems clear that this would be the case, and not just because it appears among the dispositions contained in the Fueros of Asín and Pueyo del Castellón, but because it was a typical privilege in concessions of this nature by King Sancho himself and also by his successor, Pedro I.[108] The exemption from tributes extended throughout the kingdom.

---

105 This is evident in the case of the San Cernín neighborhood, a specific locality within a wider urban area. As regards Jaca, although it remains likely that the norm may have appeared in its foundational document, it may not have been considered prudent to incorporate it in the confirmation of Ramiro II and in the later re-founding attributed to Sancho Ramírez, on account of not adapting what was established therein to the reality of the moment in which these documents were drawn up.

106 On the extent of this concurrence see my discussion above of the precept relating to foral plains.

107 Recall how the exemption from tributes in the Fuero of Jaca was a concession of Ramiro II. For its part, the original version of the Fuero of San Cernín in Pamplona does not include this norm, although it is included in an expanded version of the same fuero with a disposition, among other things, that excuses the townspeople from payment of tributes and turnpikes, which could have come about as a result of the confirmation by Sancho VI of the exemption from turnpike payments. See Lacarra and Martín Duque, *Fueros de Navarra I. Fueros derivados de Jaca: 2. Pamplona*, doc 8., and 25, 32, 85–86, and 127–28. As regards the Fuero of Estella, it concerns itself with regulating tributes in II, 59, but does not establish any exemption to the same extent as that in the fueros examined. The Fueros of Olite and Iriberri, faithful in it to their matrices, do not include the exemption.

108 That is what Sancho Ramírez did in conceding a fuero to the Navarrese town of

It is possible that its requirement, on leaving the kingdom, which is only referred to by the Fuero of Asín, was recognized as a general norm. With the exception of this clarification, the formulation of the norm is identical in all the texts, although in the Fuero of Berdún it appears applied to the Frankish and Jewish population. For its part, the Fuero of Castellón excuses not the payment of tributes but that of turnpikes on land and sea, which, without any doubt, one must attribute to an initiative of the author of the known version.[109]

Suppositions Common to the Fuero of Jaca and to the Aragonese Fueros

The seven precepts that make up this series offer similarly diverse behavior, since in there of them the variants affect basically the wording, in two also the approach but not the solution, while in a third this is affected by the distinct approach of the supposition. Likewise, the fueros that concern themselves with regulating the war levy offer a distinct and at least partial solution.

The greatest degree of similarity is found in the suppositions that deal with holding trials (§ 19), the use arms (§ 13), and trial by combat (§ 10). The first is included in the Fueros of Ainsa, Asín, and Berdún, which, like that of Jaca, exempt their inhabitants from any court appearance not held in the *villa*. The formulation of the precept, which is more unequivocal than those of Ainsa and Asín in specifying certain details, is more to the point in that of Jaca, perhaps on account of a similar wording to that of Asín, while that of Berdún, formally close to that of Jaca, reserves the possibility of development with a specific reference to that. In the second precept, common to the Fueros of Jaca and Alquézar, with the same supposition, there are still nuanced differences both in the approach and the solution. Thus, both sanction the offensive use of arms with a fine of one thousand *sueldos*, but that of Jaca offers as an alternative amputation of the hand. To that is added the fact that, here, the norm appears aimed at punishing action against a neighbor, while in that

---

Arguedas in 1092 and to those of Alquézar, Monzón, and Castellar in Aragón. Likewise, the privileges conceded by Pedro I to Huesca and Barbastro contain the exemption.

109 Recall how the tendency to exaggerate is likewise patent in this text in extending the right to exploitation within town limits to the whole kingdom. See note 101.

of Alquézar this reference is spatial in nature, in the burg or in the market, which implies that it goes beyond the demand of being part of the vicinity. In accordance with this great degree of evolution of the norm in the text of Alquézar, evident in these differences, the wording, which lacks the detailed enunciation of arms, appears implicit in its expression of intentionality, notwithstanding a possible immediate textual relationship that is difficult to clarify in the absence of other comparative elements. The norm on trial by combat is only included in the Fuero of Asín, which introduces variants on the Jaca formulation, in that it does not dwell on circumstantial aspects and offers a broader image of judicial procedure, given that it extends the prohibition to the test of red-hot iron and validity to swearing an oath. Diverse enunciations logically correspond to such differences.

Of the three norms in which the Aragonese texts differ in the approach of the same suppositions with respect to that of Jaca, two are in the Fueros of Alquézar and Asín, and the third only in the latter of these. The norm on mills (§ 21), which in the three fueros implies renunciation on the part of the sovereign of a monopoly on them, differs in its approach insofar as the Jaca text is aimed at establishing freedom of milling, while in those of Alquézar and Asín the monarch recognizes freedom of ownership on the part of townspeople. The other two dispositions are clearer for the purpose of textual transmission, given that the difference in the approach is a reflection of a gradual change in its formulation. The first of them, on penalization for homicide (§ 14), is limited in the Fuero of Jaca to establishing the amount of the sanction, but that is not the case in that of Alquézar, which in this respect introduces the limitation of responsibility to the author of the crime, at the same establishing in the solution prison and the confiscation of the killer's goods as precautionary measures in paying the fine. For its part the Fuero of Asín limits itself to exempting townspeople from responsibility for homicide occurring outside the burg. The largest formal conclusion in both texts corresponds to this difference in approach as reflected in the fact of classifying a punishable act with the term "*homicidio.*" Something similar occurs with the norm relating to fines for false accusation (§ 18), even if only with two testimonies in its evolution. The Fuero of Jaca conditions the consent of six of its dignitaries for payment for false accusation on the part of the king, while that of Asín, recognizing the latter (perhaps on the same condition), establishes the free disposition of townspeople for false accusations not reclaimed by the monarch. Given the sharp difference in approach of the norm by the different texts, as was conceivable, there is no glimmer of similarity in their wording.

The Fueros of Jaca and Asín are also the only ones to concern themselves with regulating the war levy with partially different solutions, since that of Asín, after enunciating the exemption to seven years for its townspeople and future settlers turns to that established by the Jaca text.[110] Besides this implicit reference, the Jaca origin of the exemption is testified to in the concession of "*tales fueros quomodo habent illos burzeses de Iacca*" to the *villa* of Luesia. If this reference was to a Jaca text, nowadays unknown, in which the said exemption appeared, or if the Fuero of Asín that contains it was taken as such, we do not know.[111] Whatever the case, given the privileged nature of the norm and its relation to the repopulation process of these *villas*, one would think that, having been applied in Jaca, that would have happened prior to the formulation of the norm included in its texts known today.

Suppositions Common to the Fuero of Jaca and to Those of Navarrese Towns

Apart from the relationship between the Fueros of Jaca and Estella, evident in the literal similarity of their texts that has already been examined, only one precept, in the Fuero of Puente la Reina, has a certain concurrence with the Jaca statute insofar as both turn to the prescription of one year and one day as the period for resolving their respective norms; in the former regarding the acquisition of property and in the latter with the aim of fulfilling the settlement requirement demanded in order to obtain the status of a townsperson.

---

110 Although it only states, "*et post VII annos completos quod me securratis ad lite campale,*" one supposes that it was, as in Jaca, at its own expense for three days.

111 In this regard it is worth remembering the proximity of dates between the Luesia concession of 1154 and the confirmation of the Fuero of Sangüesa by Sancho VI in 1158. See note 73.

Suppositions Common to the Navarrese
and the Aragonese Fueros that does not Include the Fuero of Jaca

The concurrences classified in this model do not have a lot of range within the set of texts as a whole insofar as they only affect four and three of them, which are never the same.

The norm that guarantees royal protection to the rights conceded about the place of settlement (§ 9) is included by the Fueros of the new burg of Sangüesa and Puente la Reina with an almost identical formulation, sanctioning indemnity in the terms conceded with a fine of sixty *sueldos*. Olite establishes this same punishment, made more severe by the involvement of royal ire, for a similar supposition, although formulated with a general scope, given that it refers to any act, not just indemnity, threatening a settler of the *villa*. Between one and the other although maintaining a certain parallelism with them, the Fuero of Ainsa refers to rights about the town limits in the same sense, but without specifying the harm or determining any sanction.

Likewise, the norm relating to the equality of fueros (§ 5) is more prevalent in Navarrese texts, with differences of nuance in its approach, since it is formulated in the sense of something of an obligatory nature with regard to subjecting people that may settle in the burg of San Cernín to its law, while on the contrary the enunciation that the other two places, Pueyo de Pintano and Iriberri, offer emphasizes its privileged character, coinciding in underscoring the personal and not local scope of this law. Beyond this concurrence, nothing in its formulation induces one to think of any closer relationship between both texts, which offer a clear divergence in their respective approaches, since the former does so in relation to the settler's potential properties in other lands in the kingdom that would thereby be "*liberas et franchas a fuero de Jaca,*" while that of Iriberri, following closely the literal content of the Pamplona text, refers specifically to Navarrese settlers, the lower nobility, and ecclesiastics accepted by the community for whom the obligatory acceptance of the fuero of that place implied the condition of freedom befitting its inhabitants.

The precept on the decimation obligation (§ 4) included in the Fueros of Puente la Reina, Asín, and Berdún, with one being an approach and a solution, the possible relationship between the two latter ones is indeed clear in that both allude to the episcopal quarter, on which that of Puente la Reina does not pronounce anything.

It is still surprising, given the burg nature of these towns, that the holding of a market is only addressed by norms in the Fueros of Alquézar (§ 5), San Cernín, and Berdún. The enunciation of the corresponding precept in the Navarrese text seems to be independent of that of its Aragonese counterparts insofar that, in accepting the holding of a market, the former limits itself to noting the place while in the Aragonese texts the circumstantial reference is of a temporal nature, coinciding in the day established, Thursdays, but not so much in the frequency, which is deduced as weekly in the Fuero of Berdún, and obligatorily every two weeks in Alquézar. The reason for this day in the Fuero of Berdún is the precedence of the market of Jaca, which was held on Tuesdays, a fact of special ineptest insofar as it reveals the priority allotted to Jaca over the rest of the towns on the Camino, at least in this specific aspect, and that even before having recognized officially its existence.[112]

Suppositions Common to the Aragonese Fueros

The close relationship between the Fueros of Alquézar and Berdún evident in the previous norm is accentuated by the presence in both, and only therein, of another norm (§ 5) by which the king makes travelers who visit the market the object of his special protection, imposing a big fine, one thousand *sueldos*, on anyone who in some way may harm them on their journey, estimated by that of Alquézar to be three days. In conceding to Jaca the right to hold a market, Pedro II likewise reveals this same favorable disposition to guaranteeing commercial traffic, which again has a bearing on pointing out the close normative link existing among Aragonese towns.

---

112 The holding of the Jaca market every week on Tuesday appears as a privilege conceded by Pedro II in 1197 (see note 14). Although the Fuero of Estella does not include any norm relating to the holding of a market, various dispositions in its fuero indicate that it also took place on Thursday (II, 59.1 and 62.4).

Finally, the concurrence pointed out between the Fueros of Berdún and Pueyo de Pintano relating to livestock grazing does not imply any normative coincidence, but it is indicative of the presence in the region of a livestock practice, governed fundamentally by custom, in which to judge by the Fuero of Berdún, the Aragonese principle of *"tortum per tortum"* prevailed.[113]

The Process of Forming Jaca Law

Such painstaking analysis could only have led to useful results when it comes to filling the void derived from a critique of Jaca foral documents and trying to reconstruct, insofar as it possible, its formation process up to the moment that the documents at our disposal allow us.

In the face of the view held up to now, by default of the critique, about one single text that was widely distributed, and despite which only began to be reflected, and that in an incomplete way, in only one of the places in which it was received, the textual critique presents a dynamic panorama in defining a formation process in which it is possible to distinguish at least two successive phases therein.

The first phase corresponds to the initiative by Sancho Ramírez to give a foundational charter by means of its express recognition of population settlements that had sprung up in his dominions, at the same time as, privileging them with the concession of a favorable statute, it ensured their growth. Hence, among other things, the Navarrese villas of Sangüesa and Estella, and Jaca, all linked originally and in their process of repopulation development stemming from the transit toward Santiago de Compostela, were the object of royal attention and received their corresponding fuero charter. These fuero charters, notwithstanding the odd difference, would contain some same norms aimed at establishing settlement conditions. As regarded space, town limits were established (except that, as could have happened in Jaca, these had already been acknowledged previously) and the rights of the local community to its use. Likewise,

---

113 See Lalinde Abadía, *Los fueros de Aragón*, 30.

each individual or family group was granted the right to acquire workable land in accordance with their possibilities within the terms outlined. Moreover, in the Navarrese *villas* the king expressed clearly the effective range of his protection of the limits, sanctioning with a fine of sixty *sueldos* any indemnity levied on his settlers.[114] Fuero equality appears guaranteed in denying the possibility of settlement to the lower nobility and perhaps also to clerics, while personal and patrimonial freedom found its normative expression in recognizing the condition of exemption for all the properties they could acquire in the kingdom. This common basis of conditions of privilege for the three *villas* was contemplated with some exemptions, which, based on the texts, would not be the same, but those that for reasons of the moment of the concession and the circumstances of the place would be most opportune. Thus, the townspeople of Sangüesa would be exempt from paying tributes in the *villas* and markets of the kingdom, while those of Estella and Jaca would be likewise exempt from aiding the king with arms for seven years.[115] This difference of content between the Fuero of Sangüesa and those of Jaca and Estella, but also the concurrences of the Navarrese fueros in limiting the indemnity sanction, as well as their greater literal proximity to that of Jaca, incline one to assume that their concession came about not simultaneously, but successively. In this chronological *"iter"* temporary priority corresponds to Sangüesa, given that, to judge by the exemption from tributes for its first settlement, its seems probable that its content was similar to that of King Sancho's other

---

114 Always on the basis of probable normative similarity and also the edition, between the primitive Fuero of Estella, today unknown, and the dispositions included in that of Puente la Reina.

115 Although neither of the known Fueros of Jaca or Estella include this exemption, this is not an unfounded statement. Its possible validity in Jaca prior to the formulation of the norm that both versions of the fuero of Sancho Ramírez include is deduced from the concession of the fero of Jaca to Luesia (see above). As regards Estella, its fuero includes the norm in the same terms in which it appears formulated in the Jaca text (I, 1.1); however, the fact that one of its final seals, *"De foro"* (III, 69/72), ratifies the said norm, thereafter explicitly stating, every now and then, a series of situations that excuse its fulfillment, could be seen as an attempt by the town authorities to thwart a contrary practice based on this first exemption. Moreover, the fact that this norm features among those included in the Fuero of Asín does not necessarily imply its validity in Sangüesa, since given the clear textual relationship of this fuero with the concessions of the Fuero of Jaca to other Aragonese *villas*, this could have been the means of receiving the said norm in its fuero.

fuero charters, while that of the war levy seems clearly exceptional.[116] Meanwhile, the greatest literal proximity between the norms in the Fuero of Sangüesa and in that of Puente la Reina incline one to situate the concession of Estella on a secondary level in order to end with that of Jaca, which ultimately coincides with the fact that it was, precisely, therein from where the right stemming from this first royal initiative was developed most intensively, paving the way for the second phase of this process.

This second phase, to judge from the results of the textual critique, culminated with the formulation and binding in writing of some norms generated by the coexistence of people settled in surroundings determined under some specific conditions guaranteeing their freedom. While the process of normative creation must have been produced equally in each of these *villas*, it would seem, on the other hand, that the wording process only took place in Jaca, disguising a certain intensity since it was settled on in various normative reviews in a not so broad lapse of time. When Alfonso I, on conceding the Fuero of Estella to Puente la Reina in 1122, restricted himself to specifying conditions relating to population settlement, turning, as regards all other issues that may be raised *"causas et faziendas"* to a somewhat verbose reference to *"tales fueros et tales usaticos vel consuetudines"* of his townspeople, it was symptomatic not of normative void, but rather of the lack of any document in which that worldly right may have appeared specified in some precise dispositions in Estella, but also in Jaca because, on the contrary, Alfonso had turned to it, as he did years later in repopulating Ainsa and the new burg of Alquézar. There is scarcely any evidence in the texts about who was in charge of this task and how it was carried out. One can only deduce information about its authors in light of the content of its norms that do not deal with population settlement, which would be a question of people knowledgeable about the customs of the land and also legal practice. Some vestiges on the way activity was undertaken can be induced from the textual critique, since substantial

---

116 On the fueros of Sancho Ramírez that contain the exemption from tributes see note 108. On the contrary, the norm on the war levy found in several of these texts (Arguedas, Ujué, Monzón, and Castellar) is that established in the previously discussed Fuero of Jaca.

and formal concurrences that are derived therefrom demand the existence of several editions.

A first would have been formed on the basis of a document by Sancho Ramírez as a development of this, consisting in its extension of a series of procedural and penal norms—the holding of trials in the *villa*, the exclusion as evidence of trial by combat, the penalization of homicide, and the use of arms for offensive objectives, as well as the disposition on established false accusations—and certain others of a privilege nature such as the freedom to mill, and those derived from the customs of new settlers such as the prescription of one year and one day. This would possibly be the text of Jaca law when its fuero was conceded to Ainsa and Pamplona, given that in the former the norm on holding trials is included, that in that of San Cernín it is still very telling that a generic reference is made, as opposed to the formula used in Puente la Reina, as in it, to "*vestras faziendas*," but also to "*vestros iudizios*." Furthermore, the presence in the Fuero of Ainsa of the clause on the exemption from tributes and its literal proximity, in general terms, to those of Sangüesa and Puente la Reina, as well as the reference ion the Pamplona fuero to "*tales fueros . . . quomodo fuerunt populatos illos populatores de Jaka*" are details revealing of the close relationship of this text to the first concession by Sancho Ramírez to Jaca, as well as its similarity to those of Sangüesa and Estella.

This text was in turn an object of revision giving rise to two new reviews, undertaken with total independence and possibly at different times and places. The first of these reviews, although linked nominally and substantially to Jaca, seems to have been created in the course of adapting its law to other communities. It is characterized by the fact that some of its norms, those of a penal and procedural nature, present a greater degree of substantial development and formal elaboration, and the addition of other news ones that are just the assumption of Jaca ways and practices in specific matters, such as holding and protecting markets and the obligation to contribute to the church with the decimation and the episcopal quarter. This text was received in the new burg of Alquézar and in Asín, where, perhaps on account of reestablishing or adapting it to the common norms of the charter conceded by Sancho Ramírez to the new burg of Sangüesa, it is presented as a fuero particular to the *villa*. Similarly, it would be used, following the version included in Alquézar, by Ramón Berenguer and Alfonso II in their concessions to Berdún and Pueyo de Pintano. The second review was carried out in Jaca, possibly already under the reign of Ramiro II. Without any immediate transcendence beyond the limits of the town, its importance was decisive given that it did not just imply the practically definitive setting of Jaca law, but it would end up achieving greater levels of diffusion on being adopted in Estella as its own fuero and, interceding or not, the express concession of the latter or with its original denomination, in San Sebastian and other *villas* in Gipuzkoa. From the substantial and formal point of view, it also implied an important re-elaboration of the previous Jaca text given that based on it, while still maintaining its attribution to King Sancho, there was, in first place, an adaptation of its norms to the new circumstances, disregarding some of the clauses contained in the privilege of Sancho Ramírez—the concession of town limits, the appropriation of land, banning the lower nobility from settling— and changing the formulation of others, whether in their content, such as in that relating to the exemption from the war levy that was now made perceptive, or whether in their wording, which was made more concise, thereby achieving the effect of greater abstraction and generality. In second place, its dispositive content was broadened with new norms in procedural matters (the loaning of bonds) and in greater penal measures (statutory rape and rape, different assaults, and disturbance of the peace) as well as those relating to community relations (falsification of measures).

Whether it was because this text was presented to the monk king for its confirmation, or whether because it may have served as the basis for elaborating the "*conscriptio*" of its own activity in which, as well as conceding other privileges, it would go on to confirm the fueros of the *villa*, it is true that it implied a definitive consecration. From that moment on it would lead its own life until arriving at forming part of the some of the documents that have arrived down to us today through a process of transmission and textual reworking of that which its document critique points to with which this study began.

With this text by Ramiro II the first cycle in the process of forming Jaca law, which I have tried to recreate here insofar as the texts at our disposal have allowed it, appears to come to an end. In any event, this only constitutes a first step in clarifying a much wider process, in no way free of mysteries (some of them pointed out here), whose resolution requires, without doubt, much greater analysis in that it would be about the texts of which there is a need, overcoming by far the chronological and spatial limits of this current proposal.

BIBLIOGRAPHY

Banús y Aguirre, José Luis. *El fuero de San Sebastián*. Zarauz: Ayuntamiento de la Ciudad de San Sebastián, 1963.

Barrero García, Ana Mª. "Las redacciones navarras del fuero de Logroño." *Príncipe de Viana* 53, no. 196 (1992): 409–28.

———. "El fuero de Carmona." In *Actas del I Congreso de Historia de Carmona. Edad Media. Congreso conmemorativo del 750 aniversario de la conquista de la ciudad de Carmona por Fernando III. 1247. Carmona (Sevilla), 22 al 25 de septiembre de 1997*. Sevilla: Centro de Estudios Ramón Areces, 1998.

———. "La difusión del fuero de Jaca en el Camino de Santiago." In *El Fuero de Jaca II: Estudios*. Zaragoza: El Justicia de Aragón, 2003.

Barrero García, Ana Mª, and Mª Luz Alonso Martín. *Textos de derecho local español en la Edad Media. Catálogo de fueros y costums municipales*. Madrid: CSIC, 1989.

———. "El proceso de formación del derecho local medieval a través de sus textos: Los fueros castellano-leoneses." In *I Semana de Estudios medievales. Nájera 1990*, edited by José

Ignacio de la Iglesia Duarte. Logroño: Instituto de Estudios Riojanos, 2001.

Canellas López, Ángel. "La cancillería real en el reino de Aragón (1035–1134)." In *Folia Budapestina*. Zaragoza: Institución Fernando el Católico; CSIC, 1983.

―――. *La colección diplomática de Sancho Ramírez*. Zaragoza: Real Sociedad Económica Aragonesa de los Amigos del País, 1993.

Du Cange [Charles du Fresne]. *Glossarium Mediae latinitatis et infimae Latinitatis*. Niort: Favre, 1883–1887.

García Larragueta, Santos, and Isabel Ostolaza Elizondo. "Estudios de diplomática sobre fuentes de la época de Sancho el Sabio." In *Vitoria en la Edad Media. Actas del I Congreso de estudios históricos celebrado en esta ciudad del 21 al 26 de septiembre de1981 en conmemoración del 800 aniversario de su fundación*. Vitoria-Gasteiz: Ayuntamiento de Vitoria-Gasteiz, 1982.

Gouron, André. "Autour de Placentin à Montpellier: Maître Gui et Pierre de Cardona." *Studia Gratiana* 19 (1976): 337–54.

Jimeno Aranguren, Roldán, ed. *Documentación histórica sobre la villa de Tiebas*. Tiebas: Concejo de Tiebas, 1999.

Lacarra, José Mª "Notas para la formación de las familias de fueros navarros." *Anuario de Historia del Derecho Español* 10 (1933): 203–72.

―――. "Alfonso el Batallador y las paces de Támara." *Estudios de Edad Media de la Corona de Aragón* 3 (1947–1948): 461–73.

―――. "Desarrollo urbano de Jaca en la Edad Media." *Estudios de la Edad Media de la Corona de Aragón* 4 (1951): 139–55.

―――. *Documentos para el estudio de la reconquista y repoblación del valle del Ebro (números 1 a 319)*. Zaragoza: Anúbar, 1982.

Lacarra, José Mª, and Ángel J. Martín Duque. *Fueros de Navarra I. Fueros derivados de Jaca: 1. Estella-San Sebastián*. Pamplona: Diputación Foral de Navarra, 1969.

————. *Fueros de Navarra I. Fueros derivados de Jaca 2. Pamplona.* Pamplona: Diputación Foral de Navarra, 1975.

Lalinde Abadía, Jesús. *Los fueros de Aragón.* Zaragoza: Librería General, 1976.

Ledesma Rubio, María Luisa. *Cartas de población del Reino de Aragón en los siglos medievales.* Zaragoza: Institución Fernando el Católico, 1991.

Martín Duque, Ángel J. "El fuero de San Sebastián. Tradición manuscrita y edición crítica." In *Congreso: El fuero de San Sebastián y su época.* San Sebastián: Sociedad de Estudios Vascos, 1982.

————. "Sancho VI de Navarra y el fuero de Vitoria." In *Vitoria en la Edad Media. Actas del I Congreso de estudios históricos celebrado en esta ciudad del 21 al 26 de septiembre de1981 en conmemoración del 800 aniversario de su fundación.* Vitoria-Gasteiz: Ayuntamiento de Vitoria-Gasteiz, 1982.

————. *Documentación medieval de Leire (siglos XI a XII).* Pamplona: Institución Príncipe de Viana, 1983.

————. "La fundación del primer burgo navarro. Estella." *Príncipe de Viana* 51, no. 190 (1990): 317–27.

————. "Navarra y Aragón." In Ramón Menénded Pidal, *Historia de España,* edited by José Mª Jover Zamora. Volume 9. *La Reconquista y el proceso de diferenciación política (1035–1217),* edited and introduced by Miguel Ángel Ladero Quesada et al. Madrid: Espasa-Calpe, 1998.

Molho, Mauricio. "Difusión del derecho pirenaico (Fuero de Jaca) en el reino de Aragón." *Boletín de la Real Academia de Buenas Letras de Barcelona* 28 (1959–1960): 265–352.

————. *El fuero de Jaca. Edición crítica.* Zaragoza: Instituto de estudios pirenáicos, 1964.

Mor, Carlo Guido. "A l'origine de l'ecole de Montpellier: Rogerius ou Placentinus?" *Recueil de mémoires et travaux. Société d'Histoire du*

Droit et des Institutions des Anciens Pays de Droit Ecrit 6 (1967): 145–55.

Morales Arrizabalaga, Jesús. *Privilegios altomedievales: El fuero de Jaca (c. 1076)*. Zaragoza: Universidad de Zaragoza, 1997.

Muñoz y Romero, Tomás. *Colección de fueros municipales y cartas pueblas de los reinos de Castilla, León, Navarra y Aragón*. Madrid: Imp. de José María Alonso, 1847.

Pavón Benito, Julia. "Fuero de Jaca y fuero de Estella. Observaciones críticas." In *XV Congreso de Historia de la Corona de Aragón. Actas. Tomo III. Jaca en la Corona de Aragón (siglos XII–XVIII)*. Zaragoza: Institución Fernando el Católico, 1994.

Ramos Loscertales, José Mª. "Textos para el estudio del derecho aragonés en la Edad Media." *Anuario de Historia del Derecho Español* 1 (1924): 397–416.

———. *Fuero de Jaca (última redacción)*. Barcelona: Universidad de Barcelona, 1927.

Sánchez Belda, Luis, ed. *Chronica Adefonsi Imperatoris*. Madrid: CSIC, 1950.

Sesma Muñoz, José Ángel. "El camino de Santiago en Aragón." In *Las peregrinaciones a Santiago de Compostela y San Salvador de Oviedo en la Edad Media. Actas del I Congreso Internacional celebrado en Oviedo del 3 al 7 de diciembre de 1990*. Oviedo: Gobierno del Principado de Asturias, 1993.

Trenchs Odena, José. "Las escribanías catalano-aragonesas desde Ramón Berenguer IV a la minoría de Jaime I." In *Folia Budapestina*. Zaragoza: Institución Fernando el Católico; CSIC, 1983.

Ubieto, Agustín. *Los "tenentes" en Navarra y Aragón en los siglos XI y XII*. Valencia: Anúbar, 1973.

Ubieto. Antonio. *Crónica de los Estados Peninsulares (Texto del siglo XIV)*. Granada: Universidad de Granada, 1955.

———. *Jaca: Documentos municipales, 971–1269*. Valencia: Cronista Almela y Vives, 1975.

————. *Documentos de Ramiro II de Aragón.* Zaragoza: Anúbar, 1988.

Vázquez de Parga, Luis, José María Lacarra, and Juan Uría. *Las peregrinaciones a Santiago de Compostela. III.* Madrid: CSIC, 1949.

Yagüe Ferrer, Mª Isabel. *Jaca: Documentos municipales (971–1324). Introducción y concordancia lematizada.* Zaragoza: Universidad de Zaragoza, 1995.

Chapter 5

Law in the Fueros of Estella
and San Sebastian

Roldán Jimeno Aranguren

We have known about law in the Fueros of Estella and San Sebastian for quite some time, since José María Lacarra began to publish his studies and works in 1927;[1] and those followed that which the distinguished Estella medievalist carried out with his disciple Ángel J. Martín Duque in 1969.[2] Prior to the latter, Gustaf Holmer published another version of the Fuero of Estella.[3] And that same year José Luis Banús y Aguirre published his edition of the Fuero of San Sebastian.[4] The proceedings resulting from the conference "El fuero de San Sebastián y su época" (The Fuero of San Sebastian and its era), organized by Eusko Ikaskuntza (the Society of Basque Studies), and held in Donostia-San Sebastian between January 19 and 23, 1981, contributed essential studies for the legal analysis

---

1   See the following by José María Lacarra: "Fuero de Estella," *Anuario de Historia del Derecho Español* 4 (1927), 404–51; "Fuero de Estella. Año 1164," *Anuario de Historia del Derecho Español* 9 (1932), 386–92; "Fuero de Estella en versión lemosina," *Anuario de Historia del Derecho Español* 9 (1932), 393–413; and "Notas para la formación de las familias de fueros de Navarra," *Anuario de Historia del Derecho Español* 10 (1933), 203–72.
2   José María Lacarra and Ángel J. Martín Duque, *Fueros derivados de Jaca I: Estella-San Sebastián* (Pamplona: Diputación Foral de Navarra, 1969).
3   Gustaf Holmer, ed., *El fuero de Estella según el manuscrito 944 de la Biblioteca de Palacio de Madrid*, Colecc. Leges Hispanicae Medii Aevi, no. 10 (Goteborg; Stockholm; Uppsala: Karlshamn, 1963).
4   José Luis Banús y Aguirre, *El Fuero de San Sebastián* (Zarauz: Ayuntamiento de la Ciudad de San Sebastián, 1963).

of the San Sebastian fuero, with those of José Luis Orella Unzué, Gabriel García Cantero, Francisco Salinas Quijada, and Paz Alonso standing out especially.[5] There were other highly useful contributions at this conference by Ángel J. Martín Duque, who provided a new edition of the text of the fuero, and Luis Alberto Basabe Martín, who accompanied its philological analysis with a translation into Spanish.[6] Orella Unzué continued to explore the topic of the Fuero of San Sebastian in more depth with his 1999 work.[7]

The latest significant contributions on the part of researchers have centered on the critical revision of the date of the first Fuero of Estella. It has come to be argued that the birth of Estella, as a particular named legal entity, occurred in the year 1090, when Sancho Ramírez repopulated lands in the settlement of Lizarrara with Franks, conceding to the settlers the Fuero of Jaca, a law embodying like no other the necessary municipal freedoms to build an urban nucleus on the Camino de Santiago. The date of 1090 was initially questioned by Martín Duque, on the supposed eight hundredth anniversary of the concession of the fuero.[8] In his work, he demonstrates that the formation of the first urban nucleus situated around the church of San Martín took place in the year 1076, so that the fuero would have been awarded to the Franks between that year and 1084, with the latter date corresponding to the denomination of the tenancy of Estella. Ana María Barrero García manages to refine that date even more in her 2003 study, in which, following an exhaustive study of the document sources in the Jaca family, she considers that the short Estella fuero was granted around the years 1076–1077.[9] This

---

5   José Luis Orella Unzué, "Estudio jurídico comparativo de los fueros de San Sebastián, Estella, Vitoria y Logroño," Gabriel García Cantero, "El Derecho civil en el Fuero de San Sebastián," Francisco Salinas Quijada, "El Derecho civil en el Fuero de San Sebastián (Y Fuero Nuevo)," and Paz Alonso, "El proceso penal en el Fuero de San Sebastián," in *El Fuero de San Sebastián y su época. Actas del VIII centenario de la Fundación de San Sebastián* (San Sebastián: Sociedad de Estudios Vascos, 1982).

6   Ángel J. Martín Duque, "El fuero de San Sebastián. Tradición manuscrita y edición crítica," and Luis Alberto Basabe Martín, "Estudio lingüístico del fuero de San Sebastián en Congreso," in ibid.

7   José Luis Orella Unzué, "El fuero de San Sebastián y su entorno histórico," in *Geografía e Historia de Donostia-San Sebastián*, ed. Javier Gómez Piñeiro and Juan Antonio Sáez García (San Sebastián: Ingeba, 1999).

8   Ángel J. Martín Duque, "La fundación del burgo navarro: Estella." *Príncipe de Viana* 51, no. 190 (1990), 317–28; reprint, *Príncipe de Viana* 63, no. 227 (2002), 761–72.

9   Ana María Barrero García, "La difusión del Fuero de Jaca en el Camino de Santiago," *El Fuero de Jaca, II, Estudios* (Zaragoza: El Justicia de Aragón, 2003), 113–60.

revision is not taken into account by later authors like Luis Javier Fortún Pérez de Ciriza, who offers a weighty analysis of the Fuero of Estella in his panoramic study of local fueros in Navarre.[10] It has, though, been embraced by others. I myself do so in two studies.[11] And Xabier Irujo dedicates a monograph to the Fuero of Estella.[12]

This abundant literature on the topic is not free of an important methodological problem, which is that those authors that have mostly looked at law in these fueros have done so on the basis of their own criteria of codification. When legal history is approached through the mere application of some criteria that did not exist in the eleventh and twelfth centuries, it implies submitting legal entities to the rigid limitation of being studied from positive civil, penal, and procedural law categories. The result is a somewhat artificial and distorting picture of reality, since the codified structure did not have anything to do with the legal nature of institutions in the Early and High Middle Ages, when law had an essentially popular character and *Ius commune* still barely existed.

The first fourteen chapters in the Fuero of Estella by Sancho Ramírez, articulated in twenty-three precepts, were copied in the longer fuero of 1164. This latter text has been published as edition *A*, written in Latin, by Lacarra and Martín Duque;[13] and is translated into Spanish by Julio Campos Ruiz.[14] Together with Gregorio Monreal Zia, I later adapted this version in 2008.[15] Both the Latin and Spanish versions were then revised in a 2016 publication of mine.[16]

Version A of the 1164 text was, in turn, the fundamental basis on which the Fuero of San Sebastian was drafted around 1180. Lacarra and Martín Duque demonstrate through textual analysis

---

10 Luis Javier Fortún Pérez de Ciriza, "Fueros locales de Navarra," *Príncipe de Viana* 68, no. 242 (2007), 881–83.
11 Roldán Jimeno Aranguren, "El municipio de Vasconia en la Edad Media," *Iura Vasconiae* 2 (2005), 63–67 and *Los Fueros de Navarra* (Madrid: Agencia Estatal Boletín Oficial del Estado, 2016), 319–26.
12 Xabier Irujo, *Giving Birth to Cosmopolis: The Code of Laws of Estella (c. 1076)* (Santa Barbara: University of California, Santa Barbara, 2011).
13 Lacarra and Martín Duque, *Fueros derivados de Jaca I: Estella-San Sebastián*, 87–149.
14 Julio Campos Ruiz, *El Fuero de Estella* (Estella-Lizarra: Ayuntamiento de Estella-Lizarra, 2005).
15 Gregorio Monreal Zia and Roldán Jimeno Aranguren, *Textos histórico-jurídicos navarros. I. Historia Antigua y Medieval* (Pamplona: Gobierno de Navarra, 2008).
16 Jimeno Aranguren, *Los Fueros de Navarra*, 327–47 (Lat.) and 348–68 (Spa.).

that both the preamble and the twenty-four precepts of the San Sebastian fuero were taken from the Fuero of Estella literally or with light variations. The parallel texts were the following:[17]

The preamble, which reproduced the inscription and protocol of the Fuero of Estella.

Chapter 1, 1 in the Fuero of Estella = Chapter 1,1 in the Fuero of San Sebastian.

Chapter 1, 13 (Estella) = Chapter 1, 17 (San Sebastian).

Chapter 1, 10 (Estella) = Chapter 1, 9 (San Sebastian).

Chapter 1, 3 (Estella) = Chapter 1, 11 (San Sebastian).

Chapter 1, 2 (Estella) = Chapter 2, 1 (San Sebastian).

Chapter 1, 4 (Estella) = Chapter 2, 2 (San Sebastian).

Chapter 1, 5 (Estella) = Chapter 2, 3 (San Sebastian).

Chapter 1, 6 (Estella) = Chapter 2, 4 (San Sebastian).

Chapter 1, 7 (Estella) = Chapter 2, 5 (San Sebastian).

Chapter 1, 8 (Estella) = Chapter 2, 6 (San Sebastian).

Chapter 1, 9 (Estella) = Chapter 2, 7 (San Sebastian).

Chapter 1, 10 (Estella) = Chapter 2, 8 (San Sebastian).

Chapter 1, 11 (Estella) = Chapter 2, 9 (San Sebastian).

Chapter 1, 12 (Estella) = Chapter 2, 10 (San Sebastian).

Chapter 1, 14 (Estella) = Chapter 2, 11 (San Sebastian).

Chapter 2, 3 (Estella) = Chapter 3, 1 (San Sebastian).

Chapter 2, 4 (Estella) = Chapter 3, 2 (San Sebastian).

Chapter 2, 5 (Estella) = Chapter 3, 3 (San Sebastian).

Chapter 2, 6 (Estella) = Chapter 3, 4 (San Sebastian).

Chapter 2, 7 (Estella) = Chapter 3, 5 (San Sebastian).

Chapter 2, 12 (Estella) = Chapter 3, 6 (San Sebastian).

---

17 Lacarra and Martín Duque, *Fueros derivados de Jaca I: Estella-San Sebastián*, 29–31.

Chapter 2, 14 (Estella) = Chapter 3, 7 (San Sebastian).

Chapter 2, 26 (Estella) = Chapter 3, 8 (San Sebastian).

Chapter 2, 11 (Estella) = Chapter 3, 9 (San Sebastian).

The authority of the Fuero of Jaca as the interpretative matrix of the other fueros was assumed from the mid-twelfth century on, since according to a testimony of Alfonso II in 1187, from the second half of that century on, "they used to come to Jaca, from Castile, Navarre, and other lands in order to learn good customs and fueros and take them to their own." From the Late Middle Ages on, people went to Jaca from Estella, Pamplona, Donostia-San Sebastian, and Fuenterrabía (Hondarribia) to carry out consultations in order to interpret their fuero and even to appeal sentences that had been pronounced in those *villas*. The historiography incorporated that reality until Esteban de Garibay reminded readers that in the early fourteenth-century *Crónica de los Estados Peninsulares*, *"Et dizen más, que Navarra e Ypuzcoa se goviernan por el fuero de Sobre Arbe; que si los reyes fuessen de Navarra, los privilegios que fueron de Navarra tenrian; et oy en dia de Ypuzcua apellan a fuero de Sobre Arbe; et los de Navarra sí fazían, si non que lo vedó el rey don Sancho 'l'Encerrado.'"*[18]

In this chapter I will analyze law in the Fueros of Estella and San Sebastian through the sources that I have just indicated. I will not include here the Fuero of Estella project of Theobald I (1234–1253), a monarch that did not end up sanctioning the fuero. This new text was written in the Romance language, introduced juridical clarifications, and added new chapters on civil and penal law based on local Estella jurisprudential practice.

Residency

Like any other medieval municipality, law in Estella and San Sebastian rested on the inhabitants of these *villas*. People's conditions were defined by being residents of the *villas* or not. The residency offered

---

18   Esteban de Garibay, *Los XL libros d'el Compendio historial de las Chronicas y vniuersal Historia de todos los reynos de España / Compuestos por Esteuan de Garibay y Çamálloa, de nación Cántabro, vezino de la villa de Mondragón, de la provincia de Guipúzcoa* (Anveres: Christophoro Plantino, 1571).

by the fuero conferred equality and legal protection, the use of common property, the possibility of participating in the council, and some freedoms, exemptions, and allowances. They were, in sum, a series of advantages conferred by the fueros with which to attract settlers. In the case of Estella and San Sebastian, moreover, these new settlers would preferably be Franks, since the Navarrese and clerics could not live in these *villas* without the consent of the king and all of the residents.[19]

The Fuero of Estella established a difference between *"poblador"* (settler) and *"vecino"* (resident) in pointing out that, if a settler were to arrive in the *villa* with the aim of putting down roots there by renting a property, they would be exempt from any tax or charge for one year and one day.[20] From that moment on, settlers would have to comply with the military draft and residency responsibilities, which would serve to make them considered residents, like the rest.[21] This most interesting and clarifying precept was not incorporated into the Fuero of San Sebastian, in which most of the dispositions allude in general to settlers, inferring them as residents, as evinced in the eloquent chapter 1, 7.2, in which the council of all the residents and the king decided jointly that the clergy and Navarrese could be "settlers in the town," that is, those people from among these social orders could accede to the status of resident. Most of the San Sebastian precepts in which there is a clear allusion to residents were taken directly from the Fuero of Estella.[22]

Not all the chapters in the Estella fuero relating to residency were incorporated by the Fuero of San Sebastian. Some of them are as illustrative as that which established full residency for widows, who had to comply with all the responsibilities of residency in the *villa*, except that of the military draft;[23] that of the obligations of

---

19 Estel   1, 13 = San Sebastian 1, 7.
20 laEstell   2, 16.1.
21 aEstell   2, 16.2.
22 aSpecifical   t   following Estella 1, 7.1 = San Sebastian 2, 5.1; Estella, 1, 8 = San
    lSebastian 2h6; Estella, 1, 13 = San Sebastian, 1, 7; Estella 1, 6.3 = San Sebastian 2,
    4.3; Estella 1, 7.1 = San Sebastian 2, 5.1; Estella, 1, 8 = San Sebastian 2, 6; Estella 1,
    9 = San Sebastian, 2, 7; Estella 2, 6.1 = San Sebastian 3, 4.1; and Estella, 2, 11.13
    = San Sebastian, 3, 9.13.
23 Estella, 2,
15.

residents to participate in the military draft;[24] that which prescribed that two residents who hoped to buy inherited property for sale could not use its residency legally, but could use kinship;[25] and the regulation on procedural questions relating to residents.[26]

Local Institutions

It is typical to find mention in the municipal fueros—and those of Estella and San Sebastian are no exception—of the authorities that governed the *villa* or that were charged with administering justice. These allusions were not accompanied by a description of the functions of these institutions.

The Fuero of Estella alludes specifically to the council of the *villa*. This professional institution made up of prominent local men hardly appears in the text, except to underscore the role carried out by the council in enclosed land;[27] or the allusion to this institution as the recipient of half of any fines imposed on outsiders who stored wine at home.[28] The Fuero of San Sebastian makes no mention of the council of the *villa*, but it does termed "twelve good residents,"[29] even if only in some dispositions that point out judicial functions. One would imagine that, as in other legal texts of the era in which there was mention of "good men," they worked on councils with municipal administrative functions, although also in meeting out justice and participating in economic and financial questions.[30] The twelve good residents would appear to have been the source of what would end up being the Council of San Sebastian, in the same way that the twelve prominent local men in the old fuero were the precursors of the Parliament of Navarre.

The institutions of the seigneur of the *villa* and of the *merino*, that is, the king's representatives in the *villa*, appear in the Fueros

---

24 Estella, 2, 69.
25 Estella, 2, 69.
26 Estella, 2, 31 and 2, 70.
27 Estella, 2, 49.
28 Estella, 2, 61.
29 San Sebastian, 2, 4.3 and 2, 4.5.
30 Beatriz Arízaga, "Las villas guipuzcoanas que reciben el fuero de San Sebastián: modos de vida de sus habitants," in *El Fuero de San Sebastián y su época. Actas del VIII centenario de la Fundación de San Sebastián* (San Sebastián: Sociedad de Estudios Vascos, 1982), 119.

of Estella and San Sebastian with identical regulation: the seigneur appears in four precepts;[31] and the merino of the king in one.[32] But as well as these precepts, these two local institutions also had their own and exclusive regulation: the seigneur of the *villa* appears in the Estella text on numerous occasions in reference to revenue from fines or other procedural questions,[33] without anything similar in that of San Sebastian. In this other text of the seigneur of the *villa* there also appear three singular precepts with regard to the Estella matrix text.[34]

Some similar happens with the *merino* of Estella.[35] The preceptor of substantial fines and different procedural competences, this is an institution that is not reflected in drawing up of the Fuero of San Sebastian, except in one singular and exclusive chapter that is not inspired by Estella forality.[36]

The fuero recognized the right of residents of San Sebastian to change annually their mayor and provost,[37] judicial institutions that, although they existed in Estella, we do not know whether they were designated annually by the *villa*, since its fuero establishes nothing in this regard. Only two precepts concerning the mayor are repeated in the two fueros.[38] The Fuero of Estella mentions this figure on countless occasions.[39] Yet such mentions are less in that of San Sebastian.[40]

The Estella fuero did not mention the figure of the admiral, a local institution with political, military, and fiscal functions, while it does appear in the San Sebastian text.[41]

---

31 Estella 2, 3.2 = San Sebastian, 3, 1.2; Estella 2, 3.2 = San Sebastian, 3, 1.2; Estella 2, 7.2 = San Sebastian 3, 5.2; and Estella 2, 7.3 = San Sebastian 3, 5.3.
32 Estella 1, 9 = San Sebastian, 2, 7.
33 Estella, 2, 1.2; 2, 8.2; 2, 8.3; 2, 21.3; 2, 25.2; 2, 30; 2, 53.1; and 2, 61.
34 San Sebastian, 4, 3.5; 4, 4.2; and 4, 4.5.
35 Estella, 2, 8.2; 2, 18.1; 2, 18.4; 2, 18.5; 2, 21.3; 2, 22.3; 2, 22.4; 2, 22.5; 2, 48.4; and 2, 50.3.
36 San Sebastian, 4, 2.2.
37 San Sebastian, 4, 8.
38 Estella 1, 6.3 = San Sebastian 2, 4.3 and Estella 1, 10.2 = San Sebastian 2, 8.2.
39 Estella, 2, 8.2; 2, 31.4; 2, 48.3; 2, 48.4; and 2, 67.
40 San Sebastian, 4, 4.7 and 4, 4.8.
41 San Sebastian, 4, 4.7.

Trials

The settlers of our two *villas* enjoyed a privileged judicial environment.[42] In the Fueros of Estella and San Sebastian men always had to be judged within the *villa*.[43] Yet if it so happened that a resident were outside the *villa* and an outsider made a complaint against him, both would go to Estella or San Sebastian, respectively, where justice would be meted out in accordance with the fuero, because he could not be judged by an external judge.[44] This legal principle was reiterated in the last chapter of the San Sebastian text, in which the monarch gave the Fuero to settlers of the *villa*, "who, wherever they were in my land or in my curia, should be judged according to the Fuero of San Sebastian."[45]

As regards the penal process in these fueros, studied by Alonso,[46] there is nothing to indicate the forms in which trials started. As we have seen, the figure of the mayor hardly appears reflected in these texts, so that we do know whether he had any kind of official initiative in persecuting a crime. The already alluded to chapter on the man from outside the *villa* who filed a complaint against a resident[47] seems to indicate that the start of judicial activity came about by motion of the accuser. This is the same idea as in other precepts that point in the same direction.[48]

There were were time-frames in which to present an accusation, at least in certain circumstances, as is deduced from the case of a women who was raped and had to make a legal claim within three days of the assault, demonstrating it with honest witnesses;[49] or likewise as is noted in the chapter on bearing false witness, for which people could not be charged once two years and one day had passed since the bearing of false witness.[50]

---

42 Alonso, "El proceso penal en el Fuero de San Sebastián," 397–98.
43 Estella 1, 10.1 = San Sebastian 2, 8.1.
44 Estella 1, 10.2 = San Sebastian 2, 8.2.
45 San Sebastian, 4, 9.
46 Alonso, "El proceso penal en el Fuero de San Sebastián," 398–405.
47 Estella 1, 10.2 = San Sebastian 2, 8.2.
48 Estella 2, 7 = San Sebastian 3, 5; Estella 1, 6 = San Sebastian 2, 4; and Estella, 2, 26 = San Sebastian, 3, 8.
49 Estella, 1, 6.5 = San Sebastian, 2, 4.5.
50 Estella, 2, 26.1 = San Sebastian, 3, 8.1.

Precautionary measures were included with a certain precision. Thus, no one could be arrested if they put down a legal or self bond.[51] In the former case, a legal guarantor guaranteed that the accused would attend the trial and, if the sentence went against him, he would comply with it. As regards the latter, it was a self-bond in which the accused himself posted the bond, promising to be held captive as a guarantee of completing the sentence.[52] There is nothing in the Fuero of Estella to indicate posting bail in penal processes. The Fuero of San Sebastian does, however, do so in a long chapter made up of ten precepts, in order to assure payment for defamation, with the aim of serving at the same time as a guarantee and an executive procedure:[53]

> Whosoever has bail through his assets, achieves security for bail.
>
> And if they were to demonstrate as bail a dead security, which may be worth a third less, accept the security, and that on the third day.
>
> But if they were to offer a living beast, accept it either sooner or later. But if the debt were to be worth more than one hundred *sueldos*, show him a horse or a female mule or a male mule or a living mare.
>
> And if his assets are worth more than one hundred *sueldos*, show him a beast that is worth twenty *sueldos*; and if fifty, show him a beast of ten *sueldos*.
>
> And if he were not able to provide security, according to that written above, show him the king's seal; and if he does not wish to show the king's seal, at an optimum time go with the seigneur of the *villa* and demand sixty *sueldos*, and put him in the king's prison until he has his assets.
>
> And the amount due for those beasts is eighteen *denarios* between day and night; and if it is an ass, nine *denarios*.

---

51 Estella 1, 5 = San Sebastian 2, 3.
52 Alonso, "El proceso penal en el Fuero de San Sebastián," 401.
53 San Sebastián, 4, 3.1–3.10.

And if the same guarantor were being held captive, he should pay sixty *sueldos* for each night for who is being kept prisoner.

And if he were to pay with those assets, return them duplicated.

And if the guarantor were to appeal to the perpetrator, give five days of peace if he is in the land of the king; and if he is outside, ten days. And if he is in Santiago, one month and one day; in San Gil one month and one day; and in Jerusalem, one year and one day. And if under the aforementioned terms he were not to come, give him assets without resistance.

And wherever he finds security give him bail so that, as an accreditor, you may take it to the debtor, show him the king's seal, and if he refuses, take it as a legal guarantor. And if it were evident, pay him or take his love; and if he were to break the king's seal, he should pay sixty *sueldos*.

The central phase of the process was made up of a test, which always fell to the accuser. He had to demonstrate the alleged facts by means of a test, and when he presented it, it does not appear that the accused presented any defense.[54] The test was generally one of testimony.[55] If there were no probatory means through witnesses and the accused was not absolved or the trial suspended, the defendant had the right to demonstrate his innocence. In the face of that unproven accusation, the accused had to banish any doubts through, above all, tests of ordeal, as befitting procedural penal law prior to the reception of *Ius commune*. These trials by God by which divinity designated the guilty[56] were in our fueros exceptional cases

---

54   As Alonso deduces from the precepts Estella 1, 6 = San Sebastian 2, 4; Estella 2, 5 = San Sebastian 3, 3; and Estella, 2, 26 = San Sebastian, 3, 8. See "El proceso penal en el Fuero de San Sebastián," 402.

55   Thus in the following precepts: Estella 1, 4.1. San Sebastian 2, 2.1; Estella 1, 4.2. San Sebastian 2, 2.2; Estella 1, 6.5 San Sebastian 2, 4.5; Estella 2, 6.4. San Sebastian 3, 4; Estella 2, 6.6. San Sebastian 3, 4.6; and Estella, 2, 26.2. San Sebastian, 3, 8.2. Likewise, Estella, 2, 13.1; 2, 13.2; 2, 19.1–19.4; 2, 22.2; 2, 22.6; 2, 22.30; 2, 25.1–25.4; 2, 28; 2, 32.2; 2, 32.3; 2, 32.5; 2, 34.1; 2, 35.2; 2, 37.1–37.3; 2, 38.3; 2, 50.1; 2, 50.2; 2, 52.1; 2, 54; 2, 55.1; 2, 55.2; 2, 55.4; 2, 55.5; 2, 62.2; 2, 63.1; 2, 63.3; 2, 64.2; 2, 66; 2, 67; 2, 68.1., and San Sebastian, 4, 4.1; 4, 4.2.

56   Monreal Zia and Jimeno Aranguren, *Textos histórico-jurídicos navarros. I. Historia Antigua y*

of trial by combat and trial by the ordeal of hot iron. The first of the ordeals appears in three precepts:

> And if someone were to pick sprouts by day in an unfenced vegetable garden, they will have to pay five *sueldos* and return what they picked; and if it were fenced, twenty-five *sueldos*. And if he cannot prove with witnesses, he will have to swear an oath that which he denied; and if he who is trying to prove this so wishes, he can demand it to be done by trial by combat.[57]

> And if any relatives of the deceased say to he who murdered the man: "you killed my relative by some other means, and not at home," the murder must be judged and proven by the iron test in order to demonstrate that he killed him at night in his home and for no other reason or enmity. And if he were to get out healthy and unharmed from the iron test, the relatives of the deceased must give him guarantees and he will not have to take responsibility for murder; they can also have a duel if both parties agree; but this is not part of the fuero.[58]

> But if he cannot prove it [false testimony] with witnesses, it can be resolved by trial by combat; and if he were to be victorious, amends will be made as written above. But if he were to be victorious in the lawsuit, he who he proves will give a fine of five hundred *sueldos* and it will be murder by he whom he wanted to prove and by his relatives.[59]

The holding of duels could only be carried out by men from the *villa* itself, since the two fueros prohibited expressly that, in the event of a lawsuit, there was a duel with men from elsewhere. In

---

Medieval, 735–36.

57   Estella 2, 6.4 = San Sebastian 3, 4.4.
58   Estella 2, 7.4 = San Sebastian 3, 5.4.
59   Estella, 2, 26.2 = San Sebastian, 3, 8.2.

place of this measure, they would appoint witnesses, one Navarrese and one Frank;[60] and if they had no witnesses, they would have to swear an oath.[61]

As regards the ordeal of hot iron, Alonso reminds us that it was reserved for casuistries that were difficult to prove on account of them coinciding with nighttime.[62] That was the case of a vineyard watchman allegedly attacked at night. The accused would suffer the iron test, but, if he did not burn himself, the watchman would have to pay sixty *sueldos*.[63] The second case, as noted already above, refers to a homicide:

> If any of the relatives of the deceased say to he who murdered the man: "you killed my relative by some other means, and not at home," the murder must be judged and proven by the iron test in order to demonstrate that he killed him at night in his home and for no other reason or enmity. And if he were to get out healthy and unharmed from the iron test, the relatives of the deceased must give him guarantees and he will not have to take responsibility for murder; they can also have a duel if both parties agree; but this is not part of the fuero.[64]

There is in the Fuero of Estella—but not in that of San Sebastian—a third example of trial by ordeal, although in this case for a civil matter, due to the payment of debts, in the chapter titled "On the man who has died."[65]

> If a man who has died owed any money to another man, and he who reclaims this cannot prove what the deceased owed him, the sons of the latter will have to swear on oath that they did not know their father owed the money; and that will be enough.

60 Estella 1, 4.1 = San Sebastian 2, 2.1.
61 Estella 1, 4.2 = San Sebastian 2, 2.2.
62 Alonso, "El proceso penal en el Fuero de San Sebastián," 404.
63 Estella 2, 6.7 = San Sebastian 3, 4.7.
64 Estella 2, 7.4 = San Sebastian 3, 5.4.
65 Estella, 2, 33.1–33.4.

The wife of the deceased will act in the same way, and if the claimant says "you knew about this," he will have to resort to the iron test.

And if he were to say to the son, "your father owes me this money," and the son replies, "he may have owed it, but he paid you back," he who is claiming the money must swear on oath and lift the hot iron, and if he demonstrates it, he will recover his money.

And if he so wishes, he who must suffer the iron test can use another man to lift the hot iron for him, because if he can use another man for the battle in his place, he can do the same to lift the iron in the trial in which the test takes place.

The Fueros of Estella and San Sebastian state nothing about the decision of the judge, but, as Alonso rightly observes, that was closely connected to the outcome of the test, so that the judge restricted himself to acknowledging this clearly, with the resulting declaration of the sentence foreseen in the fuero itself. This is what one seems to deduce from the articles in which a close relationship between test and sentence is noted;[66] the case, for example, of the chapter relating to bearing false witness.[67]

If someone appears as or bears false witness and another can prove that with other testimonies, after one year and one day has elapsed, he will make good for everything the other that he made lose has lost; and who gave the testimony will remain at the mercy of the seigneur of the land.

But if he cannot prove it with witnesses, it can be resolved by trial by combat; and if he were to be victorious, amends will be made as written above. But if he were to be victorious in the lawsuit, he who he proves will give a fine of five hundred *sueldos* and it will be murder by he whom he wanted to prove and by his relatives.

But if in the second year no appeal is made against him, he will reply no more, nor will he dare to appeal it; if he

66   Alonso, "El proceso penal en el Fuero de San Sebastián," 404.
67   Estella, 2, 26.1–26.3 = San Sebastian, 3, 8.1–8.3.

were to do so, he will be given a fine of two hundred and fifty *sueldos*.

There was no recourse before such a sentence, so that the decision was conclusive.

Military Service

The local fueros of this era usually contain a regulation concerning military service and the exemptions that the residents of foral *villas* were entitled to.[68] That is the case of the Fueros of Estella and San Sebastian, texts that granted special importance to completing military service, in that this matter was included in the first precept. In the Estella edition, which is somewhat longer, the king granted the advantageous disposition that residents did not have to complete military service, except three obligatory days when there may be a pitched battle or if the king found himself besieged by enemies. Despite that, residents could get an exemption from this obligation by sending a laborer in their possession or sixty *sueldos*.[69] The exemption from taking part in military expeditions was more restricted in the case of San Sebastian, in which the king restricted himself to pointing out that the setttlers of San Sebastian would not have to undertake military or cavalry service. The latter was a short swift horseback campaign in enemy terrain.[70] In San Sebastian, moreover, the monarch conceded that they would not wage war or fight with outside men on account of any quarrel.[71]

Taxation

The fueros of the Franks were usually characterized by the award of advantageous fiscal conditions with the aim of attracting new settlers and establishing them in the *villas*. In this sense, and as has been alluded to, the Fuero of Estella decreed that if a settler arrived

---

68 Roldán Jimeno Aranguren, "Servicio de armas en los fueros medievales de Vasconia: fonsado/hueste, cabalgada y apellido," *Iura Vasconiae* 4 (2007), 33–66.
69 Estella, 1, 1 and 1, 2.
70 San Sebastian, 1, 1.
71 San Sebastian 2, 1.

in the *villa* to put down roots there and rent out a property, he would be exempt from all taxes and charges for one year and one day. From this point on, he would have to do military service and pay residency duties, and he would be considered a resident, like any other.[72] Among those duties was the direct tax that residents had to pay the king.[73] There is no similar precept in the Fuero of San Sebastian beyond that which states that settlers will be "free and exempt from any bad fuero and any bad custom forever."[74]

The most advantageous taxation in San Sebastian was corroborated by the inclusion in this Fuero of a precept that did not exist in Estella. In the Gipuzkoan *villa* the king conceded the right of free possession for residents and their descendants of all the ovens and baths and mills they made. Moreover, the sovereign would not demand any rent from these.[75]

In both *villas* the monarch charged for the fuero substantial fines, even if there was the guarantee that the king's *merino* would never take a fine from a man of Estella, only on the agreement of six good residents.[76]

Both fueros were especially beneficial for merchants, who were partially or fully liberated from paying tributes, the tax on merchandise sold that financed the treasury.[77] Specifically, in the Fuero of Estella it was established that, on Thursdays—understood as market day—tributes would not be charged except in the case of that which was measured with a roller. The townspeople, moreover, could sell grains in their homes and they would not have to pay tributes except on Wednesdays from 3:00 pm on and until Thursday night.[78]

The Fuero of San Sebastian was more generous in this matter. The king conceded an exemption from tributes, both there

---

72   Estella, 2, 16.
73   Anotnio Sola Alayeto and Toño Ros Zuasti, *Estella, posta y mercado en la Ruta Jacobea* (Estella: Caja de Ahorros de Navarra, 1992), 12.
74   San Sebastian, 1, 1.2.
75   San Sebastian, 1, 6.
76   Estella 1, 9 = San Sebastian, 2, 7.
77   Monreal Zia and Jimeno Aranguren, *Textos histórico-jurídicos navarros. I. Historia Antigua y Medieval*, 810.
78   Estella, 2, 59.1.

and throughout the kingdom, to settlers who arrived by sea or land with their merchandise.[79] An exception was made, though, for the case of any settler who bought packages or merchandise in Baiona and was traveling through San Sebastian to sell their goods elsewhere. In that event they would have to settle the tribute payment, a tax they would not pay if selling in the *villa* itself.[80] The fuero specified that whoever took bread, wine, and meat into the *villa* would not pay any tribute.[81]

The king, moreover, decreed that vessels based in San Sebastian were free and exempt from charges, so that they would not pay transit fees (*portazgo*) or tributes;[82] in contrast, foreign vessels would have to settle payment.[83] Meanwhile, if a vessel were to run aground in San Sebastian, merchants could recover all their goods, paying ten *sueldos* and the tribute.[84]

Besides these suppositions, the San Sebastian fuero established that outsiders should give for each load of fish, six *dineros*; for each load of wax, six arrival *dineros* and its tribute, a third less than what was stated in the Fuero of Pamplona; for a load of copper, six *dineros*; for a load of tin, six *dineros* and its tribute; for a load of lead, six *dineros* and its tribute; and for each strake of hides, two *dineros*, or for half a strake, one *dinero*, and if it were less than that, there was no charge.[85]

The Rights of Merchants and Pilgrims

One of the most substantial differences between the two fueros under study here is to be found in commercial law. We have just verified this in observing in the previous section the different regulations regarding tributes and other charges levied on commerce. Yet beyond these differences there were also major similarities. Both

---

79 San Sebastian, 1, 2.1.
80 San Sebastian, 1, 2.2.
81 San Sebastian, 1, 5.
82 San Sebastian, 1, 3.1.
83 Specifically, for each vessel ten *sueldos* in the currency of Navarre, and for each package taken off the vessel, twelve arrival *dineros*, as well as its tribute, but a third less than what was stated in the Fuero of Pamplona. San Sebastian, 1, 3.2.
84 San Sebastian, 1, 10.
85 San Sebastián, 1, 4.1–4.6.

municipalities, through the fuero, would have a market, an institution that produced a commercial and industrial economy and that would be the true economic driving force of these places. Free artisans and merchants were not beholden to a seigneur, so that they were legally and economically independent.

The first Estella fuero granted special importance to boosting the local market, with different dispositions about merchants and the regulation of the market itself.[86] For example, there was the regulation that indicated that if anyone was using a false measure, weight, cubit, or cord, they would have to pay the king sixty *sueldos*. This precept is included in the Fuero of San Sebastian.[87]

There were two markets in Estella, one weekly and another daily.[88] The former appears to have been held on Thursdays. The fuero, as we have seen, decreed that no tributes would be charged on that day if it were not something that could be measured with a roller. On that day, the townspeople could sell grains in their homes, and they would not pay any tribute except between 3:00 pm on Wednesday and Thursday night.[89] The rest of the precepts relating to commerce do not appear to distinguish between the weekly and daily markets, whose co-protagonists were pilgrims. They were mixed up with the merchants themselves, even legally, since in one chapter it is stated that, "if one buys an animal from a pilgrim or a merchant and does not demand any guarantee, and they have witnesses there who will swear to it, the purchase will be valid; but if he himself swears that he bought it thus from a pilgrim with a shell and a stick, it will also be valid. It is the same for the merchant without witnesses."[90]

The Fuero of Estella protected merchants so that they would not have any major problems in their commercial activity. Thus, for example, no outsider could bear arms in the market, if he were not just passing through, and in that event, he would be left alone

---

86 Jimeno Aranguren, "El municipio de Vasconia en la Edad Media," 59–60.
87 Estella 1, 11 = San Sebastian, 2, 9.
88 Sola Alayeto and Ros Zuasti, *Estella, posta y mercado en la Ruta Jacobea*, 12–14.
89 Estella, 2, 59.1.
90 Estella, 2, 34.1.

without paying any fine.[91] The Fuero of San Sebastian was broader in the disposition that had the same aim, when it established that, "men from elsewhere, from the moment they enter San Sebastian, must not strike out or take up any sharp weapons for malevolence toward or homicide of others; and if they do so, they must pay a fine of one thousand *sueldos*. And if all the inhabitants rise up and kill that man who may have struck another, there is no defamation in that."[92]

Physical safety was tied to legal and economic security, since both fueros considered that if anyone were using false measures, weights, cubits, or cords they would have to pay the king sixty *sueldos*.[93] Both fueros also had precepts that no man could be free from debt with respect to the Franks in the *villa*.[94] Likewise, the Fuero of Estella signaled that anyone who went to the market could not get into debt, so long as they were not a debtor or guarantor.[95] In the same sense, the San Sebastian fuero stated that no man could be exempt from any debt against the Franks in the *villa*.[96] This latter text also warns that, "all the inhabitants of San Sebastian in any profession should make a living without theft or treachery."[97]

Both fueros imposed on outside merchants a tax on trading from their hostels, the so-called *hostelaje*. They were obliged to pay the owner of the premises in which they were staying and in which traders could also carry out their commercial activities. This practice must have been important, since the Estella fuero dedicated up to fourteen precepts to *hostelaje*.[98] This figure rose to thirty-two in that of San Sebastian.[99]

It does not appear that in Estella the differences between merchants and pilgrims were substantial as regards their *hospedaje*

---

91   Estella, 2, 59.3.
92   San Sebastian, 2, 11.
93   Estella 1, 11 = San Sebastian, 2, 9.
94   Estella 1, 12. San Sebastian, 2, 10. The difference in this precept is that, in the Fuero of Estella, it includes Jews alongside Franks.
95   Estella, 2, 59.2.
96   San Sebastian, 2, 10.
97   San Sebastian, 4, 1.
98   Estella, 2, 24.1–14.
99   San Sebastian, 4, 5.1–5.11 and 4, 6.1–6.21.

rights or as regards the sentences imposed for crimes committed in hostelries:[100]

> If some pilgrim or merchant lodges in a house and his baggage disappears, and he says to the head of the house or to his wife or to his sons or to his daughters: "You have my baggage and therefore you are a thief and an accomplice," and the head of the house responds: "no," the accused must take an oath and prove his innocence appearing before a judicial trial, and if he loses, he will have to surrender one third of the value of the theft to the owner of the baggage, and pay a fine of sixty *sueldos* to the king for the theft committed, and another sixty *sueldos* for the trial.
>
> And of the latter, twenty *sueldos* will be for the *merino*, another twenty for the mayor, and another twenty for the seigneur of the *villa*.
>
> Nevertheless, if the accused is not defeated in the trial, the pilgrims or the merchants will pay sixty *sueldos* to the seigneur of the *villa*.
>
> Likewise, if he who was lodging were to steal goods from the head of the house, he would have to respond by following the same judicial procedure outlined.
>
> And if by coincidence the accused did not have any goods and were declared guilty following the trial, he will have to give up publicly as a thief any personal property and real estate, with an oath that he has no more goods.

It goes without saying that the San Sebastian fuero lacks any regulation relating to the Camino pilgrimage, which demonstrates that the coastal route to Santiago did not exist in Gipuzkoa in the late twelfth century.

---

100 Estella, 2, 8.1–8.5.

The Legal Protection of Property and Possessions, and the Real Rights of Use

The strong protection of private property was a widespread characteristic of Jaca forality;[101] to the point of being able to surround it as the core power of authority, with the aim of making sure property was respected by others.[102] Property owners could own property without any taxes, on pointing out that wherever settlers brought an inherited property or they lived in it within or outside the town limits, it would be free and exempt for them, without any bad injunction or rent.[103] One could also acquire inherited property through possession for one year and one day without opposition; if, form that moment on, anyone were to claim it or take it away, they would have to pay the king sixty *sueldos* and confirm possession of the inheritance.[104] This series of measures implied an effective tutelage of property and they favored the traffic of property.

The fueros, meanwhile, developed a prominent defense in the face of forced entry of homes or any other property through numerous penal precepts.

As regards real rights of use, the king conceded to settlers in Estella the right to use fields, forests, and waters in any place they could go to and return from in a day,[105] while in San Sebastian he delimited more precisely the geographical environs of this right, in establishing it "from Undarabia to the Oria, from Arrenga up to San Martín de Arano, the whole region I possess within those limits." In the concession to San Sebastian he specified, as in Estella, that settlers would have "always and throughout my land pastures and woods and waters, just as men who live within the environs have."[106] Moreover, the monarch, owner of the means of production in those lands of the kingdom, conceded via the fuero to settlers in San Sebastian the right to establish ovens and baths and mills, and that they would

---

101 Jesús Lalinde, *Los Fueros de Aragón* (Zaragoza: Librería General, 1979), 23; García Cantero, "El Derecho civil en el Fuero de San Sebastián," 384.
102 Estella 2, 3.1–3.4. = San Sebastian, 3, 1.1–1.4.
103 Estella 1, 2.1 = San Sebastian 2, 1.1.
104 Estella 1, 2.2 = San Sebastian 2, 1.2.
105 Fuero Estella, 1.3.
106 San Sebastian, 1, 11.

be possessed by them and all their descendants, freely and exempt from charges, without the monarch being able to demand any rent from them, as we have had occasion to see above.[107]

Indebtedness and Contracts

Indebtedness

Indebtedness barely appears reflected in the legal texts being analyzed here, beyond that incurred as a result of bonds (which we will see later) and connected to the privilege the San Sebastian fuero conceded to debtors to enjoy a moratorium for the payment of debts: any debtor from the *villa* or his guarantor would not respond to the creditor until the period of two years had elapsed,[108] so any such delay did not imply guilt during this period. This was a singular precept, without any precedent in the Estella text.

Both fueros regulated in the same way the indebtedness test, which could be both under oath and in testimony.[109] The fueros anticipated, likewise, the supposition of false testimony with witnesses. One year and one day having elapsed, the person that bore false witness would have to pay for any damages and remained at the mercy of the seigneur of the *villa*, who would dictate the corresponding penal sanction.[110] In the event that there were no witnesses to be able to prove it, the alleged perpetrator of false testimony could save himself by the ordeal of trial by combat.[111]

For its part, the Fuero of Estella, without it having anything similar in that of San Sebastian, considered a dead man's debts casuistry: if he who claimed the money could not prove that the deceased owed it to him and the children of the deceased swore on oath that they did not know their father owed such money, their testimony would be enough.[112] However, if the wife of the deceased acted in the same way, and if the claimant reproached her

107 San Sebastian 1, 6.
108 San Sebastian, 1, 8.
109 Estella 1, 4.2 = San Sebastian 2, 2.2 and Estella 1, 4.1 = San Sebastian 2, 2.1.
110 Estella, 2, 26.1 = San Sebastian, 3, 8.1.
111 Estella, 2, 26.2 and 26.3; San Sebastian, 3, 8.2 and 8.3.
112 Estella, 2, 33.1.

by arguing that she did know, there would have to be a resort to trial by the ordeal of hot iron.[113] And if the debtor were to say to the son of the deceased: "your father owes me this money," and the son replied, "he may have owed it, but he paid you back," he who was claiming the money had to swear an oath and lift the hot iron, and if he demonstrated it, he would recover his money.[114]

The Buying and Selling of Property

Both the Fuero of Estella and that of San Sebastian include a rich casuistry relating to buying, selling, and renting of property, with an essentially common regulation.

Properties possessed a certain freedom in commercial dealings, which implied a powerful stimulant in attracting settlers.[115] The purchase or acquisition of an inherited property in the *villas* of Estella and San Sebastian or outside them had to be free and exempt from any kind of bad embargo or rent.[116] And, after having possessed it for one year and one day without opposition, should anyone make a claim on it, the claimant would have to pay the king sixty *sueldos* and moreover conform such possession.[117] Beyond buying and selling properties, the fueros alluded to another form of buying and selling in a chapter dedicated to the rights of stepchildren with regard to real estate that was the possession of their father, which could not be sold or pawned by their widowed stepmother.[118] In the specific case of the Fuero of San Sebastian sales are mentioned when addressing the regulation of paying tributes for the sale of merchandise.[119] And in that of Estella, four precepts are dedicated to the "purchase of farms."[120]

---

113 Estella, 2, 33.2.
114 Estella, 2, 33.3.
115 García Cantero, "El Derecho civil en el Fuero de San Sebastián," 390.
116 Estella 1, 2.1 = San Sebastian 2, 1.1.
117 Estella 1, 2.2 = San Sebastian 2, 1.2.
118 Estella, 2, 11.13 = San Sebastian, 3, 9.13.
119 San Sebastian, 1, 2.
120 Estella, 2, 25.1–25.4.

Donations

Donations were linked to family and inherence institutions.[121] If a widowed mother who had married again wished to donate some of what had belonged to her husband to her new husband or any other man, that donation would be valid so long as she gave guarantees as such.[122] This widow could also make a donation *mortis causa* of what used to belong to him, without any bond being necessary, always on the condition that there were testamentary heirs who said to God and his souls: "we hear and see this donation being made."[123] For his part, the husband could not make a donation of the possessions that belonged to his wife without her express authorization, so that he could only donate those possessions that he himself owned.[124]

Renting

The regulation of renting followed, as in other fueros of the Franks, a criterion protective of the rental owner. Renting was circumscribed to properties, with precepts relating to the duration of the contract, payment of rent, and causes for expiration.[125] The fueros were especially generous toward settlers in indicating that, "should anyone rent the house of an honorable man of the *villa*, and if the owner himself wished to move to that house, he who rented the house will have to leave the house and hand over to the seigneur the rental mount corresponding to the time he was in that house."[126]

However, when the rental was established on a winery, hay loft, granary, or other such premises, the rental agreement would remain valid until its expiration.[127]

Nor did the tenant have the right to free himself from payment of rent, not even for very important reasons such as a trip to Jerusalem or another country, or on account of a move to

---

121 García Cantero, "El Derecho civil en el Fuero de San Sebastián," 390–91.
122 Estella, 2, 11.6 = San Sebastian, 3, 9.6.
123 Estella, 2, 11.7 = San Sebastian, 3, 9.7.
124 Estella, 2, 11.10 and 11.11 = San Sebastian, 3, 9.10 and 9.11.
125 García Cantero, "El Derecho civil en el Fuero de San Sebastián," 391.
126 Estella 2, 14.1 = San Sebastian 3, 7.1.
127 Estella 2, 14.2 = San Sebastian 3, 7.2.

another *villa*.[128] Nor was taking a wife or moving to another home in the same *villa* a valid motive for finalizing a contract or being exempt from payment of the rent.[129]

When a mother who had remarried wished to rent out the inherited property of the children of her first husband, she would have the right to retain it paying the same rental amount that would be offered to any other interested party.[130]

One should point out, lastly, that the Fuero of Estella included in its epigraph "on renting" the lodging contract. This was a contract that gave full freedom, without permitting forced lodging: "should anyone rent the house of an honorable man of the villa, and if the owner himself wished to move to that house, he who rented the house will have to leave the house and hand over to the seigneur the rental mount corresponding to the time he was in that house."[131]

Bonds and Security

In the interest of achieving greater legal security in commercial transactions and all types of buying and selling, the municipal fueros regulated guarantee figures and especially bonds and security.[132] The detailed regulation that the Fuero of Estella made for these figures was barely translated in the Fuero of San Sebastian, except in very specific precepts such as that concerning the fact that no one could enter into the house of a debtor neighbor in order to reclaim the security by force, incurring in the event a sentence of twenty-five *sueldos* for the owner of the house, except if the security they were taking was by way of a bond, so that then the guarantor could take said security.[133]

---

128 Estella 2, 14.3 = San Sebastian 3, 7.3.
129 Estella 2, 14.4 = San Sebastian 3, 7.4.
130 Estella, 2, 11.17 = San Sebastian, 3, 9.17.
131 Estella 2, 14.1 = San Sebastian 3, 7.1.
132 Roldán Jimeno Aranguren, "Las figuras de garantía en los fueros medievales hispánicos occidentales," in *Historia de la Propiedad. Crédito y Garantía. V Encuentro interdisciplinar, Salamanca, 31 de mayo–2 de junio de 2006*, ed. Salustiano de Dios, Javier Infante, Ricardo Robledo, and Eugenia Torijano (Madrid: Servicio de Estudios del Colegio de Registradores, 2007), 15–79.
133 Estella, 1, 8 = San Sebastian, 2, 6.

Both fueros contain some precepts in which the obligation to guarantee is underscored, such as that of widows who wished to retain for their children real estate and personal property, in which case she had to give good bonds to the relations of the children, thereby assuring that, when they arrived at puberty, they would be given the said real estate and personal property.[134] The two texts included, likewise, the casuistry of the widow that, supplying guarantees, made a donation of her own possessions to her second and current husband or to any other man.[135]

The rest of the exhaustive regulation is privative in both fueros. That of Estella dedicated these guarantee figures fifty-four precepts;[136] and that of San Sebastian reduced the number to eleven.[137]

Marriage, Widowhood, and Second Nuptials

The texts of Estella and San Sebastian, as is typical in municipal fueros in the Middle Ages, did not regulate the institution of marriage, on account of it being a matter of canonical competence. We find allusions to marriage in sexual offenses. In this sense, what stand out are the precepts relating to rape, by which the assailant could marry the victim, seek out a husband for her, or offer her financial compensation. Specifically, the two fueros under analysis here go into great detail on the casuistry of marriage taking place after a rape.[138] Marriage was considered a form of making amends for the crime, in establishing that if any townsman forced himself on a woman, he would have to compensate her or take her as his wife.[139] This casuistry was not widespread, since distinctions were made depending on social class: if the victim was from a lower social class than her assailant, he was obliged to find her a husband in line with her position according to a ruling pronounced by the mayor and

---

134 Estella 2, 12.2 = San Sebastian 3, 6.2.
135 Estella, 2, 11.6; San Sebastian, 3, 9.6.
136 Estella, 2, 9.1–9.4; 2, 10; 2, 13.1–13.2; 2, 20.1–20.3; 2, 22.1–22.35; 2, 23.1–23.4; 2, 28; 2, 48.1–2, and 48.4.
137 San Sebastian, 1, 8; 4, 3.1–3.10.
138 Roldán Jimeno Aranguren, *Matrimonio y otras uniones afines en el Derecho histórico navarro (siglos VIII–XVIII)* (Madrid: Dykinson, 2015), 184–91.
139 Estella, 1, 6.2 = San Sebastian, 2, 4.2.

twelve good men.[140] This would be in the event of choosing not to marry her or handing himself in to the woman's relatives.[141] The fueros paused to regulate the economic dimension of marriage. Like other local normative texts of the time, they considered a system of earned goods, that is, a system that encompassed the whole set of acquisitions and earnings obtained during marriage and that with its dissolution, were divided according to that stipulated by both parties. The singularity of this system included in the Fueros of Estella and San Sebastian resided in the liquidation of the community of possessions as a result of dissolving a marriage.[142]

Another feature characteristic of the texts resided in the so-called usufruct of widowed faithfulness, which sought to guarantee family unity and the survival of the widowed spouse.[143] The widow was the usufructuary of all the possessions belonging to the deceased spouse. Although she was the transmitter of these possessions, she could not sell them, so that they passed directly from father to children when the latter came of age. The widow, moreover, could not remarry and had to raise the children and settle any outstanding debts. This woman possessed a whole series of legal powers and faculties that were outlined in the Fueros of Estella and San Sebastian: "And if the wife hears her husband make a donation, and is in that place and remains silent, if she does not authorize that donation it will not be valid. And if the wife lives and the husband dies, although there may be children, while the woman wants to remain a widow, she will be owner and in full custody of all possessions and properties."[144]

As one can observe, usufruct in the Fuero of Estella—and therefore in that of San Sebastian as well—corresponded only to the widow. The fact that the husband did not appear did not mean that

---

140 Estella, 1, 6.3 = San Sebastian, 2, 4.3.
141 "And if he should not wish to give her a husband that way, he should take her as his wife. And if he should not wish to do either of these things, he should place his body in the hands of the woman's relatives to do whatsoever they wish." Estella, 1, 6.4 = 2, 4.4. See García Cantero, "El Derecho civil en el Fuero de San Sebastián," 392; Marcelino Beroiz Lazcano, *Crimen y castigo en Navarra bajo el reinado de los primeros Evreux (1328–1349)* (Pamplona: Universidad Pública de Navarra/Nafarroako Unibertsitate Publikoa, 2005), 214.
142 Jimeno Aranguren, *Matrimonio y otras uniones afines en el Derecho histórico Navarro*, 316–19.
143 This is a summary of the text in ibid., 359–90.
144 Estella, 2, 11.11 = San Sebastian, 3, 9.11.

in practice widowers were also usufructuaries. This legal loophole was clarified by Theobald II in 1269, extending the fuero in this matter to *"todo homne ho muyller de Esteylla."*[145]

It has been noted that the widowhood included in this legal texts implied a consecration of universal widowhood as a legal institution since, in contrast to previous fueros, now it was no longer a question of simple continued conjugal community, but instead it was a whole right of usufruct established legally in favor of the surviving spouse.[146] Specifically, our fueros established the partition in half between the wife and the heirs of the husband of the earnings that existed on the death of the husband: "If a woman's husband dies and she has children by him, and later she wishes to take another husband, that woman must share out among her children half of all that she earned with her first husband, money and inheritances."[147]

In this partition an exception was made for the wife's possessions acquired before marriage, which remained at the free disposition of the surviving woman. Specifically, it was stated that if the wife had another inheritance before she took a husband, she did not have to give any part of that to her children.[148]

This universal widowhood established regarding personal property and real estate had an exception in the stepchildren's usufruct of possessions, which only applied to real estate. Personal property possessions had to be divided in a logical accordance with the matrimonial regime of the community of possessions and acquisitions included in this fuero:

> And if the wife has stepchildren and they did not divide up with their father the wife's part, those stepchildren will have the maternal personal property possessions and real estate the mother earned with their father before he may have

---

145 See doc. 8, Merche Osés Urricelqui, *Documentación medieval de Estella (siglos XII–XVI)* (Pamplona: Gobierno de Navarra, 2005), 105–6; Javier García-Granero, "Fuero General de Navarra 4, 2, 3. El cónyuge viudo que tiene fealdat ¿puede enajenar en caso de necesidad?" *Anuario de Derecho Civil* 27 (1974), 200.

146 José Luis Lacruz Berdejo, "El régimen matrimonial de los fueros de Aragón," *Anuario de Derecho Aragonés* 3 (1946), 131; García-Granero, "Fuero General de Navarra," 200.

147 Estella, 2, 11.1 = San Sebastian, 3, 9.1.

148 Estella, 2, 11.2 = San Sebastian, 3, 9.2.

taken another wife; but as regards the father's part, while the woman wished to remain a widow, they will not have the real estate possessions, but just the personal property possessions will be divided.[149]

The widow could not sell or pawn the inheritances of her stepchildren over which she had usufruct, although she could, if need be—there was express mention of "on account of hunger"—sell or pawn the property inheritances of her children.[150] The usufructuary also had the power to sell property in case of necessity, not in her condition as a widow, but on the basis of the legal authority she possessed over her children who were minors, as can be deduced form the precept that states, "if a younger child remains and later reaches legal age and claims from the mother their share of real estate and personal property possessions, they will have the right to that part of what remains of what was the patrimony of their father."[151]

The usufruct of faithfulness was lost with second nuptials, an aspect to which our fueros dedicated special regulation.[152] The widowed mother that sought to contract new nuptials had to divide up with her children, by half, everything that she had earned with her first husband, both personal property and real estate, as we saw above.[153] Exceptions were made for the wife's own possessions, in pointing out that, "if the wife had another inheritance prior to taking a husband, through patrimony or any other way, she will not have to give part of that to her children."[154]

There were no limitations as regards second, third, or more nuptials, so the liquidations of several earnings could take place: "And if she were to have two or three husbands and had children

---

149 Estella, 2, 11.12 = San Sebastian, 3, 9.12.
150 Estella, 2, 11.13 = San Sebastian, 3, 9.13.
151 Estella, 2, 11.14. San Sebastian, 3, 9.14. See José Martínez Gijón, "Los sistemas de tutela y administración de los bienes de los menores en el Derecho local de Navarra," *Anuario de Historia del Derecho Español* 40 (1970), 235–40; García-Granero, "Fuero General de Navarra," 202.
152 See the considerations of García Cantero, "El Derecho civil en el Fuero de San Sebastián," 392–93 and Salinas Quijada, "El Derecho civil en el Fuero de San Sebastián (Y Fuero Nuevo)," 367–68 and 371–72.
153 Estella, 2, 11.1 = San Sebastian, 3, 9.1.
154 Estella, 2, 11.2 = San Sebastian, 3, 9.2.

by all of them, and the children had not asked their mother for their part, and later she took another husband, then the children would come and claim their own part, the woman will give to each of her children that part of her earnings she had with their respective fathers; and nothing else."[155]

There was also consideration of the case that if the mother liquidated the conjugal state with her children from a previous marriage, she could make any donation with her part, even to a second or previous husband: "And if the children are minors and their father, on dying, appointed witnesses, they can divide up and give guarantees, if they want, and also sell and pawn the inheritance for the necessity of the children, and it will be valid. And the witnesses can compel the mother, in the name of the children, and the mother cannot compel the witnesses."[156]

A woman who remarried could also make donations *inter vivos* with her own possessions, both to her second husband and anyone else, even before dividing up her inheritance from her first spouse, but she was obliged to offer a bond, since the fueros established that, "if by chance it happens that the mother, whether she divides up or not, wished to make some donation from that which belonged to her husband or any other man, that donation will be valid if she gives some kind of guarantee."[157] For Gabriel García-Cantero this precept demonstrates the existence of an obligation to reserve a tax on the remarried woman in relations to the possessions she received from her first husband, with the objective of assuring their destiny in favor of the children of the first marriage.[158]

The widowed mother that married again could, likewise, grant testimony with regard to her own possessions, since, as indicated in the chapter already alluded to, "if the moment of death arrives and she makes a donation of what she possesses, there are no guarantors, but only witnesses, and these witnesses must not swear an oath, but

---

155 Estella, 2, 11.3 = San Sebastian, 3, 9.3.
156 Estella, 2, 11.5 = San Sebastian, 3, 9.5.
157 Estella, 2, 11.6 = San Sebastian, 3, 9.6.
158 García Cantero, "El Derecho civil en el Fuero de San Sebastián," 393.

they must say to God and his souls: 'we hear and see this donation being made'."[159]

The children of the previous marriage, who could not be obliged by the mother to divide up the possessions, could however oblige the mother to do so through a mandate of the king's justice.[160]

The Fueros of Estella and San Sebastian also considered the legal position of the spouse's widow that remarried when there were children of the original couple. Specifically, if the husband made a donation of what belonged to the wife without her authorization, it would not be valid, but it would, however, if the donation came from what belonged to him.[161] While she remained a widow, she could not sell or pawn the real estate of the stepchildren, but she could do so as regards what belonged to her children if there was a clear situation of need that could be corroborated by relatives or neighbors, as the previously discussed precept established.[162] On the other hand, if a younger child remained and later, reaching legal age, claimed from his mother that part of the real estate and personal property of his father, he would be owed his part of what remained of the father's patrimony.[163] As the fuero indicates literally: "if the son were to say, 'you have more of my father's things'; and the mother were to reply, 'no', the son could take that as an oath of his mother. And if witnesses do not want to share out and the grandfather shares out and gives bonds for his grandchildren, and received the children with authorization, it will be valid and established."[164]

When the children came to make the division, they had to do so themselves, and the father and the mother would choose from among all the inheritances.[165]

---

159 Estella, 2, 11.7 = San Sebastian, 3, 9.7.
160 Estella, 2, 11.14 = San Sebastian, 3, 9.14.
161 Estella, 2, 11.10 = San Sebastian, 3, 9.10.
162 Estella, 2, 11.13 = San Sebastian, 3, 9.13.
163 Estella, 2, 11.14 = San Sebastian, 3, 9.14.
164 Estella, 2, 11.15 = San Sebastian, 3, 9.15.
165 Estella, 2, 11.16 = San Sebastian, 3, 9.16.

Filiation

The Fueros of Estella and San Sebastian barely pause to regulate filiation, beyond acknowledging legitimate children. In contrast to other local medieval fueros, they do not mention the children born out of wedlock, although one would imagine that they existed quite normally, since consensual sexual relations with single women were not considered unlawful, or at least they were not fined.[166]

The legal capacity of parents extended to the point their children reached legal age, and as one deduces from the precept already discussed, if a younger child remained and later reached legal age and claimed from his mother part of the real estate and personal property of his father, he would be owed that part belonging to his father's patrimony.[167]

The recognition of parents was carried out bearing in mind legitimate kinship through consanguinity, and the fueros only mentioned occasionally legitimate kinship of affinity in the first degree.[168]

Donations and Inheritances

The only dispositions relating to donations that appear in the Fueros of Estella and San Sebastian were those relating to second nuptials and that would be extendable to further nuptials.[169] There existed, moreover, the particular case of he who sought to make a donation of the houses of his grandparents and who had just one house; he could not donate it, but he could give it for his soul to the church.[170] This was, then, a donation *mortis causa* or a bequest, without it being able to consider it an inheritance in the strictest sense.

The two fueros included both testamentary and intestate inheritance.[171] The ordinary forms of a witnessed will appear, naming the witnesses present. They were the executors of the last will of

---

166 Estella 1, 6.1 = San Sebastian 2, 4.1.
167 Estella, 2, 11.14 = San Sebastian, 3, 9.14.
168 Estella, 2, 11.12 = San Sebastian, 3, 9.12.
169 Estella, 2, 11; 2, 12 = San Sebastian, 3, 9; 3, 6.
170 Estella, 2, 12.6 = San Sebastian, 3, 6.6.
171 García-Granero, "Fuero General de Navarra," 394–96.

the deceased, both as regards donations and voluntary dispositions on the part of the deceased. The Estella and San Sebastian fueros mention the witnesses' functions when addressing the case of the death of a father who had left younger children and that, before dying, had designated witnesses. In such cases, they could divide up and give guarantees, if they wished, and also sell or pawn the inheritance for the need of the children. The witnesses could also compel the mother in the name of the children, and she, in turn, could not compel the witnesses.[172]

The behavior of the witnesses following a death is included in a precept that states, "if the moment of death arrives and she makes a donation of what she possesses, there are no guarantors, but only witnesses, and these witnesses must not swear an oath, but they must say to God and his souls: 'we hear and see this donation being made'."[173]

In this case it is a question of a form of voluntary inheritance (donation or *donatium*), a kind of testamentary mandate that establishes the future destiny of the possessions in an oral way in front of witnesses.

As regards intestate inheritance, a series of legal precautions were delimited to benefit the children, preventing the widowed mother from remarrying. "if someone were to die without making a will at the time of death and there were younger children, and the mother were to take another husband, the relatives of the children can divide up and acknowledge the paternal part of the children and take guarantees."[174]

There were also special testamentary forms, such as the will made before a parish priest on account of risk of death and, in the absence of this priest, making it before any man or before two legally competent women.[175] Likewise, if someone were to die in a

---

172 Estella, 2, 11.5 = San Sebastian, 3, 9.5.
173 Estella, 2, 11.7 = San Sebastian, 3, 9.7.
174 Estella 2, 12.1 San Sebastian 3, 6.1.
175 Estella, 2, 11.8 = San Sebastian, 3, 9.8.

remote place in the presence of a man or a woman, their testimony would be equally valid as that of witnesses.[176]

The two municipal fueros addressed in detail inheritance calls within family inheritance.[177]

For its part, remarrying implied a limitation on the right of disposal *mortis causa* of dividing up the inheritance and how that was carried out in such cases, as noted when addressing second nuptials.

All that remains is to highlight the presence of kinship centrality (*troncalidad*) in drawing up both fueros. This encompassed all real estate and personal property possessions inherited by the son of the deceased: "And if the mother wished to retain for her children real estate and personal property, she will have to give good bonds to the relations of the children, who will, when they arrive at puberty, give them the said real estate and personal property."[178]

There was an especially thorough regulation of kinship restitution: on the death of any children aged twelve or less, the inheritance and real estate and personal property did not go to the living mother, but instead were returned to the immediate family.[179] Kinship possessions, therefore, had to be maintained within the family through descent, and even grandchildren could not make donations of such possessions to outsiders: "No donation can be made from the inheritance from grandparents, just one vineyard, or one piece of land, or one house, if they have two or three houses, or one inherited property, and this to their son or to their daughter. But they may give from that inheritance to their sons or to their daughters when the sons take wives or the daughters husbands."[180]

---

176 Estella, 2, 11.9 = San Sebastian, 3, 9.9.
177 Estella, 2, 11.5 = San Sebastian, 3, 9.5; Estella, 2, 12.3 = San Sebastian, 3, 6.3; Estella, 2, 12.5 = San Sebastian, 3, 6.5; and Estella, 2, 12.5 = San Sebastian 3, 6.5.
178 Estella, 2, 12.2 = San Sebastian, 3, 6.2. The precept only mentions the mother, although one would think that it also applied to the father.
179 Estella, 2, 12.3–12.4 = San Sebastián, 3, 6.3–6.4.
180 Estella, 2, 12.5 = San Sebastian, 3, 6.5.

Guaranteeing the Peace and the Penal protection of People and of Possessions

Penal law in the Fueros of Estella and San Sebastian reflected a right in transformation, since it included a set of norms for diverse circumstances formulated at different periods, in which penal rules of a private nature intertwined with others of royal origins and a public nature. Next to a penal law of a private nature characterized by ordeals—analyzed above—what stood out was a penal law that sought to guarantee the peace and gradually overcome private actions based on revenge. The violation of this peace or social order gave rise to a crime and its corresponding sentence. In this sense, Alonso delimits in the Fueros of Estella and of San Sebastian the two characteristic aspects of peace in explicit references to peace in the city and peace at home: on the one hand, the prohibition on disturbing the established order through revenge; and on the other, the consequence of this violation, which implied leaving the author of the crime exposed to all those who entered into the circle of keeping the peace.[181] The importance of peace in the city is illustrated in the precept that points out that no man from outside who enters the *villa*, not on account of any enmity or homicide that one may exert on another, should strike others or use arms against another; and if they were to do so, if the men of the *villa* were to flog or kill them, they would not suffer any sentence or fine for doing so.[182] Disturbing the peace at home did not have such harsh consequences.[183]

It would entail too much to undertake here a detailed overview of the penal protection that the Fueros of Estella and San Sebastian extended to people and possessions.[184] I will restrict myself to point out that the crimes punished were robbery and theft, homicide, physical assault on people or their possessions, sexual crimes (adultery and rape), commercial deceit or fraud, and bearing false witness.

---

181 Alonso, "El proceso penal en el Fuero de San Sebastian," 399.
182 Estella 1, 14 = San Sebastian, 2, 11.
183 Estella 2, 7.1–7.4 = San Sebastian 3, 5.1–5.4
184 See on this Félix Segura Urra, *Fazer justicia. Fuero poder público y delito en Navarra (siglos XIII–XIV)* (Pamplona: Gobierno de Navarra, 2005); Beroiz Lazcano, *Crimen y castigo en Navarra;* Monreal Zia and Jimeno Aranguren, *Textos histórico-jurídicos navarros. I. Historia Antigua y Medieval,* 740–43.

The Rights of Religious Minorities

The first Fuero of Estella (c. 1076–1077) did not contain any precepts relating to Muslims, but the 1164 version included, perhaps through the influence of Jaca jurisprudence, a regulation relating to Moorish prisoners, that is, those brought from reconquered lands. The fuero restricted itself to stating that Moors had the same fuero as large beasts,[185] which was equivalent to saying that Moors had the legal status of slaves and that they were the property of owners. Likewise, the text pointed out that if a captive Moor or an animal of a townsman injured a man, and the owner refuted this, two Christian witnesses would be needed to prove it.[186] If it could not be proved, the owner of the Moor or the animal had to swear an oath that no such harm was caused; and if he did not want to swear, he would hand over the Moor or the animal.[187]

The Fuero of San Sebastian did not include any precept relating to captive Moors, but nor to Jews either, which is very eloquent since it would seem to indicate the lack of Jews in the *villa*. Furthermore, in drawing up the fuero any allusions to Jews existing in the precepts of the Estella text were deleted when it went to San Sebastian. Thus, for example, when in Estella it was pointed out that "no man can be free of a debt with regard to Franks and Jews in the *villa*," in the Gipuzkoan *villa* this was reduced to, "no man can be free of a debt with regard to Franks in San Sebastian."[188]

The Estella text of 1164 includes the particularity of the Jewish oath "on his east," perhaps by analogy with Muslims, who in their case would swear an oath by looking toward Mecca:[189] "And the Jew and the peasant will swear an oath with their own hand for any debt of more than twelve *dineros*. And the Navarrese will swear an oath on the head of his friend; and the Jew on his east for twelve *dineros* or less; and the Frank for twelve *dineros* or less must swear an

---

185 Estella, 2, 22.26.
186 Estella, 2, 52.1.
187 Estella, 2, 52.2.
188 Estella 1, 12; San Sebastian, 2, 10.
189 Monreal Zia and Jimeno Aranguren, *Textos histórico-jurídicos navarros. I. Historia Antigua y Medieval*, 967.

oath before all the men and will do so on the head of his friend or godfather."[190]

Yet, without doubt, the fuero placed most normative zeal on everything relating to the debts of Jews, to which it dedicated as many as eight precepts. As noted, the original fuero of Sancho Ramírez (c. 1076–1077) pointed out that, "no man can be free of a debt with regard to Franks and Jews in Estella."[191] Of special interest is the rubric "On the Christian and the Jew," in which five cases are included of debts contracted by Jews with respect to Christians:[192]

> If a Jew owes something to a Christian and the Jew tries to deny it, he must prove it with witnesses; if the one he owes is a Frank, he will demonstrate it with a Frank and a Jew; if he is a foreigner, with a foreigner and a Jew; and the Jew with respect to a Christian, by the same procedure.
>
> And if it so happens that the Christian has something in writing, the Jew cannot deny it because the deed of a rabbi is worth as much as witnesses against Jews. But it is necessary for the Jew to demonstrate with witnesses to he who has the deed that he has paid him, and if the claimant cannot prove it, he must swear an oath that he did not pay him, and then he will pay.
>
> And if the Jew were to die, his sons have to finish what their father should have done, according to what was written before, if the Christian has the deed.
>
> And if the Christian were to die, and his children reclaimed the debt and had the deed, then it would be necessary for the Jew to demonstrate he paid his father. And if he could not prove it with witnesses, the son who has the deed will swear an oath that his father has not been paid the money, and the Jew will pay.
>
> And if the Christian has some dispute with the Jew, whether of money, or physical, or another reason, in the

---

190 Estella, 2, 19.9.
191 Estella 1, 12.
192 Estella, 2, 55.1–55.5.

event that he did not have any deed or witnesses, the Jew will explain on oath, and will remain immune; equally the Christian will explain on oath against the Jew, if he does not have any witnesses."

Raquel García Arancón contends that Estella judges granted more importance in the fuero to a situation that must have been relatively atypical, while the more typical case, that of the Jewish creditor, was considered generically in addressing the swearing of an oath for the debts of the lower nobility, Franks, and villeins:[193]

Yet lesser nobles and Franks with respect to a villein and to a Jew will present a man, aged

fifteen or older, that should swear for ten *sueldos* or less.[194]

And the Jew and the villein will swear an oath with their own hand for any debt of more than twelve *dineros*. And the Navarrese will swear an oath on the head of his friend; and the Jew on his east for less than twelve *dineros*; and the Frank for less than twelve *dineros* must swear an oath before all the men and will do so on the head of his friend or godfather.[195]

By Way of Recapitulation

With the first Fuero of Estella, dating from around 1076–1077, there was an attempt to establish a completely new urban center, complementary to the already existing Lizarrara, which would give a different legal status to new settlers, thereby creating an urban framework blessed with services on the increasingly visited Camino de Santiago. We lack the original document of the first Estella fuero, a text that has come down to us in copied form the publication of the more extensive version of the fuero of 1164. The text is made up of fourteen chapters and twenty-three precepts, and establishes some of the defining privileges of the Franks' legal status, such as

---

193 Mª Raquel García Arancón, "Marco jurídico y proyección social de las minorías navarras: judíos y mudéjares (siglos XII–XV)," *Iura Vasconiae. Revista de Derecho Histórico y Autonómico de Vasconia* 4 (2007), 488–89.
194 Estella, 2, 19.8.
195 Estella, 2, 19.9.

the original nature of their possessions and the prescription of one year and one day to acquire them, bonds to avoid going to prison, the right to reclaim jurisdiction over the city itself, the exclusion of the *merino* in charging for defamation, punishment for falsifying weights and measures, and so on. They are the same chapters that we find in the Jaca tradition and that, from the time of Estella edition on, would be passed on with slight modifications to the Fuero of San Sebastian.

A century after its foundation, Estella was made up of different neighborhoods like Lizarra, San Pedro, San Nicolás, the Santo Sepulcro, and that of San Juan. The major novelty was that, except among the early settlements, Franks and Navarrese could settle indiscriminately. The prosperous Estella of the second half of the twelfth century needed a new legal text. Thus was born the more extensive version of the fuero, published in Latin and promulgated by Sancho the Wise in 1164. As José María Lacarra argues, this text implied an early version of the development of Jaca law, since Aragonese and Pamplona versions preserved today date from the thirteenth and fourteenth centuries. This new edition was based on some version of the Fuero of Jaca that has not been preserved. By that time, the theory of a Jaca family had already been established and consolidated, as demonstrated by the fact that in the twelfth century itself, the people of Estella went to Jaca to seek clarifications.

The dispositions in the fuero configured the life of Estella legally. Precepts appeared about the law on widowhood and inheritance that were later present in the Huesca Compilation of 1247, sometimes in almost literal form, or in extensive editions of the Fuero of Jaca, which demonstrates that Estella followed the original law of Jaca. This did not prevent Estella jurists from creating their own exclusive precepts for the city, such as those referring to the Thursday market or coexistence between Franks and Navarrese. The new text would incorporate, moreover, jurisprudence in penal, civil, fiscal, and municipal matters that was later accumulated in almost a century of history of the Frankish *villa*.

The part of the fuero published in 1164 is far more extensive than the supposed original fuero, since it has seventy chapters and two hundred forty-five precepts. The first twenty-four chapters address penal precepts. They form a catalog of crimes with their corresponding sentences, mainly pecuniary, accompanied occasionally by dispositions on their proof. The effort at systemization is most appreciable in the chapters that follow dedicated to different questions of civil law. Questions are considered such as those on security, borrowing, and renting, although the most systematized content concerns inheritance, since it establishes precisely the dividing up of earned possessions, especially when there exists a second marriage, the forms of a will—including that made before a parish priest or the particular form of doing so in a remote place—as well as usufruct rights of widowhood, and the retracting rights of a surviving spouse, an intestate will, and so on. What is more, there is the inclusion of the rights of residency and some chapters dedicated to procedural law, centering on oaths, securities, and bonds. The fuero ends with a fiscal ordinance referring to the rights to charge for *hostalaje*.

The text of the longer Fuero of Estella demonstrates a systemizing effort, at least in two of its groups of civil precepts followed by penal ones. In the former of the groups, civil questions such as debts, buying and selling, salaries, and so on come together, without any mention of the predominance of family law. This is followed by penal precepts on damages. The second group brings together civil chapters on buying and selling and securities, followed by diverse precepts on penal questions relating to certain suppositions on homicide. From chapter 2, 48 on, civil, penal, procedural, fiscal, and municipal questions intermingle more freely.

For its part, the Fuero of San Sebastian, granted by King Sancho VI the Wise around the year 1080, demonstrates a pronounced legal dependence on edition A of the Fuero of Estella. The regulation of certain matters, especially in those that seek to encourage commerce, is more advantageous for settlers in San Sebastian than that which we find in the Estella matrix text.

The most notable differences between both fueros are found, precisely, in the commercial law precepts. One must bear in mind that the Fuero of Estella was promulgated in order to establish a commercial center at a strategic point on the Camino de Santiago, while that of San Sebastian was done to create a maritime commercial nucleus for the Kingdom of Navarre. Specifically, chapters 2, 3, 4, and 5 in the first part adapt the exemption from tributes, which we know that residents of Jaca had already enjoyed since 1135, to maritime commercial customs and practices. This was an exemption that only residents that owned an inhabited house enjoyed. It illustrates the strategic interest in founding the *villa* that the payment of tributes was reduced by a third to commerce aimed at Pamplona.[196] The fourth part of the Fuero of San Sebastian, especially aimed at regulating commercial questions, had no equivalency in the Fuero of Estella. Some of the precepts in this part, such as that of the admiral, could have been inspired by some of the Pamplona versions of the Fuero of Jaca.

BIBLIOGRAPHY

Alonso, Paz. "El proceso penal en el Fuero de San Sebastián." In *El Fuero de San Sebastián y su época. Actas del VIII centenario de la Fundación de San Sebastián*. San Sebastián: Sociedad de Estudios Vascos, 1982.

Arízaga, Beatriz. "Las villas guipuzcoanas que reciben el fuero de San Sebastián: modos de vida de sus habitantes." In *El Fuero de San Sebastián y su época. Actas del VIII centenario de la Fundación de San Sebastián*. San Sebastián: Sociedad de Estudios Vascos, 1982.

Banús y Aguirre, José Luis. *El Fuero de San Sebastián*. Zarauz: Ayuntamiento de la Ciudad de San Sebastián, 1963.

---

196 San Sebastian, 1, 3.2. and 1, 4.2.

Barrero García, Ana María. "La difusión del Fuero de Jaca en el Camino de Santiago." *El Fuero de Jaca, II, Estudios*. Zaragoza: El Justicia de Aragón, 2003.

Basabe Martín, Luis Alberto. "Estudio lingüístico del fuero de San Sebastián en Congreso." In *El Fuero de San Sebastián y su época. Actas del VIII centenario de la Fundación de San Sebastián*. San Sebastián: Sociedad de Estudios Vascos, 1982.

Beroiz Lazcano, Marcelino. *Crimen y castigo en Navarra bajo el reinado de los primeros Evreux (1328–1349)*. Pamplona: Universidad Pública de Navarra/Nafarroako Unibertsitate Publikoa, 2005.

Campos Ruiz, Julio. *El Fuero de Estella*. Estella-Lizarra: Ayuntamiento de Estella-Lizarra, 2005.

Fortún Pérez de Ciriza, Luis Javier. "Fueros locales de Navarra." *Príncipe de Viana* 68, no. 242 (2007): 865–99.

García Arancón, Mª Raquel. "Marco jurídico y proyección social de las minorías navarras: judíos y mudéjares (siglos XII–XV)." *Iura Vasconiae. Revista de Derecho Histórico y Autonómico de Vasconia* 4 (2007): 459–516.

García Cantero, Gabriel. "El Derecho civil en el Fuero de San Sebastián." In *El Fuero de San Sebastián y su época. Actas del VIII centenario de la Fundación de San Sebastián*. San Sebastián: Sociedad de Estudios Vascos, 1982.

García-Granero, Javier. "Fuero General de Navarra 4, 2, 3. El cónyuge viudo que tiene fealdat ¿puede enajenar en caso de necesidad?" *Anuario de Derecho Civil* 27 (1974): 91–268.

Garibay, Esteban de. *Los XL libros d'el Compendio historial de las Chronicas y vniuersal Historia de todos los reynos de España / Compuestos por Esteuan de Garibay y Çamálloa, de nación Cántabro, vezino de la villa de Mondragón, de la provincia de Guipúzcoa*. Anveres: Christophoro Plantino, 1571.

Holmer, Gustaf, ed. *El fuero de Estella según el manuscrito 944 de la Biblioteca de Palacio de Madrid*. Colecc. Leges Hispanicae Medii Aevi, no. 10. Goteborg; Stockholm; Uppsala: Karlshamn, 1963.

Irujo, Xabier. *Giving Birth to Cosmopolis: The Code of Laws of Estella (c. 1076)*. Santa Barbara: University of California, Santa Barbara, 2011.

Jimeno Aranguren, Roldán. "El municipio de Vasconia en la Edad Media." *Iura Vasconiae* 2 (2005): 45–83.

———. "Las figuras de garantía en los fueros medievales hispánicos occidentales." In *Historia de la Propiedad. Crédito y Garantía. V Encuentro interdisciplinar, Salamanca, 31 de mayo–2 de junio de 2006*, edited by Salustiano de Dios, Javier Infante, Ricardo Robledo, and Eugenia Torijano. Madrid: Servicio de Estudios del Colegio de Registradores, 2007.

———. "Servicio de armas en los fueros medievales de Vasconia: fonsado/hueste, cabalgada y apellido." *Iura Vasconiae* 4 (2007): 33–66.

———. *Matrimonio y otras uniones afines en el Derecho histórico navarro (siglos VIII–XVIII)*. Madrid: Dykinson, 2015.

———. *Los Fueros de Navarra*. Madrid: Agencia Estatal Boletín Oficial del Estado, 2016.

Lacarra, José María. "Fuero de Estella." *Anuario de Historia del Derecho Español* 4 (1927): 404–51.

———. "Fuero de Estella. Año 1164." *Anuario de Historia del Derecho Español* 9 (1932): 386–92.

———. "Fuero de Estella en versión lemosina." *Anuario de Historia del Derecho Español* 9 (1932): 393–413.

———. "Notas para la formación de las familias de fueros de Navarra." *Anuario de Historia del Derecho Español* 10 (1933): 203–72.

Lacarra, José María, and Ángel J. Martín Duque. *Fueros derivados de Jaca I: Estella-San Sebastián*. Pamplona: Diputación Foral de Navarra, 1969.

Lacruz Berdejo, José Luis. "El régimen matrimonial de los fueros de Aragón." *Anuario de Derecho Aragonés* 3 (1946): 17–153.

Lalinde, Jesús. *Los Fueros de Aragón.* Zaragoza: Librería General, 1979.

Martín Duque, Ángel J. "El fuero de San Sebastián. Tradición manuscrita y edición crítica." In *El Fuero de San Sebastián y su época. Actas del VIII centenario de la Fundación de San Sebastián.* San Sebastián: Sociedad de Estudios Vascos, 1982.

————. "La fundación del burgo navarro: Estella." *Príncipe de Viana* 51, no. 190 (1990): 317–28; reprint, *Príncipe de Viana* 63, no. 227 (2002): 761–72.

Martínez Gijón, José. "Los sistemas de tutela y administración de los bienes de los menores en el Derecho local de Navarra." *Anuario de Historia del Derecho Español* 40 (1970): 227–40.

Monreal Zia, Gregorio, and Roldán Jimeno Aranguren. *Textos histórico-jurídicos navarros. I. Historia Antigua y Medieval.* Pamplona: Gobierno de Navarra, 2008.

Orella Unzué, José Luis. "Estudio jurídico comparativo de los fueros de San Sebastián, Estella, Vitoria y Logroño." In *El Fuero de San Sebastián y su época. Actas del VIII centenario de la Fundación de San Sebastián.* San Sebastián: Sociedad de Estudios Vascos, 1982.

————. "El fuero de San Sebastián y su entorno histórico." In *Geografía e Historia de Donostia-San Sebastián,* edited by Javier Gómez Piñeiro and Juan Antonio Sáez García. San Sebastián: Ingeba, 1999.

Osés Urricelqui, Merche. *Documentación medieval de Estella (siglos XII–XVI).* Pamplona: Gobierno de Navarra, 2005.

Salinas Quijada, Francisco. "El Derecho civil en el Fuero de San Sebastián (Y Fuero Nuevo)." In *El Fuero de San Sebastián y su época. Actas del VIII centenario de la Fundación de San Sebastián.* San Sebastián: Sociedad de Estudios Vascos, 1982.

Segura Urra, Félix. *Fazer justicia. Fuero poder público y delito en Navarra (siglos XIII–XIV).* Pamplona: Gobierno de Navarra, 2005.

Sola Alayeto, Antonio, and Toño Ros Zuasti. *Estella, posta y mercado en la Ruta Jacobea.* Estella: Caja de Ahorros de Navarra, 1992.

Chapter 6

Social Minorities in the Fuero of Estella

Xabier Irujo

Around the year 1076, the abbot of the monastery of San Juan de la Peña mentioned a piece of land located "in the burg" that was beneath the crag on which the castle of Lizarra stood (*"in burgo quod est subtus illo castro de Lizarrara"*).[1] This manuscript documents the existence of the burg of San Martín de Estella in 1076. A second text, dated 1077, shows that Lope Arnal was already the *merino* or seigneur of the land of Estella (*"Lop Arnal merino in Stela"*).[2] This new burg of San Martín constituted the oldest privileged nucleus of the future city of Estella, alongside, naturally, the site of Lizarra, the original settlement whose exact origin we do not know but whose existence would date from significantly prior to the eleventh century.[3]

The burg of San Martín extended across both sides of Pilgrims' Way, which ran parallel to the course of the River Ega with a varying width from 10 feet at its narrowest to 16 feet at its widest. It was 600 feet in length, both the center of the street and the left

---

1   Ángel J. Martín Duque, "La formación del primer 'burgo' navarro. Estella," *Príncipe de Viana* 63, no. 227 (2002), 765. See likewise Roldán Jimeno, "El municipio de Vasconia en la Edad Media," *Iura Vasconiae* 2 (2005), 45–83.

2   Diploma regio DSR, I, no. 14 (donation of the *villa* of Ucar) in José Salarrullana, *Colección de documentos para el estudio de la historia de Aragón*, vol. 3 (Zaragoza: M. Escar, 1907), 32.

3   Bronze Age remains have been found within the town limits of the current city of Estella. See *Estudios de arqueología alavesa*, vol. 6 (Vitoria: Diputación Foral de Álava, Consejo de Cultura, 1974), 59.

or inner flank, on the riverside. In light of the oldest blocks, the facades of the vestibules or original houses must have had a width of approximately 15 feet (there are those of 10 and 16 feet) and an average depth of approximately 25 to 35 feet. Today the street has 54 vestibules, but some are extremely narrow, the product of demolishing the original houses and reconstructing new blocks. In any event, a flank of 600 lineal feet among an average of 15 feet per dwelling gives us a total of 40 vestibules on the south flank and 38 on the north flank, that is, a total of 78 dwellings.[4]

These data coincide with the data that offers population registers in 1366 and 1427. The 1366 census mentions sixty-eight hearths following the scourge of the black death and that of 1427, following the plagues of 1380, 1401, 1411, 1422, thirty-six hearths or homes.[5]

The street was a stretch of the Camino de Santiago, which crossed the kingdom as a whole from northwest to southwest, which guaranteed commercial activity and economic strength for the original burg. In fact, according to the data offered by the 1266 register of accounts, two centuries after its founding Estella had become an important economic and demographic center in the Kingdom of Navarre and had 1,127 hearths or families.[6] Of these, close to 547 would have lived in the neighborhoods of San Martín and Arrabal (50 pecent), 126 in those of San Pedro and San Miguel (11.5 percent), 304 in that of San Juan (28 percent), and 113 in the Jewish quarter (10.5 percent).[7] One hundred years later and despite the negative demographic impact of the fourteenth-century plagues, Estella had 17 streets and 829 hearths, or some 4,000 inhabitants, which implied a population decrease of approximately 23 percent

---

4   Author's measurements.

5   If we accept an average of between 13 and 16 feet per vestibule, we have a total of between a minimum of 70 and a maximum of 87 dwellings that made up Pilgrims' Street.

6   As Ángel J. Martín Duque points out, noted by Peio Monteano, the concept of "hearth" used to mean "home" in the socioeconomic sense befitting "family," hence in most cases one would think that these houses were inhabited by one family, whether nuclear or extended. Ángel J. Martín Duque, in *Gran Enciclopedia de Navarra*, vol. 5 (Pamplona: CAN, 1992), 176, cited in Peio Monteano, "Navarra de 1366 a 1428: Población y poblamiento," *Príncipe de Viana* 57, no. 208 (1996), 314.

7   Mª Raquel García Arancón, "La población e Navarra en la segunda mitad del siglo XIII," *Cuadernos de etnología y etnografía de Navarra* 17, no. 46 (1985), 92.

with regard to the previous century.[8] Nevertheless, Estella entailed approximately 5 percent of the total population of Navarre and 15 percent of the population of its *merindad* or district.[9] The population survey carried out by the Crown of Navarre in 1366 distributed the Estella population into 17 streets or neighborhoods, establishing the number of hearths in each one of them: San Martín, 68; Store Street, 57; El Borc Nuel, 68; Parish of San Miguel, 192; Brotería, 5; Valdresería, 6; Arenal, 35; Asteria, 19; Old Market, 34; Neighborhood of D.ª Lamborc, 8; Parish of San Pedro de Lizarra, 49; Carrera Longa, 57; New Market, 63; Tecendería, 27; Carpintería, 15; Navarrería, 41; and Arenal, 41.[10] There were around 1,900 Jewish hearths in Navarre as a whole between the thirteenth and fourteenth centuries, approximately 5.5 percent of the kingdom.[11] In 1366, the Jewish quarter of Estella had 85 hearths, which implied 10.8 percent of the total hearths in the locality.[12] Next to that of Tudela and that of Pamplona, that of Estella was one of the three main Jewish quarters in the kingdom.[13]

As in the case of other Navarrese and European towns, the population of Estella declined again between 1366 and 1427 because of epidemics (such as those of 1380, 1401, 1411, and 1422), natural disasters, and wars. José Yanguas y Miranda states that the plague of 1422 affected Estella so much that its inhabitants could barely pay the barracks tax,[14] and in a headcount of hearths in 1427 the distribution

---

8   In the opinion of Raquel García Arancón, the Navarrese population suffered a decline of 39.2 percent in the fourteenth century. See ibid., 98–99.

9   Ibid., 98.

10   Juan Carrasco, *La población de Navarra en el siglo XIV* (Iruñea-Pamplona: Ediciones Universidad de Navarra, 1973), 85–129.

11   Juan Carrasco estimates a figure of approximately 1,591 Jewish families between 1250 and 1328, in *Sinagoga y mercado. Estudios y textos sobre los judíos del Reino de Navarra* (Iruñea-Pamplona: Institución Príncipe de Viana, 1993), 33. See likewise Juan Carrasco, "Las primeras migraciones judías en el reino de Navarra (1076–1328)," in *Movimientos migratorios y expulsiones en la diáspora occidental. Terceros encuentros judaicos de Tudela: 14 17 de julio de 1998, Universidad Pública de Navarra*, ed. Fermín Miranda García (Iruñea-Pamplona: Dirección de Publicaciones del Gobierno de Navarra. Departamento de Educación y Cultura, 2000), 37–38; and José Mª Rodríguez Ochoa, *Menahem Ben Zerah, Rabino Estellés (1310–1385). Aproximación a una cultura que floreció en Sefarad* (Iruñea-Pamplona: Gobierno de Navarra, 2011), 137.

12   Carrasco, *La población de Navarra en el siglo XIV*, 150.

13   Carrasco counts 513 Jewish hearths in Navarre, although the data are incomplete given that they lack, for example, census records for the *merindad* of Pamplona. See ibid., 149–50.

14   José Yanguas y Miranda, *Diccionario de Antigüedades del Reino de Navarra*, vol. 2 (Iruñea-

of the population was registered as 11 streets and burgs, six less than in 1366: San Nicolás, 44; Store Street, 36; Santa María Yus del Castillo, 31; Plaza de San Miguel, 51; Asteria, 29; La Garlanda de San Miguel, 37; Carrera Luenga, 45; Garlanda del Mercado Nuevo, 52; Tecendería and Carpintería, 32; Navarrería, 28; and San Pedro de Lizarra, 23. There were, then, in the city as a whole 482 closed houses and a total of 418 hearths. This was considerably less than in 1366.[15]

From its earliest times, Estella was a divers locality, populated by people from different points of Europe that spoke multiple languages, practiced different religions, and were used to varied customs and practices, which was all reflected in its fuero. In fact, this is precisely the reason behind this legal document: to organize the community life of a heterogeneous group of people that was going to populate the new city created on the old site of Lizarra. As Alfonso García Gallo and José Mª Lacarra, among others, indicate, the first population fueros took their legal regulations from Pyrenean consuetudinary law, in such a way that they constituted anthologies of legal norms.[16] In this sense, the editors of the old Fuero of Estella, which we can date to between 1054 and 1076, took from the consuetudinary law of the country some of the basic norms of coexistence, basically those that referred to commercial transactions and the freedoms and liberties that the future inhabitants of the city would be granted, and they put them in writing.[17] A century later, the king of Navarre, Sancho VI the Wise, confirmed the expansion of the original legal document, giving rise to the long fuero of 1164 that I still preserved in the city's archive.

One of the most urgent aspects of the fuero was to guarantee peace and foment the prosperity of residents of the new urban nucleus of San Martín following its founding around the year 1076, by means of a detailed regulation of judicial administration. The

---

Iruña-Pamplona, 1840), 716.

15 Jesús Arraiza Frauca, "Los fuegos de la merindad de Estella en 1427," *Príncipe de Viana* 29, nos. 110–111 (1968), 123.

16 Alfonso García Gallo, "Pirenaicos" (706), in *Manual de historia del derecho español. El origen y la evolución del derecho* (author's edition) (Madrid, 1984), 380.

17 Xabier Irujo, "Sobre la datación y naturaleza del fuero de Estella," *Terra Stellae* 7 (2016), 38–55.

Fuero of Estella includes three basic principles in relation to the public management of justice: first, justice had to be administered legally, by means of judicial confrontation, and the use of violence in order to settle accounts would be unacceptable (sections1, 4.1; 2, 30; 2, 54.1; 1, 7.1; 1,14, and 2, 50.1);[18] second, a person could only appear before a judge on those charges for which they may have been accused (2, 18.2), and, once absolved, they nor anyone else could appear for this same lawsuit on the part of the claimant (2, 18.3 and 2, 18.5); and third, no fine (or any other sanction) would be imposed without first notifying the accused of the transgression that they had committed on the part of the *alcalde* (judge), and until the accused had had the opportunity to defend themselves in a court (2, 8 and 2, 18). This precept is an antecedent of the current juridical principle of presumption of innocence.

Among the freedoms and liberties of the accused included in the Fuero of Estella we find the right to be judged before a legal judge in a court of the city and in accordance with the laws of the city (1, 10.1; 1, 10.2; 2, 31, and 2, 67), the right to be heard and to defend oneself before a court (2, 26 and 2, 18.3), to present evidence or testimonies in their defense and demand evidence or testimonies for the charges against them(1, 4.1; 1, 4.2, and 2, 37), the right to appeal the decisions of the magistrates (2, 26.3), and the right to not be detained without prior judicial order, and to not be arrested if submitting guarantees or a bond (1, 5).

There were no special courts or any different legal treatment according to social level, except in cases of immunity for public officials, such as the king's *merino*, who could not be fined in Estella except on the agreement of six good residents of the city (1, 9). Most infractions were punished by fines proportional to the offenses established "by agreement of the council of the villa" in the name of justice (2, 49.1); "and [residents] would meet any fine that they were

---

18   The original eleventh-century fuero and the longer 1164 version did not have numbered sections. The numbering was proposed by José María Lacarra and Ángel J. Martín Duque in their 1069 publication of the Fuero of Estella. I have followed this numbering to refer to the different norms in the fuero. See José María Lacarra and Ángel J. Martín Duque, *Fueros derivados de Jaca. Estella-San Sebastián* (Iruñea-Pamplona: Institución Príncipe de Viana, 1969).

given according to the will of the council. And any prohibitions they place can be maintained as long as they wish and lifted whenever they see fit, because the fuero is like that" (2, 49.2). Finally, prison sentences were very limited, in such a way that the fuero regulated that no one should be arrested or seized, either in body or possessions, having supplied a legal guarantor (1, 5),[19] and no one should be put in jail or shackled in prison, but that they should be "free of prison within the king's palace or encampment" (2, 22.3). Subsequently, this provision would be confirmed in 1253 by Theobald II "*a nostros amados burgueses de Esteilla*," both men and women: "*juramos que non soframos que ningun ome, ninguna muller del Regno de Navarra, sea preso so cuerpo nin ninguna ren de las sus cosas, eill o eilla dando fiador de dreito por tanto como su fuero mandare.*"[20] There was no death penalty for homicide in Estella until 1310.[21] As regards everything previously referred to, one deduces from the fuero that any form of violence or torture was prohibited.[22]

It is important to underscore that these norms and, in general, all those included in the fuero, were not privileges, but laws. Put another way, the norms or "good fueros" included in this legal document were not exceptions to the law but they constituted the law, a law that would remain in force "safe and decent, free and

19 This meant that preventative detention did not exist or that it was very limited.
20 Gregorio Peces-Barba, Ángel Llamas, and Carlos R. Fernández, eds., *Textos básicos de derechos humanos con estudios generales y especiales y comentarios a cada texto nacional e internacional* (Burgos: Editorial Aranzadi; Elkano, 2001), 36.
21 The Council of Estella passed a bylaw ordering that, "whosoever may kill, should die by suffocation and should pay a fine of twenty-five *libras* of *sanchetes*; whosoever may injure with a weapon, should pay a fine of twenty-five *libras*, or if they cannot pay, they should suffer one year in prison; and that any killers who may flee should be summoned or banished perpetually, paying the aforementioned fine, just as any fugitive assailants should be locked up until they complete the sentence highlighted; with exemptions for the privilege of the King Don Theobald on chance homicides and the fuero on confiscation of possessions of homicides for the king." This bylaw was ratified for five years by the governor of Navarre, Engarrán de Villers, "in Estella, on the first Monday after Pentecost, June the eighth in the year 1310." It was extended for another five years, by the king's messengers Miles, seigneur of Noyers and Alfonso de Robray, in March 1314 and it would be renewed later for another five years by Joffre de Morentaina, seigneur of Roussillon, deputy to the governor of Navarre, in Olite, the first Friday before Pentecost in the year 1320. In Pedro E. Zorrilla, *Índice cronológico de los documentos y papeles antiguos existentes en el archivo municipal de la ciudad de Estella, pertenecientes á los siglos XII á XVIII, ambos inclusive, formado por el que suscribe, en el año de 1911* (Estella, 1911), 202.
22 José Mª Satrustegi, *Comportamiento sexual de los vascos* (Donostia: Txertoa, 1981), 67. See likewise Marcelino Beroiz, *Crimen y castigo en Navarra bajo el reinado de los primeros Evreux (1328–1349)* (Iruñea-Pamplona: Universidad Pública de Navarra, 2005), 161.

frank," until they were abolished or supplanted by other disposition emanating in the form of bylaws by the city council, which was elected annually. By the same thing, the fuero established a clear distinction between disputations that were "in the fuero," that is, those legal norms that were applied to all the residents of Estella equally and prescriptively, and those formalities that "are not in the fuero" in reference to, for example, holding a duel on account of a dead relative, which in Estella remained at the discretion of the family and therefore had neither a legal or prescriptive character (2, 7.4). The fuero registers, however, its optional character precisely because Estella law entered into this point of contradiction with the customs and habits of the country, which regulated how and when burials should take place, how duels should be carried out, and even the maximum quantities that families should spend in these necessities.[23]

In this sense, the fuero is very explicit with respect to the universal character of administering justice in affirming in its last section that justice should be done with respect to the fuero and not at the expense of it, prohibiting expressly that anyone should arrive at agreements to avoid payment of fines or other impositions, under the severe penalty of sixty *sueldos*, given that in that case the council coffers would not swell "nor is justice done" and, the text adds, "the king loses with that his right, and the city loses its fuero, and the poor person loses his trial" (2, 70.1). This reference to poor people in the context of the public administering of justice is very interesting and reflects the object of the dispositions of the Fuero of Estella on this point, which is none other than guaranteeing access for all residents equally to the administration of justice. Besides the significance of a legal norm tending to protect the liberties and freedoms of a rather unprotected social minority in the eleventh and twelfth centuries, it is a very particular disposition with barely any precedent in Pyrenean and peninsular law.

---

23 These norms of a consuetudinary nature would later be incorporated into the general Fuero of Navarre in 1324 in Book III, Title XXI (On the sepultures), Chap. 1, in *Fueros del Reyno de Navarra* (Iruñea-Pamplona: Imprenta de Martín Gregorio de Zabala, 1686), 91–92. See likewise José Yanguas y Miranda, *Diccionarios de los Fueros del Reino de Navarra* (Donostia: Imprenta de Ignacio Ramón Baroja, 1828), 29 30.

There were not many local or town fueros prior to 1164. Luis Javier Fortún mentions eighty-three fueros and privileges prior to 1234 in Navarre.[24] In their *Catálogo de fueros y costums municipals* Ana Barrero and Mari Luz Alonso register some twenty peninsular *villa* and valley fueros between 1017 and 1076 and some one hundred up to 1164.[25] Specifically, both authors catalog four fueros in the seventh century, eight in the tenth century, twenty-five in the eleventh century (excluding those of Sangüesa, Estella, and Jaca), and fifty up to 1164. In preparing this chapter, I analyzed eighty-seven of these peninsular general and municipal fueros and foundational charters prior to the long version of the Fuero of Estella in 1164 with the aim of finding antecedents and parallels in that relating to the protection of interests, freedoms, and liberties of social minorities or disadvantaged groups such as the collectives of poor people and the needy.

Without claiming to be exhaustive, there are very few precedents on the collective of the poor before the 1164. One of those is the fuero of settlements by the Bishopric Santiago de Compostela granted by Bishop Diego Gelmírez (c. 1113), which registers the need to help the poor in their cases against powerful people. Under the epigraph *Episcopi ad protegendos pauperes*, the fuero decreed that the oppression of the poor and weak "had to cease, for compassion, so that they may continue to enjoy their benefits without being deprived of them."[26] The section *De causis pauperum* likewise established that "if a powerful person opens a case at trial against a poor person . . . a person of a similar standing must define clearly what the case is, lest by any means this cause be silenced, [and this will be done] to the greater glory of the justice of the poor."[27] Without any doubt, this section constitutes a lovely example of protecting the socially disadvantaged in the context of the Cistercian

---

24 Luis Javier Fortún, "Los 'fueros menores' y el señorío realengo en Navarra (siglos XI–XIV)," *Príncipe de Viana* 46, no. 176 (1985), 604.

25 Ana María Barrero and Mari Luz Alonso, *Textos de derecho local español en la Edad Media. Catálogo de fueros y costums municipales* (Madrid: Consejo Superior de Investigaciones Científicas, Instituto de Ciencias Jurídicas, 1989).

26 Henrique Flórez, *España Sagrada: Theatro geographico-historico de la Iglesia de España. Historia Compostelana* (Madrid: En la Oficina de Antonio Marín, 1754), 176.

27 Ibid., 179.

reform and it is probably the only real precedent for that contained in the Fuero of Estella.

Another example of guaranteeing the interests that by law corresponded to people who were more disadvantaged economically is the seventh title at the Council of Coyanza in 1150, in which it was decreed "that all the counts and the *merinos* of the king that may have the town that they have from the king in justice, should not pressure the poor without right in judgment, but of those that they see and they hear, and if false testimony were to be proven, there is that sentence that it is stipulated in that book that they say is of false testimonies."[28] Even though this is not a municipal fuero, the precedent is likewise worth noting.

Mention of the poor in the context of a judicial dispute is therefore common to the diverse peninsular fueros prior to 1164, that is, before the promulgation of the new Fuero of Estella. Both on account of its content and publication it was an original formulation of the freedoms of the poor in a judicial dispute, as well as a plea for the correct administration of justice, a cornerstone of a system of legitimate government. As a curiosity, after 1164 the Fuero of Madrid conceded by Alfonso VIII of Castile (c. 1202) refers likewise in its preamble that said charter is conceded "so that the rich and the poor live in peace and health."[29]

The Fuero of Estella dedicates a considerable number of sections to women. Indeed, mention of women within this rubric constitutes in itself a novelty with very few precedents in 1164, and frames this social collective as a subject in the fuero and not just as an object of law. The final formula expresses clearly that the fuero is granted by the monarch "to you, to all the inhabitants of Estella,

---

28   In the original Latin: "*Séptimo quoque titulo admonemus, ut omnes comites, seu majorini regales populum sibi subditum per justitiam regant, pauperes injuste non oprimant, in iuditio testimonium, nisi illorum pnesentium, qui viderunt aut audierunt non accipiant. Quod si testes falsi convicti fuerint, illud suplicium accipiant, quod in libro judicum de falsis testitibus est constitutum.*" In Tomás Muñoz y Romero, *Colección de fueros municipales y cartas pueblas de los reinos de Castilla, León, Corona de Aragón y Navarra*, vol. 1 (Madrid: Imprenta de Don José María Alonso, 1847), 211. Cited also by Brenda Bolton and Susan M. Stuard, *Women in Medieval Society* (Philadelphia: University of Pennsylvania Press, 1976), 93.
29   In the original Latin: "*Unde dives et pauperes vivant in pace et in salute.*" In Amalio Marichalar and Cayetano Manrique, *Historia de la legislación y recitaciones del derecho civil de España*, vol. 2 (Madrid: Imprenta nacional, 1862), 446.

both of legal age and minors, both those that will come in the future and those now, to your sons and daughters, both in your generation and for the whole of your posterity, to your descendants that will inhabit Estella." In light of the extensive list of regulations on women, this rubric is not just a mere diplomatic formula, but is instead full of legal content. We find similar formulas in the declaration of the Fueros of San Zadornin, Berbeja, and Barrio made on November 29, 953, in which both men and women (*"varones et mulieres"*) are mentioned in the formula.[30] And it is likewise present in the Fuero of Nájera confirmed by Alfonso VI (c. 1076), which, in its 1304 version, established that, "the charter is aimed in the same way at the women and at the men of Nájera" (*"tam viris quam mulieribus"*).[31] Apart from these, there are very few references to women in rubrics prior to 1164.

An exception was made for the *ius suffragiorum* (suffrage) and *ius honorum* (investiture),[32] and military questions and public order that were not guaranteed for married women. Women participated in Estella in the civil rights of residents, such as in the *ius connubii*, or right to marriage (2, 11.1 and 2, 12.5),[33] being able to marry or remain single (2, 11.12). Widows could remarry as many times as they wanted or remain widowed (2, 11.1 and 2, 11.3). The fuero makes no reference at any time to the *patria potestas* and the formula in reference to women is verbatim "wishes to take as a husband" or "take as a husband," which denotes the importance of decision-making power on the part of women (2, 11.1 and 2, 11.1). In the

---

30   In the original Latin: "*Varones et mulieres, senices et iuvenes, maximos et minimos, totos una pariter qui sumus habitantes.*" In Josep Moret, *Anales del Reino de Navarra*, vol. 9 (Tolosa: Establecimiento Tipográfico y Casa Editorial de Eusebio López, 1891), 117.

31   In the original Latin: "*Vobis plebi nagarensi, tam viris, quam mulieribus, clericis, nec non et viduis, sive maioribus, atque minoribus.*" In Muñoz y Romero, *Colección de fueros municipales y cartas pueblas*, 287.

32   In accordance with the *ius suffragiorum* and *ius honorum* only inhabitants that enjoyed legal residency had the right to vote and be elected and carry out public functions. The fuero does not specify that women were limited in exercising the *ius suffragiorum* and *ius honorum* in relation to mandates in the city, although no case is known in the eleventh and twelfth centuries. Salic law did not govern in the Kingdom of Navarre, in which five queens reigned between 816 and 1512 (14 percent of the total monarchs).

33   Navarrese women would not be divested of this freedom legally but in the parliament held in Estella in 1556, a lwa was passed that authorized legally parents to disinherit their daughters and deprive them of a dowry if they married clandestinely. See Silvia Fernández and Paco Roda, eds. *Ellas, las mujeres en la historia de Pamplona* (Iruñea-Pamplona: Concejalía de la Mujer-Emakumearen Zinegotzigoa, 1998), 104.

procedural field, the women of Estella had to be judged before a legal judge in a court in the city and in accordance with the laws of the city; and they had the right to appeal the decisions of the magistrates, habeus corpus, the right to not be arrested or seized, either in body or possessions, having supplied a legal guarantor, according to the fuero (1, 5); and the right to declare or serve as a witness in any type of litigation or legal dispute in their own name without need of an *ad litem* (1, 6.5 and 2, 11.9).[34] The fuero does not distinguish on the basis of gender those things relating to charges in which residents who infringe the law are involved and women appeared in the same way as men before the judges, on their own accounts and without any patronage. Thus for example, when Theobald II granted in 1266 the residents of Estella "that they should be some, with one single *alcalde* and provost and some jury members," he freed them from the sentence of murder, "except the death f man to man, man to women, and woman to man."[35] In an inventory made in 1339, it states that there was a man and a women being held prisoner in the castle of Estella.[36]

Likewise the participation of women in the city and, in general, the kingdom stands out in the *ius commercii* or right to carry out legal contracts[37] or pay debts, always on the condition that they were older than twelve (2, 43.1), and the right to not pay any more taxes than those agreed to by the city council (2, 15.1). The women residents of Estella had the right to possess property both within and outside the city limits in accordance with its laws, whether movable (*uxor domum habeat*) or immovable property, to head or possess

---

34 The General Fuero of Navarre decreed in Book 2, Title 6, Chap. 12, that the testimony of women could be admitted in evidence about marriage, simony, and godfatherhood. However, in Book 2, Title 7, Chap. 1, it decrees that, "we establish by fuero that no pregnant woman may swear an oath in any process judged by a judge until thirty days have passed after the birth, whether a son or a daughter is born, but she will have to provide a guarantor [to guarantee that she would swear an oath] within the time limit specified in order to swear an oath."

35 Yanguas y Miranda, *Diccionario de Antigüedades del Reino de Navarra*, 318.

36 Ibid., 167.

37 There are numerous references to businesses run by women in Estella and Navarre in general, to the extent that, "we can classify the commercial activity of women in the life of the cities studied [Tudela, Estella, and Los Arcos] as notable." See *Coloquio Mujeres de la Edad Media: escritura, visión, ciencia: Escritura, visión, ciencia. A novecientos años del nacimiento de Hildegard von Bingen* (Santiago de Chile: Universidad de Chile, Facultad de Filosofía y Humanidades, 1999), 63. See likewise Fernández and Roda, eds. *Ellas, las mujeres en la historia de Pamplona*, 69–70.

businesses, both as producers and in the role of intermediaries, and both as widows and as spinsters and even as married women (2, 11.2 and 2, 14.4), and the right to buy and sell these properties, and to grant and request loans.[38] The women of Estella were free to testify in accordance with the laws of the city as well as receive as part of aan asset any type of movable or immovable property (2, 11).[39] Daughters and sons enjoyed the same inheritance rights without any gender distinction or order of birth (the primogeniture system did not predominate). And finally, they likewise held the *ius migrationis* or right to maintain the rights of residency even when outside the city limits of Estella.

Despite the scarce existing documentation concerning the period between the eleventh and twelfth centuries, studies on the economic activity of women in Estella indicate that they were very active in a wide range of commercial activities and occupations in all sectors of the economy during that time: working as farmers and rearing livestock, in laundries and as seamstresses, as investors, traders, and moneylenders, among other activities. For example, the registers of both widowed and married Jewish women in the fourteenth century are equally indicative of the activity of women in the economic and social life of the Navarrese Jewish quarters. Among them, the following stand out: Dueña, widow of Arach Eucave; Sirnha, widow of Salomón Alberge the Older; Sorbellita, widow of Joseph Esquerra; Soloru, wife of Samuel Eder; Oroceti, wife of Josef ben Shaprut; and Oroshoel, wife of Salomon Aljarnin.[40] Mira ben Menir, wife of Nathan del Gabay in Tudela, leased to and bought land from the Navarrese treasury between 1366 and 1368.[41]

The general Fuero of Navarre regulated the fiscal obligations of men and women from in different social conditions in the Kingdom

---

38   "Husbands did not have to cover their wives' debts if they were not innkeepers or merchants." Yanguas y Miranda, *Diccionario de Antigüedades del Reino de Navarra*, 266.

39   Unfortunately, in comparison to documents concerning the period between eleventh and thirteenth century, there is much more of an abundance of documentation for the following centuries. See, for example, Merche Osés Urricelqui, ed., *Documentación medieval de Estella: siglos XII–XVI*, vol. 1 (Iruñea-Pamplona: Departamento de Cultura y Turismo del Gobierno de Navarra; Institución Príncipe de Viana, 2005), 768–70.

40   Ricardo Cierbide, "Las comunidades judaicas navarras en la Edad Media," in *Los Judíos* (Gasteiz,: Fundación Sancho el Sabio, 1992), 228.

41   Ibid., 232.

of Navarre. Although the system was complex, since situations varied from town to town or from valley to valley, as well as the nature of each of the taxes, the general fuero established as a general norm that two unmarried women would pay the same amount of taxes as a man. A disabled man who could not carry out any kind of work had to pay the same as one woman. Likewise, a young single male had to pay the same as a woman until, having reached puberty, he had "natural facial hair."[42] The Fuero of Estella, however, does not make such distinctions and decrees in the section titled "On widows" (2, 15) that they and, by extension, any woman who was the head of a family, had to fulfill all of the duties that residents of the city had, except the draft (2, 15.1). This section is very important since one deduces from the exemption from the obligation of military service that women contributed according to what was expected of them in the fuero, that is, the rights assigned to such payments were inherent.

In general terms, the Fuero of Estella establishes six general principles as regards women:

Women with the legal title of "*echandra*" or "*etxeko andre*" in the general Fuero of Navarre of 1234 were subjects in law.[43] Moreover, according to the Fuero of Estella they possessed a "legal capacity" (*sui juris*) in their condition as a "*mulier legalis*" (2, 11.9).[44]

Women had the right of residency (rubric).

The central core of Estella society was the family, which was represented by the *dominus domus* or *senior domus* (2, 2.1, 2, 7). The *dominus domus* did not exercise his authority over his wife, nor did she have a guardian and the couple administered and supervised the social and economic activity of the family nucleus in legal equality.

---

42   Book 3, Title 4, Chap. 3 in the General Fuero of Navarre. In *Fueros del Reyno de Navarra*, 45. See likewise Yanguas y Miranda, *Diccionario de Antigüedades del Reino de Navarra*, 387 and 399–400.

43   As Julio Caro Baroja reminds us, the general Fuero of Navarre refers to the "*echandra*" or "*chandra*" (*etxeko andre*) and to the "*echaun*" or "*echalaun*" (*etxeko jaun*), legal figures of great importance for the study of residency and religiosity in the country. See Julio Caro Baroja, *Etnografía histórica de Navarra*, vol. 3 (Pamplona: Editorial Aranzadi, 1972), 139.

44   There is no reference in the Fuero of Estella to the legal figure of *paterfamilias* as the only head of the family or, in general, no section that records the power of the husband over the wife in the family context.

Widows or spinsters could be heads of families with a clear character as "keepers of the hearth or home or head of the family."[45]

The married, single, and widowed woman was the "owner with full authority of all possessions and assets" of which she disposed, being able to acquire, rent, sell, pawn, mortgage, bequeath, or give as an inheritance the goods associated with her property (2, 11.11).

And women who were heads of families fulfilled all the fiscal obligations of residency that were inherent to the rights they enjoyed (2, 15).

The Fuero of Estella establishes as a principle in its first section the right that no one should take justice into their own hands, so that residents of the city were prohibited from engaging in physical conflict or duels with outsiders on account of any dispute, with the order that they should appoint witnesses, one Navarrese and one Frank, and they should settle any litigations before a court (1, 4.1). There are only partial exceptions to this rule, which are in essence requirements of a legislation that seems very early medieval, in which, in accordance with the law, the victim or parents of the victim had some capacity to make their own justice. One such case was the rape of a woman.

The fuero addressed diverse cases of rape (*mulier forciata*). If a woman was raped, she had to report it within the first three days following the assault, and she had to prove it with verified witnesses from Estella (*veridicos testes Stellenses*) because "nothing will be valid after three days" (1, 6.5). If the woman could prove it at trial, the man had to compensate her (*pariasset eam*) or marry her if that was her condition, but, if it was not, he had to find her a husband "so that she may be with him as honorable as before" (1, 6.2 and 1, 6.3). This disposition, common to several fueros of the era, has its roots in Deuteronomy (22: 28–29).[46] Apart from the compensation owed to the victim, the fuero established a fine

---

45   *Coloquio Mujeres de la Edad Media*, 56.
46   Deuteronomy, 22: *28* If a man happens to meet a virgin who is not pledged to be married and rapes her and they are discovered, *29* he shall pay her father fifty shekels of silver. He must marry the young woman, for he has violated her. He can never divorce her as long as he lives.

for rape at sixty *sueldos* that had to be paid to the king (1, 6.5). It remained in the hands of the ruling of the *alcalde* and twelve good residents of the city (*"duodecim bonorum vicinorum"*) to determine if, in effect, this man was appropriate for her or not (1, 6.5). Finally, if the rapist did not want to or could not compensate her or find a husband for the victim, his person remained in the hands of the woman's family and at their disposition (1, 6.4).

The general Fuero of Navarre that Theobald I swore an oath in 1238, seventy-four years after the passing of the new Fuero of Estella, can shine some light onto the particularities that accompanied cases of rape, since the origin of both was consuetudinary tradition. The general fuero established that any man who forced himself on a woman of a lower social status should marry her and, if he did not consent to that, he would be banished from the kingdom and all his possessions would be confiscated, "and he should count on suffering the enmity of her relatives."[47] If the woman raped was from a higher social status, the assailant had to pay a fine of six hundred *sueldos*, half for the king and the half for the woman attacked, and he would be banished and his possessions confiscated.[48]

In contrast to Estella, the general fuero likewise distinguished according to the civil status of the assailant and introduced the legal figures of abduction and adultery as circumstances of the rape. In this sense, any single man who took by force (abduction) or voluntarily (adultery) a married woman would be punished with the confiscation of all his possessions and suffer the sentence of banishment "until he may recover the favor of the king and the husband."[49] The fuero established likewise that if the husband believed that the assailant had taken his wife by force, and without her consent, having recovered his wife, "he had to continue with her as if she had done nothing wrong."[50] A married man who forced himself on a married woman would lose all his possessions and be banished. However, the wedding coins would not be confiscated

---

47 Book 4, Title 3 (On forcing women and adulteries), Chap. 3, *Fuero General de Navarra* (Pamplona: Editorial Aranzadi, 1964), 164.
48 Ibid., 164.
49 *"Daqui á que amor aya del Rey et de su marido."* Book 4, Title 3, Chap. 8, ibid., 165.
50 *"Como nuyll mal esta oviesse fecho."* Ibid.

from either the wife of the assailant or from the children of both of them; and if the wife had not received any wedding coins, half of all the assets of the parents would go to the children as well as any earned goods; and the king would confiscate the other half of all his possessions. If the assailant had participated in abducting the woman, her relatives could challenge the assailant and kill him if he refused to return her to her home. Moreover, his relatives were prohibited from giving him refuge, help, or advice. And if so happened that the assailant had children with the woman, they would have no rights to the assets. The general fuero explained that the assailant could not return to the kingdom until he regained the favor of the king and that of his wife, and that, if that happened, he was within his rights to recover all his holdings.[51] Finally, the accused could be absolved if no assault could be demonstrated, in which case he had to testify on oath "that he did not rape, nor harm her."[52]

According to a custom registered in the general Fuero of Navarre, it was prescribed that married men who had wives in the territory of their residency could not cohabit with other women;[53] that any married man who had a wife in the city limits of the *villa* should not lie with another woman; and should lie without underwear.[54] In contrast, fornication (*fornicatio*) did not constitute an offense in light of the Fuero of Estella, which regulated that consensual sexual relations between single people would not be fined (1, 6.1). As regards adultery, in light of the Fuero of Estella, it was not properly speaking an offense for women exclusively, and female adultery was not punished in any special way. Indeed, the fuero did not impose any punishment on the woman, but the man who lay with her. In the same way as the Fuero of Tudela, the Fuero of Estella established that, if a husband should catch another man with his wife at night and should kill him, he would not be fined for doing so (2, 21.2). Yet if someone caught the wife by day committing adultery, and her husband presented a complaint before the seigneur of the *villa* (the provost) or the seigneur of the land (*merino*), they should not mete

---

51 Book 4, Title 3, Chap. 9, ibid., 165–66.
52 Book 4, Title 3, Chap. 3, ibid., 164.
53 Book 4, Title 1, Chap. 2, ibid., 156–57.
54 Book 4, Title 1, Chap. 3, ibid., 157.

out justice by the imposition of a fine without taking into account the husband, "but they should mete out justice to both" (2, 21.3). The reference to meting out justice to both (*"iustitiam de ambobus facere"*) indicates that it was considered an offense against public order or social habits and customs as well as against family order, so it concerned the seigneurs of the land and the city, moreover, to mete out justice to the husband. In this same vein, the fuero establishes that if a cleric were caught with a woman—whether single or married—he should be tried by another priest and an honorable layman, and it remained in the hands of the seigneur of the land to apply the punishment (2, 27). The Jewish quarter of Estella also punished adultery, and fines were imposed by the *beth din* (rabbinical court), which supplied as unequivocal proof the advanced state of pregnancy on the part of the defendant.[55]

The general Fuero of Navarre systematizes adultery, in Title 3 of Book 4 (On forcing women and adulteries), in a similar way to that of Estella, although it excludes the right of the husband to kill his wife's lover. On the one hand, it establishes that the adulterous man and woman must pay a fine totaling half that for murder to the seigneur of the land, hence it is considered an offense against social order. On the other, the general fuero establishes that the bastard child must not be raised by any relative, or considered a sibling of the married couple's children, or have any right to inherit the possessions of the father or of the mother. More still, having reached legal age, this person cannot become a guarantor, or a cosignatory, or a witness, or an oath swearer in a church. However, in the same way as the Fuero of Estella, the general fuero protects the economic interests of the bastard child, with the father or the mother being free to give the child part of their assets according to their legal status.[56]

---

55 Carrasco, *Sinagoga y Mercado*, 76.
56 Book 4, Title 3, Chaps. 10–12, *Fuero General de Navarra*, 166. Illegitimate children could not inherit "because according to the law they should not have been born." The rights of a bastard child varied according to their legal status. The child born of two married people was termed *"campix"* (appearing for the first time in law 55 of the Fuero of Tudela, this is an Occitan word that means "found in the countryside" or illegitimate). If none of the progenitors had children, the child would inherit by law two *sueldos*, six *dineros*, and half a *peonada* of land, and everything else to the nearest relatives of the deceased. Children born to a married man and single woman were termed *"fornecinos"*

In the view of the Fuero of Estella, marriage was an economic contract in which the consent and active legal participation of the woman were imperative before, during, and after the conjugal union. While the civil status of a married woman was an important factor in restricting her social autonomy, there was nothing in the fuero to state that a married woman would enjoy more freedoms and liberties than a single woman except for those with the legal title of tenant of the hearth or head of the family. In this way, the fuero established the possibility that it would be the husband who went to live in his fiancée's house after marriage, and she would not lose ownership of the home (2, 14.4).

In the context of Pyrenean law, women were free to contract marriage and, as the Fuero of Navarre stated, neither her parents nor grandparents had the right to force their children or grandchildren to contract marriage against their will.[57] Nevertheless, in the case of the lower nobility, parents could propose a son to their daughters and the latter could refuse up to two, but they were obliged to marry a third suggestion.[58] In such cases the fuero regulated "the bride's price" or the total paid by the husband to the family of the wife for the marriage, mandating that the parents had to designate fair men and establish a date to celebrate the union, and that once both parties were in agreement, the parents of the bride would request the dowry from the husband.[59] While the Fuero of Estella did not regulate this aspect, there is a reference to it (2, 43.1), establishing that if a woman gave the dowry to her husband (or paid a debt on his behalf), it would only be valid if she gave guarantees as such and it was only valid if she was of legal age, that is, if the woman was aged twelve or older, "because it is not valid any other way." In contrast to other places in Europe, the fuero did not contemplate the gift that the groom paid the bride on the morning after the wedding

---

or out of fornication (from the Latin *fornix* or brothel) and inherited five *sueldos* and a *peonada* of land. The children of a single man and single woman were termed "out of gain" and inherited a minimum of five *sueldos* through movable possessions and a *peonada* of land, as well as whatever the parents had of their own free will. Yanguas y Miranda, vol. 1, *Diccionario de Antigüedades del Reino de Navarra*, 480.

57 Rubric 24, Art. 7, *Los fors et costumas deu Royaumme de Navarre deca-ports* (Pau: Jerôme Duproux, 1722), 76.
58 Book 4, Title 1, Chap. 2, *Fuero General de Navarra*, 156.
59 Book 4, Title 1, Chap. 1, ibid., 155–56.

night, although there were marriages that were celebrated on the condition and proof of virginity.[60] The general Fuero of Navarre did not, similarly, decree that if a servant married and his lord did not wish to grant him his freedom, the serf, "whether his lord wishes it or not" would continue on his way with his wife, abandoning the service of his lord from the day of the marriage onward, and the lord was obliged to pay him his full salary, counting the days that he had served.[61]

While the Fuero of Estella contains hardly any norms about the institution or dissolution of marriage,[62] it is very rich in norms and sections related to the management of the spouses' property. More specifically, that concerning the inheritance system in the fuero dedicates an ample section of articles to systematizing the rights of women to property on the death of their husbands. Curiously, the fuero makes no reference of widowers or their rights, which, one supposes, were identical to those of women even though there would have been fewer cases.

In the context of Pyrenean law, once a marriage was contracted, the man and woman shared their common property and possessions, so that both spouses had equal rights over that, "although the husband may have many [possessions] and the wife nothing or the wife many and the husband nothing."[63] This system of matrimonial property was characterized by the fact that, if a marriage ended and, if there were children, all the property was divided into two equal parts. If there were no children, there was no division of possessions and the system of gains was applied whereby each spouse retained their own goods and anything gained after the marriage was divided in half between them. In general,

---

60 Yanguas y Miranda, *Diccionario de Antigüedades del Reino de Navarra*, 121.
61 Book 1, Title 5, Chap. 12, *Fuero General de Navarra*, 24.
62 There is no record of any tax paid to the seigneur of the land for contracting marriage, nor was there any droit de seigneur in the country. Sumptuary norms were not regulated as regards the vestments of women in the Fuero of Estella, although certain customs in the country were observed. The fuero did not formulate any disposition about domestic violence or abuse within the environment of marriage except in an indirect way in that regarding the protection of economic interests of minors.
63 New Fuero of Bizkaia, Title 20, Law 1. This is a legal principle that we find in almost all the Basque fueros, as in the case in Rubric 25, art. 2 of the Fuero of the Kingdom of Navarre beyond the mountains in 1611; Title 9, Art. 1 in the Fuero of Lapurdi in 1514; and Title 24, Arts. 1 and 5 in the Fuero of Zuberoa in 1520.

if anyone, husband or wife, died childless, their possessions had to be returned to those relatives from whom the goods came, that is, if they were still alive, to the parents.[64] The wife was free in the view of the general Fuero of Navarre to bequeath or give as an inheritance;[65] and neither of the spouses was free to make a will without the permission or consent of the other, but instead had to do so on the basis of common agreement.[66]

The movable or unmovable possessions of a married woman were retained by her in her name and did not become in any way the property of the husband through marriage. As regards the possessions of the marriage and, following in general the principles of Pyrenean law, in the section titled "On women" (2, 43) the Fuero of Estella decrees that if a woman gave her dowry to her husband or paid off any debt, it would only be valid if guarantees of the transaction were given and if the woman were of legal age, because any other way, it would not have the force of law. In this same vein, the fuero established that the husband could not make any donation of what belonged to his wife without her authorization, although he could donate what belonged to him (2, 11.10). However, "if the wife hears that the husband is making a donation, and she is there and keeps quiet, if she does not authorize the donation it will not be valid" (2, 11.11). This principle is likewise included in the general fuero, which established that a married nobleman could not sell his wife's dowry without her consent, nor anything they may have acquired or bought together, nor the possessions that came from the wife's side. And, in the same way, a married woman could not sell her property, or transfer it, or mortgage it, or pawn it "except up to the value of a theft of bran."[67]

All of this was separate from the fact that debts contracted by spouses in the heart of the family were common according to what the fuero likewise regulated in all that relating to guarantors and creditors. In the event that a debtor did not settle their debt

---

64   Book 2, Title 4, Chap. 16, *Fuero General de Navarra*.
65   Book 4, Title 1 of the general fuero establishes the general inherence system in the kingdom. The right to receive assets is in chapter 4.
66   Book 3, Title 12, Chap. 14 and Book 3, Title 20, Chap. 8, *Fuero General de Navarra*.
67   Book 3, Title 12, Chap. 14, ibid., 112–13. "Robo de salvado" in the original versión.

and had a guarantor, the creditor had the right to go to the *alcalde* and demand entrance into the house of the guarantor to receive some security and if the latter did not come to the door, outside the house, the creditor could enter the house in order to take the corresponding security (2, 22.18). However, if at that moment the head of the family was not at home, the creditor had to inform— before witnesses—the wife of the guarantor that he had gone there to take the security; and if the guarantor was not married, he would have to inform the servants. The first time he sought to take securities, the wife had the right to deny access to officials and the creditor, and she could not be fined for doing so (2, 22.29); but from that day on, neither the wife nor the servants of the guarantor could impede the creditor from taking securities (2, 22.30). And if they did impede him, they would be fined (2, 22.31). In any event, the guarantor could show the security and in that case the creditor could not enter the house of the guarantor (2, 22.15).

In the view of the general Fuero of Navarre, women were free to bequeath or give as an inheritance and neither of the spouses was free to make a will without the permission or consent of the other, which had to be done by common agreement. This principle likewise prevailed in the Fuero of Estella, which established that the will had to be made by common agreement and always before witnesses. The witnesses were termed *"testamentarios"* and they did not have to swear an oath but, rather, certify that they had been witnesses of the free will of the spouses by means of the following legal formula: "we hear and see this donation being made" (2, 11.7). If there were no witnesses, the parish priest would suffice or in his absence, two women with a legal capacity (2, 11.8). In extreme cases, the testimony of a man or a woman without legal capacity would be valid (2, 11.9). In 1262, Theobald II ordered that any man or woman in Estella who had inherited movable possessions and possessed them in widowhood had to look after these possessions. In the event that they were farm land or vineyards, the owner had to undertake at least four working inspections annually, that is, hoe, till, prune, and trim and, if it were a case of houses, they were obliged to maintain them. And whoever did not fulfill these requirements lost the right to widowhood.[68] The reason for this norm was to protect minors.

While Deuteronomy prohibited the dissolution of marriage (22:19 and 22:29), the general Fuero of Navarre regulated the unilateral rupture of marriage, either due to the man or the woman.[69] The fuero established that if the woman did not want to stay with her husband, he would call on at least three relatives and, together with the these three plus another three residents "that should be from among the most prudent in the *villa* or the district," would inform everyone how their life together had been and both his and her way of life. If the husband could convince these people who made up a jury that the woman should stay at home, this was done. On the contrary, they would divide up their possessions and the husband kept his possessions and the wife hers, and if they had a property that had been bought or earned as a gain, it would be divided in half. By the same agreement, movable possessions and debts would be divided in half. The children too. If they had an even number of children, the father and the mother each took one half of them and, if one remained, it would be raised by both, "*diziendo estos bonos ombres: por crear estas creaturas mas vale que se aiuden esemble.*"[70] The fuero likewise decreed that any married woman that went with another man, abandoning her husband voluntarily "for her own pleasure," lost her properties that were retained by her first husband and that neither she, nor anyone else in her name, could reclaim them, although the children of both did not lose their right to inherit them.[71]

As regards the dissolution of a marriage through the death of one of the spouses, everything passed on to the surviving spouse who enjoyed all the possessions and rights of the deceased after the death. The Fuero of Estella regulated the legal usufruct of loyalty, formulating that "if the wife lives and the husband dies, even if

---

68 Yanguas y Miranda, *Diccionario de Antigüedades del Reino de Navarra*, 183.
69 Roldán Jimeno, *Matrimonio y otras uniones afines en el derecho histórico navarro (siglos VIII–XVIII)* (Madrid: Dykinson, 2015), 349–52.
70 "In order to raise these little ones, it is best that they help one another mutually." Book 4, Title 1, Chap. 1, *Fuero General de Navarra*, 155–56.
71 Book 4, Title 3, Chap. 7, ibid., 165. See likewise Jimeno, *Matrimonio y otras uniones afines en el derecho histórico navarro*, 352–53.

there are children, while the wife remains a widow she will be the owner and in full power of all the possessions and properties" of the marriage (2, 11.11). That is, on the death of the husband, everything passed into the hands of the widow and, while she did not remarry, it remained under her custody until the children of the couple came of legal age.

The freedom to make a will and enjoy usufruct was an inalienable right of the widow, although the fuero established limits according to the protection of interests of the children who were minors and whom were owed part of the inheritance. Despite that, the widow, even if she had divided the possessions the children were owed or not on the part of the father, could make "some donation of what had belonged to her husband or any other man" ("*aliquod donativum suo marito aut quolibet homini*") if guarantees were given of that (2, 11.6).

The fuero included a large number of sections ruling in the division of assets following the death of one of the spouses with special attention given to defending the interests of the mother and of minors. In general the fuero decreed that, on reaching legal age, the children could reclaim from the mother part "of what may remain" of the core possessions and assets of their father that they were owed by law (2, 11.14). In the event of litigation, if any of the children claimed that they were owed more, the mother, witnesses, and grandparents had to swear an oath (2, 11.15). It was the authority of the parents to resolve how to distribute possessions among their children (2, 11.16).

The general Fuero of Navarre regulated in Title 4 (On inheritances and successions) everything relating to this field and protected the interests of minors in relation to their testamentary rights concerning the family assets. Chapter 3 decreed that the father or the mother of the children could give and share out properties, and that it was "*abolorio*" or that part of the patrimony coming from forebears when the grandparents survived their children, parents their grandchildren. In this case, the fuero established that no possession was to be transferred as an *abolorio* to the grandchildren if the father or the mother did not die before the grandfather; if the father or the mother died after the grandfather died, then the said possession was considered patrimonial. In contrast to the Fuero of Estella, which, although with certain limits, granted the widow full authority over the possessions of the marriage before dividing them up with the children, the general fuero stipulated that the surviving spouse, father or mother, could not donate or sell anything without the consent of the children if previously the assets had not been divided up with them. Assets that came from gain and that therefore had been acquired by the husband or wife during the marriage remained excluded from this partition. The rest of the possessions corresponded by succession to being shared among the children and the parents could not disinherit them since, as established in the general fuero, "he that is disinherited from everything shall inherit everything."[72] In fact, the fuero protected fully possessions originating in a dowry, to the extent that they could not be tied to any debt.

Neither the father nor the mother could disinherit the children except in certain cases, when the son or daughter would hurt either of their parents, or if they made a serious accusation on oath, or if they pulled them by the hair or, in presence of good men, they called the parents "proven or miserable betrayers." The general fuero likewise decreed that if the couple had several children they could not give all their goods to just one, since they could not disinherit the rest even if they could give more movable assets to one of the children than to the rest, or a piece of land, or a vineyard, and add real estate by reason of marriage.[73]

The Fuero of Estella also regulated those cases in which the right of the widowed mother over the family patrimony conflicted with the protection of the interests of the minors. This was one of the few cases in which women could transmit rights that they could not enjoy. When the children were of legal age and did not want to share out their possessions, the mother could not force them to do so, but if the children wanted to share them out, being of legal

---

72   Book 2, Title 4, Chap. 3, *Fuero General de Navarra*, 40.
73   Book 2, Title 4, Chap. 8, ibid., 41–42.

age, they could force the mother into a court of justice, although in this case the widowed mother could claim poverty (2, 11.4). This is one of the first mentions to the legal figure of the poor woman or widow in the context of peninsular law. Yet in regard to what belonged to their natural sons or daughters, the widowed mother could sell or pawn any property if necessary, and if the need was obvious to relatives or neighbors, the fuero added that, "she can even sell her children due to hunger" in reference to giving them up for adoption (2, 11.13). If someone wanted to rent the inherited property of the children and the widowed mother wanted to retain it without leasing, she could do so as long as she retained it for the same price that was offered to lease it (2, 11.17).

If the woman had stepchildren and they did not divide up with her father the part of their natural mother, those stepchildren would have of the movable assets from the mother's side whatever the natural mother had gained with their father before he had taken another wife; but on the part of the father, while the woman wanted to remain in widowhood, they would not have anything of the property, but only the personal property would be divided up (2, 11.12). And while she was still a widow, she could not sell or pawn the stepchildren's property.

If someone died without having made a will, and there were still children, and the mother took another husband, the relatives of the children had to recognize the father's side of the children before witnesses and write it down (2, 12.1). And if the mother wanted to keep her children with the property and possessions, she had to give good bonds to the relatives of the children that, when they reached puberty, would be given the property and possessions that belonged to them by inheritance (2 , 12.2). If in the meantime the children died, that inheritance and property and possessions had to be returned from where it had come, to its closest relatives (2, 12.3). The children could not donate or use their inheritance before reaching the age of twelve (2, 12.4). No donation could be made from the inheritance of the grandparents, except one vineyard, one inherited property, or one house, and only if they had at least two houses, or an inherited property, and only his son or daughter to the clergy or churches. However, the widow could give that inheritance to her children and daughters freely when they got married (2, 12.5–6).

The fuero regulated harshly the absence of witnesses and the lack of deeds and penalized in such cases whoever had been involved in such omissions. In this specific case, if the deceased owed money to another person, and the claimant could not prove so with witnesses or through deeds, the latter's children had the right to swear that they did not know that their father owed such money and did not have to pay anything (2, 33.1). However, if upon claiming the money from the deceased's children, the children claimed that the deceased had returned the money, the one who claimed the money had to swear an oath and subject themselves to trial by hot iron (2, 33.3).[74] And if the plaintiff so wanted, he could put up another person to take the trial of hot iron for him, "because if he can use another man for the battle in his place,[75] he can do the same to lift the iron in the trial in which the test takes place" (2, 33.4). The wife of the deceased had the right to act in the same way, but if the claimant insisted that she knew, she was obliged to resort to the iron test (2, 33.2).

The fuero decreed with respect to bastard children that if the father gave him an inherited property, or money, after the death of his father the bastard son would not receive anything of the part that corresponded to him as a son, nor would he participate with the other legitimate children in the sharing out of the inheritance (2, 38.1), but if the father did not do that, he would have his share in the inheritance, as one of the legitimate siblings, and in the grandparents' inheritance and in that of any acquisitions (2, 38.2).

---

74   As in other parts of Europe, such ordeals fell into disuse by the end of the twelfth century, and were abolished after the Lateran Council of 1215. Specifically, canon 18 prohibited blessings of priests by the trial of hot iron and hot waters and in that of cold water and in 1222, Pope Honorius III prohibited the ordeal by the *Delecti filii* decree.

75   By virtue of the first legal norm of the Fuero of Estella, residents of the city were free and at liberty to go to war for only three days at most, and this only if it was a pitched battle, or when the king was besieged by his enemies (1, 1.1). This provision would also be regulated in the general fuero (Book 1, Title 1, Chaps. 4 and 5). The general fuero decreed likewise that if someone for some reason could not be sent to war, they could pay the amount of money necessary to send someone else in their place (a figure that is included in section 2, 69.2 of the Fuero of Estella). For this reason the Fuero of Estella decrees that if this is possible, it is also possible for one person to delegate another to carry out the test of fire.

But if on his deathbed the father did not acknowledge him as his child, and the other siblings with legitimate witnesses could prove it, he could not share in the inheritance (2, 38.3).

The fuero also decreed that if a widow, with children from her first husband, wished to marry a second time, she owed the children of her first marriage half of everything she had earned with her first husband, both money and inherited property (2, 11.1), but the woman had other inherited property or patrimony prior to her first marriage, she was not obliged to give part of that to the children (2, 11.2). And if she had had two or three husbands, and had children with all of them, she had to give each of her children the part of the gains she had made with their respective fathers "and nothing else" (2, 11.3).

The fuero regulated in great detail the guardianship of orphans in the section titled "On duties" (2, 35). If a couple died and left a child of theirs under the tutelage of another person, and the person in charge of the guardianship caused harm or deception in relation to the money or the land that corresponded to them by inheritance, or arranged for some ineffective guarantor to their detriment, even if he had had the guardianship for thirty years or more, he had to compensate the child for everything that had hurt him (2, 35.1). And he did not have to give up the guardianship on this account until the son, having reached legal age, expressed before witnesses that he did not want to continue under his tutelage (2, 35.2). The only exception to this rule is once again the protection of children on account of necessity or poverty. In this way, as minors and, if their father on his death had named witnesses, they could in cases of need share out, sell, and pawn the goods that corresponded to them according to the will, giving guarantees of this, but only to alleviate the need of the children (2, 11.5).

It is difficult, to be sure, to find legal precedents similar to those of the Fuero of Estella in peninsular legislation prior to 1164. As noted, there are very few precedents regarding the mention of women in the rubrics of legal texts. The first of these is mention of "*varones et mulieres*" in the declaration of the Fueros of San Zadornin,

Berbeja, and Barrio in 953 during the reign of García Sánchez I, king of Pamplona; and the second in the Fuero of Nájera granted by Sancho Garcés III, great grandson of the former. Nevertheless, in contrast to both legal texts, there is a surprising number of articles referring to women in the Fuero of Estella. The fuero mentions women thirty-six times, mothers sixteen times, wives five times, widows twice, daughters ten times, and on ten other occasions there is a reference to women through use of the pronoun "they," a total of seventy-nine times distributed in forty-one norms that develop the guiding principles of some of the main freedoms enjoyed by the women of Estella. This represents 15.8 percent of the total of the 258 norms in the fuero.[76] The fact that 78 percent of these norms refer to questions tied to property, inheritance, and wills is similarly very significant. Finally, the detail with which these principles are regulated in relation to the interests of women in family properties also stands out.

There are few legal precedents on the power of women in relation to the possession, use, and transfer of property as included in the Fuero of Estella between the ninth and twelfth centuries. The Fuero of Leon in 1017 contains some legal provisions on marriage, women's property, the inviolability of the home, and the immunity of the wife in the absence of the spouse. Thus, for example, the law establishes that he who marries a woman who possesses property legally in a given place could own and administer the woman's inherited property whenever she resided there, while he who married a woman who possessed a virgin property could possess it intact regardless of the place of residence (decree 10).[77]

---

76 One on fornication (1, 6.1), five on rape (1, 6.1–5), one on the theft of pilgrims' property (2, 8.1), seventeen on the section on successions (2, 11), three on inherences in the section (2, 12), one on not waiving debts contracted by a man who is going to live in his future wife's home (2, 14.4), one referring to tax charges that widows had to observe (2, 15.1), three on adultery (2, 21.1–2 y 2, 27.1), one on the protection of the wife 's movable possessions in the face of foreclosures (2, 22.20), three on the protection, on the part of the wife, of the family possessions in the face of a foreclosure as security for debts (2, 22.29–31), one on the right of daughters to not have their horse repossessed (2, 22.34), one on debts contracted by a deceased husband (2, 33.2), one on the payment of the husband's debts (2, 43.1), one on exemption from wartime service for the men of the house due to childbirth or serious illness of the mother (2, 69.2), and, finally, the epigraph dedicated to all the women of Estella.

77 Justiniano Rodríguez, ed., *Los fueros del Reino de León: Documentos*, vol. 2 (León: Leonesas, Ediciones S. A., 1981), 16.

The fuero likewise established the legal power of the husband over the wife in decreeing that no woman be imprisoned, tried, or tried in the absence of her husband (decree 42) and that no woman be taken against her will to make the king's bread, "unless she is his servant" (decree 37). Finally, the Fuero of Leon established that the female bakers who falsified the weight of the bread would, if it was their first offense, be flogged and that if they did so again they would pay five *sueldos* to the king's *merino* (decree 35). Women bakers owed the king's *sayón* (a legal official) a weekly amount of two silver *sueldos* (decree 43). Finally, decree 25 mandated that if a husband committed homicide and had no money to pay, the *sayón* took half of his personal property, and the other half was reserved for his wife, children, or relatives, with the houses and all the inheritance.[78]

The Fuero of Nájera established in article 31 that a widow (*"vidua de Naiara"*) who did not have children should not pay the war tax (nor did clerics or land tenants pay this tax).[79] No one could ask for lodging the house of a widow or single woman, nor threaten her honor (Article 30).[80] Article 44 regulated the freedom to make a will, stating that if a man or woman did not have children or natural heirs, they could leave their movable and immovable property in inheritance to anyone they wanted, except a lesser noble.[81] Finally, poor women are mentioned in the Fuero of Nájera, in the decree that, if the king or seigneur of the country were in dire need, they could send the *sayón* to requisition chickens of poor women, but he had to pay for each a special price, a sheepskin.[82]

The antecedents of the regulations on rape are more common since they have their roots in biblical texts. For example, the Fuero of Miranda de Ebro in 1099 established the death penalty for rape. This also likewise established that if a man or woman wounded a married man or woman, they should pay a fine of sixty *sueldos*; and if there was no blood, thirty *sueldos*. Moreover, it stipulated that "if

---

78   Ibid., 16–23. See likewise the original Latin text in Flórez, *España Sagrada*, 340–47.
79   *Boletín de la Real Academia de la Historia*, vol. 19 (Madrid: Real Academia de la Historia, 1891), 79.
80   Ibid., 79.
81   Ibid., 82.
82   Ibid., 83.

a man or woman, moved by lasciviousness, were to grab a married man by the hair, by the beard, or by the testicles, he should redeem their guilt by paying a fine of half a murder; and in the event of note being able to pay, he should remain in prison for thirty days and thereafter beaten from one side of the *villa* to the other."[83] The Fuero of Marañón in Navarre (c. 1124) also regulated rape via the payment of a fine of 300 *sólidos* ("*Toto homine qui rapuerit filiam de vicino de Maraione*").[84] The fuero of the towns in the bishopric of Santiago de Compostela in 1113 dedicated likewise a section to the rape or abduction of women ("*mulieris violationis, quod vulgo raptum dicitur*");[85] and the Fuero of Toledo in 1118 prohibited rape on the sentence of death ("*morte moriatur in loco*").[86] Finally, the Fuero of Nájera established a prohibition on raping virgin women, although it did not fix a sentence attached to the offense ("*neque virginem forciare*").[87]

There are also few precedents on systematizing the rights of minors regarding inheritance and it is truly difficult to find written legal norms that regulate in such detail the power of minors in regard to inheritance from their parents prior to 1164. There are fifty-seven references to minors in the Fuero of Estella included in twenty-eight norms, practically all of them in relation to their inheritance rights and their protection and tutelage, something certainly new in that century.

The Fuero of Estella also regulated in great detail some of the freedoms and liberties of Jews in the burg of San Martín initially, and then the whole city. There are nineteen mentions of Jews in the fuero, grouped into eight legal norms, most of which refer to commercial transactions: within their own neighborhood or Jewish quarter, surrounded by the city walls, with a synagogue and a cemetery, and they had their own bylaws and institutions. In 1170, Sancho the Wise conceded to the Jews of Tudela the fuero of those of Nájera,[88]

---

83   Muñoz y Romero, *Colección de fueros municipales y cartas pueblas*, 348.
84   Ibid., 496.
85   Ibid., 404.
86   Ibid., 366.
87   Ibid., 290.
88   With many prerogatives such as, "that they should move to the town castle, with the power to sell the homes that they left behind in their neighborhood: they should not pay tributes, but with the duty to repair the castle: they should not pay for murder, if, on being attacked in the castle, they kill some Christians; with many other advantages,

and the Navarrese communities were organized thereafter by means of a municipal government with a *beth din* at the head, aldermen and juries and the other positions befitting Christian councils, who enjoyed a wide margin of autonomy. The legal norms that governed life in the Jewis quarter, known as *takkanot* or *takkanah*, were passed like bylaws of the Christian communities, in the municipal assembly whose sessions were held in the synagogue.[89] Thus, for example, the Jewish quarter of Tudela passed new municipal bylaws in 1363, "imposing penalties on those who did not obey the agreements of the twenty *regidores* that they appointed, and those who raised false witness."[90]

Despite having their own bylaws, the Fuero of Estella obliged the Jews to comply with the laws of the city concerning commerce in the same way as all the other residents were obligated. In this sense, the text of the fuero does not distinguish in that relating to murders, injuries, or insults between Jews and Christians, applying the same legal measures to all of them (1, 14) and, therefore, it is likewise very explicit in that relating to the legal status of Jews when affirming that lesser nobles, Franks, villeins, and Jews are on the same level legally (2, 19.8–9).

The Fuero of Estella includes at least four principles that, in general, govern the legal treatment of Jews in the Kingdom of Navarre as a whole: first, Jews were subject to law (1, 14; 2, 19.8–9); second, they were free (1, 14; 2, 19.8–9); third, they could trade freely and have access to property (2, 55). The bulk of their patrimony came from the breach of credit commitments contracted by Christians, Muslims, and Jews;[91] and fourth, they enjoyed legal protection (1, 12). They maintained their own legal system, jurisprudence, and judges for the internal matters of their community in religious and civil affairs. In criminal matters, they could administer low justice, since in Navarre criminal justice corresponded to the royal authority, with

---

among them, that of not paying tithes for inherited estates, and only for those that they acquired from Christians." Marichalar and Manrique, *Historia de la legislación y recitaciones del derecho civil de España*, 363–64.

89   Carrasco, *Sinagoga y Mercado*, 34.

90   Marichalar and Manrique, *Historia de la legislación y recitaciones del derecho civil de España*, 364.

91   Carrasco, *Sinagoga y Mercado*, 52.

exceptional cases made for jurisdictional seigneuries and immunities. The enforcement of judgments and the collection of fines was the responsibility of royal power.

The merchants of Estella and their interests were protected by the authorities of the kingdom and, also, by those of the neighboring kingdoms of Castile and Aragon. In its first section, regarding the freedoms and liberties of the residents of the city, the Fuero of Estella stated that no man could be free of a debt contracted with the Franks or Jews of Estella (1, 12).

In general terms, the Fuero of Estella makes explicit mention of Jews in those aspects that concern the two religious communities in the city, the Jews and Christians, since there was no Muslim population in Estella. In the context of a judicial dispute, Jews could and had to swear by their own creed (2, 19.9) and rabbinical letters had the same value as the writings or testimonies of Christians (2, 55.2). This freedom has its immediate origin in the charter that Alfonso I granted to the Muslims of Tudela in 1119, ordering that, "if a Moor were to have a trial with a Christian, or a Christian with a Moor, the judge of the Moors shall judge Moors according to his *sunnah*, and the judge of the Christians to Christians according to their fuero."[92]

The chapter entitled "On Christians and Jews" mainly referred to legal action over deeds, debts, or purchases and sales and, in general, legal battles between the Christians and Jews of Estella, established a system of total equality between the faithful of the two religions; in this way, if a Christian had a lawsuit against a Jew, either on account of money or physical confrontation or for any other matter, in the event that there were no deeds or witnesses, Jew justified themselves by an oath and remained free; likewise, Christians could be justified by oath in their litigation with Jews if they had no witnesses (2, 55.5).

In this same sense, the fuero distinguished between Frankish and Navarrese witnesses (coming from other parts of the kingdom), priests and laymen, and Christians and Jews. In the context of a lawsuit

---

92 Peces-Barba, Llamas, and Fernández, eds., *Textos básicos de derechos humanos*, 31–32.

between Jews and Christians, for whatever cause, two witnesses had
to testify, one Jewish and the other Christian (2, 55.1). As it was said,
in the event that they did not have deeds or witnesses, both could
be justified by an oath, and they were free of any charge (2, 55.5).
In the context of legal action over debts, Christians could take to
the trial a deed of the rabbi from the Jewish quarter demonstrating
they had made the payment (2, 55.2), in which case Jews had to
demonstrate with witnesses to those that had such deeds that they
had not been paid. In the event of the death of a Jew or Christian,
the children had to pay the debt contracted by their father, as long
as the creditor had made a deed or there was evidence of it (2, 55.3).
When a Christian died and his heirs claimed a debt owed to a Jew,
they had to prove it with deeds, and if the Jew could not prove
with witnesses that the debt had indeed been canceled, he had to
pay the debt (2, 55.4). In the event of debts of less than ten *sueldos*
of lesser nobles and Franks with respect to villeins and Jews, the
former only had to present as a witness an adult man, aged fifteen
or more, who gave sworn testimony (2, 19.8). For their part, Jews
and villeins had to swear by their own hands on debts of more than
twelve *dineros* (2, 19.9). In cases of amounts less than twelve *dineros*,
Navarrese had to swear "before all men" and "on the head of his
friend," Jews "on the east," and Franks "on the head of his friend
or his godfather" (2, 19.9).

The protection granted by the law to the Jewish population
of Estella, together with the protection enjoyed by the monarchs,
made Navarre a place of refuge for many Jewish exiles between
the mid-eleventh and late sixteenth centuries. The invasion of the
Almoravid dynasty in 1086, and later the Almohad Caliphate from
1147 on, encouraged a Jewish migration of communities that were
living in Muslim lands toward Navarre from the second half of the
eleventh century on. Simultaneously, starting with the first crusade
of Pope Urban II in 1096 and the provisions against the Jews that
followed them, such as those ordered by Philip II in 1182, the
measures of the Lateran Council of 1215, the measures adopted in
the course of the Albigensian Crusade between 1209 and 1244, and
the edicts of Louis IX in 1242 and 1254 (massacres and expulsion)

in the context of the seventh crusade, encouraged many Jewish communities to find refuge in the Kingdom of Navarre.

The repressive policies of the Kingdom of France and other corners of Europe contrast with the measures adopted by Theobald I in 1237 who, supported by Pope Innocent IV, openly declared his protection of the Jewish minority "to the point of avoiding forced baptisms and seeking reimbursement of their debts."[93] The *villas* of Viana and Laguardia, frontier towns with Castile, gave shelter to seventy and fifty Jewish families respectively in the early thirteenth century.[94] In 1234, Pope Gregory IX reminded King Theobald that Navarre did not comply with the provisions of the Lateran Council, which forced Jews to wear different attire to that of Christians, in order to identify themselves publicly.[95] The 1266 census records twenty-nine houses in the whole of the Jewish quarter of Estella, all contributors to the royal treasury of Navarre, and records, among other services to the crown, the important loan of 1,700 *libras* given to the monarch by the community.[96] As Juan Carrasco states, "the tolerance and treatment dispensed to the refugees made Navarrese soil a true land of exile, especially after 1274, since the anti-Semitic policy by the house of France led to successive waves of Jewish emigrants."[97]

But the violence also affected Navarrese Jews and in 1276 the French forces of Philip III attacked and destroyed the Navarrería and with it the Pamplona Jewish quarter. A year after the destruction of the Navarrería, the king of France, acting as tutor of the Queen of Navarre, ordered that those who had lent money or supplies with interest to Nuño González, should consent to the payment of the main debt and that the Jews of Estella should grant eight years to their debtors for the payment of the debt, charging each year the eighth part of it. In this same vein, in 1278 he ordered that limits be placed on the interest that the Jews imposed on the residents of Murillo el Fruto and Cabanillas, and that those of Araciel and Corella should

93   Carrasco, "Las primeras migraciones judías en el reino de Navarra," 24.
94   Ibid., 27.
95   Yanguas y Miranda, *Diccionario de Antigüedades del Reino de Navarra*, 516.
96   Carrasco, "Las primeras migraciones judías en el reino de Navarra," 25.
97   Carrasco, *Sinagoga y Mercado*, 58.

not pay the Jews the interest but just the main debt, and ordered that the Jews grant the residents of San Adrián and Azagra three years to pay what they owed.[98] While between 1277 and 1280 the kingdom approved a series of provisions aimed at safeguarding the people and interests of the Jewish communities of the *merindad* of Estella, setting a cap of 2,000 *libras* on the annual tribute payment, in 1280 the king ordered likewise that the Jews of Tudela should not bother the residents of Ribaforada for the interests that they owed and that they should only charge the residents of Buñuel for the capital they owed. In this same vein, in 1299 the king consort of Navarre, Felipe I, ordered unsuccessfully that there should be an observance in the kingdom an ordinance by Louis of France, by virtue of which the obligations contracted by usury with the Jews were condoned and they were executed by means of the return of the capital received.[99]

But, despite such measures, the Jewish exodus attracted new migrations to Navarre from the anti-Semitic measures that took place between 1292 and 1306 in different parts of the continent, the systematic plundering of properties, arrests, special taxes, and confisactions that culminated in the expulsion ordered by Philip IV in 1306 and the sixth expulsion of the Jews from France, Languedoc, and Burgundy in 1322. Consequently, during the reign of Jeanne II of Evreux (1329–1349), there was a new wave of Jewish immigration to Navarre, with Tudela and Estella welcoming most of the exiles, 65 percent of the total. In the early fourteenth century, the Jewish quarter of Estella had grown to become the third in the kingdom by virtue of its contribution to the treasury and in a flourishing focus of economic and cultural activity.[100]

---

98 In 1256 Pope Alexander IV authorized King Theobald II to appropriate goods acquired by the Jews through the nonpayment of loans and return them to their owners or use them for pious purposes, and in 1330 King Felipe III limited, in an amendment of the fueros, extending loans at an interest higher than the 20 percent, although this order did not produce the effects suggested by the legislator because of the necessity incurred even by the crown itself to avoid it. See Yanguas y Miranda, *Diccionario de Antigüedades del Reino de Navarra*, 502 and 516.

99 Ibid., 517. Between 1277 and 1280, the kingdom approved a series of provisions aimed at safeguarding the people and interests of the Jewish communities of the *merindad* of Estella, setting a maximum of 2,000 *libras* in the annual payment of tributes.

100 Carrasco, *Sinagoga y Mercado*, 74.

The Jews of Estella were subject to the jurisdiction of the seneschal, who took some of them prisoner in 1308, which provoked the protest of the Jewish community before King Luis the Stubborn. After hearing the case, the latter ordered the Estelle seneschal to cease exercising that jurisdiction and deliver it to Pamplona with the keys of the Jewish quarter and to release the prisoners. At the same time the king ordered the seneschal of Pamplona to defend the interests of the Jews and their property. In 1326, the Jews of Estella complained again against the tax collector, Juan García, because he had demanded fifty *sueldos* per day "for a long time" to collect taxes (*pechas*) owed to the king, which meant an increase in their tax burden. After listening to the case, Juan García had to renounce his position as tax collector of the Jewish community, and thereafter they administered it themselves, as was the custom previously.[101]

From the spring of 1320, the shepherds' crusade movement had sown terror in the Jewish quarters in various parts of Europe. As Yanguas and Miranda points out, Christians in Estella were increasingly irritated at the protection that the crown granted to the Jews, "who were envied for their riches."[102] Taking advantage of the death of the monarch, Carlos I the Bald, on February 1, 1328, anti-Semitic movements in Navarre began and a great number of Estella Jews were killed at the hands of a crowd instigated by Pedro Ollogoien, a friar in the convent of San Francisco, which attacked the Jewish quarter on the night of March 5 to 6.[103] Following the massacre, the kingdom carried out some justice by executing a condemnatory sentence and imposing severe fines on individuals and even those *concejos* in which some of their residents had taken part in lynching, a difficult legal procedure, to be sure, because of the large amount of people involved in the crime and sentenced by the courts.[104] Brother Pedro Ollogoien was arrested in Estella by the king's officials and handed over to the bishop of Pamplona.[105]

101 Yanguas y Miranda, *Diccionario de Antigüedades del Reino de Navarra*, 517.
102 Ibid.
103 José Goñi Gaztambide, "La matanza de judíos en Navarra, en 1328," *Hispania Sacra* 12 (1959), 5–33.
104 Fernando Mendoza, "Con los judíos de Estella," *Príncipe de Viana* 44–45 (1951), 261.
105 José Goñi Gaztambide, *Historia Eclesiástica de Estella*, vol. 2 (Iruñea-Pamplona: Gobierno de Navarra, Departamento de Educación, Cultura y Deporte, 1990), 85.

Prosecuted and condemned to death for his intervention in the events of 1329, his sentence would be commuted later by the ecclesiastical authorities. In addition to the individual fines, the king imposed a fine of 10,000 *libras* on the residents of the city of Estella, payable in ten years and the king inherited, according to custom, the possessions of the Jews who died without heirs.

Despite the extent of the massacre, only a year later the Jewish community of Estella in particular and Navarre in general began to experience a new boom and in 1329 the Jews of Estella contributed 1,600 *libras* of aid to the royal coffers.[106] The policy of the new sovereigns of Navarre with respect to the Jewish population continued to be protectionist, as reflected in the treatment given to this social, religious, and cultural minority in the improvement of the general Fuero of Navarre enacted in 1330. At first, Tudela became the place of destination of the majority of Jewish exiles, although from 1334 on—with Henri de Sully as governor—Tudela, Estella, and Sangüesa would be the destinations for 64 percent of the expatriate Jews and the six localities in the land of Estella welcomed thirty-six families or almost 34 percent of the total.[107] At the same time, in 1336 the governor of Navarre, Salhadin de Angleura, ordered the rebuilding of the Jewish quarter of Navarreria that had been destroyed in 1277. The new Jewish quarter was to be walled and protected by the order that no Jew should build his house in another part of the city.[108]

In 1331, 1340, and 1361, the courts in Portugal carried out anti-Semitic measures by which ghettos were created in towns in which more than ten Jewish families resided.[109] And the abuses of 1355, and those recorded between 1366 and 1369 in the context of the first civil war in Castile by the troops of Enrique de Trastámara, meant that Navarre once more became a more welcome destination and the kingdom continued to protect the interests of Jews.[110]

---

106 Carrasco, *Sinagoga y Mercado*, 77.
107 Ibid., 69.
108 Yanguas y Miranda, *Diccionario de Antigüedades del Reino de Navarra*, 518.
109 María José Pimenta, *Los judíos en Portugal* (Madrid: Mapfre, 1992), 72 and 110.
110 Joseph Pérez, *Los judíos en España* (Madrid: Marcial Pons, 2005), 121–23. See likewise Béatrice Leroy, "Recherches sur les juifs de Navarre à la fin du Moyen Age," *Revue des études juives* 140 (1981), 319–432.

In 1370, Queen Juana I ordered that the Jews of Calahorra and Castile who had been exiled to Navarre should be protected, each contributing, *por cabezaje* y *brazaje*, two florins a year, and that both rich and poor should pay. She further ruled "that the Jewish quarters of the kingdom should not be obliged to contribute, except for the quota of wine and meat, as well as the other Jews; and that they could not be accused of excommunication or *aztama*."[111] Moreover, in order to avoid abuses, Christians or Muslims were prohibited from buying property from Jews without the king's license. In 1366, the Jewish quarter of Estella had eighty-five hearths, 10 percent of the population of the Jewish quarters of the lands of Estella, and almost 11 percent of the population of the city. At that time the tax collector for the Jews of the *merindad* was Jeuda Levi.[112] In 1375, the Jewish quarter of Estella was still the third most important in terms of contributions to the royal treasury.[113] International pressure on the Jewish people prompted many of them to sell their movable properties in order to facilitate mobility, so in 1380 Carlos II imposed a new contribution of five *sueldos* per *libra* on all the properties sold by Jews to Christians or Muslims.[114]

The massacre of 1391 in the kingdoms of Castile and Aragon and the seventh expulsion edict ordered by Charles IV of France in 1394, by which Jewish communities had forty-five days to sell their property before going into exile, caused new waves of immigration to Navarre.[115] In 1386, King Carlos II excused the Jews of Tudela from 431 *libras* that they owed in taxes, "on account of their poverty, since of the five hundred tax payers there used to be in times past, barely two hundred remained."[116] Carlos III again pardoned the Jewish quarter of Tudela 120 *libras* of its ordinary tax contribution so that they could repair the main synagogue that was

---

111 Yanguas y Miranda, *Diccionario de Antigüedades del Reino de Navarra*, 518.
112 Béatrice Leroy, *The Jews of Navarre in the Late Middle Ages* (Jerusalem: Magnes Press; Hebrew University, 1985), 94 and 119.
113 The Jewish quarter of Tudela paid the king monthly taxes of 521 florins, 7 *sueldos*, and 2 *dineros*; that of Pamplona 261 florins, 14 *sueldos*, and 11 *dineros*; and that of Estella 119 florins and 9 *dineros*.
114 Yanguas y Miranda, *Diccionario de Antigüedades del Reino de Navarra*, 519.
115 Béatrice Leroy, "Le royaume de Navarre et les juifs aux XIV et XV siècles: entre l'accueil et la tolerance," *Sefarad* 38 (1978), 263–92.
116 Yanguas y Miranda, *Diccionario de Antigüedades del Reino de Navarra*, 519.

in bad state and in 1435 the king again forgave them 342 *libras* of the ordinary tax.[117] In 1469, Jews living outside the Jewish quarter of Pamplona were ordered to return to live there and to renovate the houses that were part of the royal patrimony; and in 1482 the assembly of Tafalla passed a bylaw by which, on feast days, Jews should not leave their quarters or walk the streets among Christians until after the functions had been carried out.[118]

Nevertheless, the pressure of the Catholic monarchs began to affect the welcoming role of the Navarrese Jewish quarters from the mid-fourteenth century on.[119] In 1492, Estella, Tafalla, and Tudela welcomed the Jews expelled from Castile and Aragon, although in 1498, six years after the expulsion of the Jews from these kingdoms, Catherine of Navarre had to yield to the threat of excommunication.[120] During the wars of the conquest of Navarre, converts lent their support to the legitimate cause of the Navarrese kings, so in 1521, sanctions were imposed against people of Jewish origin. Many years after the conquest, in 1561, some inhabitants of Tudela still requested "that the ban on obtaining public offices and benefits should not be extended to future generations of the new Christians."[121] With the aim of distinguishing converted families from those of "old Christians," it was decreed that the names of the Jewish converts should be recorded on large "blankets," which hung in public view in churches. That of Tudela, hanging in the chapel of Cristo del Perdón in the cathedral, was one of the largest with almost two hundred registered names.[122] And "so that the ignominy of the families was perpetuated," the municipality of Tudela stated in 1610 that, "these names were written on the blanket, so that cleanliness was maintained in the city and elsewhere, and it was known how to distinguish those who descended from such people, so that over time the memory of their ancestors was not obscured

117 Ibid.
118 Ibid., 520.
119 Carrasco, *Sinagoga y Mercado*, 34.
120 Cierbide, "Las comunidades judaicas navarras en la Edad Media," 241. See likewise Benjamin R. Gampel, *The Last Jews on Iberian Soil: Navarrese Jewry 1479/1498* (Berkeley: University of California Press, 1989).
121 Yanguas y Miranda, *Diccionario de Antigüedades del Reino de Navarra*, 523.
122 This is where the expression *"tirar de la manta"* comes from. See Julio Caro Baroja, *Los judíos en la España moderna y contemporánea* (Madrid: Istmo, 1978), 38.

or extinguished, and it was known how to and distinguish the quality of noble men."[123] In the late eighteenth century, these blankets were still being displayed in many Navarrese churches, and the Tudela blanket remained on show until the late nineteenth century.[124]

Among the closest antecedents regarding provisions on the activity and interests of the Jewish populations in Navarre, one should cite the Fuero of Nájera, which was aimed at lesser nobles, clerics and monks, Jews and Moors, townsfolk, plebeians and villeins, and the residents of Nájera. This fuero established that homicide of lesser nobles, monks, or Jews would imply a fine of 250 *sueldos* while the death of a villein would be 100 *sueldos*, and for a Muslim 12.5 *sueldos*. In many aspects, the fuero out Christians and Jews on the same level. In the late eleventh century they were granted a statute by which they could buy and sell properties within the Jewish quarter, they were exempt from paying tributes, the royal *merino* was their appeals judge, and they were in charge of maintaining the city walls of the Jewish neighborhood. Alfonso I granted the Muslims of Tudela the Fuero of Nájera after taking the city in 1119. By this fuero, any trials or legal action were to be in the hands of their judge and clerks, "as it was in the time of the Moors."[125] The Muslims had the right to appoint their own judges and to have them "in their honors as they were in the time of the Moors, honorably." If a Muslim had a lawsuit with a Christian, the Muslim judge should judge the Muslim according to the *sunnah*, and the Christian judge the Christian according to their fuero and each should swear oaths according to their own creed and customs.[126] The fuero decreed, moreover, that if there were any suspicion that a Muslim had committed an offense, the testimony of a Muslim would only be lawful, and not that of a Christian.[127]

---

123 Marichalar and Manrique, *Historia de la legislación y recitaciones del derecho civil de España*, 365.
124 Yanguas y Miranda, *Diccionario de Antigüedades del Reino de Navarra*, 525.
125 Alfonso García Gallo, *Metodología histórico-jurídica. Antología de fuentes del derecho español* (Madrid: Artes Gráficos, 1975), 540.
126 Ibid., 541.
127 Other antecedents are the Fuero of Calatayud granted by Alfonso I of Aragon (c. 1131) punished the flagrant death of Jews with 300 *sólidos* and decreed that Jews could swear before the law. The foundational charter of Lerma in 1148 established that lesser nobles and Jews enjoyed the same fuero as the residents of Lerma.

By way of conclusion, the legal treatment of women in the Fuero of Estella stands out because it was not typical in other fueros of the time or prior to then, in terms of the number of articles devoted to this particular legal area and the thoroughness with which the legal precepts were synthesized and put in writing. The same can be said with regard to the mention of the poor in the context of a legal dispute or the protection of the interests of minors, which was settled in a very complex and complete way. Likewise very exceptional was the loyal casuistry regarding widowhood and indigence, as well as cases related to minors affected by poverty in the context of a guardianship on account of being minors.

The original fuero prior to 1077 and its expansion in 1164 undoubtedly constitute two of the most notable factors in the population and demographic success experienced by the original small burg of San Martín, which in just over 150 years multiplied fifteen times, from about 78 hearths in the late eleventh century to constituting a city with 1,127 hearths, divided into seventeen districts, in 1266. Socioeconomic and political factors undoubtedly played a decisive role in this growth, but the fuero constituted its foundation and its development made this growth possible in a sustainable manner, mainly because it attracted and retained new settlers and because it established a stable framework of legal guarantees suitable for all its inhabitants without distinction of class.

As regards situation of the Estella Jews, the law of the city and the crown provided a degree of security that was not comparable to that of many other places in Europe. In this case, too, the nature of the fuero as well as the crown's defense of the interests of the Jewish community made the city of Estella in particular and the Kingdom of Navarre in general a place of destination for a large number of Jewish exiles between the eleventh and fourteenth centuries.

BIBLIOGRAPHY

Arraiza Frauca, Jesús. "Los fuegos de la merindad de Estella en 1427." *Príncipe de Viana* 29, nos. 110–111 (1968): 117–47.

Arrechea, Horacio. "Algunas correspondencias sobre el fuero de Estella y el fuero de Tudela." Special issue, "Segundo Congreso General de Historia de Navarra. 2. Prehistoria, Historia Antigua, Historia Medieval." Annex 14. *Príncipe de Viana* 14 (1992): 315–24.

Barrero, Ana María, and Mari Luz Alonso. *Textos de derecho local español en la Edad Media. Catálogo de fueros y costums municipales.* Madrid: Consejo Superior de Investigaciones Científicas, Instituto de Ciencias Jurídicas, 1989.

Beroiz, Marcelino. *Crimen y castigo en Navarra bajo el reinado de los primeros Evreux (1328–1349).* Iruñea-Pamplona: Universidad Pública de Navarra, 2005.

Boletín de la Real Academia de la Historia. Volume 19. Madrid: Real Academia de la Historia, 1891.

Bolton, Brenda, and Susan M. Stuard. *Women in Medieval Society.* Philadelphia: University of Pennsylvania Press, 1976.

Caro Baroja, Julio. *Etnografía histórica de Navarra.* Pamplona: Editorial Aranzadi, 1972.

———. *Los judíos en la España moderna y contemporánea.* Madrid: Istmo, 1978.

Carrasco, Juan. *La población de Navarra en el siglo XIV.* Iruñea-Pamplona: Ediciones Universidad de Navarra, 1973.

———. *Sinagoga y mercado. Estudios y textos sobre los judíos del Reino de Navarra.* Iruñea-Pamplona: Institución Príncipe de Viana, 1993.

———. "Las primeras migraciones judías en el reino de Navarra (1076–1328)." In *Movimientos migratorios y expulsiones en la diáspora occidental. Terceros encuentros judaicos de Tudela: 14–17 de julio de 1998, Universidad Pública de Navarra,* edited by

Fermín Miranda García. Iruñea-Pamplona: Dirección de Publicaciones del Gobierno de Navarra. Departamento de Educación y Cultura, 2000.

Cierbide, Ricardo. "Las comunidades judaicas navarras en la Edad Media." In *Los Judíos*. Gasteiz,: Fundación Sancho el Sabio, 1992.

Coloquio Mujeres de la Edad Media: escritura, visión, ciencia: Escritura, visión, ciencia. A novecientos años del nacimiento de Hildegard von Bingen. Santiago de Chile: Universidad de Chile, Facultad de Filosofía y Humanidades, 1999.

Estudios de arqueología alavesa. Volume 6. Vitoria: Diputación Foral de Álava, Consejo de Cultura, 1974.

Fernández, Silvia, and Paco Roda, eds. *Ellas, las mujeres en la historia de Pamplona*. Iruñea-Pamplona: Concejalía de la Mujer-Emakumearen Zinegotzigoa, 1998.

Flórez, Henrique. *España Sagrada: Theatro geographico-historico de la Iglesia de España. Historia Compostelana*. Madrid: En la Oficina de Antonio Marín, 1754.

Fortún, Luis Javier. "Los 'fueros menores' y el señorío realengo en Navarra (siglos XI–XIV)." *Príncipe de Viana* 46, no. 176 (1985): 603 73.

Fueros del Reyno de Navarra. Iruñea-Pamplona: Imprenta de Martín Gregorio de Zabala, 1686.

Fueros del Reyno de Navarra. Iruñea-Pamplona: Longas, 1815.

Fuero General de Navarra. Pamplona: Editorial Aranzadi, 1964.

Gampel, Benjamin R. *The Last Jews on Iberian Soil: Navarrese Jewry 1479/1498*. Berkeley: University of California Press, 1989.

García Arancón, Mª Raquel. "La población e Navarra en la segunda mitad del siglo XIII." *Cuadernos de etnología y etnografía de Navarra* 17, no. 46 (1985): 87–101.

García Gallo, Alfonso. *Metodología histórico-jurídica. Antología de fuentes del derecho español*. Madrid: Artes Gráficas, 1975.

———. *Manual de historia del derecho español. El origen y la evolución del derecho.* Author's edition. Madrid, 1984.

Goñi Gaztambide, José. "La matanza de judíos en Navarra, en 1328." *Hispania Sacra* 12 (1959): 5–33.

———. *Historia Eclesiástica de Estella.* Iruñea-Pamplona: Gobierno de Navarra, Departamento de Educación, Cultura y Deporte, 1990.

Irujo, Xabier. "Sobre la datación y naturaleza del fuero de Estella." *Terra Stellae* 7 (2016): 38–55.

Jimeno, Roldán. "El municipio de Vasconia en la Edad Media." *Iura Vasconiae* 2 (2005): 45–83.

———. *Matrimonio y otras uniones afines en el derecho histórico navarro (siglos VIII–XVIII).* Madrid: Dykinson, 2015.

Lacarra, José María, and Ángel J. Martín Duque. *Fueros derivados de Jaca. Estella-San Sebastián.* Iruñea-Pamplona: Institución Príncipe de Viana, 1969.

Leroy, Béatrice. "Le royaume de Navarre et les juifs aux XIV et XV siècles: entre l'accueil et la tolerance." *Sefarad* 38 (1978): 263–92.

———. "Recherches sur les juifs de Navarre à la fin du Moyen Age." *Revue des études juives* 140 (1981): 319–432.

———. *The Jews of Navarre in the Late Middle Ages.* Jerusalem: Magnes Press; Hebrew University, 1985.

Los fors et costumas deu Royaumme de Navarre deca-ports. Pau: Jerôme Duproux, 1722.

Marichalar, Amalio, and Cayetano Manrique. *Historia de la legislación y recitaciones del derecho civil de España.* Madrid: Imprenta nacional, 1862.

Martín Duque, Ángel J. "La formación del primer 'burgo' navarro. Estella." *Príncipe de Viana* 51 (1990): 317–27; reprint, *Príncipe de Viana* 63, no. 227 (2002): 761–72.

Mendoza, Fernando. "Con los judíos de Estella." *Príncipe de Viana* 44–45 (1951): 235–71.

Monteano, Peio. "Navarra de 1366 a 1428: Población y poblamiento." *Príncipe de Viana* 57, no. 208 (1996): 307–44.

Moret, Josep. *Anales del Reino de Navarra.* Tolosa: Establecimiento Tipográfico y Casa Editorial de Eusebio López, 1891.

Muñoz y Romero, Tomás. *Colección de fueros municipales y cartas pueblas de los reinos de Castilla, León, Corona de Aragón y Navarra.* Madrid: Imprenta de Don José María Alonso, 1847.

Osés Urricelqui, Merche, ed. *Documentación medieval de Estella: siglos XII–XVI.* Iruñea-Pamplona: Departamento de Cultura y Turismo del Gobierno de Navarra; Institución Príncipe de Viana, 2005.

Peces-Barba, Gregorio, Ángel Llamas, and Carlos R. Fernández, eds. *Textos básicos de derechos humanos con estudios generales y especiales y comentarios a cada texto nacional e internacional.* Burgos: Editorial Aranzadi; Elkano, 2001.

Pérez, Joseph. *Los judíos en España.* Madrid: Marcial Pons, 2005.

Pimenta, María José. *Los judíos en Portugal.* Madrid: Mapfre, 1992.

Rodríguez, Justiniano, ed. *Los fueros del Reino de León: Documentos.* León: Leonesas, Ediciones S. A., 1981.

Rodríguez Ochoa, José Mª. *Menahem Ben Zerah, Rabino Estellés (1310–1385). Aproximación a una cultura que floreció en Sefarad.* Iruñea-Pamplona: Gobierno de Navarra, 2011.

Salarrullana, José. *Colección de documentos para el estudio de la historia de Aragón.* Zaragoza: M. Escar, 1907.

Satrustegi, José Mª. *Comportamiento sexual de los vascos.* Donostia: Txertoa, 1981.

Yanguas y Miranda, José. *Diccionarios de los Fueros del Reino de Navarra.* Donostia: Imprenta de Ignacio Ramón Baroja, 1828.

———. *Diccionario de Antigüedades del Reino de Navarra.* Iruñea-Iruña-Pamplona, 1840.

Zorrilla, Pedro E. Índice cronológico de los documentos y papeles antiguos existentes en el archivo municipal de la ciudad de Estella, pertenecientes á los siglos XII á XVIII, ambos inclusive, formado por el que suscribe, en el año de 1911. Estella, 1911.

Chapter 7

The Jewish Minority in the Fuero of Estella

Amaia Álvarez Berastegi

The wars and economic crisis that Europe experienced in the ninth and tenth centuries provoked the migration of Jewish communities, which were already diasporas, in search of safety and prosperity. Although it could be the case that the first Navarrese synagogue was founded in Pamplona around 905, the first Jewish quarters of towns were established in the Ribera zone under Islamic rule. In the Kingdom of Pamplona, as in other Christian kingdoms, the Jewish presence was accepted on the basis of criteria of legality and legitimacy, and this was awarded through the protection of the monarchs. The Jews, a distinct community with restricted rights, remained under the protection and shelter of the monarchs, from whom they received rights directly.[1]

The drive to develop the Camino de Santiago during Sancho the Great's reign was followed by a considerable growth in the number of pilgrims that, already by the time of the kingdoms of the Navarrese-Aragonese monarchs, as expressed in planning to create new settlements made up of urban populations.[2] The migratory flows

---

1   Fernando Suárez Bilbao, "La comunidad judía y los procedimientos judiciales en la Baja Edad media," *Cuadernos de Historia del Derecho* 2 (1995), 100.
2   Luis Javier Fortún Pérez de Ciriza, "Fueros locales de Navarra," *Revista Príncipe de Viana* 68, no. 242 (2007), 869–70. The only good *villa* on the Camino de Santiago that did not possess the fuero de Jaca, in its Estella or Pamplona version, was Los Arcos, which in 1176 received from Sancho VI its own fuero, aimed above all at attracting settlers,

in the last third of the ninth century summed up in the process of creating *villas* on the part of the Kingdom of Pamplona coincided in time with Jewish migrations, so that both occurred at the same time, contributing to the economic growth of the kingdom and, most especially, to the creation of new urban centers.[3] The new money-based economy acted as a potent focus of attracting Jews.[4] They were privileged owing to their economic capacity and, most especially, their contributions to the crown.[5] Despite the fact that the monarchs saw in them efficient collaborators in the government and administration of its territories, at the same time Christian society was fomenting, within the frame of European anti-Semitism, an anti-Jewish reaction nourished from pulpits and that made them responsible, among other things, for the death of Jesus.[6]

Estella was created around 1076–1077 by means of a municipal fuero. Although the town of Lizarra existed previously beneath the castle of the tenancy of Lizarra or Lizarrara, the transformation of this settlement into an urban center took place in the second half of the ninth century. Its evolution was tied to the commercial activity along the Camino de Santiago and the markets created around the route. Configured initially around the neighborhood surrounding San Martin street, it was transformed into a privileged site to attract traders and moneylenders who worshipped Yahweh. The presence of Jewish settlers is attested from the final third of the eleventh century on.[7] And soon, the two Jewish quarter of Estella, made up

---

among whom included both Franks and the lesser nobility and farmers.

3   Ricardo Cierbide Martinena, "La lengua de los francos de Estella: intento de interpretación," *Sancho el Sabio: Revista de cultura e investigación vasca* 3 (1999), 115; Ángel J. Martín Duque, "La fundación del primer burgo navarro: Estella," *Príncipe de Viana* 63, no. 227 (2002), 317–28.

4   There is an extensive collection of documents concerning Jews in Navarre in Juan Carrasco, Fermín Miranda García, and Eloísa Ramírez Vaquero, *Los judíos del reino de Navarra. Documentos 1093–1333* (Pamplona: Gobierno de Navarra, 1994).

5   Fermín Miranda García, "El precio de la fe. Rentas de la corona y aljamas judías en Navarra (siglos XII–XIV)," *Príncipe de Viana* 58, no. 210 (1997), 51.

6   José Ramón Hinojosa Montalvo, "Los judíos de la España medieval: de la tolerancia a la expulsion," in *Los marginados en el mundo medieval y moderno. Almería, del 5 al 7 de noviembre de 1998*, ed. María Desamparados Martínez San Pedro (Almería: Instituto de Estudios Almerienses, 2000), 27.

7   Juan Carrasco Pérez, "Juderías y Sinagogas en el reino de Navarra," *Príncipe de Viana* 63, 225 (2002), 115.

of two distinct districts, became one of the most influential in the kingdom, although it always remained behind that of Tudela.[8]

The Jewish minority was not only protected by the monarchy; the local fuero itself granted them rights, which came to resemble those of the Franks in many aspects;[9] although they never reached the same level, with the latter enjoying more fiscal exemptions.[10] Both the concession of the short fuero (1076–1077) and the conformation of the extensive fuero (1164) coincided with a moment in which the Jewish population grew in both Europe and Navarre, hence also the generous protective measures of the fueros during these centuries. However, growing anti-Semitism from the thirteenth century on, as a result of mistrust on the part of papacy and other reasons, led to a restriction of their rights, as could be seen in later legal texts, although this was still not part of the reform project promoted by Theobald I.[11]

The legal regulation of different aspects related to Jews also appears in other Navarrese municipal fueros granted from the eleventh century on with the objective of awarding a series of privileges and rights to the inhabitants of recently formed municipalities. As is well known, far from forming a homogenous group, the towns with fueros were made up of collectives of Franks, Navarrese, Jews, and Moors—the latter limited in the Ribera zone—so that local fueros included precepts to regulate relations among the diverse groups. Given their typical condition of moneylenders, in the case of the Jewish population, the local fueros made a special point of regulating the economic relations of this community with the rest of the collectives. This was also included in the Fuero of Estella,

---

8 Antonio Sola Alayeto and Toño Ros Zuasti, *Estella, posta y mercado en la Ruta Jacobea* (Pamplona: Caja de Ahorros de Navarra, 1992), 8.
9 Xabier Irujo, *Giving Birth to Cosmopolis: The Code of Laws of Estella (c.1076)*, Basque Law Series 1, Barandiaran Basque Studies Chair (Santa Barbara: University of California, 2011), 113.
10 Roldán Jimeno Aranguren, "El municipio de Vasconia en la Edad Media," *Iura Vasconiae* 2 (2005), 63.
11 During the reign of Theobald I (1234–1253), preparations were probably made, although it was not promulgated officially, for a new edition of the fuero of 1164, with a few lexical tweaks. Ángel J. Martín Duque, "El fenómeno urbano medieval en Navarra," in *El fenómeno urbano medieval entre el Cantábrico y el Duero: revisión historiográfica y propuestas de estudio*, ed. Jesús Ángel Solórzano Telechea and Beatriz Arízaga Bolumburu (Santander: Asociación de Jóvenes Historiadores de Cantabria, 2002), 737.

which, although a fuero for Franks, included norms that regulated the relations among the diverse social groups that populated Estella.

In this chapter I will focus on analyzing the relationship of the Jewish community with the Fuero of Estella during the eleventh and twelfth centuries. Following an initial section in which I will observe the principal features of the Estella Jewish quarter, in the second art I will analyze the precepts of the Estella fuero aimed specifically at the Jewish collective.

The Estella Jewish Quarter

Basic Features of the Estella Jewish Quarter

The Jews were organized into autonomous quarters, although they were integrated into Christian urban centers. The Jewish quarter was a legal institution that grouped together the Jews of a locality, and in each one there was a synagogue and a rabbi, although, above him was the chief rabbi of all the Jews in the Kingdom of Navarre. The Jewish quarters were organized like a council, with their *beth din* (rabbinical court) and juries, they had internal bylaws (*takkanot*) and they organized and judged themselves on that basis. The Jewish quarter took responsibility for providing for rabbis, the synagogue, and its own cultural institutions, as well as raising taxes in the community. Each Jewish quarter was autonomous and elaborated its own statutes by which it governed itself, which were granted or ratified by the monarch.[12] The legal powers of the Jewish quarters were relative to low justice.[13] And transgressions within the Jewish community were punished with fines or even expulsion from the community (*herem*). The basic core of social organization in each Jewish quarter was the family, understood as a conjugal family organized according to its strict patriarchal system.[14] The Hebrew communities that lived in the Jewish quarters, as well as holding government posts and those

---

12 Hinojosa Montalvo, "Los judíos de la España medieval," 36.
13 Mª Raquel García Arancón, "Marco jurídico y proyección social de las minorías navarras: judíos y mudéjares (siglos XII y XV)," *Iura Vasconiae* 4 (2007), 459–516.
14 Enrique Cantera Montenegro, "La mujer judía en la España medieval," *Espacio, Tiempo y Forma, Serie III, Historia medieval* 2 (1989), 38–39.

of tax collectors, worked as moneylenders, traders, and specialized professions like doctors.[15]

The lack of accounts registers and other sources that facilitate calculating statistics prevents us from calculating how many Jews lived in the Jewish quarter of Estella during the era in which the fuero was promulgated and the extensive version confirmed. We know that in the period that followed, in the thirteenth and fourteenth centuries, Jews represented 7.5 percent of the Navarrese population, some 1,500 families in total. The Estella Jewish quarter, the second most important in the kingdom, came to house 150 families and still counted 85 after the ravages suffered in 1328.[16]

Despite the fact that the first specific mentions of Jews in Estella came in several sections of the fuero, shortly afterward, in 1093, another document shows them to having been settled in both Estella and the original town of Lizarra, and it already attributes them with their own taxes as a community in both enclaves (legal action, homicides, exchanges).[17] The *villa* was populated above all by Franks, but there were also Jewish and Navarrese settlers that come to live there. By the end of the eleventh century, the Jewish quarter had already emerged, as well as the burgs of San Martín and Nuevo, the "old *villa*" of San Miguel, and the districts of San Juan and the Arenal.[18] The Jewish population expanded in Estella as the burg of Franks took shape, whose boom was likewise associated with the concession of the fuero around 1076–1077.

The urban center of Estella was created in very favorable conditions for developing a city-market befitting of the Early Middle Ages.[19] During this era, the city on the River Ega had three important

---

15   Josef Rapoport, "Los médicos judíos y su actividad en el reino de Navarra. 1349–1425," *Príncipe de Viana* 64, no. 229 (2003), 338. Jewish doctors in Navarre enjoyed great professional prestige compared to their Christian colleagues, and in one of the documents specific mention is made of that.

16   Martín Duque, "La fundación del primer burgo navarro," 737.

17   José Miguel Legarda Sembroiz, "La judería Nueva de Estella. Intervención Arqueológica, 2008," *Trabajos de Arqueología de Navarra* (TAN) 21 (2009): 325.

18   José María Jimeno Jurío, *Merindad de Estella. I. Historia de Estella/Lizarra*, Obras completas no. 33 (Pamplona: Pamiela; Udalbide; and Euskara Kultur Elkargoa, 2006), 170.

19   Juan Ignacio Alberdi Aguirrebeña, "La actividad comercial en el espacio urbano medieval: el ejemplo de Estella," *Vasconia. Cuadernos de sección. Historia-Geografía* 21 (1993), 101–2.

functions: a defensive function (with a castle and city walls); a religious-hospital function lined to the Camino de Santiago; and a commercial function associated with its important market.[20] Navarre was in a strategic position due to the flow of people going on pilgrimages and Estella became a crossroads both on the Camino and for different commercial routes. Shepherds from the north and south of the kingdom mixed with foreign merchants, Franks, and Jews in the Estella markets.[21] The principal weekly market was controlled by Franks, but there was also a daily market in the neighborhood of San Martín and another outside the city, in the neighborhood of San Miguel, which was sanctioned by Theobald I.[22] The markets of Estella, in fact, competed with those of Pamplona and Logroño, both cities located twenty-five miles away from the municipality. The Champagne dynasty was especially important in promoting the merchant fairs and the growing commercial activity encouraged the need to seek out a maritime outlet. Precisely with this aim there, links were developed with French counties, Baiona, and also with San Sebastian, the locality that acquired the Fuero of Estella in 1180.[23]

The growing commercial activity in Estella attracted, as noted, a Jewish community, with one of the most important Jewish quarters in the kingdom taking shape little by little; it was even more important than those of Tudela and Pamplona, since despite the fact that the Tudela Jewish quarter had a greater number of inhabitants, that of Estella contributed more, proportionally, through taxes. Jewish quarters were also established in Funes and Viana, but they played less of an important role.

As well as the small Jewish quarter of Lizarra or Lizarrara— the original Jewish quarter next to the castle of Lizarra—the Jewish population in Estella was organized into two Jewish quarters, the new one and the old one in Elgazena, both located between the castles

20   Vicente Bielza de Ory, "Estella, estudio geográfico de una pequeña ciudad Navarra," *Príncipe de Viana* 29, nos. 110–111 (1968), 53.
21   Martín Duque, "La fundación del primer burgo navarro," 766.
22   Sola Alayeto and Ros Zuasti, *Estella, posta y mercado en la Ruta Jacobea*, 14.
23   José María Lacarra and Ángel J. Martín Duque, *Fueros derivados de Jaca. I. Estella-San Sebastián* (Pamplona: Diputación foral, 1969).

of Zalatambor, the castle of La Atalaya, the castle of Belchemer, and the Gate of the Sepulcher.[24] That of Olgazena or the old Jewish quarter was the first and oldest in the kingdom, and its origins and growth coincided with the era of the dynastic union with Aragon (1076–1134).[25] The new Jewish quarter, located on one side of a steep east-leaning slope, ended up being delimited with a boundary of strong walls, probably constructed between the Castilian attack of 1203 and the construction of the castle of Belchemer, which crowned the hill, around 1276–1278.[26]

The Jews payed contributions collectively and high amounts,[27] so the Jewish community had to pay more taxes than Christians. The main economic contribution of the Jews was the annual tax. In the late thirteenth century, the prosperity of the time and the favors of the Capetian dynasty toward the Jewish quarter of Estella, meant that it even surpassed that of Tudela (880 to 900 *libras*) as regards its fiscal capacity.[28] The inhabitants of the Estella Jewish quarter contributed with more than 1,500 *libras*, which represented almost 10 percent of the crown's total income.[29] In Estella, Jews contributed four times as much per person than Christians, and in Tudela and Pamplona their contribution amounted to approximately half of all income.[30]

Originally, the Jewish quarter in Estella was under lock and key, within the city walls, and had royal protection. As Fernando de Mendoza states, during the twelfth century the Estella Jewish quarter was surrounded by walls and formed an island "that was growing endlessly."[31] The signs of royal protection for the Jews during the twelfth century were evident, and in fact, this collective participated actively in determining the burgs of Franks.[32] In the

---

24 Carrasco Pérez, "Juderías y Sinagogas en el reino de Navarra," 156.
25 Ibid., 115.
26 Legarda Sembroiz, "La judería Nueva de Estella," 326. In 2008, the Centro de Estudios Tierra Estella, through a volunteer program, carried out the first excavation of the Jewish quarter with three surveys.
27 Sola Alayeto and Ros Zuasti, *Estella, posta y mercado en la Ruta Jacobea*, 45.
28 Carrasco Pérez, "Juderías y Sinagogas en el reino de Navarra," 118.
29 Ibid.
30 García Arancón, "Marco jurídico y proyección social de las minorías navarras," 478.
31 Fernando de Mendoza, "Con los judíos de Estella," *Príncipe de Viana* 44–45, (1951), 236.
32 Carrasco Pérez, "Juderías y Sinagogas en el reino de Navarra," 116.

thirteenth century, this community had already taken shape; during the first third of the century the number of inhabitants that made up the Estella Jewish quarter could have been around 150, which was equivalent to 10 percent of the residents in the municipality.[33]

Judicial Autonomy in the Jewish Quarter

During the Early Middle Ages, the Jewish quarters enjoyed an autonomy that allowed them to administer their own justice on the basis of justice according to Hebraic law. The Estella Jewish quarter also had a limited amount of legal autonomy and its own bylaws. Its juridical powers were, however, limited, given that, criminal justice, for example, corresponded exclusively to the king. The execution of sentences and payment of fines was likewise a royal power. Moreover, the royal tax office was practically the only beneficiary of the numerous fiscal exactions of these protected groups.[34]

Jewish law applied only in disputes between Jews and their bylaws or *takkanot* could not be published without the consent of the king. The bylaws also included penal norms, but in practice their application was very complex. Christians, moreover, did not appear before Hebraic courts.

The synagogue was the seat of the Hebraic court, and it was composed of three judges that formed part of the elite in the Jewish quarter. Especially important among the offenses judged by the court was defamation or betrayal of the community, which was castigated with the punishment of the sentence of *herem* or expulsion, or even with lighter sentences like temporary exclusion or *nidduy*.[35]

The Crisis in the Estella Jewish Quarter

Legal autonomy for the Jews declined in the Late Middle Ages, a time in which more powers were transferred to the royal courts.

---

33   Ibid.
34   García Arancón, "Marco jurídico y proyección social de las minorías navarras," 493.
35   Ibid., 486.

These measures coincided with a rise in European anti-Semitism. The hostile attitude of the papacy toward Jews promoted in the thirteenth century result in major acts, such as the well-known canon 67 of the Fourth Council of the Lateran (1215), which prohibited Christians from doing business with Jews. As regards the situation in Navarre, Pope Gregory IX's bull of June 7, 1233, sent to Sancho VII the Strong, rejected the mixing of Christians and Jews in the kingdom; and two decades later, on October 5, 1257, Pope Alexander IV requested Theobald II to restrain the usury of Jews.[36] However, by that time, the house of Champagne had come to maintain some very different criteria with regard to Jews, and the prosperous Jewish quarters began to fulfill the exclusive function of serving as an effective source of direct income for the crown.[37]

The support of the Navarrese monarchy could not prevent European anti-Semitism also taking root in the kingdom. There are precedents from the High Middle Ages that had as a consequence occasional expropriations of Jewish communities, such as that which took place in Olgazena, Estella, in 1135.[38] The economic difficulties and tumultuous politics of the fourteenth century in Europe aggravated social tensions and anti-Semitism among the Christian urban oligarchies and popular masses grew. Within this new context, the Jews were the scapegoats for the difficulties of the century and were accused, among other things, of propagating epidemics of the plague or of poisoning the waters.[39] The persecution of Jews increased, above all, through the fourteenth century, reaching an apex with the well-known massacre of 1328, which was especially bloody in Estella;[40] and which we know through the eyewitness testimony of the Estella Talmudic scholar Menahem ben Zerah.[41] On the death of the last Capetian monarch, Charles IV the Fair, king of France and of Navarre, most of the Jews living in Navarre suffered the most unforgiving attack in their history. Only two

---

36   Miranda García, "El precio de la fe," 54.
37   Ibid., 55.
38   Sola Alayeto and Ros Zuasti, *Estella, posta y mercado en la Ruta Jacobea*, 52.
39   Hinojosa Montalvo, "Los judíos de la España medieval," 28.
40   José Goñi Gaztambide, "La matanza de judíos en Navarra en 1328," *Hispania Sacra* 23 (1959), 5–33.
41   José María Rodríguez Ochoa, *Menahem ben Zerah, rabino estellés (1310–1385). Aproximación a una cultura que floreció en Sefarad* (Pamplona: Gobierno de Navarra, 2011).

months after the razing and sacking of March 6, 1328, the internal life of the Jewish quarter was beginning to get back on its feet.[42] But the most immediate consequence of this slaughter was the emigration of Jews to other kingdoms—especially Aragon—and the weakening of royal assets as a result of the close ties between the Jewish community and the king.[43]

In 1381 the Navarrese monarch Carlos II imposed a special tax, consisting of five *sueldos* per *libra* (25 percent), on all goods sold or pawned by Jews in his kingdom to Christians in the previous fifty years.

The Legal Regulation of Jews in the Fuero of Estella

Jews in the Fuero of Estella: General Aspects

The general conditions that guaranteed a Jewish presence in Christian kingdoms in the Iberian Peninsula during the Early and High Middle Ages were diverse in type. There were general guarantees about ownership of their assets and homes, particular and communal (synagogues, and so on). They only paid taxes to the king and they did so directly to the royal treasury, enjoying in exchange legal and administrative autonomy.[44] In the case of Estella, the rights and privileges of the Jewish community were regulated initially by the municipal fuero of 1076–1077. Thus, in line with other municipal fueros, that of Estella granted its settlers their own jurisdictional environment, a sweetening procedural and penal right, guarantees of the common peace and the inviolability of the home, freedom to buy, sell, and possess inheritances, and few military obligations, among other privileges.[45] This law also extended to future inhabitants:

---

42   Juan Carrasco Pérez, "El libro del menidaje en Estella (1328–1331)," *Miscelánea de Estudios Árabes y Hebráicos* 30 (1981): 109.

43   Juan Carrasco Pérez, "Propiedades de judíos en la merindad de Estella (1330–1381)," in *En la España medieval: estudios en memoria del profesor D. Salvador de Moxó*, vol. 1 (Madrid: Universidad Complutense de Madrid, 1982), 275.

44   Suárez Bilbao, "La comunidad judía y los procedimientos judiciales en la Baja Edad media," 101.

45   Roldán Jimeno Aranguren, *Los Fueros de Navarra, Leyes Históricas de España* (Madrid: Boletín Oficial del Estado, 2016).

This aforementioned fuero and privilege I grant, concede, and conform to you, to all the inhabitants of Estella, both of legal age and minors, both those that will come in the future and those now, to your sons and daughters, both in your generation and for the whole of your posterity, to your descendants that will inhabit Estella, they should be kept safe and decent, free and frank for ever and ever, amen.[46]

As regards the fuero of 1164, it established differences among the Frankish, Navarrese, and Jewish communities. It differentiated, *grosso modo*, three estates: (1) the lower nobility and Franks, put on the same level and differentiated from (2) Jews, farmers, Navarrese, and lower social orders from the *villa*, and (3) Jews and Navarrese that are not from the *villa* (*de foris*).[47] In various areas of the fuero Jews were put in the same level as Christians.[48] However, the fuero of 1164 distinguished, on the one hand, between those of Frankish origin that were beneficiaries of special prerogatives and were put on the same level as the lower nobility; and on the other, the lower social orders, Navarrese, and Jews, who were separated because of their lower status.[49]

The main objective of the fuero was to attract Frankish settlers to the *villa*, but also to regulate the relations among the different existing communities, above all among Franks, Jews, and Navarrese. As regards the Moorish population, the Fuero of Estella makes its inferior legal status clear. Medieval Jewish and Mudejar communities shared characteristics in regard to their internal cohesion, as well as their distinct languages and religions, but, however, their legal situation was quite different. In the case of the Fuero of Estella, it likened the Mudejar or Moorish population to beasts: "The Moor has the same fuero as a large beast."[50] Yet, in contrast to the Jews, there

---

46   Fuero of Estella, Title III. Spanish translation of Fuero of Estella in ibid., 368.
47   José Luis Orella Martínez, "Los judíos en las fuentes jurídicas medievales del pueblo vasco," *Revista internacional de los estudios vascos-Eusko ikaskuntzen nazioarteko aldizkaria* 29, no. 2, (1984), 270.
48   Carrasco Pérez, "Juderías y Sinagogas en el reino de Navarra," 2.
49   Jimeno Aranguren, *Los Fueros de Navarra*, 58.
50   Fuero of Estella, Title II, 22.26.

was no Mudejar community in the *villa* of the Ega, so in practice those chapters in the fuero lacked any practical application.

The precepts relating to the Jewish population in the Fuero of Estella refer above all to economic relations, focusing above all on the most conflictive aspects of a contractual (loans) or procedural (witnesses, guarantors, oaths) nature.[51]

The Oath of the Jews

The municipal fueros of Jaca origin included numerous articles referring simultaneously to Jews and Moors. That was the case of the Fuero of Pamplona and also of Estella, in which, although they did not have Mudejar communities, their local fueros made references to both communities.[52] In the same vein, the Fuero of Estella included the particularity that the oath of the Jew "on his east," perhaps by analogy with Muslims that, in their case, would swear an oath looking toward Mecca:[53]

> And the Jew and the villein will swear an oath with their own hand for any debt of more than twelve *dineros*. And the Navarrese will swear an oath on the head of his friend; and the Jew on his east for twelve *dineros* or less; and the Frank for twelve *dineros* or less must swear an oath before all the men and will do so on the head of his friend or godfather.[54]

The requirements for debts that we find in early medieval municipal fueros referred to people of the three religions, and the swearing of an oath was adapted to the customs of each religion. The norms on oaths that we find in the Fuero of Estella, in the same way as in that of Pamplona, indicates that it was not obligatory in every case and varied according to the number of *dineros*. In contrast to the fuero for Jews granted to the Hebraic communities in Tudela and Funes, which did develop a procedure for swearing

---

51 García Arancón, "Marco jurídico y proyección social de las minorías navarras," 493.
52 Ibid., 469.
53 Gregorio Monreal Zia and Roldán Jimeno Aranguren, *Textos histórico-jurídicos navarros. I. Historia Antigua y Medieval* (Pamplona: Gobierno de Navarra, 2008), 967.
54 Fuero of Estella, 2, 19.9.

an oath with a detailed list of oaths and curses, the Fuero of Estella restricted itself to mentioning, without any more explanation, that the Jewish swearing of an oath would be, in the case of more than twelve *dineros*, "by his own hand," and in the case of less than twelve *dineros*, "on his east" (*secundum orientem*), that is, on the Torah or the Law of Moses.

The Regulation of Loans

The most typical activity among Jews in the medieval West was loaning money in different ways. The Fuero of Estella regulated economics relations among debtors, guarantors, and moneylenders, and equated Jews and Franks in significant economic aspects. For example, the fuero protected these two communities from potential nonpayments: "And that no man may be free of a debt with respect to Franks and Jews I Estella."[55]

Every supposition in the Fuero of Estella relating to the Jews refers to loans. The fuero incudes cases in which Jews owed Christians, but this was not a typical situation, given that it was much more normal for Jews to be the creditors. The measures against interest dictated by the papacy began to be applied in the era of Theobald II and, therefore, the Fuero of Estella docs not include measures against usury that were implemented from the thirteenth century on. The Fuero of Estella does include, however, differences according to the diverse collectives when it comes to loan conditions.

The regulation on loans varied according to the amount vouched for. A bond of more than ten *sueldos* meant that the loan conditions were more severe. In this context, the privileges of the Franks resembled those of the lower nobility:

> Among Franks, there will be legal action for more than ten *sueldos*, and the litigants must be Franks, from the Logroño bridge to here, and from Sangüesa to here, and the same from Pampona.[56]

---

55 Fuero of Estella. Title I, 12.
56 Fuero of Estella. Title II, 19.6.

> For less than ten *sueldos*, a Frank will present another Frank of fifteen years of age or more in order to swear an oath.[57]

> The same must be said for lesser nobles with regard to Franks, and for Franks with regard to lesser nobles.[58]

The norms relating to bonds varied according to whether the bond was agreed on with respect to villeins and Jews, or Navarrese:

> Yet lesser nobles and Franks with respect to a villein and to a Jew will present a man, aged fifteen or older, that should swear an oath for less than ten *sueldos*.[59]

> And the Jew and the villein will swear an oath with their own hand for any debt of more than twelve *dineros*. And the Navarrese will swear an oath on the head of his friend; and the Jew on his east for twelve *dineros* or less; and the Frank for twelve *dineros* or less must swear an oath before all the men and will do so on the head of his friend or godfather.[60]

The fuero also contemplated in detail the different conditions applied to diverse settler communities in Estella when it came to presenting evidence in legal action over the nonpayment of debts:

> If a Jew owes something to a Christian and the Jew tries to deny it, he must prove it with witnesses; if the one he owes is a Frank, he will demonstrate it with a Frank and a Jew; if he is a foreigner, with a foreigner and a Jew; and the Jew with respect to a Christian, by the same procedure.[61]

In such lawsuits, the fuero recognized the status of the deed of the rabbi, although it demands that Jews prove that same deed with witnesses:

> And if it so happens that the Christian has something in writing, the Jew cannot deny it because the deed of a rabbi is

---

57 Fuero of Estella. Title II, 19.7.
58 Fuero of Estella. Title II, 19.5.
59 Fuero of Estella. Title II, 19.8.
60 Fuero of Estella. Title II, 19.9.
61 Fuero of Estella. Title II, 55.1.

worth as much as witnesses against Jews. But it is necessary for the Jew to demonstrate with witnesses to he who has the deed that he has paid him, and if the claimant cannot prove it, he must swear an oath that he did not pay him, and then he will pay.[62]

In the event of death, the debt was transferred to the children of the deceased, but in the case that nonpayment was attributed to Jews on the part of Christians, Jews had to fulfill harsher conditions of settlement, and if they could not prove that the debt had been paid by their father and the son with a written oath that he had not been paid, Jews were obliged to pay:

> And if the Jew were to die, his sons have to finish what their father should have done, according to what was written before, if the Christian has the deed.[63]

> And if the Christian were to die, and his children reclaimed the debt and had the deed, then it would be necessary for the Jew to demonstrate he paid his father. And if he could not prove it with witnesses, the son who has the deed will swear an oath that his father has not been paid the money, and the Jew will pay.[64]

In any event, justification through swearing an oath was applied both to the Jewish and the Christian population:

> And if the Christian has some dispute with the Jew, whether of money, or physical, or another reason, in the event that he did not have any deed or witnesses, the Jew will explain on oath, and will remain immune; equally the Christian will explain on oath against the Jew, if he does not have any witnesses.[65]

---

62 Fuero of Estella. Title II, 55.2.
63 Fuero of Estella. Title II, 55.4.
64 Fuero of Estella. Title II, 55.3.
65 Fuero of Estella. Title II, 55.5.

Jews, therefore, had similar privileges to Christians, despite the fact there were variances according to whether they were the debtors. Jews were obliged to swear more costly oaths with their own hands, while Franks and lesser nobles could do so by delegating. Jews, moreover, had to present more witnesses in the vent of evidentiary legal action. In any event, one should not forget that the assumption of Jews as debtors was not very typical, so in effect the Estella fuero acknowledges similar privileges for the Frankish and Jewish population.

Conclusion

In the eleventh and twelfth centuries, the Jewish community was a cohesive heterogeneous group that received royal support and protection. It was a period of economic growth in Western Europe and of resettlement within the framework of the Reconquest in the Iberian Peninsula. In this context, the Navarrese monarchs put into practice a series of measures designed to attract European pilgrims and establish Frankish settlements in their territories. Royal protection for these groups fostered the creation of the first medieval burgs, which, in turn, fomented commerce and urban development in the kingdom. The cash economy soon attracted a Jewish population, and Jewish quarters emerged in the new Frankish burgs. The Jewish collectives arrived in the kingdom attracted by the growing economic activity, and, thanks to their common condition as moneylenders and traders, their presence favored the economic growth of the Kingdom of Navarre.

The Jewish quarter in Estella was one of the most important in the kingdom. Estella was in a strategic location to foment commerce in Navarre and protect it militarily, and the development of the Camino de Santiago on the part of Sancho the Great toward La Rioja meant that, in time, the central part of the Estella territory needed to accommodate a larger population. The Fuero of Estella, conceded by Sancho Ramírez around 1076–1077, fostered the legal protection of new settlers in the *villa*, among whom there were above all Franks, although Jews as well. The fuero regulated relations among the diverse collectives and protected the Jews specifically in matters relating to economic transactions. The fuero established harsher conditions for Jews in the event that they had requested loans, but this supposition was rare in practice because it was not very typical for Jews to ask for money. It was more customary for Jews to be creditors.

The Fuero of Estella, therefore, constitutes one of the most significant historical documents for sketching the legal, political, and social situation of the Kingdom of Navarre in the eleventh and twelfth centuries. The text protected the Frankish and Jewish communities, encouraged the creation of urban settlements, and established the first rights and privileges for settlers in the new municipalities. The text also demonstrated royal protection in the era for the Jewish population, a protection that, however, changed in tone in the thirteenth century and was transformed into persecution and slaughter from the fourteenth century on.

BIBLIOGRAPHY

Alberdi Aguirrebeña, Juan Ignacio. "La actividad comercial en el espacio urbano medieval: el ejemplo de Estella." *Vasconia. Cuadernos de sección. Historia-Geografía* 21 (1993): 99–114.

Bielza de Ory, Vicente. "Estella, estudio geográfico de una pequeña ciudad Navarra." *Príncipe de Viana* 29, nos. 110–111 (1968): 53–115.

Cantera Montenegro, Enrique. "La mujer judía en la España medieval." *Espacio, Tiempo y Forma, Serie III, Historia medieval* 2 (1989): 37–64.

Carrasco Pérez, Juan. "El libro del menidaje en Estella (1328–1331)." *Miscelánea de Estudios Árabes y Hebráicos* 30 (1981): 109–20.

———. "Propiedades de judíos en la merindad de Estella (1330–1381)." In *En la España medieval: estudios en memoria del profesor D.*

Salvador de Moxó. Volume 1. Madrid: Universidad Complutense de Madrid, 1982.

———. "Juderías y Sinagogas en el reino de Navarra." *Príncipe de Viana* 63, 225 (2002): 113–56.

Carrasco, Juan, Fermín Miranda García, and Eloísa Ramírez Vaquero. *Los judíos del reino de Navarra. Documentos 1093–1333*. Pamplona: Gobierno de Navarra, 1994.

Cierbide Martinena, Ricardo. "La lengua de los francos de Estella: intento de interpretación." *Sancho el Sabio: Revista de cultura e investigación vasca* 3 (1999): 115–45.

Fortún Pérez de Ciriza, Luis Javier. "Fueros locales de Navarra." *Revista Príncipe de Viana* 68, no. 242 (2007): 865–900.

García Arancón, Mª Raquel. "Marco jurídico y proyección social de las minorías navarras: judíos y mudéjares (siglos XII y XV)." *Iura Vasconiae* 4 (2007): 459–516.

Goñi Gaztambide, José. "La matanza de judíos en Navarra en 1328." *Hispania Sacra* 23 (1959): 5–33.

Hinojosa Montalvo, José Ramón. "Los judíos de la España medieval: de la tolerancia a la expulsión." In *Los marginados en el mundo medieval y moderno. Almería, del 5 al 7 de noviembre de 1998*, edited by María Desamparados Martínez San Pedro. Almería: Instituto de Estudios Almerienses, 2000.

Irujo, Xabier. *Giving Birth to Cosmopolis: The Code of Laws of Estella (c.1076)*. Basque Law Series 1, Barandiaran Basque Studies Chair. Santa Barbara: University of California, 2011.

Jimeno Aranguren, Roldán. "El municipio de Vasconia en la Edad Media." *Iura Vasconiae* 2 (2005): 45–83.

———. Los Fueros de Navarra, Leyes Históricas de España. Madrid: Boletín Oficial del Estado, 2016.

Jimeno Jurío, José María. *Merindad de Estella. I. Historia de Estella/ Lizarra*. Obras completas no. 33. Pamplona: Pamiela; Udalbide; and Euskara Kultur Elkargoa, 2006.

Lacarra, José María, and Ángel J. Martín Duque. *Fueros derivados de Jaca. I. Estella-San Sebastián.* Pamplona: Diputación foral, 1969.

Legarda Sembroiz, José Miguel. "La judería Nueva de Estella. Intervención Arqueológica, 2008." *Trabajos de Arqueología de Navarra* (TAN) 21 (2009): 325–37.

Martín Duque, Ángel J. "El fenómeno urbano medieval en Navarra." In *El fenómeno urbano medieval entre el Cantábrico y el Duero: revisión historiográfica y propuestas de estudio*, edited by Jesús Ángel Solórzano Telechea and Beatriz Arízaga Bolumburu. Santander: Asociación de Jóvenes Historiadores de Cantabria, 2002.

———. "La fundación del primer burgo navarro: Estella." Príncipe de Viana 63, no. 227 (2002): 317–28.

Mendoza, Fernando de. "Con los judíos de Estella." *Príncipe de Viana* 44–45, (1951): 235–71.

Miranda García, Fermín. "El precio de la fe. Rentas de la corona y aljamas judías en Navarra (siglos XII–XIV)." *Príncipe de Viana* 58, no. 210 (1997): 51–65.

Monreal Zia, Gregorio, and Roldán Jimeno Aranguren. *Textos histórico-jurídicos navarros. I. Historia Antigua y Medieval.* Pamplona: Gobierno de Navarra, 2008.

Orella Martínez, José Luis. "Los judíos en las fuentes jurídicas medievales del pueblo vasco." *Revista internacional de los estudios vascos-Eusko ikaskuntzen nazioarteko aldizkaria* 29, no. 2, (1984): 261–98.

Rapoport, Josef. "Los médicos judíos y su actividad en el reino de Navarra. 1349–1425." *Príncipe de Viana* 64, no. 229 (2003): 333–51.

Rodríguez Ochoa, José María. *Menahem ben Zerah, rabino estellés (1310–1385). Aproximación a una cultura que floreció en Sefarad.* Pamplona: Gobierno de Navarra, 2011.

Sola Alayeto, Antonio, and Toño Ros Zuasti. *Estella, posta y mercado en la Ruta Jacobea.* Pamplona: Caja de Ahorros de Navarra, 1992.

Suárez Bilbao, Fernando. "La comunidad judía y los procedimientos judiciales en la Baja Edad media." *Cuadernos de Historia del Derecho* 2 (1995): 99–132.

Chapter 8

The Family of the Fueros of Estella and San Sebastian from 1200 on

Nere Jone Intxaustegi Jauregi

The fueros, whose name originates etymologically from the Latin term *forum*, were constructed as a source par excellence of medieval Spanish law.[1] The fueros were concessions of freedoms and privileges, that is, they were legal advantages conceded to the inhabitants of a specific place by the king or by a seigneur. It must be said that the fueros did not symbolize the total autonomy of that locality, but, to be sure, they did create a differentiated and privileged environment in the municipality with respect to the peripheral rural framework.[2] The fueros were the result of an evolution in which different elements converged, and their final version has come down to us today, that is, when they were expressed in writing.[3] Within that evolution there were different types of fueros, such as shorter or longer ones, or good and bad fueros. Another fuero archetype were the municipal ones, which have to be seen as groups of medieval

---

1   José Antonio Escudero, *Curso de Historia del Derecho. Fuentes e Instituciones político-administrativas* (Madrid: Edisofer, 1995), 406.
2   Francisco Tomás y Valiente, *Manual de Historia del Derecho Español* (Madrid: Editorial Tecnos, 2012), 145.
3   José Sánchez-Arcilla Bernal, *Historia del Derecho. Colección jurídica general* (Madrid: Editorial Dykinson, 2009), 148

norms used to configure legally residential communities, and whose principal characteristic would be its complexity as regards this.[4]

Within this latter variety one example is the term "family of fueros" that refers to the different texts that were related to one principal from which the rest emerged;[5] in other words, there was a principal fuero that was conceded to a locality and, later, that same fuero was used in other areas. Therefore, we are speaking about the diffusion of a fuero. However, as Ana María Barrera García shows, in this regard one should mention some problems, given that it was often the case that the text reproduced did not coincide with that it was said had been conceded. For example, the Fuero of Santo Domingo de Silos in the year 1135 says that is has been reproduced from that of Sahagún, although it does not coincide with any of the fueros preserved in that *villa* in Leon; and in 1182 the Navarrese king, Sancho the Wise, conceded to the *villas* of Antoñana and Bernedo in Araba the Fuero of Languardia, which does not coincide with that known text from the latter locality, although it does with that of Arganzón in 1191.[6] These examples reflect the fact that the diffusion of the fueros was not a simple matter, and in those cases it could be that a fuero was awarded to them, but that later extensions may have transformed and changed it almost completely, yet the fuero continued to be known by its original name.[7] Moreover, one should ask why some fueros were diffused and others not. In the face of such an approach, the response of legal historians in this respect indicates that the transmission was closely related to the juridical appeal of the content of those fueros, which meant that certain localities also sought to enjoy the same freedoms and privileges as other municipalities.[8]

---

4   Ana María Barrero García, "El proceso de formación del derecho local medieval a través de sus textos: Los fueros castellano-leoneses," in *I Semana de Estudios medievales. Nájera 1990*, ed. José Ignacio de la Iglesia Duarte (Logroño: Instituto de Estudios Riojanos, 2001), 89.
5   Escudero, *Curso de Historia del Derecho*, 409.
6   Barrero García, "El proceso de formación del derecho local medieval a través de sus textos," 101.
7   José María Lacarra de Miguel, "Notas para la formación de las familias de fueros navarros," *Anuario de Historia del Derecho Español* 10 (1933), 204.
8   Tomás y Valiente, *Manual de Historia del Derecho Español*, 147.

It is also possible to observe that the family of fueros implied a decrease in the diversity of fueros and it was an atomization of local laws.[9] In other words, it had the effect of not producing a high and varied number of fueros, given that it was a tool to control the very number of them.

Moreover, as José María Lacarra de Miguel indicates, examining this subject of medieval fueros and the families of fueros is no simple task, given that, typically, not many original fueros have been preserved, and the researcher must settle for copies or references. It is true that there are cases in which the original has indeed been preserved, but it cannot be accessed, so that the problems and mysteries persist.[10]

Despite the reactions that the subject elicits, it is true that the historical context helps to clarify things. In this way, on the one hand, one must not forget the Reconquest and resettlement that was carried out during those centuries. Thus, while Christians fought Muslims in order to regain occupied territory, in the reconquered lands a process of resettlement was carried out, using, in order to do so, the fueros to attract people, both from within the Iberian Peninsula and form beyond the Pyrenees, to these new areas. Moreover, on the other hand, one should not forget the phenomenon of the Camino de Santiago, which also served, among other thigs, to attract (mainly European) people.

In our case, we know that the Fuero of San Sebastian, which was granted in 1180, did come from that of Estella in 1164, and the latter, for its part, originated in that of Jaca. Furthermore, that of San Sebastian ended up being conceded to other Gipuzkoan *villas*, such as Hondarribia and Zarautz, as well as Castilian towns like San Vicente de la Barquera. Therefore, in this chapter I am going to focus on the families of fueros that shaped these two fueros.

---

9   Alfredo José Martínez González, "El Fuero de Estella: instrumento de atracción en las peregrinaciones europeas." In El Mediterráneo en el origen: IX Congreso Internacional de Asociaciones Jacobeas," ed. Amparo Sáncez Ribes (Valencia: Asociación Amigos del Camino de Santiago de la Comunidad Valenciana, 2012), 78.
10   Lacarra de Miguel, "Notas para la formación de las familias de fueros navarros," 203.

The Fuero of Estella and its Family of Fueros

In 1164 Sancho VI the Wise confirmed the Fuero of Estella, which is considered the oldest extensive fuero in Navarre.[11] However, one should remark that the locality already had a previous fuero, the so-called short Fuero of Estella. This was granted by Sancho V Ramírez, although we do not know when exactly; the date has traditionally been understood as 1090, although other years have been suggested, until Ana María Barrero García estimated that this original fuero was awarded around 1076–1077.[12]

The Fuero of Estella is considered the oldest application in the Kingdom of Navarre and with a known date of the Fuero of Jaca;[13] in fact, it goes back farther still and is an early version of the development of the Fuero of Jaca at a wider and not just Navarrese level, although one should add that it also possesses its own local singularity, given that it includes precepts specific to the *villa*, such as, for example, questions relating to markets being held on Thursdays and the regulation of relations between Navarrese and Franks.[14] Moreover, the Estella fuero gained such renown that, when it was extended to other localities, it was cited as Estella and not Jaca, the original text.[15]

Because this chapter explores the families of fueros, before proceeding to develop the Fuero of Estella, I will focus on that of Jaca given that, as noted, it was the precursor of that of Estella. First, this Aragonese locality was one of the neuralgic points in the creation, transmission, and divulgation of medieval law.[16] Indeed, the Fuero of Jaca served as a source in the formation of different Navarrese fueros, not just in Estella but also in other localities such as Sangüesa and San Cernín in Pamplona. What is more, it was also used in other places throughout the peninsula, such as

---

11   Luis Javier Fortún Pérez de Ciriza, "Fueros locales de Navarra," *Príncipe de Viana* 68, no. 242 (2007), 881.
12   Roldán Jimeno Aranguren, *Los Fueros de Navarra. Leyes Históricas de España* (Madrid: Boletín Oficial del Estado, 2016), 319.
13   Lacarra de Miguel, "Notas para la formación de las familias de fueros navarros," 219.
14   Jimeno Aranguren, *Los Fueros de Navarra*, 320.
15   Lacarra de Miguel, "Notas para la formación de las familias de fueros navarros," 204.
16   Pedro J. Arroyal Espigares, "Las fuentes del Derecho de los fueros de la Familia Cuenca-Teruel: el fuero de Jaca," *Baetica. Estudios de Arte, Geografía e Historia* 2, no. 1 (1979), 168.

Teruel and Cuenca. In this way, in questions relating to securities and guarantors, the inheritance of children born through adultery, bonds, and disputes between clerics and lay people, the literal nature of the articles demonstrates clearly that the Fuero of Jaca served as an inspiration in these lands.[17]

Jaca was the first capital of the Kingdom of Aragon, founded in 1063 when King Sancho Ramírez granted a fuero to the *villa*, converting it into a city.[18] This monarch, who reigned in both Aragonese and Navarrese territory, broke the theoretical legal unity of the Kingdom of Aragon in that he singled out a locality from the rest of the Aragonese *villas* in granting it distinct privileges.[19] This early medieval policy was framed within resettlement practices carried out by different monarchs whose objective was to attract people to certain places in exchange for freedoms and privileges. In fact, around 1137, it is estimated that the Jaca population was 21.5 percent Aragonese and 78.85 percent from beyond the Pyrenees.[20] A high percentage of these colonists were foreign and especially French.[21] And, together with soldiers that had taken part in the Reconquest and traders that settled along the Camino de Santiago, they were very influential during that peninsular medieval era, especially in Aragon.[22] In fact, in the Fuero of Jaca one can read how it was aimed at people from everywhere, "*omnibus hominibus qui sunt usque in oriente, et occidente, et septentrionem, et meridiem,*" and, as Pilar García Mouton notes, one can see how it includes totally exceptional freedoms for the eleventh century such as, for example, that of decreeing personal liberty and the inviolability of the home.[23] In this way, those precepts, like others related to acquiring property for the possession of one year and one day, limiting trial by combat as a

---

17 Ibid., 176.
18 Josep Serrano Daura, "El Fuero de Jaca," *Boletín de la Real Academia de Buenas Letras de Barcelona* 49 (2003–2004), 532.
19 Mauricio Molho, "Difusión del derecho pirenaico (Fuero de Jaca) en el reino de Aragón," *Boletín de la Real Academia de Buenas Letras de Barcelona* 28 (1960), 268.
20 Miguel Ángel Ladero Quesada, *La formación medieval de España. Territorios. Regiones. Reinos* (Madrid: Alianza Editorial, 2006), 113.
21 The French origin of many (although not all) of them meant that these Christian European settlers were considered "Franks."
22 Pilar García Mouton, "Los franceses en Aragón (siglos XI–XIII)," *Archivo de filología aragonesa* 26–27 (1980), 7.
23 Ibid., 10.

means of proof, being tolerant in the punishment of sexual crimes, and establishing multiple guarantees of a procedural character[24] help to explain to perfection the success of the Fuero of Jaca. Indeed, both this and other fueros of the era contained so many freedoms and privileges that the expression "law of Franks" would end up becoming a synonym for "law of freedoms."[25]

Unfortunately, no Jaca compilation from that medieval era has been preserved to this day.[26] In fact, of the original text only four chapters have survived, and the rest are a set of dispositions of which some originated in Jaca and the rest in other localities.[27] Nevertheless, seeing the similarities between that of Estella and that of Jaca, clearly at that time some compilation reached the Navarrese locality.[28] First, both localities are geographically situated along the Camino de Santiago, considered one of the most complex phenomena of the Middle Ages in the peninsula.[29] Estella, alongside Pamplona and Sangüesa, was one of the main recipients of Christian migrations from beyond the Pyrenees;[30] indeed, as occurred in Jaca, it was founded with the objective of attracting settlers; thus, from the late ninth century on, one can detect the installation of Frankish colonists in the Kingdom of Navarre.[31] What is more, as Miguel Ángel Ladero Quesada observes, the Camino de Santiago was an interregional route through the northern lands, creating the main east–west line of communication,[32] which explains the influence of Jaca in towns situated to the west and following the Camino.

---

24 Escudero, *Curso de Historia del Derecho*, 464.
25 Enrique Gacto Fernández, Juan Antonio Alejandre García, and José María García Marín, *Manual Básico de Historia del Derecho (Temas y antología de textos)* (Madrid: Editorial Dykinson, 1997), 102.
26 As Mauricio Molho points out, there are five known extensive editions and two fragmentary ones. See "Difusión del derecho pirenaico (Fuero de Jaca) en el reino de Aragón," 267.
27 Sánchez-Arcilla Bernal, *Historia del Derecho*, 168.
28 Jimeno Aranguren, *Los Fueros de Navarra*, 320.
29 Francisco Ruiz Gómez, "El Camino de Santiago: circulación de hombres, mercancías e ideas," in *IV Semana de Estudios Medievales de Nájera, 2 al 6 de agosto de 1993*, ed. José Ignacio de la Iglesia Duarte (Logroño: Instituto de Estudios Riojanos, 1994), 167.
30 Angel J. Martín Duque, "El fenómeno urbano medieval en Navarra," in *El fenómeno urbano medieval entre el Cantábrico y el Duero: Revisión historiográfico y propuestas de estudio*, ed. Jesús Ángel Solorzano Telechea and Beatriz Arízaga Bolumburu (Santander: Asociación de Jóvenes Historiadores de Cantabria, 2002), 755.
31 Fortún Pérez de Ciriza, "Fueros locales de Navarra," 867.
32 Ladero Quesada, *La formación medieval de España*, 105.

The first mention we have of Estella is related to its etymology. Thus, from the year 958 on the name of Lizarrara appears.[33] And by 1076 there is already documentation of the formation of a burg by people beneath the castle of Lizarrara.[34] For its part, already from 1084 on the name Estella was being used.[35] It was the Romance form of the Latin Stella.[36] However, as Ángel J. Martín Duque points out, one cannot identify Estella with Lizarrara because the former was created as site for Frankish settlers,[37] while the latter already existed. Indeed, the fact that no Navarrese was permitted to become a resident without the consent of the king and the local authorities (including, among others, mayors[38] (*"el quod ullus navarrus vel presbiter de foras non possit populare in Stella sine voluntate regis et omnium stellensium"*), reflected the fact perfectly that this new urban site had been designed by the monarch to house Franks exclusively. Therefore, it is possible to see that, in the same way as the Fuero of Jaca, that of Estella was designed clearly to attract foreign settlers, who were grouped around the chapel of San Martín, spreading out later to other areas in the original Estella. The importance of this Frankish population, especially people from the Languedoc and Gascony,[39] can be seen clearly in the documentation. This is because up to the fourteenth century many legal documents like censuses, real estate contracts, and accounts were written in Occitan.[40] However, although in principle the indigenous population remained at the margins, by the time of Sancho the Wise locals were included in the confirmation of the fuero.[41] Nevertheless, Theobald I's project

---

33 José María Jimeno Jurío, "Estella/Lizarra. Toponimia," *Fontes Linguae Vasconum: Studia et documenta* 77 (1998), 135.
34 Carlos Laliena Corbera, *La servidumbre y las transformaciones de la organización* (Zaragoza: Prensas Universitarias de Zaragoza, 2013), 396.
35 Fernando González Ollé, "Etimología del topónimo Estella," *Príncipe de Viana* 190 (1990), 329.
36 Jimeno Jurío, "Estella/Lizarra. Toponimia," 136.
37 Ángel J. Martín Duque, "La fundación del primer burgo navarro. Estella," *Príncipe de Viana* 227 (2002), 320.
38 Martínez González, "El Fuero de Estella," 82.
39 Ricardo Cierbide Martinena, "La lengua de los francos de Estella: intento de interpretación," *Sancho el Sabio: Revista de cultura e investigación vasca* 3 (1993), 118.
40 José Luis Orella Unzué, "La gasconización medieval occidental del Reino de Navarra," *Lurralde: investigación y espacio* 33 (2010), 181.
41 Lacarra de Miguel, "Notas para la formación de las familias de fueros navarros," 220.

included, once again, social differences in relation to the population that would be affected by the Estella fuero.[42]

As noted, the date of the Fuero of Estella remains unclear, but not that of the confirmation by King Sancho VI. Later, during the era of Theobald I, a new version was likely prepared, also written in Latin with some lexical tweaks, although it was never promulgated. However, in the late thirteenth century two simple versions of the same juridical body of 1164 were composed, in which precepts from the era of Theobald I were not included.[43] In the face of this situation, in the words of Horacio Arrechea Silvestre, one could say that, "from that date on, Estella law was paralyzed."[44] In other words, when we speak about the Fuero of Estella we are referring to the conformation by King Sancho VI the Wise and not later confirmations or projects.

Moreover, one should point out that we have not just different versions of the Fuero of Estella, but also in different languages, like the original in Latin and Romance for the Frankish colonists. Therefore, this fuero is not just significant legally but also linguistically.[45]

Finally, the Fuero of Estella was disseminated among the *villas* along the Camino de Santiago and mid-Navarre. In this way, concessions were given to Puente la Reina (1122), Olite (1147), Monreal (1149), Tiebas (1264), Torralba (1264), Urroz (1286), Tafalla (1423), Artajona (1423), Huarte Araquil (1461), and Mendigorría (1463).[46] As indicated at the beginning of the chapter, many fueros that originated in another one acquired such legal importance and significance that, when they were granted to other localities, there was no mention of the original fuero from which they came but just the name of the locality that had received that fuero. And this is precisely what happened with that of Estella, given that when it was granted to the aforementioned Navarrese *villas*, at no time was

---

42   Roldán Jimeno Aranguren, "El municipio de Vasconia en la Edad Media," *Iura Vasconia* 2 (2005), 58.

43   Martín Duque, "El fenómeno urbano medieval en Navarra," 737.

44   Horacio Arrechea Silvestre, "Algunas correspondencias entre el Fuero de Estella y el Fuero de Tudela," *Príncipe de Viana* 14 (1992), 318.

45   Gustaf Holmer, *El Fuero de Estella según el Manuscrito 944 de la Biblioteca de Palacio de Madrid* (Goteborg, Stockholm, and Uppsala: Almqvist and Wiksell, 1963), 5.

46   Fortún Pérez de Ciriza, "Fueros locales de Navarra," 870.

the original Fuero of Jaca mentioned, but instead it was referred to directly as the Fuero of Estella.[47]

The Fuero of San Sebastian

The Fuero of San Sebastian was the first municipal fuero in Gipuzkoa of great importance since it marked the beginning of a transcendent legal metamorphosis of the human communities in that part of the Cantabrian coast.[48] Despite its importance, we currently lack the original text. For that reason, it has been customary to use copies and editions, although the most rigorous specific text of the Fuero of San Sebastian that exists today is based on two documents: the royal confirmation of King Juan II in 1424 and the notary copy of 1474.[49]

One should note that, although in most of the municipal fueros the figure of the king appears as the grantor of the fueros, in reality, frequently it was the councils that chose the law that interested them. A reflection of that reality was the propagation of some fueros to nearby places and encompassing extensive districts, that is, it seems clear that many localities wanted the prevailing law of their neighbors.[50] We find a good example of that precisely in the Fuero of San Sebastian, since it was granted to the neighboring coastal Gipuzkoan *villas* of Fuenterrabia (Hondarribia, 1203), Getaria (1204–1609?), Motrico (Mutriku, 1256), Zarauz (Zarautz, 1237), Rentería (Errenteria, 1320), Oiartzun (1320), Zumaia (1347), Usurbil (1371), Orio (1379), and Hernani (before 1379); and not just to Gipuzkoan *villas*, but also to others such as the case of the Cantabrian town of San Vicente de la Barquera in 1210. This was undoubtedly a coastal fuero since, for their part, the inland Gipuzkoan *villas* used the Fuero of Logroño.[51]

---

47   Lacarra de Miguel, "Notas para la formación de las familias de fueros navarros," 221.
48   José Luis Banús y Aguirre, *El Fuero de San Sebastián* (San Sebastián: Ayuntamiento de San Sebastián, 1963), 1.
49   Ángel J. Martín Duque, "El Fuero de San Sebastián. Tradición manuscrita y edición crítica," in *Congreso: El fuero de San Sebastián y su época (San Sebastián 19–23 de enero de 1981) / Donostiako forua eta bere garaia (Donostia, 1981ko urtarrilaren 19tik 23ra)* (San Sebastián: Eusko Ikaskuntza / Sociedad de Estudios Vascos, 1982), 699.
50   Lacarra de Miguel, "Notas para la formación de las familias de fueros navarros," 204.
51   Beatriz Arizaga Bolumburu, "Las villas guipuzcoanas que reciben el Fuero de San

As the Fuero of San Sebastian belonged to the family of the Fuero of Estella, it reproduced the Estella text of 1164. However, it also made original contributions, specifically relating to maritime law,[52] which was logical bearing in mind the geographical location not just of Estella but also of Jaca. Moreover, that original contribution in relation to commercial matters explains clearly why the other *villas* situated on or near the coast also obtained the Fuero of San Sebastian while as regards the foundation of inland *villas*, as mentioned, the Fuero of Logroño was used.

For his part, the aforementioned Sancho VI the Wise did not just confirm the Fuero of Estella in 1164, but he also granted San Sebastian its fuero in 1180, which transformed the Gipuzkoan *villa* into the port of the Kingdom of Navarre. However, as Gipuzkoa was incorporated into Castile in 1200, different Castilian kings such as Alfonso VIII, Alfonso X, and Alfonso XI awarded the Fuero of San Sebastian to the abovementioned *villas*. In other words, the Castilian monarchs conceded a fuero that was first conceded by a Navarrese king.

Nevertheless, it does not appear that there was a close relationship between the Gipuzkoan and Navarrese localities. Proof of that is the evidence we have that in the fifteenth century, when the people of San Sebastian had some doubts about certain precepts in the fuero, they went to Jaca and not Estella in search of help to solve their juridical qualms.[53] These contrasts with that of Estella, since it does not cite the city of Jaca or its fuero, nor does it appear that there was any later relationship between the two places.[54] Therefore, in the face of the existing debate about whether the Fuero of Estella really came from that of Jaca or not, this seems to indicate that, in effect, that dependence and relationship did indeed exist.

Sebastián: modos de vida de sus habitants," in *Congreso: El fuero de San Sebastián y su época (San Sebastián 19–23 de enero de 1981) / Donostiako forua eta bere garaia (Donostia, 1981ko urtarrilaren 19tik 23ra)* (San Sebastián: Eusko Ikaskuntza / Sociedad de Estudios Vascos, 1982), 113–14.

52   Gregorio Monreal Zia and Roldán Jimeno Aranguren, *Textos histórico-jurídicos navarros. I Historia Antigua y Medieval* (Pamplona: Instituto navarro de Administración Pública, 2008), 330.

53   Gacto Fernández, Alejandre García, and García Marín, *Manual Básico de Historia del Derecho*, 129.

54   Holmer, *El Fuero de Estella*, 4.

We have already seen that in Jaca and in Estella the Camino de Santiago was a key factor; indeed, the central centuries during the Middle Ages, when these towns were founded, are considered the golden age of the Camino.[55] In this sense, the *villa* of San Sebastian was also situated on the Camino, precisely ion what was termed the coastal route to Santiago, which was a costal offshoot of the French route.[56] However, the historiography is divided over this branch of the Camino: thus, on the one hand, Juan Eduardo Cirlot and Ramón Menéndez Pidal defended the notion that this particular route was created early on, even prior to what is today termed the French route. In contrast, Lacarra de Miguel thought that this route was not used until the thirteenth century, because it was not safe prior to that on account of the local population.[57] Therefore, it is unclear whether the *villa* of San Sebastian was founded at a place where there already existed a route to Santiago or that route was developed thereafter. However, there is certainly no doubt that the *villa* was situated on one of the Camino routes, as were Jaca and Estella.

Furthermore, as had happened in those two places, the monarch, on granting the fuero, also sought to attract Franks to settle in San Sebastian. In order to do so, one can read repeatedly throughout the Fuero of San Sebastian that it is aimed at settlers, excluding non-settlers from the benefits of the fuero.[58] Nevertheless, those differences did not, in the long run, last too long since by the end of the fourteenth century the universal nobility project treated all Gipuzkoans juridically equally. Indeed, before the king proclaimed universal nobility, the province itself, at a meeting of its general councils in Getaria in 1397, considered that all Gipuzkoans were nobles, and one year later Enrique II confirmed it.[59]

---

55   Luis Martínez García, "Formación y desarrollo del Camino de Santiago en la Edad Media. Algunos aspectos generals," *Estudio e investigación* 24 (2009), 249.

56   Francisco Alonso Otero, "Santiago y los Caminos de Santiago: un paisaje cultural, una cultura del paisaje," *Boletín de la A. G. E.* 51 (2009), 209.

57   Astrid de Sas van Damme, "Peregrinación a Santiago y Oviedo por la ruta costera en la Edad Media," *Estudios Medievales Hispánicos* 3 (2014), 176.

58   Francico Salinas Quijada, "El derecho civil en el Fuero de San Sebastián y sus relaciones con el derecho civil en los fueros navarros," in *Congreso: El fuero de San Sebastián y su época (San Sebastián 19–23 de enero de 1981) / Donostiako forua eta bere garaia (Donostia, 1981ko urtarrilaren 19tik 23ra)* (San Sebastián: Eusko Ikaskuntza / Sociedad de Estudios Vascos, 1982), 313–14.

59   Arizaga Bolumburu, "Las villas guipuzcoanas que reciben el Fuero de San Sebastián,"

By Way of an Epilogue

First, one must focus on the concept of the family of fueros, which was a way of avoiding or impeding disproportionate growth in the granting of fueros and, as such, it was a means of channeling and controlling this medieval juridical phenomenon. Moreover, Alfonso García-Gallo grouped the fueros into four areas: those of Aragon-Navarre, those of Extremadura in Leon, those of Extremadura in Castile, and those of Catalonia. The Fueros of Jaca and Estella mentioned here were, precisely, part of that first group. The latter was of Jaca origin and we have already seen how it was conceded to other areas both in and outside Navarre; therefore, a chain of transmission of the law was formed from Jaca throughout all these areas when, politically, they were not Aragonese.[60]

Among the Fueros of Jaca, Estella, and San Sebastian it is possible to find a series of similarities of content, which is logical bearing in mind that the Jaca fuero served as the basis of the other two. What is more, they also shared other questions, such as the absence of original fueros. This lack has given rise to problems in different areas, such as the different hypotheses surrounding the exact date the fueros were granted. Likewise, it has also been possible to observe how the Camino de Santiago was related to the three places, which were founded with the objective of attracting foreign settlers.

For their part, the three places were *villas* originally. However, both Jaca and Estella, in 1483, obtained the status of city;[61] while San Sebastian maintained the original title of *villa*, something it has preserved to this day.[62]

Lastly, the fueros were granted and confirmed by monarchs. In this way, the fueros that have been the subject of this chapter, that of Estella and that of San Sebastian, share a royal figure, given that, on the one hand, the Navarrese monarch Sancho the Wise granted

---

120.
60 Tomás y Valiente, *Manual de Historia del Derecho Español*, 151.
61 Serrano Daura, "El Fuero de Jaca," 532; Martín Duque, "El fenómeno urbano medieval en Navarra," 738.
62 At the time of publication (2019).

the Fueros of Vitoria and San Sebastian, yet he also confirmed those of Estella and Logroño.[63] This makes him a significant figure in the question of Basque-Navarrese fueros.

BIBLIOGRAPHY

Alonso Otero, Francisco. "Santiago y los Caminos de Santiago: un paisaje cultural, una cultura del paisaje." *Boletín de la A. G. E.* 51 (2009): 203–18.

Arizaga Bolumburu, Beatriz. "Las villas guipuzcoanas que reciben el Fuero de San Sebastián: modos de vida de sus habitantes." In *Congreso: El fuero de San Sebastián y su época (San Sebastián 19–23 de enero de 1981) / Donostiako forua eta bere garaia (Donostia, 1981ko urtarrilaren 19tik 23ra).* San Sebastián: Eusko Ikaskuntza / Sociedad de Estudios Vascos, 1982.

Arrechea Silvestre, Horacio. "Algunas correspondencias entre el Fuero de Estella y el Fuero de Tudela." *Príncipe de Viana* 14 (1992): 315–24.

Arroyal Espigares, Pedro J. "Las fuentes del Derecho de los fueros de la Familia Cuenca-Teruel: el fuero de Jaca." *Baetica. Estudios de Arte, Geografía e Historia* 2, no. 1 (1979): 167–76.

Banús y Aguirre, José Luis. *El Fuero de San Sebastián.* San Sebastián: Ayuntamiento de San Sebastián, 1963.

Barrero García, Ana María. "El proceso de formación del derecho local medieval a través de sus textos: Los fueros castellano-leoneses." In *I Semana de Estudios medievales. Nájera 1990,* edited by José Ignacio de la Iglesia Duarte. Logroño: Instituto de Estudios Riojanos, 2001.

---

63 José Luis Orella Unzué, "Estudio jurídico comparativo de los Fueros de San Sebastián, Estella, Vitoria y Logroño," in *Congreso: El fuero de San Sebastián y su época (San Sebastián 19–23 de enero de 1981) / Donostiako forua eta bere garaia (Donostia, 1981ko urtarrilaren 19tik 23ra)* (San Sebastián: Eusko Ikaskuntza / Sociedad de Estudios Vascos, 1982), 255.

Cierbide Martinena, Ricardo. "La lengua de los francos de Estella: intento de interpretación." *Sancho el Sabio: Revista de cultura e investigación vasca* 3 (1993): 115–48.

Escudero, José Antonio. *Curso de Historia del Derecho. Fuentes e Instituciones político-administrativas*. Madrid: Edisofer, 1995.

Fortún Pérez de Ciriza, Luis Javier. "Fueros locales de Navarra." *Príncipe de Viana* 68, no. 242 (2007): 865–99.

Gacto Fernández, Enrique, Juan Antonio Alejandre García, and José María García Marín. *Manual Básico de Historia del Derecho (Temas y antología de textos)*. Madrid: Editorial Dykinson, 1997.

García Mouton, Pilar. "Los franceses en Aragón (siglos XI–XIII)." *Archivo de filología aragonesa* 26–27 (1980): 7–98.

González Olle, Fernando. "Etimología del topónimo Estella." *Príncipe de Viana* 190 (1990): 329–44.

Holmer, Gustaf. *El Fuero de Estella según el Manuscrito 944 de la Biblioteca de Palacio de Madrid*. Goteborg, Stockholm, and Uppsala: Almqvist and Wiksell, 1963.

Jimeno Aranguren, Roldán. "El municipio de Vasconia en la Edad Media." *Iura Vasconia* 2 (2005): 45–83.

———. *Los Fueros de Navarra. Leyes Históricas de España*. Madrid: Boletín Oficial del Estado, 2016.

Jimeno Jurío, José María. "Estella/Lizarra. Toponimia." *Fontes Linguae Vasconum: Studia et documenta* 77 (1998): 133–64.

Lacarra de Miguel, José María. "Notas para la formación de las familias de fueros navarros." *Anuario de Historia del Derecho Español* 10 (1933): 203–72.

Ladero Quesada, Miguel Ángel. *La formación medieval de España. Territorios. Regiones. Reinos*. Madrid: Alianza Editorial, 2006.

Laliena Corbera, Carlos. *La servidumbre y las transformaciones de la organización*. Zaragoza: Prensas Universitarias de Zaragoza, 2013.

Martín Duque, Ángel J. "El Fuero de San Sebastián. Tradición manuscrita y edición crítica." In *Congreso: El fuero de San Sebastián y su época (San Sebastián 19–23 de enero de 1981) / Donostiako forua eta bere garaia (Donostia, 1981ko urtarrilaren 19tik 23ra).* San Sebastián: Eusko Ikaskuntza / Sociedad de Estudios Vascos, 1982.

———. "El fenómeno urbano medieval en Navarra." In *El fenómeno urbano medieval entre el Cantábrico y el Duero: Revisión historiográfico y propuestas de estudio,* edited by Jesús Ángel Solorzano Telechea and Beatriz Arízaga Bolumburu. Santander: Asociación de Jóvenes Historiadores de Cantabria, 2002.

———. "La fundación del primer burgo navarro. Estella." *Príncipe de Viana* 227 (2002): 317–27.

Martínez García, Luis. "Formación y desarrollo del Camino de Santiago en la Edad Media. Algunos aspectos generals." *Estudio e investigación* 24 (2009): 247–61.

Martínez González, Alfredo José. "El Fuero de Estella: instrumento de atracción en las peregrinaciones europeas." In *El Mediterráneo en el origen: IX Congreso Internacional de Asociaciones Jacobeas,* edited by Amparo Sáncez Ribes. Valencia: Asociación Amigos del Camino de Santiago de la Comunidad Valenciana, 2012.

Molho, Mauricio. "Difusión del derecho pirenaico (Fuero de Jaca) en el reino de Aragón." *Boletín de la Real Academia de Buenas Letras de Barcelona* 28 (1960): 265–352.

Monreal Zia, Gregorio, and Roldán Jimeno Aranguren. *Textos histórico-jurídicos navarros. I Historia Antigua y Medieval.* Pamplona: Instituto navarro de Administración Pública, 2008.

Orella Unzué, José Luis. "Estudio jurídico comparativo de los Fueros de San Sebastián, Estella, Vitoria y Logroño." In *Congreso: El fuero de San Sebastián y su época (San Sebastián 19–23 de enero de 1981) / Donostiako forua eta bere garaia (Donostia, 1981ko urtarrilaren 19tik 23ra).* San Sebastián: Eusko Ikaskuntza / Sociedad de Estudios Vascos, 1982.

————. "La gasconización medieval occidental del Reino de Navarra." *Lurralde: investigación y espacio* 33 (2010): 177–208.

Ruiz Gómez, Francisco. "El Camino de Santiago: circulación de hombres, mercancías e ideas." In *IV Semana de Estudios Medievales de Nájera, 2 al 6 de agosto de 1993*, edited by José Ignacio de la Iglesia Duarte. Logroño: Instituto de Estudios Riojanos, 1994.

Salinas Quijada, Francisco. "El derecho civil en el Fuero de San Sebastián y sus relaciones con el derecho civil en los fueros navarros." In *Congreso: El fuero de San Sebastián y su época (San Sebastián 19–23 de enero de 1981) / Donostiako forua eta bere garaia (Donostia, 1981ko urtarrilaren 19tik 23ra)*. San Sebastián: Eusko Ikaskuntza / Sociedad de Estudios Vascos, 1982.

Sánchez-Arcilla Bernal, José. *Historia del Derecho. Colección jurídica general*. Madrid: Editorial Dykinson, 2009.

Sas van Damme, Astrid de. "Peregrinación a Santiago y Oviedo por la ruta costera en la Edad Media." *Estudios Medievales Hispánicos* 3 (2014): 173–206.

Serrano Daura, Josep. "El Fuero de Jaca." *Boletín de la Real Academia de Buenas Letras de Barcelona* 49 (2003–2004): 532–40.

Tomás y Valiente, Francisco. *Manual de Historia del Derecho Español*. Madrid: Editorial Tecnos, 2012.

Chapter 9

Notes on the Fuero of San Sebastian:
Its Expansion, Validity, and Modernity,
and an Analysis of its Texts

Mª Rosa Ayerbe Iribar

T he concession of the Fuero of San Sebastian, believed to
have been around 1180 (since no date has been discovered),[1] by
the Navarrese King Sancho VI the Wise, marked a fundamental
milestone in Gipuzkoan municipal organization. The ancient valleys
into which the territory was organized gradually disappeared to give
rise to a more limited and specific municipality, from the territorial
point of view, yet more developed and compact, from the public-
institutional perspective.

Within this concession there was a clear demarcation of the
jurisdictional limits of the new *villa*, constructed on an existing town
sheltered by Mount Urgull, between the bay and the mouth of the
River Urumea (the most favorable site within the surroundings of
San Sebastian for the defensive and economic interests of the king
of Navarre), in granting it the geographical space in the kingdom

---

1   There are many different and notable opinions on its dating, but here the view of
    José Mª Lacarra is followed. It is based on the problematic political context of the
    Kingdom of Navarre in the face of Castilian pressure, and the consequent need to
    secure repopulation and border defenses.

that, "*de Hundarribia usque ad Oriam et de Arenga usque ad Sanctum Martinum de Arano.*"

Historiography in general has seen in this demarcation the inclusion in the territory thus conceded of the very limits of Fuenterrabia (Hondarribia). When speaking about Fuenterrabia, Pablo de Gorosabel restricted himself to saying that it was one of the oldest towns in Gipuzkoa and there was mention of it, with the name "Undarribia," in the concession of the fuero to San Sebastian in 1180, "which hints at a much earlier existence."[2] When speaking about San Sebastian and the concession of the fuero he already included Fuenterrabia within its limits alongside Irun, Oyarzun (Oiartzun), Rentería (Errenteria), Lezo, Pasajes (Pasaia), Astigarraga, Hernani, Urnieta, Lasarte, Usurbil, and Orio, the *universidad* (community) of Andoain and part of Zubieta, Aduna, and Alquiza (Alkiza).[3]

I am, however, of the opinion that such an expression indicates that the new limits of San Sebastian "extended from" the limits of "Hundarribia," in the same way they extended to the "Sanctum Martinum de Arano," but that in both cases these population centers remained excluded from the jurisdiction of the new *villa*. The jurisdiction of San Sebastian, a town in the Hernani Valley, would thus be delimited by the port of Pasajes[4] and the River Oria toward Navarre. And within its jurisdiction the new *villas* of Hernani, Usurbil, and Orio later emerged, but not that of Fuenterrabia (which belonged to the Oyarzun Valley), to where the Fuero of San Sebastian would be extended by express concession in 1203, once the area that had always been Navarre was incorporated into Castile up to the River Urumea.[5]

---

2   Pablo de Gorosabel, *Diccionario histórico-geográfico-descriptivo de los pueblos, valles, partidos, alcaldías y uniones de Guipúzcoa, con un apéndice de cartas-pueblas y otros documentos importantes* (Tolosa, 1862; Bilbao: La Gran Enciclopedia Vasca, 1972), 171.

3   Ibid., 436.

4   Identified by almost all authors by the term "Arrenga," although Juan Ignacio Gamón argues that this referred to Mount Renga in Lesaca (Lesaka).

5   In the words of Gonzalo Martínez Díez, in 1200 Alfonso VIII "had not only regained all the territory that had one day belonged to [his great-great-grandfather] Alfonos VI: the whole of Araba and Gipuzkoa up to the Urumea, but he had also, crossing this river, incorporated a district that had always been under Navarrese sovereignty, the land of the Rivers Urumea and Bidasoa." See *Alfonso VIII, rey de Castilla y Toledo (1158–1214)* (Burgos: La Olmeda, 1995), 95.

Not for nothing did the concession of the fuero to Fuenterrabia in 1203 delimit its jurisdictional limits *"de ribo de Oyarzum vsque ad ribum de Fonte Rabia [Bidasoa], et de Pena de Aia usque ad mare, et de Lesaca usque ad mare, et de Belfd⁶ usque ad mare, et terminum de Yrun cum omnibus inde habitantibus."* In other words, the River Oyarzun delimited both jurisdictions. And the fuero included the port of "Astuuiaga,"[7] and the merging town of Lezo (*"Et dono uobis Guillelmum de Lacon et socios suos, ut sint uestri uicini"*).

It makes no sense for the Wise King, seeking to foster loyalty among the inhabitants of San Sebastian that included an important core population of Gascon people (which, although it formed part of the Kingdom of Navarre, shifted, some time previously, between Navarre and Castile), to put under his jurisdiction the loyal population of Fuenterrabia, which had been and was Navarrese, and that only passed into the hands of Castile in 1200 through "conquest."

Nor should we forget that these jurisdictional limits of Fuenterrabia belonged and would continue to belong to the Diocese of Baiona,[8] while the San Sebastian limits belonged to Diocese of Pamplona.

That interpretation, which was already old, was consolidated possibly in a bad translation from Latin to Spanish by José Luis Banús y Aguirre in his works *El límite oriental de San Sebastián y el Puerto de Pasajes* (1950) and *El Fuero de San Sebastián* (1963),[9] and those that followed him without any more reflection. The Latin fuero he

---

6   Identified as Vera de Bidasoa (Bera).

7   A port in the northeastern part of the *villa*.

8   By a papal bull of Celestine III, given in the Archbasilica of St John Lateran on November 13, 1194, an accord signed by the bishop and canons of Baiona (during the Pontificate of Urban III in 1186) was confirmed, and a new allocation was made of the church of Baiona in this way: *"Vallem quæ dicitur Oyarzu usque ad Sanctum Sebastianum,"* by this, their bishopric included not just the towns of Gipuzkoa between the River Bidasoa and San Sebastian, but also the towns of Navarre that made up the valleys of Lerín, Baztan, and the Five *Villas* (which remained under its domain, with some intermittences, until 1566, when they separated definitively). The towns of the "Archpriestship of Fuenterrabia" (later termed "lesser Archpriestship") thus belonged to the Bishopric of Baiona, and those of the Archpriestship formerly termed "of Gipuzkoa" (and later "greater Archpriestship") to Pamplona.

9   José Luis Banús y Aguirre, "El límite oriental de San Sebastián y el Puerto de Pasajes," in *Homenaje a Don Julio de Urquijo*, vol. 3 (San Sebastián: Real Sociedad Vascongada de Amigos del País, 1950) and *El Fuero de San Sebastián* (San Sebastián: Ayuntamiento de San Sebastián, 1963).

publishes delimits clearly the jurisdiction of San Sebastian, saying (art. I-11): "*Eciam terminum dono al popullatores de Sancto Seuastiano, de Hundarribia usque ad Oriam, et de Arrenga usque ad Sanctum Martinum de Arano; scilicet quod ego habeo sub terminum illum et totum quod ibi est de rreyalengo.*" It is clear that they were granted limits that were demarcated from Fuenterrabia to the Oria and from Arrenga (Pasajes) to Arano (Navarre).

And yet, the translation states that, "as limits, to the settlers of San Sebastian, from the Bidasoa to the Oria, and from Arrenga to San Martín de Arano; that is, what I possess within those limits and everything there that is part of the kingdom."[10] Limits that begin within the very limits of Fuenterrabia are not the same as limits that mark an end, on the boundary of this town with Navarre.

This inclusive vision is shared by Leandro Silván, Beatriz Arizaga Bolumburu,[11] and all the other authors who follow and cite, directly or indirectly, the inadequate translation highlighted.

The First Granting of Fueros to the Coastal Villas and their Surroundings

The early loss of the original fuero (before 1396, according Doctor Gonzalo Moro) has prevented and prevents any physical examination of the text. Nevertheless, its granting and concession to other towns, on the basis of its very confirmation for San Sebastian by the Castilian King Alfonso VIII (the architect of the incorporation of Gipuzkoa into the Crown of Castile in 1199–1200),[12] has allowed

---

10   Banús y Aguirre, *El Fuero de San Sebastián*, 84. The full translation (in Latin and Spanish, 79–110) is based on that of Juan de Sorola, September 26, 1474.

11   Leandro Silván, *El término municipal de San Sebastián: su evolución histórica* (San Sebastián: Grupo Doctor Camino de Historia Donostiarra, 1971); Beatriz Arizaga Bolumburu, "Las villas guipuzcoanas que reciben el Fuero de San Sebastián: modos de vida de sus habitants," in *Congreso: El fuero de San Sebastián y su época (San Sebastián 19–23 de enero de 1981) / Donostiako forua eta bere garaia (Donostia, 1981ko urtarrilaren 19tik 23ra)* (San Sebastián: Eusko Ikaskuntza / Sociedad de Estudios Vascos, 1982).

12   "*Notum sit tam presentibus quam futuris quod ego Aldefonssus Dey gratia Rex Castelle et Toleti, vnaque cum uxore mea Alienor, Regina, et cum fillio meo Fernando, libente animo et boluntate espontanea concedo in rregno meo et confirmo uobis vniuersso concillio de Sancto Seuastiano presenti et futuro omnes foros et consuetudines et liuertates, videlicet de terminis de foris et consuetudinibus et pedagiis liuertatibus et alliis rrebus quas Sancius, fillius Regis Garsie, quondam Rex Nauarre abunculus meus nobis dedit et concessit in rregno suo cum eandem villam de nobo construxit, sicut in instrumentyo ab eodem nobis condito plenius et expressius continetur. Et vt omnia predicta firmus*

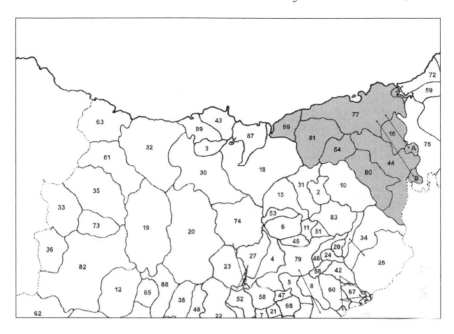

Map 1. The Jurisdictional Limits of San Sebastian in 1180

and allows us to know and figure out its meaning and content. It was linked to the Fuero of Jaca and extended, in an initial phase, to all the Gipuzkoan coastal *villas* (except Deba) and San Vicente de la Barquera in Cantabria (1210).[13] This is how the fuero was received:

Fuenterrabia (Alfonso VIII, Palencia, April 18, 1203)

"Dono et concedo uobis concilio de Fonte Rabia presenti et futuro forum de Sancto Sebastiano perpetuo hauendum."[14]

---

obseruentur \et/ presens sigilum meum plumbeum aponi precepi. Si quis bero contra hoc preceptum egerit rrogem indignacionem incurrat et rregia parti .M°. aures in tanto persoluat daptum super hoc illatum rrestituat duplicatum. Facta carta apud Burgos rrege esprimete, XVI° die menssy augusti, era M° CC° XL°." [AGG-GAO CO LCI 4, fols. 76 r°-vto.].

13 Its municipal charter has not been preserved, but there is a copy in Gervasio Eguaras Fernández, *Colección de Documentos para la Historia de la Provincia de Santander* (Santander, 1865–1867) in which it is stated that, "*dono itaque vobis et concedo forum de Santo Sebastiano, quantum ad illud scilicet quod vos vicini villa dare debitis.*" Cited in Banús y Aguirre, *El Fuero de San Sebastián*, 215.

14 Doc. 4, in Gonzalo Martínez Díez, Felix J. Martínez Llorente, and Emiliano González Díez, *Colección de documentos medievales de las villas guipuzcoanas (1200–1369)* (Donostia-San

Guetaria (Alfonso VIII, San Sebastian, September 1, 1209)

"Dono itaque vobis et concedo forum Sancti Sebastiani, ut illud perpetuo habeatis in montibus, pascuis, aquis et in omnibus causis, eo modo quo rex Navarre illud dedit vobis habendum."[15]

Motrico (Alfonso VIII, San Sebastian, September 1, 1209)

The original concession of the fuero was lost, but Fernando III confirmed it from Vitoria on March 23, 1237, and Alfonso X from Burgos on May 16, 1256, in which it was stated that, *"do vos demás e otorgo vos aquellas libertades e franquezas por todo mio regno que han los de San Sebastián"; y en la carta puebla de Zumaya se dice que "ayan los que en ella poblaren el fuero de San Sabastián, así como los de San Sabastián an el fuero de Iaca e segund que lo an e son poblados al dicho fuero las villas de San Sabastián e de Guetaria e de Motrico."*

Zarauz (Fernando III, Burgos, September 28, 1237)

"Dono itaque vobis et concedo pro foro quia detis mihi duos solitos de qualibet domo annuatim in festo Sancti Martini, et si maraveritis aliquam baleam detis in [mihi] unam tiram a capite usque ad caudam, sicut forum est; et in ombibus aliis causis habeat illud forum, quod habet concilium de Sancto Sevastiano."[16]

Villanueva de Oyarzun or Rentería (Alfonso XI, Valladolid, April 5, 1320)

"E que assí los que agora y poblaren commo los que fueren moradores en esta dicha villa de Villanueua de Oyarço, a tanbién fiiosdalgo commo otros omnes qualesquier, que ayan el fuero de Sant Sauastián, por que se iudguen segund que lo ouieron en tiempo que los otros rreyes onde

---

Sebastián: Juntas Generales de Gipuzkoa; Diputación Foral de Gipuzkoa, 1991), 20.
15 Doc. 5, in ibid., 21.
16 Doc. 12, in ibid., 28.

nos venimos e en el nuestro fasta aquí quando se llamaua conceio de Oyarço."[17]

Hernani (before 1332)

The original concession of the fuero was lost.

Villagrana de Zumaya (Alfonso XI, Valladolid, July 4, 1347)

"*tovímoslo por bien que fagan villa en el dicho lugar Çumaia e le çerquen de muros e torres lo meior que ellos entendieren que cunple para nuestro seruiçio, e que aya nonbre el dicho logar Villagrana de Çumaya, e que ayan los que en ella poblaren el fuero de San Sabastián, así como los de San Sabastián an el fuero de Iaca e segund que lo an e son poblados al dicho fuero las villas de San Sabastián e de Guetaria e de Motrico; e ayan e pongan sus alcaldes, preboste e iurados e escriuanos públicos e fieles e ofiçiales segund que lo an e ponen en Sant Sabastián e en Guetaria e en Motrico, e de los iuizios e sentençias de los alcaldes de dicho lugar de Villagrana de Çumaya que ayan las alçadas para San Sabastián e de San Sabastián para la nuestra Corte.*"[18]

Belmonte de Usúrbil (Enrique II, Toro, September 11, 1371)

"*e hayades el fuero e las franquezas e libertades e los buenos usos e las buenas costumbres que ha la nuestra villa de San Sebastián, e usedes de todo ello según que mejor e más cumplidamente los han e usan de ellos en la dicha villa de San Sebastián.*"[19]

Villarreal de San Nicolás de Orio (Juan I, Burgos, July 12, 1379)

"*E que ayades el fuero de la villa de Sant Sabastián e todas las franquezas e libertades e buenos vsos e buenas costunbres que el dicho conçeio de la dicha villa de Sant Sabastián an de los rreyes onde yo*

17 Doc. 141, in ibid., 143.
18 Doc. 238, in ibid., 253.
19 Banús y Aguirre, *El Fuero de San Sebastián*, 221 and appendix 10.

vengo e de mí, e que pongades en la dicha villa por cada anno alcalles e preuoste, iurados e escriuanos e otros ofiçiales qualesquier segund en la dicha villa de Sant Sabastián los an e suelen poner."[20]

All of these places, except Rentería and Usurbil, are coastal *villas*. And the reason that these two inland *villas* received the fuero is due, without doubt, to the fact that, in the case of Usurbil, it entered into the municipal limits of San Sebastian when it was founded in 1180 and when, thereafter, it segregated from the latter and became a *villa* itself in 1371, the king granted it a fuero, known and practiced for more than a century. As regards Rentería, it emerged as a *villa* in the Oyarzun Valley with the name Villanueva de Oyarzun, and it seems that already prior to 1320 the Oyarzun Valley was regulated by Fuero of San Sebastian, as was noted when speaking about the valley.

The only exception to this general rule of conceding the Fuero of San Sebastian to Gipuzkoan coastal *villas* was that of the *villa* of Monreal de Deva (Deba), which, being a coastal town, would receive the Fuero of Vitoria from Alfonso XI, from the site of Algeciras, on June 17, 1343:

Por rrazón que el conçeio de la villa de Monrreal, que es en Guypuzca, nos enbiaron dezir que ellos que sson poblados al ffuero de Bitoria e el rrey Don Ssancho, nuestro auuelo, que Dios perdone, que les dio ssus priuillegios e ffranquezas e libertades, e porque en aquel logar do sson poblados no podían auer las cosas assy commo les era menester para ssu mantenimiento, porque están alongados del agua e de las lauores del pan, e que en término de la dicha villa de Monrreal que á vn suelo en que non á ninguna puebla, que es çerca del agua de Deva en la rribera de la mar, e que era su voluntad de poblar ally e nos pedían merçed que nos ploguyese ende.

Nos por esto, e por fazer bien e merçed al conçeio de la dicha villa de Monrreal, tenemos por bien que puedan poblar e pueblen en el dicho suelo que es çerca del agua de Deua; e aquella puebla que se y

---

20   Doc. 382, in Martínez Díez, Martínez Llorente, and González Díez, *Colección de documentos medievales de las villas guipuzcoanas*, 101.

fecier que aya nonbre Monrreal, e aquellos que y poblaren e moraren de
aquí adelante que ayan aquel fuero e aquellas ffranquezas e libertades
que agora an en aquel logar do sson poblados, e ellos que nos ffagan
aquellos ffueros rreales que nos agora ffazen e sson tenudos a fazer, e
nos den aquellos pechos e ffueros e derechos que agora auemos e deuemos
auer en la dicha villa de Monrreal.[21]

This "apparent contradiction" as Elena Barrena Osoro accurately terms it,[22] was due, without doubt, to the fact that the original concession of the Vitoria fuero was made to the site of Icíar (Itziar) (in Valladolid, June 24, 1294), an elevated settlement inland from the coast whose inhabitants were involved in an economy more in keeping with the assumptions included in that fuero rather than in that of San Sebastian. And when its center of operations, that is, its status as a *villa*, was transferred to the coast, the fuero was taken along as well, despite the fact that the subsequent activities it would prioritize were more and better reflected in the very Fuero of San Sebastian.

Thus, with the exception of Deba, on their foundation the rest of the Gipuzkoan coastal *villas* received the Fuero of San Sebastian. But there is another problem when it comes to considering the study of the concession of fueros in Gipuzkoa: it is the case of the *villa* of Hernani, whose municipal charter had already disappeared by the end of the fifteenth century. Indeed, in the General Council of Tolosa in 1491, it was said of Hernani that, "the archive of papers it had, had been burned some time ago."[23]

Basque historiography has always understood the foundation of Hernani as the work of King Enrique II or Juan I, prior to 1380 (power changed hands in May 1379), and as such it should have been granted the Fuero of San Sebastian. However, Navarrese documents mention Hernani as a walled *villa* already in 1332, and the reference date that has been followed in order to consider its founding date

---

21   Doc. 224, in ibid., 236.
22   Elena Barrena Osoro, "El Fuero de Vitoria en la villa de Deva. Aparentes contradicciones geopolíticas," in *Congreso: El fuero de San Sebastián y su época (San Sebastián 19–23 de enero de 1981) / Donostiako forua eta bere garaia (Donostia, 1981ko urtarrilaren 19tik 23ra)* (San Sebastián: Eusko Ikaskuntza / Sociedad de Estudios Vascos, 1982).
23   Banús y Aguirre, *El Fuero de San Sebastián*, 223.

as prior to 1380 is only a neighborly or good relations contract signed "among equals" with the neighboring *villa* of San Sebastian on August 2, 1379, in which the main aspect was the regulation of commercial and economic ties between the two *villas* that would characterize the whole subsequent era.

Hernani must also have been constituted as a *villa* in the second half of the thirteenth century, insofar that the foundational policy followed by Alfonso X (1252–April 4, 1284) appears to have prioritized safeguarding the route from Araba, following the course of the Oria, to San Sebastian. On the basis of this policy, between 1256 and 1268, the king founded the *villas* of Segura, Villafranca (Ordizia), and Tolosa, built at similar distances from one another, as boundary markers and reference points for users of the highways; and the non-concession at that time of a fuero to the villa of Hernani would imply the existence of an important lacuna on that route, in that the royal highway that went from Tolosa to San Sebastian passed through Andoain-Lizaur, Urnieta, and Hernani, from whose river ports goods were transported in boats of *"alas"* to the port or market of Santa Catalina in San Sebastian, after passing through the toll of Murguía, in Astigarraga.

I argued, until quite recently and following Luis Murugarren Zamora and Luis Miguel Díez de Salazar Fernández,[24] that in this concession of the status of *villa* to Hernani, the Fuero of Vitoria rather that of San Sebastian should have been taken in the same way as in the *villas* of Segura, Villafranca, and Tolosa. This is because, like those places, it lacked a coastline and should have been constituted as a *villa* jointly with them; and moreover, because its later domestic life and organization did not resemble at all the institutions particular to the San Sebastian fuero (especially the figures of the provost and dual mayoralty). The foundational logic and loss of the original text that allowed for its status as a *villa* (always before 1332), on account of numerous fires in the *villa* as a result of French incursions, led me to this conclusion. However, I now believe with total certainty that

---

24 Luis Murugarren Zamora, *Hernani y su historia e instituciones* (San Sebastián: Caja de Ahorros Municipal, 1970); Luis Miguel Díez de Salazar Fernández, "La vecindad de Hernani (1379–1429)," *Anuario de Estudios Medievales* 18 (1988): 367–77.

the *villa* of Hernani was also founded on the basis of the fuero de San Sebastian, as it is stated in the bylaws of the *villa* in 1518, prior to their confirmation in 1542: "*Yten, que pues esta villa esta aforada con San Sabastián que se guarde el preuillejo de no sacar de casa por devda çebil a ningún vezino ny estrano.*"[25]

That explains the numerous references that, in this 1518 municipal set of laws in Hernani, were made to the very municipal set of laws of San Sebastian:

> *Sobre las ynjurias y rrenzillas de entro vozinos, que se pongan las hordenanças de San Sabastián que sobre esto hablan.*

> *Que conforme a la carta e prouysión rreal de San Sabastián, los alcaldes no proçedan de ofiçio syn pidimiento de parte sobre palabras d'entre vezinos donde no ay armas ny sangre, y las partes fueren amigos.*

> *Yten, que pues esta villa esta aforada con San Sabastián que se guarde el preuillejo de no sacar de casa por devda çebil a ningún vezino ny estrano.*

> *Yten que quando ay acusador sobre heridas e ynjurias que se goarden las hordenanças que la villa de San Sabastián tiene sobre ello.*

---

25 AGSimancas. Consejo Real. Escribanías, 236-5. The Council of Hernani asked for the council bylaws to be confirmed, which was undertaken by a royal provision of July 8, 1518, in 125 chapters. Juan de Ilarreta and other residents of the *villa* were opposed to this. They presented certain deeds on sentences and other questions, with annotations and comments in the margins by the *corregidor* Attorney Navia, in his report of January 31, 1540. I am grateful to Iago Irijoa Cortés for facilitating this information.

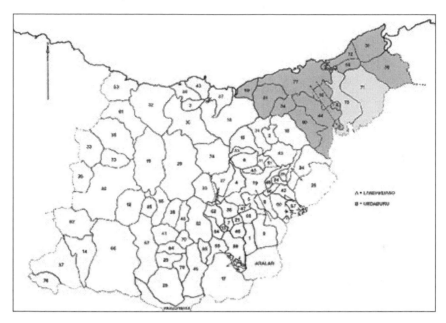

Map 2. The Process of Granting the Fuero of San Sebastian to Medieval Villas, 1180–1379

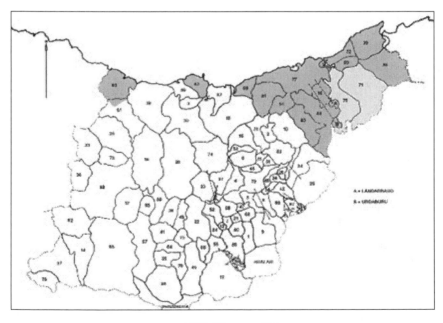

1203 (Fuenterrabia)
1209 (Guetaria and Motrico)

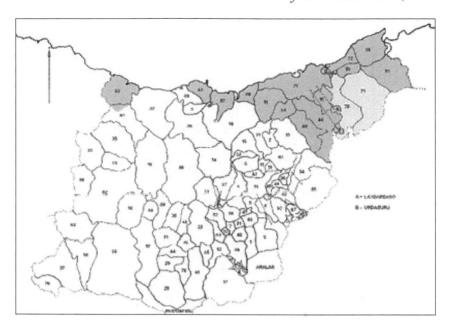

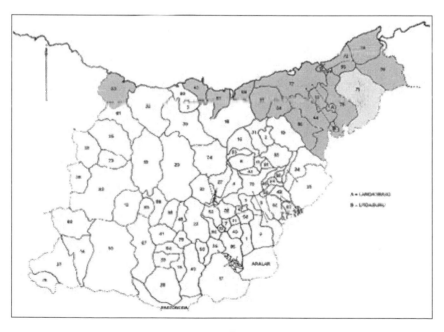

1237 (Zarauz)
1320 (Rentería)

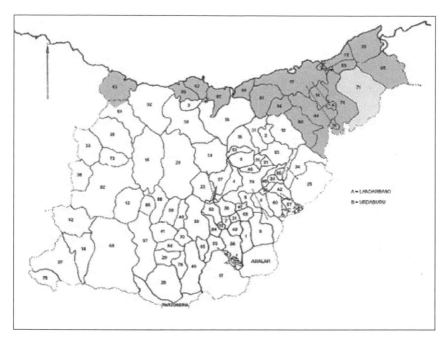

1347 (Zumaya), 1371 (Usurbil), and 1379 (Orio)

The Expansion of this Fuero Granting Inland

Besides the twenty-five *villas* that were founded through two centuries (1180–1383), whether on the basis of the Fuero of Jaca-Estella-San Sebastian or the Fuero of Logroño-Vitoria, there were in Gipuzkoa small population nuclei termed in the documents of the era *anteiglesias* (parishes), *universidades* (communities), *parroquias* (parishes), *colaciones* (congregations), or, later, *aldeas* (villages). They did not enjoy the privileged law of *villas* and, but were instead subject to traditional law and under the influences of the seigneurs of the land, the landed nobility or *parientes mayors* (senior lincage heads), the owners of important lands dedicated to agricultural and livestock activities, in contrast to the artisanal, commercial, and industrial activities befitting the foral *villas*.

For that reason, from the fourteenth century on, the improving everyday conditions implied by possessing a fuero conceded to the *villas*, especially insofar that it brought with it security and royal protection as opposed to seigniorial pressure. From the fifteenth century on, and especially on account of the economic convenience, many of those *universidades* or communities (and even individuals and particular houses) began to sign neighborly contracts with the villas in their districts.

Such were the cases of the *villas* of San Sebastian, which incorporated Andoain (until 1475, when it passed over to Tolosa), part of Zubieta, Igueldo (Igeldo)and Ibaeta (connected in 1379), Aduna and Alquiza (which were passed over from Tolosa to San Sebastian in 1478), twenty-nine houses in Urnieta, and Alza (Altza)and Pasajes *de Aquende, de San Sebastian*, or *de San Pedro*; of Fuenterrabia, which incorporated Irun Uranzu, inserted into the foundation of the villa within its jurisdictional limits, as were Lezo and Pasajes *de Allende, de Fuenterrabía*, or *de San Juan*; the *villa* of Tolosa, which incorporated Berrobi, Gaztelu, Irura, Leaburu and Oreja (Orexa), Abalcisqueta (Abaltzisketa), Albistur, Alegría (Alegia), Alzo (Altzo), Amasa, Amézqueta (Amezketa), Anoeta, Baliarrain, Belaunza (Belauntza), Berástegui (Berastegi), Cizúrquil (Zizurkil), Elduayen (Elduaien), Hernialde, Ibarra, Icazteguicta (Ikaztegieta), Lizarza (Lizartza), and Orendain (connected between 1374 and 1392), Aduna, Alquiza (which passed over to San Sebastian in 1475), and Asteasu (connected in 1386), *Larraul* and *Soravilla* (which, with Asteasu, would go on to form part of the *alcaldía mayor* (senior mayoralties) de Aiztondo), Andoain (separated from San Sebastian, it was joined to Tolosa in 1475), and wondered about Villabona; the *villa* of Segura, which incorporated Astigarreta, Cegama (Zegama), Cerain (Zerain), Gaviria (Gabiria), Gudugarreta, Idiazabal, Legazpia, Mutiloa, and Ormaiztegui (Ormaiztegi), joined in 1384, and for a time Ezquioga and Zumarraga; the *villa* of Villafranca, which incorporated Alzaga (Altzaga), Arama, Ataun, Beasain, Gainza (Gaintza), Isasondo (Itsasondo), Legorreta, and Zaldivia (Zaldibia), connected in 1399, and eight houses in Lazcano (Lazkao); the *villa* of Mondragon (Arrasate), which would incorporate, in 1353, Garagarza, Udala, Guesalíbar (Gesalibar), Uríbarri, Herenuzqueta, Isasigaña, and Oleaga, splitting away from those in Léniz (Leintz) Valley; the villa of Vergara (Bergara), which incorporated Zumarraga in 1383, although on account of the opposition of Segura it would thereafter separate, becoming head of the *alcaldía mayor* of Arerí; the *villa* of Usurbil, which incorporated Aguinaga and Urdayaga, integrated since their establishment in the *villa*, and part of Zubieta since 1379; the *villa* of Hernani, which incorporated sixteen houses in Urnieta between 1402 and 1429; the *villa* of Deva, which incorporated Icíar, since its establishment, and Garagarz; the *villa* of Elgoibar, which incorporated Alzola (Altzola) and Azpilgoeta; the *villa* of Zumaya (Zumaia), which incorporated Aizarnazabal in 1480, and Oiquina (Oikia); and the *villa* of Cestona (Zestoa), which incorporated Aizarna since its establishment, an after some time, Aizarnazabal, until 1480 (when it went over to Zumaya).

The *villas* this made up an organizational mechanism for the territory by which small villages and rural districts were linked to a main town of "head of jurisdiction," thus termed because its mayor held the power of royal civil and criminal jurisdiction. The *aldeas*, *colaciones*, or *universidades* linked to these towns therefore experienced a fairly low level of institutional development, with practically no role in the town councils. Only *colaciones* like Anzuola and Oxirondo (linked to Vergara) or Aguinaga (linked to Usurbil) achieved more active and proportional participation in municipal (and later provincial) government thanks to agreements and *cartas partidas* (shared charters) by which they managed to subscribe to their *villas*.

In general, the *villas* organized the life of their *colaciones*, leaving them free to act on those questions that did not surpass initiatives that may have been harmful to their own interests. From a political perspective, they appointed local mayors, whose powers were limited by the very competences of the ordinary mayors of the *villas*. They did, though, allow some autonomy in their internal organization, in which the interests of the *villas* and their oligarchs played a fundamental role, with their opinions being decisive when it came to planning activities and the system of benefiting from their use. Economic matters, on the other hand, as well as tax issues, were strongly centralized and controlled from the *villas*.

Yet despite all the problems that, in time, emerged, the movement to establish these neighborly connections in Gipuzkoa was so widespread, that, by the late fifteenth century, with the exception of three *alcaldías mayores* (Arería, Sayaz, and Aiztondo), the two valleys (Léniz and Oyarzun), and some singularities (that would continue to term themselves *parientes mayores*), all Gipuzkoa was subject to the law of the Fueros of San Sebastian or Vitoria-Logroño.

Thus, through this "neighborly connection" method, the Fuero of San Sebastian was extended to Andoain (until 1475, when it established a neighborly connection with Tolosa, and switched to having the Fuero of Logroño-Vitoria), Igueldo, Ibaeta, and part of Zubieta (connected in 1379), and twenty-nine houses in Urnieta (from the late fourteenth century on), Aduna, Alquiza, and extending also to Alza and Pasajes de San Pedro (communities integrated since its granting of the fuero to San Sebastian).

Andoain

Andoain-Leizaur was a *colación* that had an important iron industry already by the late fourteenth century, halfway between Tolosa and San Sebastian, and which opted to link itself to the latter. This neighborly relation was confirmed by Enrique II in Valladolid, on February 28, 1379, alongside similar agreements with Zubieta, Igueldo, and Ibaeta.[26] This royal provision was later completed with another, dated March 3 that same year, in which the king gave residents of the *villa* the right to select mayors and the *aldeas* of their jurisdiction, mayors that had to swear an oath in San Sebastian, go to the *villa* on the occasion of any appeal, and treat only cases of less than four *maravedís*.[27]

---

26 Thus registered by Luis Cruzat, and verified according to him with his lead seal in fol. 5 vto., in his *Inventario de los papeles que la ciudad de San Sebastián tiene en su archivo* (1581), published in *Colección de documentos inéditos para la historia de Guipúzcoa*, vol. 2 (San Sebastián: Diputación Provincial 1958), 73. The same reference is published in José Luis Banús y Aguirre, *El Archivo Quemado. Inventarios antiguos y acervo documental de la M.N. y M.L. Ciudad de San Sebastián antes de la destrucción de 1813* (San Sebastián: Grupo Doctor Camino de Historia Donostiarra; Caja de Ahorros Municipal de San Sebastián, 1986), 32.

27 José Antonio de Camino y Orella, "Historia civil-diplomática-eclesiástica, antigua y moderna de la ciudad de San

The impossibility of consulting the document, due to its destruction in the 1813 fire of San Sebastian, means that we cannot be sure if in 1379 Andoain established a neighborly agreement or confirmed such an agreement (or both things), as well as the reasons put forward for the parts or the conditions, obligations, and benefits that such a union of neighborly relation entailed. In fact, the review undertaken by Luis Cruzat in his inventory stated that, "*Privilegio del rey Don Enrique de la vecindad de Zubieta, de Igueldo, de Ybaeta y de Andoayn,*" and Banús y Aguirre says it was a "privilege of King Enrique that confirmed the lands of Zubieta, of Igueldo, of Ybaeta, and of Andoayn as places within its neighborly relationship."

We only know, through the charter of protection that the monarchs gave to San Sebastian on its right to exercise jurisdiction over the terrain of Andoain, aright disputed by the villa of Tolosa and registered in Medina del Campo, on March 10, 1475,[28] that this union was made voluntarily and in perpetuity ("*de su propia voluntad la dicha tierra e universidad de Ahinduán se obligaron por contrabto de no salir de dicha vesindad, so çiertas penas*"); that it subjected Andoain to the jurisdiction and court of the villa, both in civil and criminal proceedings; and that it obliged the land and the *universidad* of Andoain to pay one thousand *maravedís* annually "*por respeto de dicha vezindad.*"

The connection between Andoain and San Sebastian ended in 1475, when the former decided to establish a neighborly relation definitively with the nearby *villa* of Tolosa, thereby also changing its fuero. The confrontation that generated between San Sebastian and Tolosa ended in 1479, when both *villas* agreed to forgive one another for previous offences and promised to aid each other in the provincial councils and other places.[29]

Sebastián." Euskal-Erria 17 (1887), 377–79, 444–46, and 569–71; and 18 (1888), 27–28 and 41–45.

28   AGSimancas (RGS), III-1475, fol. 293.

29   All of this is covered in Mª Rosa Ayerbe Iribar and Luis Miguel Díez de Salazar Fernández, *Andoain, de Tierra a Villazgo (1379–1615). Un caso modélico de preautonomía municipal en Gipuzkoa* (Andoain: Ayuntamiento "Leyçaur, 0", 1996).

Zubieta

The current neighborhood of Zubieta matches that of the neighborly agreement that one part of the population of this *colación* or *universidad* made with the *villa* of San Sebastian in 1379, with the other part reaching an agreement with the nearby *villa* of Usurbil. Worth noting is that this division of neighborly relations was reflected in the parish church itself, which still today has two doors of access that are differentiated according to which of the two sides the worshipers come from.

Because the annexation document has been lost, we know nothing of its conditions, although we do know that the agreement will have allowed Zubieta to enjoy the privileges of the Fuero of San Sebastian, because Usurbil subscribed to that as well.

Igueldo and Ibaeta

The current neighborhoods of Igueldo and Ibaeta were originally well-defined *colaciones* that had their own parishes, which were distinct from the wholly San Sebastian parishes of Santa María and San Vicente (located in the center of the *villa*) and that of San Sebastian el Antiguo or San Sebastian de Hernani situated in the outskirts of the *villa*, far outside the city walls, the first settlement of what would later be San Sebastian.

In all likelihood they were within the jurisdictional limits conceded to San Sebastian in the Fuero of 1180, but the limited exercise of this municipal authority on the part of its officials there, and the character of their inhabitants—who always demonstrated a strong personality, especially those of Igueldo; and those of the Antiguo as well, although with it being closer to the walls and the San Sebastian patricians having more vested interests there, it was subjected more strictly to the jurisdiction of the villa[30]—meant that

---

30   One can see this clearly in Mª Rosa Ayerbe Iribar, *El Monasterio Dominico de San Pedro González Telmo (San Sebastián). De centro religioso a centro cultural y museístico de primer orden de la ciudad* (San Sebastián: Grupo Doctor Camino de Historia Donostiarra; Kutxa Fundazioa, 2012), 215–60.

they managed to defend their own interests and lead a life free of official and patrician pressure.

This was possibly reason why, in 1379, they subscribed (along with the residents of Zubieta and Andoain) to a neighborly contract with the *villa*, as distinct population entities outside the jurisdiction of San Sebastian. The loss of this contract, however, also prevents us here from knowing the conditions and obligations agreed to by both parts.[31]

Urnieta

The *universidad* or *colación* of Urnieta appears through history within the *alcaldía mayor* of Aiztondo, alongside the towns of Asteasu (its head), Astigarraga (minus Murguia), Larraul, and Soravilla.

In the process of establishing neighborly relations that developed in Gipuzkoa, the residents of Unriniet were split on what they wanted to do as regards linking with either San Sebastian or Hernani, remaining in the *alcaldía* of Aiztondo, until its constitution as a *villa* in 1615.[32]

The numerous privileges and exemptions that the oldest *villa* in Gipuzkoa, San Sebastian, gradually received from the Castilian kings, who were in favor of promoting its development both within and outside its own city limits, must have been important reasons for why a majority of Urnieta residents made the decision to request its incorporation into a neighborly relation with that *villa*.

We do not know the background, or the date of its incorporation and the specific conditions that underpinned its commitment, because no document sealing the agreement has been preserved in any of its archives. Yet we do know that the part annexed to the jurisdiction of San Sebastian, in the late fourteenth or early fifteenth century, constituted the most important part of

---

31   The neighborly agreement was communicated by Luis Cruzat in his *Inventario* (1581), in *Colección de documentos inéditos para la historia de Guipúzcoa*, vol. 2, 73; see also Banús y Aguirre, *El Archivo Quemado*, 32.

32   On its history see Mª Rosa Ayerbe Iribar, *Urnieta, de Tierra a Villazgo (1402–1615)* (Urnieta: Urnietako Udala/Ayuntamiento de Urnieta, 2015).

Urnieta, and was made up of the parish church of San Miguel and the twenty-nine most economically powerful farms and houses in Urnieta: Adarraga, greater Alaricu (or Alarizu), lesser Alaricu (or Alarizu), Alcibar, Almorza, Amitesarobe, Arancibia, Araneder, Ayerdi, Azconobieta, Barcardaztegui or upper Barcaiztegui,[33] Basoaltu, Berasaberro, Berrasoeta, Dendaltegui (or Tendategui), Elqueta, Elquezabal, Embutodi, Erauso-andia, Ermutegui, Galardi, Guerez, upper Larburu (or Arburu), middle Larburu (or Arburu), upper Lasarte, Loperdi, Orcayen (or Acain), Oyanume, and Oyarbide; to which in time were added the houses and farms of Berazaburu, Echeverria, Florencia, Garmendia, Querin, and Urmeneta.[34] On not possessing the document agreed to by both parts we cannot know precisely the conditions agreed on.

For their part, sixteen farms and houses in Urnieta would establish neighborly relations with Hernani, a *villa* with the Fuero of San Sebastian. The first fifteen of these did so by a contract signed in the apple orchard of Arreizola (in Hernani) on January 19, 1402:[35] Aguirre, Altuna, Arizola, Artoloniaga or Artolea, Azteguieta, Bidarte, the two in Egurrola, Erauso, Garraza, Gorostiaga, Guruceta, Idiazabal, Izaguirre, and Zucinaga. In this neighborly agreement, made in perpetuity, those who subscribed to it acted freely "on our own free will and authority, without any reward or pressure," for themselves and their heirs, to better serve the king, and for their own security ("for the benefit and protection of said land"). They

---

33 Although Gorosabel states that it was the lower Barcardaztegui house that established a neighborly relation with San Sebastian, it was the upper one, with the lower one going over to Hernani.

34 The latter appear with the former when, in 1615, the *corregidor* gave over their possession to the *villa* of San Sebastian, on the king reverting to the exemption previously conceded for its conversion into a *villa*.

35 The residents and inhabitants of the *colación* of "Urrieta" committed to that contract were: "*Martín de Çuçinaga dueño y señor de la casa y casería de Çuçinaga, e doña María Joan de Ydiaçabal dueña de la casa y casería de Ydiaçábal, e Joan de Çaldu dueño y señor de la casa y casería de Vidarte, e Pedro de Otálora dueño y señor de la casa y casería d'Egurrola, e Miguel señor de la casa y casería d'Egurrola, e Joan de Artoloniaga dueño y señor de la casa y casería de Artoloniaga, e Pedro de Estierreche dueño y señor de la casa y casería de Altuna, e Lope de Sarrudegui e Michelco de Aguirre dueño y señor de la casa y casería de Azteguieta, e Miguel de Areyçola señor de la casa y casería de Areiçola, e García de Artoloniaga señor de la casa y casería de Gurruçeta, e Joan señor de la casa y casería de Yçaguirre, e Miguel de Herauso señor de la casa y casería de Erauso, y Miguel de Ychurça e Pedro de Garraça dueño e señor de la casa y casería de Garraza, e Joan de Gorostiaga señor de la casa y casería de Gorostiaga.*" A. Marqueses de Rocaverde, "Mayorazgo Ayerdi-Epela," Caja 1, doc. 9, dated in the catalog in 1520, in Díez de Salazar Fernández, "La vecindad de Hernani," 378–79.

maintained the right to not have to carry out night watchman services if they did not want to and the free enjoyment of their own ciders.

In exchange, the council and good men of the *villa* received them within the neighborly relations under the promise of *"vos ajudar e sostener e anparar y defender y aconsejar como a nuestros propios vecinos,"* facilitating land to graze for their animals in the hills and public lands of the *villa*, grazing on its grass and drinking its water freely, and their pigs on council hills. Only one use was denied them: the felling of any trees "small or big" without a council license, as any of its other residents was obliged to do.

This neighborly agreement would be completed on November 6, 1429 in the church cemetery San Juan de Hernani, with the joining of a new neighbor (the sixteenth): Ochoa de Areizmendi, nicknamed "Ochoalaza," *"duenno e sennor de la casa e casería nueba que agora tengo començada a faser en la dicha tierra e collaçión de Urrieta, en el logar qu'el disen Oyharbide."*[36]

This neighborly agreement was made for them and their heirs "for the rest of known time," *"e segund e commo lo han acostunbrado de faser besindad con vos el dicho conçejo los otros besinos de la dicha tierra e collaçión de Urrieta,"* in 1402, with them enjoying *"prestaçiones et livertades et franquesas que los otros vuestros besinos de Urrieta han en los términos de vos el dicho conçejo et de todas las otras cosas."* The *villa*, as in the previous case, promised to *"vos dar ajuda e sostener et anparar et defender et consejar bien et lealmente commo a nuestro besino, et segund e de la forma e manera que a los otros nuestros besinos de la dicha tierra e collaçión de Urrieta."* And both parts committed to maintaining good neighborly relations and asking for and obtaining royal confirmation.

There is no mention in either case of the enjoyment of the Fuero of San Sebastian, which one supposes was implied, since both *villas* shared that fuero.

---

36   AM Hernani C/5/V/1/1. Parchment in bad state, in Díez de Salazar Fernández, "La vecindad de Hernani," 380–81.

Aduna and Alquiza

We know little about these *colaciones* that were added on March 23, 1386, together with Asteasu, to the *villa* of Tolosa, taking its fuero with respect to possessions and people, but maintaining the administration of its rents and the use of its mountainous lands. The differences arising between these *colaciones* and the *villa* led both of them to join San Sebastian in 1450. That provoked strong tensions between the two *villas* (they were competing over Asteasu as well), which ended in the 1479 agreement, in which Andoain (which was joined to San Sebastian) went over to Tolosa and Aduna and Alquiza (which were attached to Tolosa) went over to depend on San Sebastian. Alquiza obtained its *villa* status in 1731, and Aduna obtained municipal autonomy in 1883.

Alza and Pasajes de Aquende, de San Sebastián, or de San Pedro

Since its establishment, both towns remained within the jurisdiction of the villa of San Sebastian, with the benefits of its fuero, therefore, being extended to them.

Lezo, Pasajes de Allende, de Fuenterrabia, or de San Juan, and Irun

Yet besides these towns, which enjoyed the fuero through their link with or integration into the municipality of San Sebastian, there were others that enjoyed the same fuero through their link with or integration into *villas* already possessing the Fuero of San Sebastian. This was the case of Lezo, Pasajes de Allende, de Fuenterrabia, and de San Juan, and Irun.

Integrated into the jurisdiction of Fuenterrabia, they enjoyed the Fuero of San Sebastian since the foundation of the *villa* in 1203. Today, Lezo is still a *universidad* and constitutes its own municipality, Pasajes is a *villa* (made up of three Pasajes: de San Juan, de San Pedro, and Ancho), and Irun is a city.

Others

Aguinaga and Urdayaga, integrated since its founding into the *villa* of Usurbil (1371), as well as part of Zubieta since 1379. Today they make up neighborhoods in the municipality.

Aizarnazabal, an official neighbor of Zumaya since 1480 (today it is an indoendent municipality), and Oiquina, integrated into the *villa* since its founding in 1347 (today it is one of its neighborhoods).

Mendaro, constituted as an independent municipality in 1983, enjoyed the Fuero of San Sebastian insofar as it belonged to the *villa* of Motrico (from which it split away), with the other part linked to the Fuero of Logroño-Vitoria possessed by the villa of Elgoibar, from which its other part split away when both of them came to make up a new municipality.

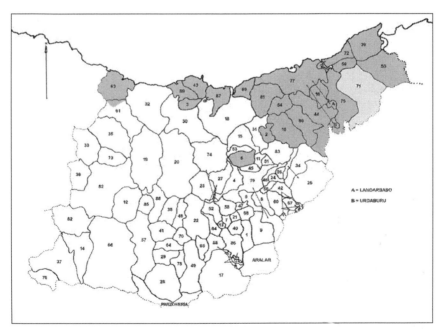

Map 3.
Villas and Aldeas with Neighborly Ties to the Fuero of San Sebastian

Aizarnazabal (with Zumaya), Aduna and Alquiza (with San Sebastian), Andoain (for a while, since it later went over to Tolosa), while the rest were already in the orbit of the San Sebastian fuero.

The Second Concession of the Fuero of San Sebastian to *Alcaldías Mayores* and Valleys

Following the constitution of the twenty-five medieval *villas* in Gipuzkoa and their linking to smaller towns (*anteiglesias, colaciones,* and *universidades*) through the neighborly contracts, all that remained of the older valley organization were three *alcaldías mayores* (Arería, Sayaz, and Aiztondo) and two valleys (Léniz and Oyarzun). Both were made up of small population settlements or *universidades* that were organized among themselves. The former, however, were subject to an *alcalde mayor*, appointed by the king, who generally delegated his functions to *tenientes de alcalde* or *alcaldes de partido* (with the holder of the post or *alcalde mayor* living at court, taking with him rents and rights). The lands or valleys, for their part, were organized in a different way, with that of Léniz being subject to the authority of the seigneury of the Guevara family until 1556 (when it went over to the kingdom), even though in 1493 its residents obtained the right to appoint their own mayor and *merino*, passing their appeals to the *alcalde mayor* of the seigneury. The Oyartzun Valley followed a different process, being governed by its own officials. Both, however, achieved political maturity and participated directly in the provincial councils.

The Oyarzun Valley originally extended from the Pasajes Channel to the River Bidasoa. When it split away from Fuenterrabia in 1203 (with Irun, Lezo, and Pasajes *de Allende de Fuenterrabía* or *de San Juan*) and Rentería in 1320 (as Villanueva de Oyarzun, built on the village of Orereta), the alley was made up of the villages of Elizalde (head), Alcíbar, and Iturrioz.

The Léniz Valley was originally integrated by the *anteiglesias* of Arrasate (which became a *villa* in 1260 by the name of Montdragon), Garagarza, Udala, Guesalíbar, Uríbarri, Herenuzqueta, Isasigaña, and Oleaga, (whiuch were integrated into the *villa* in 1353, splitting away from the valley), and Arechavaleta (Aretxabaleta) and Escoriaza (Eskoriatza) (which disputed the position of head settlement until their separation and the constitution of Escoriaza as a *villa* in 1630), Aozaraza, Arenaza, Bedoña, Galarza, Goronaeta, Isurieta, and Larrino (which would remain with Arechavaleta), and Apózaga, Bolíbar, Marín, Mázmela, Guellano, Mendiola, and Zarimuz (which would remain with Escoriaza).

The *alcaldía mayor* of Aiztondo was integrated originally by Asteasu (head of jurisdiction), Cizúrquil (which would move over to Tolosa in 1391, until its constitution as a *villa* in 1615), and Aduna and Alquiza (which would go from Tolosa to San Sebastian in 1479), which remained there until the elimination of Larraul, Soravilla, Astigarraga, and part of Urnieta (with those residents not in a neighborly agreement with either Hernani or San Sebastian).

The *alcaldía mayor* of Arería was integrated originally by Zumarraga (head of jurisdiction until its constitution as a *villa* in 1661), Lazcano (except the eight residents or houses in a neighborly relationship with Villafranca), Olaberría, Ichaso, Arriarán, Gaviria, and Ezquioga.

And the *alcaldía mayor* of Sayaz, integrated by Aya (Aia) (head of jurisdiction), Beizama, Goyaz, Régil (Erregil), and Vidania (Bidania).

In principle, because they had not received a fuero or had not come to a neighborly agreement, these small settlements continued to be governed by consuetudinary law. However, because of their limited size and proximity to *villas* with fueros, from the mid-fifteenth century on they also gradually came to be governed (except the Léniz Valley) by the Fuero of San Sebastian.

The Oyarzun Valley

This was, without any doubt, the area that was most likely to be influenced early on by the Fuero of San Sebastian. It would appear that following the separation of Fuenterrabia (with Irun, Lezo, and Pasajes *de Allende de Fuenterrabía* or *de San Juan*), in order to augment and consolidate its population (which was very close geographically to France and Navarre), Alfonso VIII had to grant it a privilege.[37] By an expanded privilege of Fernando III (Vitoria, March 20, 1237) aimed at the "*concilio* of Oiarso," the king confirmed therein the fueros, habits, customs, and exemptions that his grandfather (Alfonso VIII) had given, whose thanks "you had and have until death." He conceded, likewise, the limits, mountains, pastures, and grazing land that the former had pointed out, so that people there could enjoy them in perpetuity on oath of heredity, and ordered the residents of San Sebastian "to help and defend you." All this was confirmed later by Alfonso XI in Valladolid, on June 15, 1318.

More reliable is a 1318 reference to a charter underwritten by Fernando III and directed at the very same "*concejo* of Oyarzun," in which he speaks of some "charters on how they are related to the fuero that those of San Sebastian have," whose original has been lost. The fact is that, when the *villa* of Villanueva de Oyarzun (Rentería) was founded in 1320, the Fuero of San Sebastian already prevailed in the Oyarzun Valley.

In the *Memorial del fecho del pleito con Rentería*, cited by Banús y Aguirre and questioned by Gamón,[38] it is said that, in a legal dispute between San Sebastian and Rentería over control of the port of Pasajes, the villa of San Sebastian presented a charter starting ABC that was agreed to with the land of Oyarzun, before Fernando III (1217–1252), establishing that uninhabited terrain was common to both parts, and that those of Oyarzun should live according to the Fuero of San Sebastian and, "*que fiziesen vecindad con ellos en todas las cosas, salvo que no les ayudasen a velar la villa ni a cercarla, e que los de Oyarçun huviessen preboste e iurado e alcalde, assí como lo mandava el fuero de San Sebastián.*" According to Amalio Marichalar and Cayetano Manrique, in 1237 Fernando III confirmed the Fuero of San Sebastian for the whole Oyarzun Valley.[39]

---

37 Gorosabel, *Diccionario histórico-geográfico-descriptivo*, 378–79. The point is clarified by Banús y Aguirre, *El Fuero de San Sebastián*, 216–17.

38 Fols. 6 vto-7 rº in the *Memorial*, in Banús y Aguirre, *El Fuero de San Sebastián*, 218; Juan Igancio Gamón, *Noticias Históricas de Rentería* (San Sebastián: Nueva Editorial, 1930), 95.

39 Amalio Marichalar and Cayetano Manrique, *Historia de la Legislación y recitaciones del Derecho Civil de España*, vol. 8, *Fueros de Navarra, Vizcaya, Guipúzcoa y Álava* (Madrid: Impr. Gasset-Loma, 1868), 485.

The serious problems and confrontation that arose between the *villa* of Villanueva and the Oyarzun Valley in jurisdictional matters led the valley in 1453 to ask the king to sanction the complete separation of jurisdiction in the *villa*. The petition was founded on the numerous scandals, disputes, debates, conflict and fights, men's deaths, burning of houses, felling of apple trees, and other misconduct ion the part of the *villa* inhabitants, as well as the many bad things that they had to put up with as a result of criminals of their own and from outside (from Navarre, Baiona, and Lapurdi) on account of not having in their district their own mayors or judges. Therefore, on June 20, 1453 Juan II, from Escalona, exempted all good men and denizens of the valley (the inhabitants of Elizalde, Iturrioz, and Alcibar) from all jurisdiction, including that of the *villa* of Villanueva de Oyarzun-Rentería, and put them under his own jurisdiction, ordering that henceforth they should have a separate head and council and therefore granting them the Fuero of San Sebastian:

> *E otrosí, demás de esto, es mi merced que la dicha tierra e todos los vecinos e moradores de ella que sean aforados al fuero de la villa de Sant Sebastián, que es en la dicha Provincia de Guipúzcoa, e que hayan el fuero de ella, e todas las otras franquezas, exenciones, libertades, privilegios, usos e costumbres según que los han en la dicha villa de San Sebastián.*[40]

This privilege was confirmed by the same King Juan II three months later, on September 13, 1453, from Becerril de Campos. And although in 1463, in the face of a complaint by Rentería, Enrique IV revoked the favor conceded to Oyarzun by his father, when he passed through the valley on his way to France and saw that there were more people there than in Rentería, and that it formed a border with France and Navarre, he confirmed it and ordered that Juan II's favor be retained, by a privilege awarded in Valladolid on September 24, 1470, and by another in Segovia on October 10, 1472.

---

40 See under "Oyarzun" in appendix to Gorosabel, *Diccionario histórico-geográfico-descriptivo*, 700. Gorosabel also cites it when he discusses Oyarzun in the text, stating that in 1453 the conceded "to its inhabitants the fuero, freedoms and exemptions, privileges and customs of the then villa of San Sebastian" (384).

The Catholic monarchs also confirmed it in Seville, on February 20, 1484.[41]

The Alcaldía Mayor of Arería

It originally included the settlements of Lazcano, Olaberria, Ichaso, and Arriarán (today a neighborhood of Beasain), to which were added later those of Ezquioga, Gaviria, and Zumarraga (which would act as the head). In 1661 the latter three separated, with the *alcaldía* just made up of the first four.

The baton of the *alcaldía* had, since time immemorial, been in the hands of the house of Lazcano, until the death of Martín López de Lazcano. The king then conceded the baton to Fortuño de Nuncibay, who ceded his rights to the councils of the mayoralty, authorizing them to appoint m mayors annually to administer both civil and criminal justice. Seeing this, the Brotherhood of Gipuzkoa (Hermandad de Guipúzcoa), meeting in a council session in Vergara in 1460, requested of King Enrique IV that he approve Fortuño de Nuncibay's withdrawal and authorize the councils of the mayoralty to appoint their mayors and have a council, common coffers, and any seal they wanted. Therefore, on March 12, 1461 and from Segovia, Enrique IV approved Nuncibay's withdrawal and conceded them what they had asked for, extending the fuero de San Sebastián to the *alcaldía*: "*E demás d'esto es mi merced e voluntad que el dicho concejo e alcaldía e todos los vecinos e moradores de ella sean aforados e vivan e se rijan por el fuero de la villa de San Sebastián, que es de la dicha Provincia de Guipúzcoa, e viva e rija otrosí por los usos e costumbres d'ella segund que los han en la dicha villa de Sant Sebastián.*"[42] The Catholic monarchs confirmed this favor in Segovia, on September 15, 1476.[43]

---

41   Ibid., 385.
42   See under "Arería" in appendix to ibid., 673.
43   Ibid., 52.

The Alcaldía Mayor *of Sayaz*

It was composed of the villages of Aya (head of the *alcaldía*), Beizama, Goyaz, Regil, and Vidania. And although Aya was also a coastal village, it did not receive the San Sebastian fuero in the Middle Ages.

Known as the "five mountain villages," it was governed by different *alcaldes mayores* appointed by the king until Queen Juana conceded the baton of the *alcaldía* to Francisco Pérez de Idiaquez, a resident of Azcoitia (Valladolid, May 2, 1545).

His residence at court meant that the five mountain villages were governed by *tenientes* in civil and criminal matters. The lack of administration and the subsequent complaints of people meant that, when Francisco Pérez renounced the baton, in 1563 the general councils meeting in Cestona asked the king for permission to authorize their villages to appoint their mayors. Therefore, from Monzón (Aragon), on December 23, 1563 Felipe II granted the privilege of the baton of the *alcaldía* to its own villages, and the San Sebastian fuero: "And likewise it is our wish that the said council and mayoralty and all the residents and inhabitants there should be given the fuero and should live and be governed by the Fuero of the *villa* of San Sebastian, in said province."[44]

The Alcaldía Mayor *of Aiztondo*

Integrated by Asteasu (its head), with Larraul and Soravilla, they also came to form part of Astigarraga itself without Murguia and Urnieta (in that part that did not have a neighborly agreement with San Sebastian or Hernani, especially the area of Lasarte).

In the sixteenth century the baton of the *alcaldía* was in the hands of Don Juan de Borja. On his death in 1608, seeing that the towns lacked justuce and faced with the attempts of Asteasu to become their head, Urnieta and Astigarraga began legal action in the royal council. But the king appointed to the post of *alcalde mayor* Don Francisco de Borja y Aragón, the Prince of Esquilache (son of Don Juan), who tried to sell the baton in 1612 for 2,000

---

44   See under "Sayaz" in appendix to ibid., 718.

ducados. Before the proposed purchase presented by Urnieta and Astigarraga, San Sebastian and Hernani offered 3,000. But when Don Francisco left for the Americas to become Viceroy of Peru, without taking up the baton, the matter was left hanging. On his death, the general council, meeting in Tolosa in 1651, in the name of the towns of the *alcaldía*, requested the handing over of the baton to them. On December 22, 1659, from Madrid, Felipe IV conceded the privilege of the baton to the *alcaldía*, ordering that: "in the selection and appointment you may make of the said baton you must observe and maintain the same form that is observed and maintained in the other valleys and councils of the said province, to which I have done the favor of this baton, without this being able to change in any way in any time."[45]

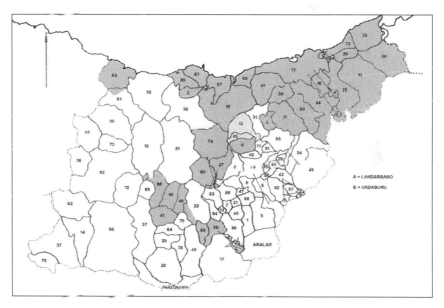

Map 4. T
he Fuero of San Sebastian in Gipuzkoa in the Sixteenth Century

---

45   See under "Aiztondo" in appendix to ibid., 670.

There is no mention on this occasion of the Fuero of San Sebastian being awarded, but its circumstances were very special. Urnieta and Astigarraga were within the limits of influence of the fuero granted to San Sebastian in 1180. Larraul and Soravilla were very small settlements and subjected to the major influence of Asteasu. And we should not forget that Asteasu, although it joined Tolosa in 1386, soon split away from it, achieving, it would seem, the category of *villa* (we do not know when), and has been termed "a noble and loyal *villa*" for a long time.

Oyarzun Valley, apparently with Alfonso VIII, but documented in 1453; *Alcaldía Mayor* of Arería in 1461; *Alcaldía Mayor* of Sayaz in 1563.

The Validity and Modernity of the Fuero of San Sebastian in the Sixteenth Century

As regards the Fuero of San Sebastian, there were early material losses as a result of the fire suffered in 1397.[46] Despite that, we know the content of the fuero through several copies that have come down to us since its confirmation by Alfonso VIII in 1202.[47] The analyses of José Luis Banús y Aguirre, José Mª Lacarra, Ángel J. Martín Duque, and José Luis de Orella coincide with that of Serapio Múgica in stating that it was composed of its own articles, added to articles taken from the Fuero of Estella (1090) and that of Jaca (1063).

They do not however agree on how many there were in total, since while the others mention forty, Múgica counts thirty-seven (although he doubts Sancho VI conceded so many), of which twenty-five were linked to the Fuero of Estella, including thirteen of which that came from Jaca via Estella.[48] He even cites José de Yanguas y Miranda, who states that, when arriving at article 35,

---

46 According to Banús y Aguirre, *El Fuero de San Sebastián*, 63.
47 When the original copy was lost to the fire, Alfonso VIII's confirmation came to serve as the original. See Serapio Múgica, "Donación a Leire. Orígenes de San Sebastián. Iglesias de Santa María, San Vicente y San Sebastián," *Revista Internacional de Estudios Vascos* 26 (1935), 393–422.
48 Ibid.

which begins with "*Omnis troselus,*" and through "*et si hospes*" in the same chapter, "it seems, according to its different language, that it was inserted at a later time, as happened in many other fueros."[49] What is more, speaking about the fuero, Gabriel de Henao himself remarked that, "in this instrument the old Fueros of San Sebastian came to be confirmed and many other very favorable ones were added, and laws were made for businesses, contracts, etc."[50]

According to the above-mentioned authors, there are two clearly defined parts in the composition of the fuero: articles making up the new statute of freedoms and liberties, which derives, with little variation, from the Fuero of Estella (1090), which in turn came, with little variation, from that awarded to Jaca in 1063; and an original set of articles, which makes up a code of maritime law according to *usus mercatorum* in the Atlantic area of the time.

The articles that make it up do not have, however, any explanatory structure, and their content can be divided according to the following general subjects: concession of royal possessions; concession of a legal status of freedoms and liberties to its settlers; fiscal privileges; private law, especially in inheritance matters of possessions; public and administrative civil law; procedural law; penal law; and maritime law.

And while its original content served to change the politico-juridical status of a community, like all the other fueros that were disseminated during the Early and Late Middle Ages throughout the Kingdom of Castile, in the case of the Fuero of San Sebastian its validity did not end, as was the case with other localities and *villas*, despite the new law they were producing by means of municipal bylaws; rather, it continued to be valid until at least (according to documents) the seventeenth century.

The Fuero of San Sebastian was a living fuero that was cited frequently in legal action among the people who had been

---

49   José Yanguas y Miranda, *Diccionario de antigüedades del Reino de Navarra*, vol. 3 (Pamplona, 1840), 314.

50   Gabriel de Henao, *Averiguaciones de las antiguedades de Cantabria: endereçadas principalmente a descubrir las de Guipuzcoa, Vizcaya y Alaba, prouincias contenidas en ella*, vol. 5 (Salamanca: por Eugenio Antonio Garcia, 1689), 333.

granted the privilege in inheritance matters, even in the sixteenth and seventeenth centuries. The historical context in which it was cited was always a dispute over the inheritance of possessions, an institution included in the San Sebastian fuero, and that did not need to be confirmed in charters awarded and similar documents in places with this fuero, in that it was inherent to the fuero. This was not the case with those towns that had the Fuero of Logroño-Vitoria, whose awarded charters had to confirm clearly the inheritance return.[51] That institution, regulated so early on in the fuero, said clearly:

> *De homine mortuo*
>
> *Si quis moritur et non fecerit testamentum ad obitum mortis et rremanserint parui filii et mater ducit alium maritum, parentes filiorum possunt partire et cognoscere partem filiorum patris et dare fermens et accipere. Et sy mater boluerit tenere fillos suos cum honore et habere debet dare mater bonas fidanças parentibus filliorum, quod quando filii peruenerint ad perfectam hetatem rreddat illis predictum honorem et haberem.*
>
> *Et sy filii interim obiuntur, illam hereditatem et honorem et hauere debet tornare vnde venit parentibus suis.*

The application of that inheritance disposition in the fuero, then, would be that which kept it alive and the reason it was cited and copied as a document of proof in different lawsuits that were settled in courts regarding the return of granted or core possessions.

As Luis Miguel Díez de Salazar pointed out in 1980,[52] this inheritance tradition implied the existence of a consanguineous relative and granted or core possessions (properties) that had been owned by a common ancestor. Under the principle that, "the core returns to the core and the root to the root," on the death of a childless owner (or on the death of his children without making a will or before coming of age to make a will), the possessions of

---

51 Luis Miguel Díez de Salazar Fernández, "Un nuevo manuscrito del Fuero de San Sebastián," in *Congreso: El fuero de San Sebastián y su época (San Sebastián 19–23 de enero de 1981) / Donostiako forua eta bere garaia (Donostia, 1981ko urtarrilaren 19tik 23ra)* (San Sebastián: Eusko Ikaskuntza / Sociedad de Estudios Vascos, 1982), 533.

52 Luis Miguel Díez de Salazar Fernández, "Vigencia y aplicación del principio de la troncalidad de bienes según el Fuero de San Sebastián," *Boletín de Estudios Históricos sobre San Sebastián* 14 (1980), 275–95.

the deceased had to be returned to his family of origin without his surviving spouse being able to inherit (as was the case in Castilian law). Parents did not pass down to their children, but instead possessions were simply returned to the core family.

This is what happened in the lawsuit settled before the *corregidor* Gómez de la Puerta in 1581, between María López de Ambulodi and Tomás de Sarasa, residents of Oyarzun, who were disputing the possessions of their common ancestor Joanes de Sarasa.[53] In order to defend her right, María López requested of the *corregidor* the transfer of the fuero so that, "*los asçendientes no suçedan a los deçendientes avintestato, sino que buelban los bienes al tronco.*" As such, on February 11, 1581 in San Sebastian (where the trial was being held), the *corregidor* ordered the scribe of the *villa*, Marcos de Garay, to copy the copy made by the scribe Juan Bono de Tolosa on December 22, 1552.[54]

And the same thing happened in 1632 in the legal action carried out by the brothers Juanes and Miguel de Echeverría against their widowed brother-in-law Juanes de Leguía the older, which demanded the restitution to the blood family of the possessions and inheritance of his son (and their nephew), Juanes de Leguía the younger, according to a clause in the Fuero of San Sebastian.[55] And there are numerous examples of inheritance return within the jurisdiction of the *corregidor* until well into the eighteenth century.

Texts of the Fuero of San Sebastian

I should point out that not all the published copies of the Fuero of San Sebastian are exactly the same. The loss of the original and attempts to reconstruct it have even given rise to a series of variants, sometimes important on account of the growing distance between them and the original. They are errors in the reading and transcription, printing errors, or different orthographic variants;

---

53 AGG-GAO CO ECI, 425 (a fols. 99 vto.-113 vto. Inserted in the fuero).
54 According to the author, in another hand, and in its first folio, it is recorded that, "this privilege is from the *villa* of San Sebastian, and not from the valley [of Oyarzun] . . . this valley has the privilege of this fuero; especially since the witnesses of . . . the said Oyarzun Valley do not have it or appear to." In Díez de Salazar Fernández, "Un nuevo manuscrito del Fuero de San Sebastián," 533–34.
55 AGG-GAO CO LCI 830.

or they may change the meaning of or contradict dispositions in the texts.

The copies that were kept in the municipal archive of San Sebastian before 1813 should have been more reliable, but it does not seem that this was the case. Indeed, for Marichalar and Manrique, the fuero published in the Royal History Academy's dictionary by Don Joaquín de Camino y Orella is "extremely ruined by the errors of copyists and printers."[56] And within its pages one notes the omissions of several words and even whole sentences, "on account, surely, of not having taken sufficient care in correcting printing proofs."[57]

I offer here a list of the texts of the fuero that I have found in manuscript or printed form, in Latin, Spanish, or Basque, so that researchers can appreciate for themselves the variants that different copyists or authors have introduced into the original text.

Manuscripts

Medieval Era

1. The confirmation of Juan II of the Fuero of San Sebastian to the *villa* of Guetaria (Simancas, July 12, 1426), preserved in the library of the Royal History Society, Salvá Collection, 9-22-7, 4307. Original parchment of 800x670 mm. Made up of:

> 1. The protocol of the confirmation of Juan II.
>
> 2. The protocol of the confirmation of Juan I.
>
> 3. The protocol of the confirmation of Alfonso XI.
>
> 4. The concession of the Fuero of San Sebastian made by Alfonso VIII to the *villa* of Guetaria (San Sebastian, September 1, 1209).
>
> *3 bis*: the regulation and eschatocol of the confirmation of Alfonso XI (Burgos, April 11, 1332).

---

56 Marichalar and Manrique, *Historia de la Legislación*, vol. 8, *Fueros de Navarra, Vizcaya, Guipúzcoa y Álava*, 354.
57 Múgica, "Donación a Leire," 410.

5. The copy of the fuero de San Sebastian granted by Sancho VI (1180).

6. And of the confirmation of Alfonso VIII in 1202.

2 bis: the regulation and eschatocol of the confirmatory rounded privilege of Juan I (Burgos, November 15, 1379).

7. The royal charter (*albalá*) of Juan II ordering the expediting of the confirmation (September 20, 1424).

And *1 bis*: the regulation and eschatocol of the confirmation of Juan II (Simancas, July 12, 1426).

It appears that this was used by Juan Antonio Llorente, and that Pablo de Gorosabel followed him. It would be used for comparison with the following version by José Mª Lacarra and Ángel J. Martín Duque.

2. Copy done on September 26, 1474 by the scribe from Tolosa, Juan de Sorola, and preserved in a lawsuit of 1543 that Juan de Zaldivar brought against Juan de Ayerdi and Clara de Luscando in the Gipuzkoan *corregimiento* (jurisdiction of the *corregidor*), kept in AGG-GAO CO LCI, 4. Inserted in the process at fols. 72 vto.–76 rº. It is made up of:

1. Introductory clauses of the scribe Sorola.

2. Protocol of the confirmation of Enrique IV.

3. Protocol of the confirmation of Enrique III.

4. Introductory clauses of the copy ordered by Doctor Gonzalo Moro and authorized by the scribe Alfonso Fernández of Oviedo.

5. Copy of the fuero de San Sebastian granted by Sancho VI (1180), undersigning of Gonzalo Moro.

6. Confirmation of Alfonso VIII (August 16, 1202).

4 bis: final clauses of the copy prepared by Gonzalo Moro (Guetaria, February 23, 1396).

7. The royal charter (*albalá*) of Enrique III ordering the expediting of the confirmation (September 29, 1402).

8. The ruling of Chancellor Domingo Fernández de Candamo ordering the drafting of the confirmation (no date).

3 bis: the regulation and eschatocol of the confirmatory rounded privilege of Enrique III (Valladolid, April 14, 1403).

2 bis: the regulation and eschatocol of the confirmatory rounded privilege of Enrique IV (Medina del Campo, June 15, 1403).

And *1 bis*: the final clauses of the copy of Juan de Sorola (San Sebastian, September 26, 1474).

Published by Jesús Mª de Leizaola in 1935, this is the basis of the study and edition of the fuero by José Luis Banús y Aguirre, who inserted its images in the book. It was used as a contrast with the previous text by José Mª Lacarra and Ángel J. Martín Duque.

Modern Era: Sixteenth Century

1. Copy made by the scribe Juan Bono de Tolosa on December 22, 1552 (today lost), the basis of many later copies.

2. Copy by the scribe Marcos de Garay, on the orders of the *corregidor* Gómez de la Puerta, on February 11, 1581, in the lawsuit between María López de Ambulodi and Tomás de Sarasa, residents of Oyarzun, who were disputing the possessions of their common forebear Joanes de Sarasa. It is in AGG-GAO ECI, 425 (at fols. 99 vto.–113 vto), which must have been copied from the copy of the scribe Juan Bono de Tolosa on December 22, 1552.

This was published by Luis MiguelDíez de Salazar Fernández.

Modern Era: Seventeenth Century

1. Copy authorized by the scribe of Fuenterrabia Esteban de Lesaca on July 24, 1632, from the copy (today lost) done by

the scribe Juan Bono de Tolosa (San Sebastian, December 22, 1552) of the confirmation of Enrique IV in 1457 to Fuenterrabia, in the lawsuit concerning Juanes and Miguel de Echeverria against Juanes de Leguía. It is in AGG-GAO CO LCI, 830, fols. 153 r°–159 vto. (at fols. 147–172 with the copy of 1474).

2. Copy authorized by the scribe of Fuenterrabia Martín Sanz de Laborda on March 27, 1653, in the lawsuit concerning Gabriel de Astarbe and María de Ugarte against Pedro de Candia. It only includes the text of the fuero and the concession of Alfonso VIII to the *villa* (Palencia, April 19, 1203). It is in AGG-GAO CO LCI, 1250, at fols. 80 r°–83 vto. (on the 1474 copy of Sorola).

Modern Era: Eighteenth Century

1. Simple copy of "Privilegio de fundación de la ciudad de San Sebastián, en latín," kept in the Municipal Archive of San Sebastian, B/I/4/I/I (followed by José Antonio Camino y Orella).

2. Simple copy of "Confirmación del privilegio de la refundación de la villa de San Sebastián," kept in the Municipal Archive of San Sebastian, B/I/4/I/2 (which is a copy of that which features in the *libro becerro* (code book) of the city, now disappeared and which must have been published by the Royal History Academy in its dictionary, and followed by Mariano de Zuaznabar and José Yanguas y Miranda).

3. Copy by the master Brother Lorenzo Frías of the confirmation of the fuero in favor of Guetaria by Juan II in 1424. In the library of the Royal History Academy, ms. 9-22-7, fols. 52–60.

4. Copy of the copy for Fuenterrabia by the scribe Juan Bono de Tolosa (San Sebastian, December 22, 1552). In the library of the Royal History Academy, Vargas Ponce Collection, Volume 25, fols. 22–41. There it states that, "It

exists in the first *libro becerro* in the archive in Irun; it was and is its first document, although it is on paper and a copy, even if authorized."

5. Copy of the translation of the fuero by the *corregidor* Don Pedro Cano y Mucientes, authorized by the scribe Juan Bautista de Landa on July 8, 1757. In the library of the Royal History Academy, Vargas Ponce Collection, Volume 24, in 8 fols. Under the title of "Copia traducida del latín al castellano del real priuilegio expedido por el señor Rey Don Sancho para la refundación de la Muy Noble y Muy Leal Ciudad de San Sevastián, y testimonio de las confirmaciones reales posteriors." Cited by Juan Ignacio Gamón, *Noticias Históricas de Rentería* (San Sebastián: Nueva Editorial, 1930), 224.

Published Works

Anabitarte, Baldomero. *Colección de documentos históricos del Archivo Municipal de San Sebastián (1200–1813)*. San Sebastián: Ayuntamiento, 1895. It includes a flawed version of the fuero in Spanish, 7–15.

Ayerbe Iribar, Mª Rosa. *Fuentes normativas y documentales del País Vasco*. At https://ocw.ehu.eus/course/view.php?id=57.

Banús y Aguirre, José Luis. *El Fuero de San Sebastián*. San Sebastián: Ayuntamiento, 1963. 259 pp + 18 sheets. Following the copy of Juan de Sorola on September 26, 1474. Latin and Spanish, 79–110.

Basabe Martín, Alberto. "Estudio lingüístico del Fuero de San Sebastián." In *Congreso: El fuero de San Sebastián y su época (San Sebastián 19–23 de enero de 1981) / Donostiako forua eta bere garaia (Donostia, 1981ko urtarrilaren 19tik 23ra)*. San Sebastián: Eusko Ikaskuntza / Sociedad de Estudios Vascos, 1982. Translation into Spanish, 27–68.

Camino y Orella, José Antonio de. "Historia civil-diplomática-eclesiástica, antigua y moderna de la ciudad de San Sebastián." *Euskal-Erria* 17 (1887): 377–79, 444–46, and 569–71; and 18 (1888): 27–28 and 41–45.

Diccionario Auñamendi. Under "San Sebastián." Taking the Latin transcription of Ángel J. Martín Duque and the Spanish translation of Alberto Basabe, in the published proceedings of the conference "El fuero de San Sebastián y su época," 333–36.

Echegaray, Carmelo de. *Fuero de repoblación de San Sebastián, concedido por Don Sancho VI el Sabio (Rey de Navarra). Trabajo sobre ese tema presentado al Concurso abierto por la Comisión Municipal de Fiestas Euskaras de San Sebastián el año 1906 por Don Carmelo de Echegaray, Cronista de las Provincias Vascongadas.* San Sebastián: Sociedad Española de Papelería, 1909. 67 pp. In Basque, 31–47 and in Spanish, 49–69. The Basque text is included in the *Revista Internacional de Estudios Vascos* (RIEV) II (1908): 111–87.

Gorosabel, Pablo de. *Diccionario histórico-geográfico-descriptivo de los pueblos, valles, partidos, alcaldías y uniones de Guipúzcoa, con un apéndice de cartas-pueblas y otros documentos importantes.* Tolosa, 1862. The fuero is at fols. 730–741; Bilbao: La Gran Enciclopedia Vasca, 1972. 734 pp. At 707–14. It seems to follow Juan Antonio Llorente.

Lacarra de Miguel, José María, and Ángel J. Martín Duque. *Fueros de Navarra. 1. Fueros derivados de Jaca. I. Estella-San Sebastián.* Pamplona: Diputación Foral de Navarra, 1969. 364 pp + 20 sheets. At 269–86, comparison of the confirmation of Juan II to the *villa* of Guetaria of the fuero in 1426, with the copy by Juan de Sorola in 1474.

Llorente, Juan Antonio. *Noticias históricas de las tres provincias vascongadas: Álava, Guipúzcoa y Vizcaya.* Madrid: 1808. The fuero is included in vol. 8, 244–54. It appears to follow the confirmation of Juan II of the fuero to Guetaria in 1426.

Marichalar, Amalio, and Cayetano Manrique. *Historia de la Legislación y recitaciones del Derecho Civil de España.* Volume 8. *Fueros de Navarra, Vizcaya, Guipúzcoa y Álava.* Madrid: Impr. Gasset-Loma, 1868. 682 pp. At 354–61. In note 1, from a text kept in the San Sebastian archive, "extremely ruined by the errors of copyists and printers."

Martín Duque, Ángel J. "El Fuero de San Sebastián. Tradición manuscrita y edición crítica." In *Congreso: El fuero de San Sebastián y su época (San Sebastián 19–23 de enero de 1981) / Donostiako forua eta bere garaia (Donostia, 1981ko urtarrilaren 19tik 23ra).* San Sebastián: Eusko Ikaskuntza / Sociedad de Estudios Vascos, 1982. At 3–25, comparison of the confirmation of Juan II to the *villa* of Guetaria of the fuero in 1426, with the copy of the fuero (in the confirmation of Enrique IV in 1457) by Juan de Sorola, scribe of Tolosa, in 1474.

Real Academia de la Historia. *Diccionario histórico-geográfico-histórico de España. Sección I, comprehende el reyno de Navarra, señorío de Vizcaya y provincias de Álava y Guipúzcoa.* 2 volumes. Madrid: Real Academia de la Historia, 1802. In volume 2, 541–57.

Yanguas y Miranda, José. *Diccionario de antigüedades del Reino de Navarra.* 3 volumes. Pamplona, 1840; plus one addition, Pamplona, 1843. In volume 3, 302–16; and in vol. 3, Pamplona: Institución Príncipe de Viana , 1964, 19–29.

Zuaznabar, José María. *Ensayo histórico-crítico sobre la legislación de Navarra.* 4 volumes. San Sebastián: Imprenta de Ignacio Ramon Baroja, 1827. In vol. 2, 205–15.

Appendix

Towns included in the maps

1.   Abalcisqueta

2.   Aduna

3.   Aizarnazabal

4.   Albiztur

5.   Alegría de Oria

6.   Alquiza

7.   Alzaga

8.   Alzo

9.   Amézqueta

10.   Andoain

11.   Anoeta

12.   Anzuola

13.   Arama

14.   Arechavaleta

15.   Astuasu

16.   Astigarraga

17.   Ataun

18.   Aya

19.   Azpeitia

20.   Azcoitia

21.   Baliarrain

22.   Beasain

23.   Beizama

24.   Belaunza

25. Berástegui
26. Berrobi
27. Bidegoya (Vidania-Goyaz)
28. Cegama
29. Cerain
30. Cestona
31. Cizurquil
32. Deva
33. Eibar
34. Elduayen
35. Elgoibar
36. Elgueta
37. Escoriaza
38. Ezquioga
39. Fuenterrabia
40. Gainza
41. Gaviria
42. Gaztelu
43. Guetaria
44. Hernani
45. Hernialñde
46. Ibarra
47. Icazteguieta
48. Ichaso
49. Idiazabal
50. Irun
51. Irura

52. Isasondo

53. Larraul

54. Lasarte-Oria

55. Lazcano

56. Leaburu

57. Legazpia

58. Legorreta

59. Lezo

60. Lizarza

61. Mendaro

62. Mondragón

63. Motrico

64. Mutiloa

65. Olaberria

66. Oñate

67. Oreja

68. Orendain

69. Orio

70. Ormáiztegui

71. Oyarzun

72. Pasajes

73. Placencia

74. Régil

75. Rentería

76. Salinas de Léniz

77. San Sebastian

78. Segura

79.   Tolosa

80.   Urnieta

81.   Usurbil

82.   Vergara

83.   Villabona

84.   Villafranca de Oria-Ordizia

85.   Villarreal de Urrechua

86.   Zaldivia

87.   Zarauz

88.   Zumarraga

89.   Zumaya

BIBLIOGRAPHY

Arizaga Bolumburu, Beatriz. "Las villas guipuzcoanas que reciben el Fuero de San Sebastián: modos de vida de sus habitantes." In *Congreso: El fuero de San Sebastián y su época (San Sebastián 19–23 de enero de 1981) / Donostiako forua eta bere garaia (Donostia, 1981ko urtarrilaren 19tik 23ra)*. San Sebastián: Eusko Ikaskuntza / Sociedad de Estudios Vascos, 1982.

Ayerbe Iribar, Mª Rosa. *El Monasterio Dominico de San Pedro González Telmo (San Sebastián). De centro religioso a centro cultural y museístico de primer orden de la ciudad*. San Sebastián: Grupo Doctor Camino de Historia Donostiarra; Kutxa Fundazioa, 2012.

———. *Urnieta, de Tierra a Villazgo (1402–1615)*. Urnieta: Urnietako Udala/Ayuntamiento de Urnieta, 2015.

Ayerbe Iribar, Mª Rosa, and Luis Miguel Díez de Salazar Fernández. *Andoain, de Tierra a Villazgo (1379–1615). Un caso modélico de preautonomía municipal en Gipuzkoa*. Andoain: Ayuntamiento "Leyçaur, 0", 1996.

Banús y Aguirre, José Luis. "El límite oriental de San Sebastián y el Puerto de Pasajes." In *"Homenaje a Don Julio de Urquijo" ofrecido por la Real Sociedad Vancongada de los Amigos del País*. Volume 3. San Sebastián: Real Sociedad Vascongada de Amigos del País, 1950.

————. *El Fuero de San Sebastián*. San Sebastián: Ayuntamiento de San Sebastián, 1963.

————. *El Archivo Quemado. Inventarios antiguos y acervo documental de la M.N. y M.L. Ciudad de San Sebastián antes de la destrucción de 1813*. San Sebastián: Grupo Doctor Camino de Historia Donostiarra; Caja de Ahorros Municipal de San Sebastián, 1986.

Barrena Osoro, Elena. "El Fuero de Vitoria en la villa de Deva. Aparentes contradicciones geopolíticas." In *Congreso: El fuero de San Sebastián y su época (San Sebastián 19–23 de enero de 1981) / Donostiako forua eta bere garaia (Donostia, 1981ko urtarrilaren 19tik 23ra)*. San Sebastián: Eusko Ikaskuntza / Sociedad de Estudios Vascos, 1982.

Camino y Orella, José Antonio de. "Historia civil-diplomática-eclesiástica, antigua y moderna de la ciudad de San Sebastián." *Euskal-Erria* 17 (1887): 377–79, 444–46, and 569–71; and 18 (1888): 27–28 and 41–45.

Colección de documentos inéditos para la historia de Guipúzcoa. Volume 2. San Sebastián: Diputación Provincial, 1958.

Díez de Salazar Fernández, Luis Miguel. "Vigencia y aplicación del principio de la troncalidad de bienes según el Fuero de San Sebastián." *Boletín de Estudios Históricos sobre San Sebastián* 14 (1980): 275–295.

————. "Un nuevo manuscrito del Fuero de San Sebastián." In *Congreso: El fuero de San Sebastián y su época (San Sebastián 19–23 de enero de 1981) / Donostiako forua eta bere garaia (Donostia, 1981ko urtarrilaren 19tik 23ra)*. San Sebastián: Eusko Ikaskuntza / Sociedad de Estudios Vascos, 1982.

————. "La vecindad de Hernani (1379–1429)." *Anuario de Estudios Medievales* 18 (1988): 367–82.

Gamón, Juan Igancio. *Noticias Históricas de Rentería.* San Sebastián: Nueva Editorial, 1930.

Gorosabel, Pablo de. *Diccionario histórico-geográfico-descriptivo de los pueblos, valles, partidos, alcaldías y uniones de Guipúzcoa, con un apéndice de cartas-pueblas y otros documentos importantes.* Tolosa, 1862; Bilbao: La Gran Enciclopedia Vasca, 1972.

Henao, Gabriel de. *Averiguaciones de las antiguedades de Cantabria: enderezadas principalmente a descubrir las de Guipuzcoa, Vizcaya y Alaba, prouincias contenidas en ella.* Salamanca: por Eugenio Antonio Garcia, 1689.

Marichalar, Amalio, and Cayetano Manrique. *Historia de la Legislación y recitaciones del Derecho Civil de España.* Volume 8. *Fueros de Navarra, Vizcaya, Guipúzcoa y Álava.* Madrid: Impr. Gasset-Loma, 1868.

Martínez Díez, Gonzalo. *Alfonso VIII, rey de Castilla y Toledo (1158–1214).* Burgos: La Olmeda, 1995.

Martínez Díez, Gonzalo, Felix J. Martínez Llorente, and Emiliano González Díez. *Colección de documentos medievales de las villas guipuzcoanas (1200–1369).* Donostia-San Sebastián: Juntas Generales de Gipuzkoa; Diputación Foral de Gipuzkoa, 1991.

Múgica, Serapio. "Donación a Leire. Orígenes de San Sebastián. Iglesias de Santa María, San Vicente y San Sebastián." *Revista Internacional de Estudios Vascos* 26 (1935): 393–422.

Murugarren Zamora, Luis. *Hernani y su historia e instituciones.* San Sebastián: Caja de Ahorros Municipal, 1970.

Silván, Leandro. *El término municipal de San Sebastián: su evolución histórica.* San Sebastián: Grupo Doctor Camino de Historia Donostiarra, 1971.

Yanguas y Miranda, José. *Diccionario de antigüedades del Reino de Navarra.* 3 volumes. Pamplona, 1840; plus one addition, Pamplona, 1843.

Chapter 10

The Development of Maritime Law Following the Fuero of San Sebastian

Margarita Serna Vallejo[1]

From the twelfth century on, coinciding with the concession of the fuero and its immediate growth, the *villa* of San Sebastian was incorporated into the Atlantic maritime tradition, as attested to by numerous testimonies that document the wishes of its residents and authorities to consolidate and prolong relations with the men and the places of the rest of the European Atlantic coastline. In this sense, it is sufficiently illustrative to recall the testimonies that tell of the presence of the same vessels in the port of San Sebastian and in other Atlantic port enclaves; of the mixed composition of the crews that were made up, mostly, of individuals from different points on the Atlantic coast, including those from San Sebastian; of the participation of Gipuzkoa in signing various good relations treaties, also known as commercial exchanges (*conversas comerciales*), with the French province of Labourd (Lapurdi) and the *Cuatro Villas de la Costa* (four coastal *villas*); and the settlement of a Gascon

1   This work is part of the task of a national project, "Culturas urbanas en la España Moderna: policía, gobernanza e imaginarios (siglos XVI–XIX)," reference no. HAR2015-64014-C3-1-R, financed by the Ministry of the Economy and Competitiveness, and the European project "Rebellion and Resistance in the Iberian Empires, 16th–19th centuries," which has received financing from the European Union Horizon 2020 research and innovation program by virtue of the grant agreement Marie Skłodowska-Curie No 778076.

population from Baiona, closely connected to the maritime world and its activities, in San Sebastian.

And in the context of this Atlantic maritime tradition, so tied to the history of San Sebastian, one must call attention to the prominent place of law in all this, once the legal norms stemming from this tradition came to shape the fundamentally commercial and fishing maritime activities practiced on the European Atlantic coast by its navigators. This allows us to speak of the existence of Atlantic maritime law in the medieval and modern eras.

At the heart of this law, which served to organize the commercial and fishing activities of seafarers on the European Atlantic coasts, including an important number of residents of San Sebastian, different kinds of norms were included of distinct origins and reach. Here I am interested in two main areas: on the one hand, the juridical body that was common to all Atlantic seafarers in that it was a consuetudinary-based law created by these same people to keep pace with the practice of maritime activities, and in whose formation there was no participation of either jurists or the heads of political power; and on the other, the set of dispositions of a municipal and/or corporate nature elaborated by the municipal governments of the coastal *villas* and by distinct professional corporations, such as the important maritime guilds of the Cantabrian corniche, with a fundamentally local territorial application and, therefore, considerably more limited than that of the previous area.

What did not exist in the Middle Ages and for most of the Modern Era were national maritime laws or those specifically pertaining to each of the kingdoms bathed by the Atlantic, because the political leaders of France, England, Castile, and the rest of the national bodies took considerable time in demonstrating a real interest in what was happening at sea and in legislating on maritime matters. Proof of that is that we understand the first important national maritime legislation in Europe to be the French Maritime Ordinance of 1681. Prior to that, European monarchs had restricted themselves to pronouncing dispositions with maritime content in an isolated casuistic manner and, what is more, only once in a while, which prevented any suggestion of the existence of maritime laws specific to the European nations prior to 1681.[2]

The two expressions of maritime law originating in the medieval period on European coasts mentioned above applied in San Sebastian following the concession of its fuero in 1180.[3] Thus, commercial and fishing practice on the part of San Sebastian seafarers was organized and, at the same time, by that maritime law common to all navigators on the European Atlantic coasts and by the maritime law created by the council of the *villa* and by the Santa Catalina and San Pedro guilds, two of the guilds of seafarers, fishermen, and navigators established on the coasts of Bizkaia and Gipuzkoa in the Middle Ages.[4]

The *Rôles d'Oléron* and the Fuero of San Sebastian

The most important source of maritime law common to Atlantic seafarers was the custom stemming from commercial and fishing practice itself, a consuetudinary system that was partially written down in the mid-thirteenth century, giving rise to the text known as the *Rôles d'Oléron* or *Fuero de Layron* in Spanish.[5] This is a work that we should clearly pay some attention to after authors like José Ángel García de Cortázar, José Luis Orella Unzué, and Soledad Tena García link it to the maritime content of the San Sebastian foral text.

However, I believe that the relationship these authors establish between both texts is not fully accurate in some of their more

2   On the French ordinance, see Margarita Serna Vallejo, "La Ordenanza francesa de la marina de 1681unificación, refundición y fraccionamiento del derecho marítimo en Europa," *Anuario de Historia del Derecho* 78–79 (2008–2009), 233–60.

3   Here I use the edition of the fuero published in José Luis Banús y Aguirre, *El Fuero de San Sebastián* (San Sebastián: Ayuntamiento de San Sebastián, 1963), 79–110.

4   Besides works published on different Basque maritime guilds, there is a general study of these institutions in Josu Iñaki Erkoreka Gervasio, *Análisis histórico-institucional de las cofradías de mareantes del País Vasco* (Vitoria-Gasteiz: Servicio Central de Publicaciones del Gobierno Vasco, 1991) and Ernesto García Fernández, "Las cofradías de mercaderes, mareantes y pescadores vascos (siglos XIV a XVI)," in *Ciudades y villas portuarias del Atlántico en la Edad Media. Nájera, Encuentros Internacionales del Medievo: Nájera, 27–30 de julio 2004*, ed. Beatriz Arízaga Bolumburu and Jesús Ángel Solórzano Tellechea (Logroño: Instituto de Estudios Riojanos, 2005), 257–94.

5   On this text, see Margarita Serna Vallejo, *Los Rôles d'Oléron. El coutumier marítimo del Atlántico y del Báltico de Época medieval y moderna* (Santander: Centro de Estudios Montañeses, 2004).

debatable, from my point of view, statements. Specifically, they point out, on the one hand, that in the Fuero of San Sebastian there are dispositions taken from or based on the *Rôles d'Oléron*. And, on the other, they contend that this work is merely a collection of consuetudinary-based sentences elaborated in the late eleventh century.[6] Yet why do I not share these views?

The chapters in the Fuero of San Sebastian contain, in effect, as García de Cortázar points out, an important number of previsions concerning business activity.[7] However, I believe that not all of them enter into the concept of maritime law; and that, despite the fact that commercial traffic is understood mainly in the San Sebastian text as, precisely, seaborne commerce.

If one starts from the basis of considering maritime law as a set of already consuetudinary and legal norms that govern the relations that are established among all of those involved in maritime fishing and commercial voyages, there should be no place in this concept for the previsions included in the Fuero of San Sebastian that concern terrestrial commerce exclusively; those that can be considered common to both terrestrial and maritime commercial traffic; and also those that fall within the orbit of what today would be considered tax or fiscal law and whose objective was to levy commercial exchanges with different taxes or, on the contrary, exempt them from some levies.

---

6   See José Ángel García de Cortázar, "Una villa mercantil. 1180–1516," in *Historia de Donostia-San Sebastián*, ed. Miguel Artola (San Sebastián: Editorial Nerea, 2004), 22; José Luis Orella Unzué, "Estudio jurídico comparativo de los Fueros de San Sebastián, Estella, Vitoria y Logroño," in *Congreso: El fuero de San Sebastián y su época (San Sebastián 19–23 de enero de 1981) / Donostiako forua eta bere garaia (Donostia, 1981ko urtarrilaren 19tik 23ra)* (San Sebastián: Eusko Ikaskuntza / Sociedad de Estudios Vascos, 1982), 275; José Luis Orella Unzué, "El Fuero de San Sebastián y su entorno histórico," in *Geografía e Historia de Donostia-San Sebastián*, ed. Juan Antonio Sáez and Javier Gómez Piñeiro (San Sebastián: Ingeba, 2013), at: http://www.ingeba.org/liburua/donostia/43fuero/43fuero.htm (last accessed September 13, 2013); and Soledad Tena García, "Composición social y articulación interna de las cofradías de pescadores y mareantes. (Un análisis de la explotación de los recursos marítimos en la Marina de Castilla durante la Baja Edad Media)," *Espacio, Tiempo y Forma, Serie III, Historia Medieval* 8 (1995), 113.

7   He calculates that one third of the 146 dispositions in the foral text are related to commercial activity and, in particular, with three operations: the transport of merchandise by land and by sea, the storage of merchandise, and transactions in guest homes or inns. See García de Cortázar, "Una villa mercantile," 24.

This approach, then, leads me to contend that, in reality, the San Sebastian fuero only includes, in the strictest sense, one single disposition of maritime law. Specifically, it is chapter I-10, which, on the one hand, protects the property rights of merchants[8] regarding merchandise recovered after a shipwreck, in terms of both regular and commercial vessels, and independent of whether the accident occurred as a result of chance (because of a storm, for example) or of human activity (such as an attack by pirates, corsairs, or enemies, or the placing of false lighthouses); and, on the other, it establishes the payment to the council for certain economic rights as a requisite for traders to be able to recover any of their goods that may be salvaged from a shipwreck. The prevision is specified in the payment of "ten *sueldos* and its tribute;"[9] the same rights that chapter I-3 established for vessels from outside San Sebastian that arrived at the port there.[10]

The disposition in chapter I-10 implied that San Sebastian had relinquished the practice of *ius naufragii*, which had been at one time more extensive along the European coastline with the patronage or support of the river authorities that, frequently, were the first beneficiaries of the custom. It consisted of taking or appropriating the remains of shipwrecks by anyone who should come across them. Among the critiques that were raised against *ius naufragii* at different points on the European coast and that ultimately led to its prohibition as in the case of San Sebastian here, the Church played a decisive role, once it declared itself in favor of the ban.[11]

And if one accepts that the Fuero of San Sebastian contained exclusively this one disposition on maritime law, one should view the

---

8   The term "merchants" used in this chapter of the fuero should be understood as including all those who shipped their goods by sea, that is, traders in the strictest sense, but also ship owners because the precept refers equally to the recovery of the remains of merchandise and shipwrecked vessels.

9   Chapter I-10: "If it should happen that a ship were to sink within the limits of San Sebastian, the vessel's merchants may recover the vessel and all its merchandise by giving ten *sueldos* and its tribute according to [what is determined] above." Banús y Aguirre, *El Fuero de San Sebastián*, 83.

10   Chapter I-3: "But foreign vessels should pay a tribute: for each vessel, ten *sueldos* in my money; and for each package that may be salvaged from the vessel, twelve *denarios* for entry into the harbour as well as its tribute, but deducting a third part."

11   On the position of the Church, see Domenico. Schiappoli, *Il ius naufragii secondo il Diritto della Chiesa* (Roma: Societè Editrice del Foro Italiano, 1938).

arguments of García de Cortázar and Orella Unzué as exaggerated, in the sense that the text combines dispositions originating in the Fuero of Estella and the *Rôles d'Oléron*, and that the juridical sources of the local text are based on this latter work. In order to accept such claims, it would be necessary for the Fuero of San Sebastian to have included some ore maritime previsions. And that is not the case.

But it is moreover the case that nor can the statement that the chapter relating to ownership of goods recovered from a shipwreck was taken from the *Rôles d'Oléron* be considered correct, given that none of the chapters in the four versions there were of the maritime text—the original version, the Spanish version, the English version, and the Breton version—refer to that institution.[12] This is a confirmation that obliges us to question on what basis the considerations of García de Cortázar, Orella Unzué, and Tena García were made.

Although none of these authors says so specifically, I believe I know the justification for their approach. It is a case of an explanation related to what was known about the *Rôles d'Oléron* when their works were published and the edition of the *Rôles d'Oléron* that was being used by historiography at that time as the model of the maritime text.

At the time these authors published their works most experts, both in Spain and abroad, still believed that the *Rôles d'Oléron* was just a collection of sentences and it was occasionally referred to as being on a consuetudinary base, and created in the late eleventh century, thereby following the nineteenth-century thesis of Jean-Marie Pardessus.[13] Therefore the model text of the work was the edition used by Pardessus in his monumental contribution to the history of maritime law.[14] This was a version of the maritime code constructed artificially by Pardessus that did not correspond to any of the four versions established by European navigators.

---

12 On the four versions that came to shape the *Rôles d'Oléron* see Serna Vallejo, *Los Rôles d'Oléron*.

13 Jean-Marie Pardessus, *Collection des lois maritimes anterieures au XVIII siècle*, vol. 1 (Paris: L'Imprimerie Royal, 1828–1845), 300–3.

14 Ibid., 323–55.

The articles in the *Rôles d'Oléron* published by this French author originated in his desire to publish a critical edition.[15] It was constructed on the basis of different manuscripts and previous editions of the text by Pierre Garcie and Etienne Cleirac.[16] These editions were also the result of accumulating different material on the part of their authors, and achieved a certain diffusion in specific circles in Europe.[17]

The result of the copying carried out by Pardessus was a text made up of fifty-six chapters that had little to do with the four versions in circulation of the *Rôles d'Oléron*, but which did contain various precepts relating to the property of goods recovered from shipwrecks; chapters that had already appeared in the texts by Garcie and by Cleirac (chapters 36 to 56).

And in light of this data, it is not difficult to conclude that the arguments of García de Cortázar, Orella Unzué, and Tena García made sense when they were formulated on the basis of the study and edition of the *Rôles d'Oléron* by Pardessus. Yet in fact, according to what we know currently about the *Rôles d'Oléron*, they cannot be considered valid; nor can one consider the precept on shipwrecks included in the Fuero of San Sebastian as stemming from the *Rôles d'Oléron*, because, as noted, in none of the four versions of the text is there any reference to this issue.

And, moreover, nor can one continue to claim that the *Rôles d'Oléron* is a collection of sentences now that we know for sure that the work was, in reality, a maritime *coutumier*. In other words, it was a collection of consuetudinary maritime law.[18]And, finally,

---

15 Margarita Serna Vallejo, "La historiografía sobre los Rôles d'Oléron (siglos XV a XX)," *Anuario de Historia del Derecho Español* 70 (2000), 486–87.

16 Pierre Garcie, *Le Grand routier et pillotage et enseignement pour encrer tant ès ports, havres que lieux de la mer, tant des parties de France, Bretaigne, Engleterre, Espaigne, Flandres et haultes Alemaignes...* St. Gilles-sur-Vie: 1483–1484, 1st known ed., Poitiers, 1520; 2nd ed., 1521, in David Watkin Waters, *The Rutters of the Sea: The Sailing Directions of Pierre Garcie; A Study of the First English and French Printed Sailing Directions, with Facsimile Reproductions* (New Haven and London: Yale University Pres, 1967), 376–93; Etienne Cleirac, *Us et coutumes de la mer divisées en trois parties* (1st ed., Bordeaux: Guillaume Millanges, 1647; 6th ed., Rouen: E. Viret, 1671), 7–135.

17 On the origins and features of these editions of the *Rôles d'Oléron* see Serna Vallejo, "La historiografía sobre los Rôles d'Oléron (siglos XV a XX)," 473–79.

18 The postscript *"Et cest le jugement en ceo cas"* with which the precepts conclude, and that led Pardessus to believe that it was a collection of dispositions of judicial origin, was

in relation to its dating, the idea that the work had been published originally in the eleventh century has also been ruled out, following the consolidation of the thesis that it was actually published in the mid-thirteenth century.[19]

Therefore, the dates presented lead me to contend that the *Rôles d'Oléron* could not have influenced the Fuero of San Sebastian because this maritime text was published after the fuero had been conceded. This argument is not, however, an obstacle to understanding that the prevision relating to protecting the ownership of goods salvaged from shipwrecks contained in the San Sebastian fuero did form part of the same Atlantic tradition to which the *Rôles d'Oléron* belonged. And, precisely, this common belonging to the Atlantic cycle is what justified Garcie, Cleirac and, later, Pardessus, to include in their texts chapters reserved for *ius naufragii*.

The existence of this link between the prevision on *ius naufragii* in the Fuero of San Sebastian and the Atlantic juridical-commercial tradition or culture was outlined accurately in the early twentieth century by Bonifacio de Echegaray Corta.[20] It was later embraced by José Luis Banús y Aguirre in connecting the fuero precept on goods in shipwrecks to the previsions, along similar lines, included in other Atlantic texts.[21] These included, in his opinion, a privilege by Richard I of England, the *Assises de la court des barons* (Assizes of Jerusalem), and the law of the Isle of Oléron, the latter of which should not be confused with the *Rôles d'Oléron*.[22] I would add to this that its spirit is also linked to the Fuero Real (IV, XXV, 1) and in the headings (V, IX, 7) and, ultimately, to Roman law because already by that time, gradually, the necessary judicial framework had been constructed to protect the property of the remains of shipwrecks, in such a way that only at an early stage of Roman legal history could

---

just a recourse used by the compiler of the work to give it greater authority than that of dispositions of a consuetudinary background that made up the text before judicial bodies. See Serna Vallejo, "La historiografía sobre los Rôles d'Oléron (siglos XV a XX)," 65–67.

19 On these issues, see ibid., 55–75.
20 Bonifacio de Echegaray Corta, "La vida civil y mercantil de los vascos a través de sus instituciones jurídicas," *Revista Internacional de Estudios Vascos* 13, 4 (1922), 588–97.
21 Banús y Aguirre, *El Fuero de San Sebastián*, 152–57.
22 Ibid., 154–57.

the goods associated with shipwrecks be considered *res nullius* and, therefore, susceptible to appropriation by anyone who found them.[23]

Having thus examined this issue, as a means of concluding this section, one can now ask whether the *Rôles d'Oléron* was valid for San Sebastian seafarers. To date, we lack any kind of clear testimony to conform that the Atlantic maritime *coutumier* was used by San Sebastian navigators. This is in contrast to those at other points on the Castilian coast from which we have different testimonies that demonstrate, without any doubt, the use of the text by their residents and seafarers. This is the case, among others, of Seville, Pontevedra, and San Vicente de la Barquera.[24]

Nevertheless, the *Rôles d'Oléron* achieved widespread diffusion along the Atlantic coast, which is documented through diverse sources such as the more than one hundred copies of its articles we know of to date. Moreover, the very French monarchy allowed Castilian seafarers to be governed from 1364 on by the *Fuero de Layron*, the Castilian version of the work. Added to this, there were close links between the inhabitants of San Sebastian and Gascony, where the *Rôles d'Oléron* was most likely formulated, and people from San Sebastian participated actively in medieval Atlantic commerce organized, precisely, by this code. On the basis of all this, it does not seem too speculative to suggest that the *Rôles d'Oléron* must have been used, alongside Atlantic maritime custom, by San Sebastian seafarers. Although only the discovery of new documents will enable us to confirm this hypothesis.

The Maritime Law Established by the Council of San Sebastian and the Guilds of Santa Catalina and San Pedro

Leaving to one side reflections on maritime law common to the Atlantic and the *Rôles d'Oléron*, I will continue in my study by focusing on a second demonstration of maritime law. I am referring to the maritime law established by the Council of San Sebastian and by the

---

23   On Roman law and shipwrecked goods, see José Luis Zamora Manzano, "El salvamento y la asistencia marítima en el Derecho romano," *Revue Internationale des Droits de l'Antiquité* 48 (2001), 373–403.
24   See Serna Vallejo, *Los Rôles d'Oléron*, 120, 169–71.

guilds of Santa Catalina and San Pedro. This was a very important law for San Sebastian seafarers due to its proximity and immediacy, although it had considerably less validity, both in territorial and personal terms, than the maritime law common to the whole Atlantic area once its dispositions only applied to those who were in the *villa* and the members of each of those brotherhoods.

From this perspective, which has as its focus local maritime law, agreements with some maritime content that the governing bodies in the *villa* adopted occasionally were less important than maritime dispositions included in the bylaws of the Council of San Sebastian and the bylaws of each of the two maritime guilds established in the Gipuzkoan capital since the Middle Ages. Hence, I will now focus my attention on the bylaws, leaving for another occasion an analysis of the random agreements made by the *villa* on maritime issues. But before analyzing these bylaws, I should offer some reflections of a more general nature.

As regards the municipal bylaws of towns located on the coast, as in the case of San Sebastian, one should note that maritime previsions were, in general, more important in situations in which the governing councils were attempting to control, with varying degrees of success, the activity of residents who worked in the maritime field and, especially, the navigators', seafarers', and fishermen's guilds, than in other situations in which the councils avoided the possibility of exercising any kind of control over those residents.

To this one should also add the fact that the councils, controlled by local oligarchs, were more concerned with intervening in maritime affairs after they became aware that the maritime guilds could be a threat to their interests at the same time as these corporations were becoming or trying to become political articulators of the common people in different towns. This was an interest that the maritime brotherhoods demonstrated as a consequence of the fact that most of the residents that made up the common people of many of these towns were precisely people who were engaged in maritime activities, who were members of maritime guilds, and because of their social situation were excluded from municipal governments.

From these two perspectives, the case of the Council of San Sebastian is of special interest because it presents some significant particularities in comparison with what happened at the same time in most of the maritime *villas* in the surrounding area, both in Gipuzkoa and in Bizkaia, such as the judgement of the *corregimiento* (a territorial subdivision presided over by the *corregidor*, the king's royal official) of the Cuatro Villas de la Costa.

And at the same time San Sebastian is also a special case as regards the bylaws of its maritime guilds because it was one of the few towns on the Cantabrian coast whose seafarers, navigators, and fishermen, instead of being grouped in just one guild—although in each one of them a specific collective linked to the sea, whether in fishing or commercial terms, could predominate, as was typical on the northern Castilian coast—had been organized since the Late Middle Ages in two different brotherhoods. That is why we come across bylaws for the guild of Santa Catalina drawn up to organize commercial activity, and others to govern the fishing practice of residents in the *villa* grouped into the guild of San Pedro.[25]

Municipal Bylaws and the Bylaws of the Guilds of Santa Catalina and San Pedro in 1489

Since the fifteenth century, the four most important seafaring guilds in the *corregimiento* of the Cuatro Villas de la Costa were the political articulators of the common people in San Vicente de la Barquera, Santander, Laredo, and Castro Urdiales.[26] It was, moreover, a similar situation in Lekeitio.[27] In response, there was a logical opposition on

25 Soledad Tena García mentions a third guild, that of San Nicolás, of which for now we have no further information. See "Cofradías y concejos: encuentros y desencuentros en San Sebastián a finales del siglo XV," in *Sociedades urbanas y culturas políticas en la Baja Edad Media castellana*, ed. José María Monsalvo Antón (Salamanca: Ediciones Universidad de Salamanca, 2013), 233.

26 Margarita Serna Vallejo, "El conflicto político entre las gentes del mar y las oligarquías locales en el Corregimiento de las Cuatro Villas de la Costa en el Antiguo Régimen," in *La vida inquieta. Conflictos sociales en la Edad Moderna*, ed. Ofelia Rey Castelao, Rubén Castro Redondo, and Camilo Fernández Cortizo (Santiago de Compostela: Universidad de Santiago de Compostela, 2018), 119–43.

27 Erkoreka Gervasio, *Análisis histórico-institucional de las cofradías de mareantes del País Vasco*, 402–5; Tena García, "Composición social y articulación interna de las cofradías de pescadores y mareantes," 133–34.

the part of local governments because this function carried out by the maritime guilds was not to the liking of municipal governance, nor the oligarchs that controlled it. In the case of San Sebastian, the guilds never came to carry out this political function, despite having attempted to do so at one time. Their attempt failed because the government of San Sebastian, with the express support of the monarchy, prevented the possibility.

This must be placed in the context of elaborating and confirming the municipal bylaws of San Sebastian in 1489.[28] Likewise, one should bear in mind the bylaws of the guild of Santa Catalina;[29] and of San Pedro, both dating from the same year, 1489.[30]

The bylaws of these two guilds are remarkably similar. In reality, many precepts are the same in both texts, and the only differences are the chapters that regulate the particular activities practiced by the members of each of them. The reason for this similarity is that they were drawn up simultaneously, with the same objective, and by the same person, the *bachiller* Diego Arias de Anaya, investigating judge in the *villa*, after he himself had abolished both bodies and they had been reestablished by the Catholic monarchs.

However, one also observes certain points in common between the guild and municipal bylaws that same year that merit some explanation. A joint reading of the three texts reveals that

---

28 Municipal bylaws of San Sebastian, approved by the Catholic monarchs on July 7, 1489, in María Rosa Ayerbe Iríbar, "Las ordenanzas municipales de San Sebastián de 1489," *Boletín de Estudios Históricos de San Sebastián* 40 (2006), 14–91.

29 Bylaws of the guild of Santa Catalina of masters, merchants, pilots, and seafarers, given by the Catholic monarchs on July 7, 1489. They were later confirmed by Carlos I in 1539, and reformed in 1642. See José Luis Banús y Aguirre, "Ordenanzas de la Cofradía de Santa Catalina," *Boletín de Estudios Históricos de San Sebastián* 8 (1974), 90–106.

30 Bylaws of the guild of seafarers of San Pedro given by the Catholic monarchs in 1489, in María Rosa Ayerbe Iríbar, "Ordenanzas de la cofradía de mareantes de San Pedro, en San Sebastián (1489)," *Boletín de Estudios Históricos de San Sebastián* 41 (2007), 428–37. There is no specific date in the text, but Ayerbe Iríbar (ibid., 428n34) dates the bylaws to July 7, 1489 in accordance with a statement by Pedro Manuel Soraluce based on their confirmation in 1539. See Pedro Manuel de Soraluce, "Las cofradías de marcantes de San Sebastián desde la Edad Media hasta nuestros días," *Euskal-Erria* 28 (1893), 410. However, I do not agree with this date because the 1539 conformation was, in effect, of the bylaws of Santa Catalina, as indicated in the previous note, and not those of San Pedro. Later, specifically in 1491, the bylaws of the guild of San Pedro were also confirmed. See Erkoreka Gervasio, *Análisis histórico-institucional de las cofradías de mareantes del País Vasco*, 461–69.

the seafarers and fishermen of the *villa*, who made up most of the common people of San Sebastian, had become, at least in the eyes of the oligarchs that controlled the municipal government, a threat and a motive for concern. This was because, after having organized themselves into guilds, they attempted to intervene in the governing council in order to defend their interests, just at a moment, moreover, in which municipal government was going through a bad time.[31] One should not forget the terrible fire the *villa* suffered in January 1489, which forced the reconstruction of the city with the explicit help of the Catholic monarchs.[32] And during those months, the guilds had been excessive in attempts to impose on the council, by force, some agreements favorable to their demands, which were contrary to the decisions made by the local authorities.

Therefore, the council bylaws and the two maritime guild texts of 1489 responded to the same objective of fortifying the government of the people, controlled by the local oligarchy, at a moment of profound institutional crisis for the governing body; limiting the power and protagonism that the guilds could exercise in the *villa*; and intensifying the control of the local authorities over the maritime guilds. These were objectives for which the municipal authorities counted on the inestimable support of the Catholic monarchs.

31   As regards the medieval oligarchy of San Sebastian, it was established initially around the Gascon Mans Engómez family. Then, in a dual lineal temporal process, it first brought in other Gascon families present in the *villa* and, thereafter, still more families originating in Gipuzkoa that had also settled in the *villa*. On this, see the work of Soledad Tena García: "Los Mans-Engómez: el linaje dirigente de la villa de San Sebastián durante la Edad Media," *Hispania* 185 (1993), 987–1008; *La sociedad urbana en la Guipúzcoa costera medieval: San Sebastián, Rentería y Fuenterrabía (1200–1500)* (San Sebastián: Fundación Social y Cultural Kutxa, 1997); "Los linajes urbanos de las villas del Puerto de Pasajes (San Sebastián, Rentería y Fuenterrabía). Dos modelos de formación de las oligarquías municipales," in *La lucha de bandos en el País Vasco: de los Parientes Mayores a la Hidalguía Universal: Guipúzcoa, de los bandos a la provincia (siglos XIV a XVI)*, ed. José Ramón Díaz de Durana (Bilbao: Universidad del País Vasco, 1998), 323–39. And on the population of San Sebastian not connected with these oligarch families, see Ernesto García Fernández, "La comunidad de San Sebastián a fines del siglo XV: un movimiento fiscalizador del poder concejil," *Espacio, Tiempo y Forma, Serie III, Historia Medieval* 6 (1993), 543–72.

32   On the fire and the aid of Fernando e Isabel to help rebuild the *villa*, see two works by José Luis Banús y Aguirre: "Viejas ordenanzas de construcción en San Sebastián," *Boletín de la Real Sociedad Vascongada de Amigos del País* 1 (1945), 185–94; and "Los Reyes Católicos y San Sebastián. El incendio de 1489 y la reconstrucción de la villa," *Boletín de la Real Sociedad Vascongada de Amigos del País* 17 (1961), 283–304.

The *bachiller* Diego Arias de Anaya, sent to the *villa* to look into the conflict stemming from the municipal elections, abolished the guilds of Santa Catalina and San Pedro in San Sebastian, arguing that guilds and gangs were detrimental for the republic, the common good, and the monarchy itself,[33] and argument that also justified, once they had been reestablished, maintaining them under the control of the council.

In reality, the reasoning behind the harm that was inferred from the existence of the guilds was nothing new because different complaints had been made for some time, sometimes in a general way and sometimes the charge was more particular, against them using justifications similar to those of Arias de Anaya. Such complaints had been made by the monarchy;[34] by the parliament;[35] and by the brotherhood of Gipuzkoa.[36] It is not clear, however, whether on each occasion such pronouncements were made, the goal was to abolish the guilds and unions more generally, or just to eliminate their political nature or that of individuals therein who carried out some kind of political function, who caused problems for public order in the towns and had not come to terms with the requisites demanded by legislation.[37]

---

33 In the preamble to the bylaws, both those of San Pedro and of Santa Catalina, there were references to problems among the people because of the guild members' "town halls" and other institutions.

34 Suspicion on the part of these institutions had been evident since the reign of Alfonso X as one can see in the text *Partidas* (Partidas, V, VII, 2). And they were reiterated by some of his successors such as Enrique IV in 1460, when he went to the guild of San Pedro to complain about the noise and disturbance that had occurred in the *villa* as a result of actions against the royal judge. See Real Academia de la Historia, Colección Vargas y Ponce, vol. 39, 9/4207, cited in José Damián González Arce, "Asociacionismo, gremios y restricciones corporativas en la España medieval (siglos XIII–XV)," *Investigaciones de Historia Económica* 10 (2008), 21–22; and Carlos I in 1552 (Pragmática de 1552, chap. 16. NoR, XII, XII, 13 (=NR VIII, XIV, 4).

35 Parliament of Toledo in 1462 (Petition 36. Novísima Recopilación (NoR), XII, XII, 12 (=NR VIII, XIV, 3) and of Santa María de Nieva in 1473 (Petition 31. NoR, XII, XII,12). And, later, there were similar complaints in the Parliament of Madrid in 1534 (Petition 29. NoR, XII, XII, 12).

36 Chap. 136 in the *Cuaderno Viejo de Ordenanzas de la Hermandad de Guipúzcoa, aprobado por Enrique IV en Vitoria el 30 de marzo de 1457*; and chaps. 177 and 180 in the *Cuaderno Nuevo de Ordenanzas de la Hermandad de Guipúzcoa, elaborado en la Junta General celebrada en Mondragón, con los Comisarios nombrados por Enrique IV, el 13 de junio de 1463*, in Elena Barrena Osoro, *Ordenanzas de la Hermandad de Guipúzcoa (1357–1463)* (San Sebastián: Sociedad de Estudios Vascos, 1982).

37 On this debate, see González Arce, "Asociacionismo, gremios y restricciones corporativas en la España medieval."

In light of the unequal treatment that different Cantabrian guilds received not just through the centuries more generally but also at specific moments, it seems prudent to state that, in reality, the goal of such prohibitions was to make the guilds, which had become gangs, disappear. In other words, they had become leagues or pressure groups that exerted an influence on the residents and governments of different places with the aim of imposing favorable measures for their own interests and to the detriment of the rest,[38] pursuing, therefore, a "bad end," as it was termed in the *Diccionario de Autoridades*.

As regards the unequal treatment meted out by the monarchy to the guilds, it is enough to recall here that the same Catholic monarchs that supported the subjugation of the guilds of Santa Catalina and San Pedro to the Council of San Sebastian, depriving them of their autonomy, endorsed and strengthened in a very obvious way the maritime guilds in other places on the Cantabrian coast. Hence, I believe that if the monarchy were convinced firmly that the guilds were such a threat to the common good, as one deduces from the documents concerning the guilds of San Sebastian, it would have opposed clearly all the guilds, which it did not do. In reality, as in many other circumstances and matters, the attitude of the monarchy with respect to the guilds depended on the interests that, at a given moment, could have been affected by political activity on the part of maritime brotherhoods and, most especially, by the pressure that local governments and the elites that controlled them exercised before the royal institution.

And in the case of San Sebastian, it seems clear that the municipal government convinced the Catholic monarchs that the guilds of Santa Catalina and San Pedro constituted a threat to the everyday lives of the population, to its good government, and to its safety through the political activity that they were trying to carry out, as articulators of the common people, coinciding with a difficult moment for the government of San Sebastian.

38　Álvaro Aragón Ruano and Xabier Alberdi Lonbide, "El proceso de institucionalización de las cofradías guipuzcoanas durante la Edad Moderna: cofradías de mareantes y de podavines," *Vasconia. Cuadernos de Historia-geografía* 30 (2000), 207.

This would explain why the Catholic monarchs supported the decision to suppress the San Sebastian guilds and, when they decided to reestablish them, attending to the demands presented in this regard by the guilds in different institutions, they decided to subject them to the municipal authorities and reduce considerably their responsibilities, thereby restricting any possibility of effective political activity.

This explained why the bylaws banned leagues and gangs; why in order to convoke meetings of members for strictly professional reasons it was necessary to obtain the consent of the municipal council; why permanent and stable participation of guild members in council meetings was vetoed, ordering their participation in official acts only on the basis of prior arrangement on the part of the town council with the guild spokesmen; and why the intervention of these representatives of the guilds in official meetings was limited to debating specific matters for which they had been called.

And this is precisely one of the most notable differences that existed between the maritime guilds of San Sebastian and those of other places on the Cantabrian coast that, as well as carrying out professional, charitable and welfare, religious, and legal functions, also carried out important political activity.

As noted, the reestablishment of these guilds required mobilizing their members. They went to the Catholic monarchs to get them to reverse the decision made by the *bachiller* Diego Arias de Anaya. On raising their petition, as was to be expected, the members of the institutions remained silent on account of the disorder that had taken place in the *villa*, in which they had participated actively, and for which the governing council held them responsible. They therefore restricted themselves, in the two cases, from demonstrating the positive aspects of their work in the preceding years and that, from their point of view, justified their reestablishment.

As such, the members of San Pedro, in order to defend, before the monarchy, the suitability of reestablishing the guild, reminded it of the important services it had offered while it existed. Specifically, thanks to them, there was light in the city, that is, a lighthouse, to guide arriving ships into the port; the guild overseer administered justice, resolving any differences that emerged from the practice of fishing, in accordance with a simple, fast, and inexpensive procedure; and the guild had saved many poor people. While those of Santa Catalina reminded it that they had constructed a wharf and a dock in the *villa*; and that they had also helped many poor people.

Maritime Previsions in the Municipal Bylaws of San Sebastian in 1489

The previsions contained in the municipal bylaws of San Sebastian in 1489 that affected directly members of the maritime guilds were aimed mainly at supplying certain products for the residents of the *villa*, given their scarcity; regulating the price, quality, and sale of fish there; avoiding fraud in the sale of fishing resources; favoring direct commerce and avoiding the intervention of intermediaries; controlling, at least in some aspects, fishing activity; guaranteeing order and safety among the population; and preventing any deterioration in hygiene and the health of residents through the spread of bad odors. These were proposition that, in general terms, coincided with those covered by municipal bylaws in other Cantabrian towns, including those in Gipuzkoa.[39]

In this way, with the aim of guaranteeing order and safety, the bylaws of 1489 prohibited the formation of leagues and gangs in order avoid the scandals and disturbances that had occurred in the *villa* on account of the existence of such institutions, as the decisions of mayors and judges could be contradictory (chapter 20). And it was established that, in the event of convening guild meetings or councils, a prior official license was required (chapters 40 and 41). These provisions affected the maritime guilds immediately and established the bases for the control and dominance of the town

---

39   Ernesto García Fernández, "Para la buena gobernación e regimiento de la villa e sus vecinos e pueblo e republica: De los Fueros a las Ordenanzas municipales en la Provincia de Guipúzcoa (siglos XII–XVI)," in *El triunfo de las elites urbanas guipuzcoanas: nuevos textos para el estudio del gobierno de las villas y de la Provincia (1412–1539)*, ed. José Ángel Lema, Jon Andoni Fernández de Larrea, Ernesto García, Miguel Larrañaga, José Antonio Munita, and José Ramón Díaz de Durana (San Sebastián: Diputación Foral de Gipuzkoa, 2002), 27–58.

council over the guilds of Santa Catalina and San Pedro following their reestablishment.

Chapters 103, 104, and 105 blocked "in the landscape of our vicinity" the loading and unloading of wheat, salt, fish, or any other merchandise without a license from the mayors and governors of the *villa*;[40] the drying of any fishing resource; and people from Pasajes bringing barley or wheat to San Sebastian by sea, except if they had the appropriate license to do so issued by the local authorities.

The main aim of chapters 110 through 117 was to safeguard the correct provision of fish to the *villa*, which justified the regulation of the methods, features, and conditions of the sale of fish in the streets of the town, but also the fish that may arrive in the *villa* of San Sebastian from Pasaje de Fuenterrabía, the current Pasajes de San Juan (Pasai Donibane), or any other port outside the town. And chapter 117 established the system that had to be observed for renting out nets in certain places.

The Content of the Bylaws of the Guilds of Santa Catalina and San Pedro

And, as regards the content of the bylaws of the guilds of Santa Catalina and San Pedro, the aspect that most calls attention is that in their chapters, there was no prevision with regard to the government of each of these guilds, and that the dispositions relating to other questions usually considered in the bylaws of maritime guilds were quite scarce. This was the case with those relating to the economic resources of the guilds, the organization of their members' professional activities, and the carrying out of charitable, welfare, and religious functions that guilds associated with the sea typically fulfilled.

On the contrary, in both texts much importance is given to administering justice among members on the part of the overseer of each of the guilds. And attention was paid, likewise, to questions that, as well as interesting members of each of the guilds, must have concerned the local authorities, such as those relating to maintaining

---

40   Reference here is to the current port of Pasajes de San Pedro (Pasai San Pedro), formerly known as the port of Oyarzun (Oiartzun), which was the most important port of the four San Sebastian had in the Middle Ages.

and cleaning the docks and the maintenance of the fire with which the lighthouse functioned. The fact that the guild of Santa Catalina had taken responsibility for constructing and maintaining the dock and that of San Pedro was responsible for the "fire" that served the lighthouse in the town, and that both points would have been put forward by members of the two institutions when they asked the Catholic monarchs to reestablish the guilds, explains the central importance of these matters in the San Sebastian bylaws.

The set of particularities that we observe in these bylaws and that, in general, are not observed in most of the maritime guilds of the Cantabrian coast, is related to the previsions in the municipal bylaws of 1489 aimed at limiting the sphere of activity of the guilds and submitting them to the control of the council authorities; and, especially, with a desire that meetings among navigators, seafarers, and fishermen in San Sebastian were just occasional affairs and always controlled by the local authorities.

The dependence on and subjection to the town council on the part of the guilds of Santa Catalina and San Pedro from 1489 on was an exceptional case on the Cantabrian corniche. In general, medieval seafaring guilds on the northern Castilian coast enjoyed a wide margin of autonomy with respect to municipal governments, counting for that on the explicit support of the monarchy. And what is more, they managed to incorporate themselves into the local governments of the *villas*, which allowed them to participate in council decision-making and be permanently and directly informed of any matters resolved at council meetings that affected their interests. Guilds at other points on the Castilian coastline achieved this presence in local governments, enjoying permanent representation in the councils and/or managing that certain municipal professions were obligatorily allotted to members of the seafaring guilds.

And another particularity that the bylaws of the San Sebastian seafaring guilds offered compared to most of the other guilds on the Cantabrian coast had to do with the institution that drew them up. As a general rule, it was typical, at least in the Middle Ages (there were certain changes in the modern era), for members themselves to draw up the guild bylaws, which were later sent to the Council of Castile so that the monarchy, through this means, could proceed to confirm them after verifying and checking the suitability of their content. As a previous step to confirmation, the texts of the bylaws used to be sent to the local councils of the towns in which the guilds were based with the aim of the municipal authorities agreeing to the text or proposing any modifications they thought appropriate, which, in that event, could be taken into account by the Council of Castile and incorporated definitively into the text approved by the monarchy.

However, the procedure followed for elaborating the bylaws of Santa Catalina and San Pedro was quite distinct. The wording was in the hands of the *bachiller* Arias de Anaya, instead of their members, although taking account of older guild bylaws and, above all, being very aware of the interests of the government in San Sebastian.

Nonetheless, with the passage of time, the control on the part of the local authorities of residents engaged in maritime activities, at least in some aspects, must have been eased; hence the later bylaws of the guild of Santa Catalina, confirmed by the Council of Castile in 1642, were drawn up by the members themselves and their overseer, without detriment to the fact that the processing of its approval before the Council of Castile was undertaken by the local council, justice, and governing authority of San Sebastian.[41] Yet, on the contrary, the authorization for members of the municipal government to be admitted as elected and chosen members in elections to the guild (chapter 2) continued to subject the guild to the authority and control of local government.

As I have been indicating in the previous pages, the new bylaws of the guilds of San Pedro and Santa Catalina were aimed mainly at annulling the political power of both guilds so that already in the preamble of both bylaws, there was a ban on any official meeting as a "council" in the name of the guild, under the penalty of being punished with sentences contained in the bylaws and sentences established in the general legislation for sedition and troublemaking

---

41 The text of the new bylaws of the guild of Santa Catalina, confirmed on April 7, is in Banús y Aguirre, "Ordenanzas de la Cofradía de Santa Catalina," 101–6.

in towns. This was a prevision reiterated in chapter 1 of both bodies of bylaws, and in the chapter that both devoted to the exercise of jurisdictional functions on the part of the overseers.

The sentences established for anyone not complying with this order were, to be sure, serious: a sentence of one thousand *maravedíes* and banishment from the *villa* and its jurisdiction for two years, which for the insolvent would be changed to the sentence of thirty days on the floor of the tower and a two-year banishment. And the sentences were even more serious for anyone leading disturbances that ended up causing blood wounds because in this case it was the death penalty.

The participation of guild members in local government meetings was provided for in chapter 1 of both bylaws, in considering that those who were not in agreement with council decisions, believing them to be detrimental to the republic, could attend sessions in the city hall to demonstrate their point of view.

The only meetings permitted for guild members were those whose aim was to resolve questions concerning the professions exercised by these members, but in order to proceed to calling a meeting, as already noted, the prior consent of the local authorities was necessary, under threat of the death penalty and the confiscation of possessions (chapter 2 in both bylaws).

Thereafter, in both texts, and in light of that put forward as a merit by the members of both institutions in relation to the jurisdictional function that the overseers were fulfilling, it was contemplated that within the framework of the two brotherhoods, these officials should continue to administer justice in the guilds in claims of no more than six thousand *maravedís* that derived from maritime activities, whether fishing or commercial. The procedure foreseen for the selection of overseers of the guilds was shrouded in a certain complexity, whose results were applied for a long period of ten years and that entailed the annual appointing of an overseer and two examiners of the overseer's accounts. These accounts had to be prepared on finalizing the carrying out of the position for inspection by the two examiners in the presence of two or three principal members from each guild.

Both texts contemplated a second petition in the judicial process once an appeal had been accepted against the sentences dictated by the overseer of each guild before a court made up of four ship's captains and seafarers, in the case of the guild of Santa Catalina, and four ship's captains or fishermen in the case of the guild of San Pedro.

With the aim that the overseers could count on the help of an official and carry out in the best way possible their jurisdictional responsibilities, the texts established that this help would be given by a beadle.

In the final part of both texts the salaries to be received by both the overseers and the beadles in exercising their functions were outlined.

And finally, within this sphere, it was foreseen that the execution of the sentences dictated in the first or second petition within the framework of each of the guilds corresponded to the provost of the *villa*, who, attending to the order of the overseer, had to proceed to carry them out both as regards people and goods.

There also existed a similarity in the precepts of each guild aimed at regulating the charitable, welfare, and religious functions that both the guild of Santa Catalina and that of San Pedro had to fulfill. This was the case of the precepts that established the masses that had to be held in the guilds, together with the method for paying for them and the dates they were to be held; the alms that had to be handed in order to help the infirm and elderly who were no longer in any condition to carry out maritime activities; assistance with burying deceased members; and respect for the festivals to be upheld established by the diocese in which it was prohibited from pitting out to sea.

The section in which, naturally, there were more differences between one set of bylaws and the other was that referring to the professional activities of the members of Santa Catalina and San Pedro.

In the case of the fishing guild rules for selling fish in the *villa* were established, including for that bought from foreigners, and both how often and how much; and for the care and maintenance of the firelight, positioned at the entrance to the port to help guide in ships, which required the overseer to appoint someone annually for its upkeep. And in the Santa Catalina text there was a prevision for a system to honor contracts for crew recruitment; a prohibition on loading and unloading on holidays; the ballast conditions in the dock; holding embarkations, both large and small, in the port; a ban on throwing garbage out at the wharf; a ban on abandoning ships not fit to set sail in the port; for foreign merchandise; and maintenance of the dock.

BIBLIOGRAPHY

Aragón Ruano, Álvaro, and Xabier Alberdi Lonbide. "El proceso de institucionalización de las cofradías guipuzcoanas durante la Edad Moderna: cofradías de mareantes y de podavines." *Vasconia. Cuadernos de Historia geografía* 30 (2000): 205–22.

Ayerbe Iríbar, María Rosa. "Las ordenanzas municipales de San Sebastián de 1489." *Boletín de Estudios Históricos de San Sebastián* 40 (2006): 11–91.

———. "Ordenanzas de la cofradía de mareantes de San Pedro, en San Sebastián (1489)." *Boletín de Estudios Históricos de San Sebastián* 41 (2007): 417–37.

Banús y Aguirre, José Luis. "Viejas ordenanzas de construcción en San Sebastián." *Boletín de la Real Sociedad Vascongada de Amigos del País* 1 (1945): 185–94.

———. "Los Reyes Católicos y San Sebastián. El incendio de 1489 y la reconstrucción de la villa." *Boletín de la Real Sociedad Vascongada de Amigos del País* 17 (1961): 283–304.

————. *El Fuero de San Sebastián*. San Sebastián: Ayuntamiento de San Sebastián, 1963.

————. "Ordenanzas de la Cofradía de Santa Catalina." *Boletín de Estudios Históricos de San Sebastián* 8 (1974): 73–106.

Barrena Osoro, Elena. *Ordenanzas de la Hermandad de Guipúzcoa (1357–1463)*. San Sebastián: Sociedad de Estudios Vascos, 1982.

Cleirac, Etienne. *Us et coutumes de la mer divisées en trois parties*. 1st ed., Bordeaux: Guillaume Millanges, 1647; 6th ed., Rouen: E. Viret, 1671.

Echegaray Corta, Bonifacio de. "La vida civil y mercantil de los vascos a través de sus instituciones jurídicas." *Revista Internacional de Estudios Vascos* 13, 3 (1922): 273–336; 13, 4 (1922): 582–613; and 14, 1 (1923): 27–60.

Erkoreka Gervasio, Josu Iñaki. *Análisis histórico-institucional de las cofradías de mareantes del País Vasco*. Vitoria-Gasteiz: Servicio Central de Publicaciones del Gobierno Vasco, 1991.

García de Cortázar, José Ángel. "Una villa mercantil. 1180–1516." In *Historia de Donostia-San Sebastián*, edited by Miguel Artola. San Sebastián: Editorial Nerea, 2004.

García Fernández, Ernesto. "La comunidad de San Sebastián a fines del siglo XV: un movimiento fiscalizador del poder concejil." *Espacio, Tiempo y Forma, Serie III, Historia Medieval* 6 (1993): 543–72.

————. "Para la buena gobernación e regimiento de la villa e sus vecinos e pueblo e republica: De los Fueros a las Ordenanzas municipales en la Provincia de Guipúzcoa (siglos XII–XVI)." In *El triunfo de las elites urbanas guipuzcoanas: nuevos textos para el estudio del gobierno de las villas y de la Provincia (1412–1539)*, edited by José Ángel Lema, Jon Andoni Fernández de Larrea, Ernesto García, Miguel Larrañaga, José Antonio Munita, and José Ramón Díaz de Durana. San Sebastián: Diputación Foral de Gipuzkoa, 2002.

————. "Las cofradías de mercaderes, mareantes y pescadores vascos (siglos XIV a XVI)." In *Ciudades y villas portuarias del Atlántico en la Edad Media. Nájera, Encuentros Internacionales del Medievo: Nájera, 27–30 de julio 2004*, edited by Beatriz Arízaga Bolumburu and Jesús Ángel Solórzano Tellechea. Logroño: Instituto de Estudios Riojanos, 2005.

Garcie, Pierre. *Le Grand routier et pillotage et enseignement pour encrer tant ès ports, havres que lieux de la mer, tant des parties de France, Bretaigne, Engleterre, Espaigne, Flandres et haultes Alemaignes...* St. Gilles-sur-Vie: 1483–1484. 1st known edition, Poitiers, 1520; 2nd ed., 1521. In David Watkin Waters, *The Rutters of the Sea: The Sailing Directions of Pierre Garcie; A Study of the First English and French Printed Sailing Directions, with Facsimile Reproductions*. New Haven and London: Yale University Pres, 1967.

González Arce, José Damián. "Asociacionismo, gremios y restricciones corporativas en la España medieval (siglos XIII–XV)." *Investigaciones de Historia Económica* 10 (2008): 9–34.

González Arce, José Damián, and Joaquín Gil Sáez. "El puerto de San Sebastián y su cofradía de mareantes de Santa Catalina (1450–1550)." *Tst. Transportes, Servicios y telecomunicaciones* 21 (2011): 84–111.

Orella Unzué, José Luis. "Estudio jurídico comparativo de los Fueros de San Sebastián, Estella, Vitoria y Logroño." In *Congreso: El Fuero de San Sebastián y su época (San Sebastián 19–23 de enero de 1981) / Donostiako forua eta bere garaia (Donostia, 1981ko urtarrilaren 19tik 23ra)*. San Sebastián: Eusko Ikaskuntza / Sociedad de Estudios Vascos, 1982.

————. "El Fuero de San Sebastián y su entorno histórico." In *Geografía e Historia de Donostia-San Sebastián*, edited by Juan Antonio Sáez and Javier Gómez Piñeiro. San Sebastián: Ingeba, 2013. At: http://www.ingeba.org/liburua/donostia/43fuero/43fuero.htm (last accessed September 13, 2013).

Pardessus, Jean-Marie. *Collection des lois maritimes anterieures au XVIII siècle*. 6 volumes. Paris: L'Imprimerie Royal, 1828–1845.

Schiappoli, Domenico. *Il ius naufragii secondo il Diritto della Chiesa*. Roma: Societè Editrice del Foro Italiano, 1938.

Serna Vallejo, Margarita. "La historiografía sobre los Rôles d'Oléron (siglos XV a XX)." *Anuario de Historia del Derecho Español* 70 (2000): 471–98.

———. *Los Rôles d'Oléron. El coutumier marítimo del Atlántico y del Báltico de Época medieval y moderna*. Santander: Centro de Estudios Montañeses, 2004.

———. "La Ordenanza francesa de la marina de 1681unificación, refundición y fraccionamiento del derecho marítimo en Europa." *Anuario de Historia del Derecho* 78–79 (2008–2009): 233–60.

———. "El conflicto político entre las gentes del mar y las oligarquías locales en el Corregimiento de las Cuatro Villas de la Costa en el Antiguo Régimen." In *La vida inquieta. Conflictos sociales en la Edad Moderna*, edited by Ofelia Rey Castelao, Rubén Castro Redondo, and Camilo Fernández Cortizo. Santiago de Compostela: Universidad de Santiago de Compostela, 2018.

Soraluce, Pedro Manuel de. "Las cofradías de mareantes de San Sebastián desde la Edad Media hasta nuestros días." *Euskal-Erria* 28 (1893): 380–84, 407–14, and 459–66.

Tena García, Soledad. "Los Mans-Engómez: el linaje dirigente de la villa de San Sebastián durante la Edad Media." *Hispania* 185 (1993): 987–1008.

———. "Composición social y articulación interna de las cofradías de pescadores y mareantes. (Un análisis de la explotación de los recursos marítimos en la Marina de Castilla durante la Baja Edad Media)." *Espacio, Tiempo y Forma, Serie III, Historia Medieval* 8 (1995): 111–34.

————. *La sociedad urbana en la Guipúzcoa costera medieval: San Sebastián, Rentería y Fuenterrabía (1200–1500)*. San Sebastián: Fundación Social y Cultural Kutxa, 1997.

————. "Los linajes urbanos de las villas del Puerto de Pasajes (San Sebastián, Rentería y Fuenterrabía): dos modelos de formación de las oligarquías municipales." In *La lucha de bandos en el País Vasco: de los Parientes Mayores a la Hidalguía Universal: Guipúzcoa, de los bandos a la provincia (siglos XIV a XVI)*, edited by José Ramón Díaz de Durana. Bilbao: Universidad del País Vasco, 1998.

————. "Cofradías y concejos: encuentros y desencuentros en San Sebastián a finales del siglo XV." In *Sociedades urbanas y culturas políticas en la Baja Edad Media castellana*, edited by José María Monsalvo Antón. Salamanca: Ediciones Universidad de Salamanca, 2013.

Zamora Manzano, José Luis. "El salvamento y la asistencia marítima en el Derecho romano." *Revue Internationale des Droits de l'Antiquité* 48 (2001): 373–403.

LIST OF CONTRIBUTORS

José Ángel Lema Pueyo teaches at the University of the Basque Country (UPV-EHU). Born in Donostia-San Sebastian in 1960, he holds a doctorate in history from the University of Deusto (Donostia-San Sebastian campus). He is currently associate professor in the Faculty of Arts at the UPV-EHU (Vioria-Gasteiz campus), where he teaches medieval history, paleographic history, and document history. His research has been dedicated to two fields: the twelfth-century monarchy and institutions in Navarre and Aragon; and Basque society at the end of the Middle Ages, with publications on sources and studies. He is a member of the consolidated research group "Society, power, and culture," led by José Ramón Díaz de Durana, professor in the Department of Medieval History and the Americas in the abovementioned faculty.

Javier Ilundain Chamarro teaches at the International University of La Rioja (UNIR). HE holds a BA in history from the University of Navarre and an international doctorate in history from the same institution, having received an extraordinary award (2014). He taught in the Department of History and the Institute of the Spanish Language and Culture at this university between 2006 and 2012. He has been, moreover, a researcher at the CSIC Institute of History and at the Centre for English Local History at the University of Leicester, UK. He has been a professor at the UNIR since 2014. He is the author of the monograph *Los buenos hombres de Olite (s XII–XIV). Sociedad, poder y élites urbanas* (Gobierno de Navarra, 2017).

Iosu Etxezarraga Ortuondo holds a BA in history and cultural patrimony from the University of Deusto (2003) and a PhD in history from the University of the Basque Country (UPV-EHU) and the University of Valladolid (2017). His main research has addressed the study of churches as a source to understand the transformation of political, social, and territorial configuration, as well as the role of secular figures in ecclesiastical organization in Gipuzkoa during the Middle Ages. However, he has also worked on other research subjects, in the main linked to the historical use of field resources (the paleo-iron industry, *seles*, livestock and forestry establishments, and so on). His more than twenty years of experience in archeology have enabled him to include it in his research, in tandem with written documentation. He currently works on historico-archeological research into cultural heritage and its divulgation.

Ana Mª Barrero García holds a doctorate from the University of Salamanca. She is a retired researcher at the Higher Scientific Research Center (CSIC) in the field of the history of law. She has been a numbered member of the International Institute of the History of Spanish-American Law since 1978, holding the post of secretary there between 1992 and 1995. Likewise, she has managed the publication of the *Anuario de Historia del Derecho Español* as vice secretary and secretary for fifteen years. A specialist in the study of historico-legal sources, she has focused especially on the medieval fueros from the methodological and technical perspective of textual critique. She is the coauthor of the work *Textos del derecho local medieval. Catálogo de Fueros y Costums municipales* (1989). Among her works are several monographs on diverse groups of fueros in different peninsular kingdoms.

Mª Rosa Ayerbe Iribar teaches at the University of the Basque Country (UPV-EHU) and holds a PhD from the same institution. An expert in the history of Basque law, especially that of Gipuzkoa, she has published more than fifty books and eighty articles. She was awarded the National Heraldry Prize in 2008 and is currently editor of the *Boletín de la Real Sociedad Bascongada de los Amigos del País* and a member of the society's editorial board; editor of the *Fuentes Documentales Medievales del País Vasco* document collection published by Eusko-Ikaskuntza, the Society of Basque Studies; secretary of the Foundation for the Study of Historical and Autonomous Law and subeditor of its journal *Iura Vasconiae*; she collaborates in the *Boletín de Estudios Históricos sobre San Sebastián* published by the Kutxa Foundation; she is corresponding member for Gipuzkoa of the Royal Academy of History; and the author of thirty-five volumes (to date) of the *Juntas y Diputaciones de Gipuzkoa (1550–1700)* collection, published by the foral provincial government and general councils of Gipuzkoa.

Nere Jone Intxaustegi Jauregi is a professor in the Department of Public Law at the University of Deusto, where she teaches classes on the history of law and political science: state theory and constitutional systems. She holds a PhD in history from the University of the Basque Country (UPV-EHU) (2017) and a BA in law from the University of Deusto (2013). Her main areas of research focus on the history, society, and institutions of Bizkaia in the Modern Age.

Roldán Jimeno Aranguren is associate professor of law at the Public University of Navarre (UPNA-NUP). He holds a BA in law from the UNED, a BA in history from the University of Navarre, having received an extraordinary award and third place national end of degree prize, and a PhD in history from the same university as well as a PhD in philosophy and education sciences from the University of the Basque Country (UPV-EHU) and a PhD in law from the University of Deusto. He has spent different research visits in academic centers in Ireland, the United States, Venezuela, Italy, and France. He is the author of some twenty books, and some one hundred articles in specialized journals and in collaborations in collective works. He is the coordinator of *Iura Vasconiae. Revista de Derecho histórico y Autonómico de Vasconia* and editor of the journal *Príncipe de Viana*. As regards the municipal fueros, he is the author of the work *Los Fueros de Navarra* (Madrid: Agencia Estatal Boletín Oficial del Estado, 2016).

Xabier Irujo is director of the Center for Basque Studies at the University of Nevada, Reno, where he is professor of genocide studies. He was the first Guest Research Scholar of the Manuel Irujo Chair Fellowship at the University of Liverpool and has given classes on genocide at Boise State University and the University of California, Santa Barbara. He holds a bachelors degrees in philology, history, and philosophy, and two doctorates in history and philosophy. He has been an advisor for numerous doctoral dissertations and forms part of the executive committees of five academic and university publishers. He is the author of more than fifteen books and diverse articles in specialized journals and has perceived awards and distinctions at the national and international level. Among his latest books, the following stand out: *Giving Birth to Cosmopolis: The Code of Laws of Estella (c. 1076)* (Barandiaran Chair of Basque Studies, University of California, Santa Barbara, Santa Barbara, 2013) and *Gernika: Genealogy of a Lie* (Sussex Academic Press, Eastbourne, 2019.)

Margarita Serna Vallejo holds a PhD from the University of Cantabria (1995). She is currently professor of history in the Department of Private Law at the same university. Her research work has been developed mainly in the field of the history of private law and, in particular, in the history of property and in the history of sources and in maritime institutions during the medieval and modern eras, a research area in which the work published in this volume is framed. This has not stopped her from dealing occasionally with the study of topics in public law such as territorial and local organization in historical Cantabria. She has been a member of the editorial boards of several historico-legal journals, is secretary of the journal *Iura Vasconiae*, and in charge of the "Spanish pages" for the Italian journal *Historia et Ius*.

Amaia Álvarez Berastegi holds a PhD in law from Ulster University in Northern Ireland (2016). She is currently a researcher and lecturer in the history of law at the Public University of Navarre (UPNA-NUP). She has various publications in international impact journals and two years' experience as a researcher at the University of the Basque Country (UPV-EHU). She has participated in some twenty conferences and carried out a research stay in the Faculty of Jurisprudence at the University of Rosario in Colombia.

Made in the USA
San Bernardino, CA
22 February 2020

64689547R00226